The Edge of Revolution

David Torrance

THE EDGE OF REVOLUTION

The General Strike that Shook Britain

DAVID TORRANCE

BLOOMSBURY CONTINUUM
LONDON · OXFORD · NEW YORK · NEW DELHI · SYDNEY

BLOOMSBURY CONTINUUM
Bloomsbury Publishing Plc
50 Bedford Square, London, WC1B 3DP, UK
Bloomsbury Publishing Ireland Limited
29 Earlsfort Terrace, Dublin 2, D02 AY28, Ireland

BLOOMSBURY, BLOOMSBURY CONTINUUM and the
Diana logo are trademarks of Bloomsbury Publishing Plc

First published in Great Britain 2026

Copyright © David Torrance, 2026

David Torrance has asserted his right under the Copyright, Designs and Patents Act, 1988,
to be identified as Author of this work

For legal purposes the Acknowledgements on p. 295 constitute an extension of this
copyright page

All rights reserved. No part of this publication may be: i) reproduced or transmitted in
any form, electronic or mechanical, including photocopying, recording or by means of
any information storage or retrieval system without prior permission in writing from the
publishers; or ii) used or reproduced in any way for the training, development or operation
of artificial intelligence (AI) technologies, including generative AI technologies. The rights
holders expressly reserve this publication from the text and data mining exception as per
Article 4(3) of the Digital Single Market Directive (EU) 2019/790

Bloomsbury Publishing Plc does not have any control over, or responsibility for, any
third-party websites referred to or in this book. All internet addresses given in this book
were correct at the time of going to press. The author and publisher regret any inconvenience
caused if addresses have changed or sites have ceased to exist, but can accept no
responsibility for any such changes

A catalogue record for this book is available from the British Library

Library of Congress Cataloging-in-Publication data has been applied for

ISBN: HB: 978-1-3994-2359-5
       ePUB: 978-1-3994-2361-8
       ePDF: 978-1-3994-2363-2

2 4 6 8 10 9 7 5 3 1

Typeset by Lumina Datamatics Ltd
Printed and bound in Great Britain by Clays Ltd, Elcograf S.p.A.

To find out more about our authors and books visit www.bloomsbury.com and sign up for
our newsletters
For product safety related questions contact productsafety@bloomsbury.com

CONTENTS

	Dramatis Personae	vii
	The General Strike Timeline	xii
1	'The Great Trek'	1
2	The Origins of the General Strike	9
3	'The road to anarchy and ruin'	25
4	'Anxious times'	43
5	'Blacklegs'	53
6	'Napoleon-Churchill'	69
7	'Raised passions and frayed tempers'	83
8	'The Big Three'	99
9	'The stupidest men in England'	115
10	The Archbishop, the Cardinal and the Moderator	127
11	'That Wuthering Height'	141
12	The Civil Commissioners	153
13	'An utterly illegal proceeding'	169
14	The Judgement of Samuel	181
15	'A grotesque tragedy'	195
16	Afterlives	207
17	The General Strike Reconsidered	223

Appendix	235
Endnotes	237
Bibliography	284
Acknowledgements	295
Index	297

DRAMATIS PERSONAE

Sir Charles Stewart Addis (1861–1945), a Scottish banker who was a director of the Bank of England between 1918 and 1932

Prince Albert, Duke of York (1895–1952), the second son of King George V; later King George VI (1936–52)

Leopold (Leo) Amery (1873–1955), a Conservative MP and Secretary of State for the Colonies between 1924 and 1929

Sir John Anderson (1882–1958), a Scottish civil servant and permanent secretary at the Home Office between 1922 and 1931

Robert (Robin) Page Arnot (1890–1986), a Scottish political activist and founder member of the Communist Party of Great Britain

Herbert Henry Asquith, 1st Earl of Oxford and Asquith (1852–1928), Liberal Prime Minister between 1908 and 1916 and leader of the Liberal Party until October 1926

John Astbury, Mr Justice Astbury (1860–1939), a judge in the Chancery Division of the High Court of England and Wales between 1913 and 1929

Stanley Baldwin (1867–1947), a Conservative politician who served as Prime Minister between 1924 and 1929

John Milne Barbour (1868–1951), Minister of Commerce in the Government of Northern Ireland and also its Chief Civil Commissioner during the general strike

Ernest Bevin (1881–1951), a trade unionist and general secretary of the Transport and General Workers' Union between 1922 and 1940

Arthur John Bigge, 1st Baron Stamfordham (1849–1931), private secretary to King George V between 1910 and 1931

Cardinal Francis Bourne (1861–1935), Catholic Archbishop of Westminster from 1903 until 1935; elevated to the cardinalate in 1911

William Bridgeman (1864–1935), another Conservative politician and First Lord of the Admiralty from 1924 until 1929

Fenner Brockway (1888–1988), an Independent Labour Party activist
John (Jack) Bromley (1876–1945), general secretary of the Associated Society of Locomotive Engineers and Firemen (ASLEF) from 1914 to 1936 and Independent Labour Party MP for Barrow-in-Furness (1924–31)
John Colin Campbell (J. C. C.) Davidson (1889–1970), a Conservative politician and Deputy Chief Civil Commissioner during the general strike
Neville Chamberlain (1869–1940), a Conservative politician and Minister of Health between 1924 and 1929
Henry 'Chips' Channon (1897–1958), a Chicago-born socialite and diarist
Winston Churchill (1874–1965), a journalist, writer and Conservative politician who served as Chancellor of the Exchequer from 1924 until 1929
Walter Citrine (1887–1983), acting general secretary of the Trades Union Congress between 1925 and 1926
Arthur James Cook (1883–1931), general secretary of the Miners' Federation of Great Britain from 1924 until his death in 1931
Duff Cooper (1890–1954), a Conservative politician and diarist
Major William Cope (1870-1946), a Conservative politician and Junior Lord of the Treasury between 1924 and 1928 as well as Civil Commissioner for London and the Home Counties during the general strike
Philip Cunliffe-Lister (1884–1972), a Conservative politician and President of the Board of Trade from 1924 until 1929
Randall Davidson (1848–1930), an Edinburgh-born Anglican bishop who served as Archbishop of Canterbury from 1903 until 1928
Prince Edward, Prince of Wales (1894–1972), eldest son of King George V and Prince of Wales between 1911 and 1936; later King Edward VIII (1936)
Patrick Dollan (1885–1963), a long-standing Independent Labour Party councillor and activist in Glasgow
Hamilton Fyfe (1869–1951), a journalist who edited the *Daily Herald* between 1922 and 1926 and the *Daily Worker* during the general strike
Kingsley Game, a Londoner who experienced the general strike
William Garnett, a volunteer special constable at Toynbee Hall

DRAMATIS PERSONAE

George V (1865–1936), King of the United Kingdom of Great Britain and Ireland during the general strike

Sir Maurice Hankey (1877–1963), a civil servant who served as Cabinet Secretary from 1919 until 1938 and Clerk of the Privy Council between 1923 and 1938

Dr James Harvey (1859–1950), Moderator of the General Assembly of the United Free Church of Scotland from 1925 to 1926

Cuthbert Headlam (1876–1964), a Conservative politician and diarist

Arthur Henderson (1863–1935), an iron moulder and Labour politician who served as general secretary of the Labour Party between 1912 and 1934

Major George Hennessy (1877–1953), a Conservative politician who was Vice-Chamberlain of the Household between 1925 and 1928 and Civil Commissioner for the North Western Division during the general strike

Samuel Hoare (1880–1959), a Conservative politician who served as Secretary of State for Air between 1924 and 1929

Sir Douglas Hogg (1872–1950), a Conservative politician who served as Attorney General for England and Wales from 1924 until 1928

Thomas Jones (1870–1955), a Welsh civil servant who was Deputy Secretary to the Cabinet during the general strike

Sir William ('Jix') Joynson-Hicks (1865–1932), a Conservative politician who served as Home Secretary between 1924 and 1929

John Maynard Keynes (1883–1946), a Liberal economist and philosopher

David Kirkwood (1872–1955), the Independent Labour Party MP for Dumbarton Burghs between 1922 and 1950

David Lloyd George (1863–1945), a former Liberal Prime Minister who led his party in the House of Commons during the general strike

James Ramsay MacDonald (1866–1937), a Scottish Labour politician who served as the UK's first Labour Prime Minister; between 1924 and 1929 he was Leader of the Opposition

Harold Macmillan (1894–1986), the Conservative MP for Stockton-on-Tees between 1924 and 1929

Thomas Marlowe (1868–1935), a journalist who edited the *Daily Mail* from 1899 until 1926. He published the notorious Zinoviev Letter during the 1924 general election campaign.

Sir William Mitchell-Thomson (1877–1938), a Scottish Conservative politician who served as Postmaster General between 1924 and 1929 and as Chief Civil Commissioner during the general strike

Sir Adam Nimmo (1866–1939), a Scottish coal owner and vice-president of the Mining Association of Great Britain from 1918 until his death

John Paton (1886–1976), a Scottish Independent Labour Party organizer

Joseph (Jack) Pease, 1st Baron Gainford (1860–1943), a Durham coal owner and Liberal politician who served as chairman of the British Broadcasting Company between 1922 and 1926

Arthur Pugh (1870–1955), a trade unionist who was president of the Trades Union Congress during the general strike

John Reith (1889–1971), a Scottish broadcasting executive who was the British Broadcasting Company's general manager from 1922 until 1927

Shapurji Saklatvala (1874–1936), the Indian-born Communist MP for North Battersea between 1924 and 1929

Sir Herbert Samuel (1870–1963), a Liberal politician and the first British High Commissioner for Palestine (1920–25) who chaired the Royal Commission on the Coal Industry between 1925 and 1926

Sir Philip Sassoon, 3rd Baronet (1888–1939), an aristocrat and Conservative politician who served as the junior minister for air between 1924 and 1929 and Civil Commissioner for the Eastern Division during the general strike

Sir John Simon (1873–1954), a Liberal politician and former Attorney General for England and Wales

Sir Henry Slesser, KC (1883–1979), Solicitor General for England and Wales in the first Labour government (1924)

Frederick Edwin Smith, 1st Earl of Birkenhead (1872–1930), a Conservative politician and barrister who was Secretary of State for India between 1924 and 1928

Herbert Smith (1862–1938), a trade unionist who served as president of the Miners' Federation of Great Britain between 1922 and 1929

Philip Snowden (1864–1937), a socialist politician who served as the first Labour Chancellor of the Exchequer in 1924

Sir Arthur Steel-Maitland, 1st Baronet (1876–1935), a Conservative politician who served as Minister of Labour between 1924 and 1929

DRAMATIS PERSONAE

John St Loe Strachey (1860-1927), a journalist who edited the *Spectator* between 1887 and 1925

James Henry (Jimmy) Thomas (1874-1949), a Welsh trade unionist and Labour politician who served as general secretary of the National Union of Railwaymen between 1916 and 1931

Edward Turnour, 6th Earl Winterton (1883-1962), a Conservative politician who was junior minister for India between 1924 and 1929 and Civil Commissioner for the South Midland Division during the general strike

Charles Stewart Henry Vane-Tempest-Stewart, 7th Marquess of Londonderry (1878-1949), an Ulster Unionist politician and Durham coal owner

George Herbert Hyde Villiers, 6th Earl of Clarendon (1877-1955), junior minister for dominion affairs between 1925 and 1927 and Civil Commissioner for South Wales during the general strike

William Watson, KC (1873-1948), a Scottish Unionist politician who served as Lord Advocate between 1924 and 1929

Beatrice Webb (1858-1943), a social reformer, economist and diarist

John White (1867-1951), a minister in the Church of Scotland who served as Moderator of the General Assembly of the Church of Scotland from 1925 until 1926

John Henry Whitley (1866-1935), a Liberal politician and the last to serve as Speaker of the House of Commons between 1921 and 1928

'Red' Ellen Wilkinson (1891-1947), a Labour politician and MP for Middlesbrough East during the general strike

Evan Williams (1871-1959), a Welsh industrialist who served as president of the Mining Association of Great Britain during the general strike

Havelock Wilson (1859-1929), a trade unionist who founded the National Sailors' and Firemen's Union in 1887 and served as its president until his death

Sir Horace Wilson (1882-1972), a civil servant who was permanent secretary at the Ministry of Labour between 1921 and 1930

Sir Kingsley Wood (1881-1943), a Conservative politician who served as junior minister for health between 1924 and 1929 and Civil Commissioner for the Northern Division during the general strike

Virginia Woolf (1882-1941), an English writer and diarist

THE GENERAL STRIKE TIMELINE

1917
February   The government takes control of coal mines as a wartime measure

1919
26 February   The *Coal Industry Commission Act 1919* establishes an inquiry into the coal industry chaired by Sir John Sankey
June   The 'Sankey Commission' recommends four separate approaches ranging from full nationalization to continued private ownership; the government rejects nationalization

1920
29 October   The *Emergency Powers Act 1920* receives Royal Assent

1921
31 March   The government returns the coal mines to private ownership
15 April   Black Friday: The 'Triple Alliance' collapses when a miners' strike fails to win support from railwaymen and other transport workers

1924
29 October   Conservative leader Stanley Baldwin wins a landslide in the general election; this brings to an end the first Labour government

1925
28 April   Chancellor Winston Churchill announces the UK's return to the Gold Standard; this leads to a reduction in British coal exports

30 June	Coal owners announce the termination of a national agreement on miners' wages agreed in 1924
29 July	Prime Minister Stanley Baldwin says the government will not grant a subsidy to maintain miners' wages
31 July	The government U-turns, offering a nine-month subsidy and announcing another Royal Commission
5 September	A Royal Commission on the Coal Industry chaired by Sir Herbert Samuel is established
7–12 September	The Trades Union Congress (TUC) meets at Scarborough and empowers itself to call a general strike
25 September	The voluntary Organisation for the Maintenance of Supplies is formed

1926

11 March	The 'Samuel Commission' reports, recommending coal industry reorganization, wage reductions and no further subsidy
30 April	The government's coal subsidy ends and the coal owners post final terms for miners' pay and hours
1 May	May Day: A special conference of trade union executives approves TUC proposals for a general strike to begin at midnight on 3 May
	The King proclaims a state of emergency under the *Emergency Powers Act 1920*, giving his government authority to take emergency measures
2 May	The TUC and Prime Minister continue to negotiate
3 May	When the Cabinet learns that printers at the *Daily Mail* have refused to print an article denouncing the strike, it calls off negotiations with the TUC
	King George V and Queen Mary return to London from Windsor
4 May	First day of the general strike: 'First-line' workers in transport, printing and 'productive' industries stop work
	The Communist MP Shapurji Saklatvala is arrested and charged with making a 'seditious' speech

5 May	Home Secretary Sir William Joynson-Hicks appeals for volunteers to sign up as special constables in a BBC broadcast
	The first edition of the government-produced *British Gazette* is published
	Hansard, the Official Report of parliamentary proceedings, is suspended
6 May	The first edition of the TUC-facilitated *Daily Worker* goes on sale
	Sir Herbert Samuel returns to London from Italy
	In the House of Commons, the Liberal MP Sir John Simon declares the general strike illegal
7 May	Sir Herbert Samuel offers the TUC his services as a mediator
	Randall Davidson, the Archbishop of Canterbury, proposes terms for a settlement; the BBC refuses to broadcast them
8 May	The Archbishop's appeal is published in the *British Worker* but not the *British Gazette*
	The Governor of Northern Ireland declares a state of emergency in that part of the United Kingdom
	A convoy of lorries carrying flour travels from the London Docks to Hyde Park
	Stanley Baldwin broadcasts to the nation via the BBC
9 May	Cardinal Bourne declares the general strike to be 'a sin' against the duty owed to 'constituted authority and to God'
10 May	The Scottish Trades Union Congress publishes the first issue of the *Scottish Worker*
	Four people are killed in railway accidents caused by volunteer-driven trains at Edinburgh and Bishop's Stortford
11 May	All engineering and shipbuilding workers are instructed to stop work at midnight
	The *Flying Scotsman* service is deliberately derailed at Cramlington
	In *obiter* remarks, Mr Justice Astbury states that the general strike is illegal

THE GENERAL STRIKE TIMELINE

	The Cabinet decides to defer legislation declaring strikes illegal
	The BBC finally broadcasts details of the Archbishop's appeal
	The TUC decides to call off the strike, with or without the miners
12 May	The TUC informs the Prime Minister of an 'unconditional' end to the general strike
14 May	Stanley Baldwin submits new proposals to the miners and coal owners
20 May	A miners' delegate conference rejects the Prime Minister's proposals
21 May	The coal owners also reject the proposals
27–30 November	Miners return to work on lower pay and at longer hours

1927

20–21 January	A conference of trade union executives reviews the general strike
29 July	The *Trade Disputes and Trade Unions Act 1927* receives Royal Assent; this declares unlawful any strike whose purpose is to 'coerce' the government

Source: https://warwick.ac.uk/services/library/mrc/collections/digital/gs/timeline/

1

'The Great Trek'

It's the great, great trek
Thro' the thronged City streets,
It's the trek to the shops And the tall office-seats;
The roads are thick with people Cheek by jowl, neck and neck,
As the walkers thro' the City Make the great, great trek.[1]

The BBC called it 'The Great Trek'. From the early hours of Tuesday, 4 May 1926 hundreds of thousands of office workers began to walk from their suburban homes towards the City of London. With no regular and underground trains, trams or buses, they had little choice. Most were good-humoured. The whole thing was a novelty, and the prospect of reaching the office an hour late not altogether unpleasant. Looking out of his window at the Admiralty, the Conservative minister J. C. C. Davidson saw 'an endless army of men and women trudging eastward in their thousands'.[2]

The streets were crowded with bicycles as well as pedestrians, including bowler-hatted businessmen 'uncomfortably balanced on decrepit bicycles'.[3] Sir Charles Stewart Addis, a director of the Bank of England, 'pedalled comfortably by back streets' and parked his 'trusty bicycle' on Threadneedle Street.[4] Behind the bicycles came 'old cars that were really almost beyond their last gasp, cars that had been used by their owners as purely week-end vehicles, cars that had chugged a way up from the trainless country'.[5] This too presented a memorable sight, for by ten o'clock there was a traffic jam stretching for miles on every main road leading into central London. 'The roads are a sight for the Gods,' wrote the trade unionist and Labour MP Jimmy Thomas, 'nothing but private cars, myriads of them.'[6]

In many cases, those who had embarked upon the great trek arrived at their destination as soon as the motorists. The journalist Hamilton Fyfe saw carts and lorries 'filled with lucky clerks and typists' rumbling alongside 'expensive, shining sports cars and limousines'.[7] By late morning, central London had become 'the biggest car park the country has ever seen'.[8] Cars were even deposited inside the Royal Exchange. There were yet stranger sights. The *Guardian* reported sight of an old stagecoach, businessmen on horseback and a man in Holborn on a child's scooter.[9]

There were similar scenes in much of mainland Britain. Landing at Southampton that day was Alan Turing, who found the city 'full of people' and, determined to start school (Sherborne) on time, had 'a lovely ride' on his bicycle to the Dorset market town.[10] In South Wales most vital services had ground to a halt; in Manchester, almost all trains had stopped. Sheffield's great iron, steel and engineering firms were 'closed or just ticking over'.[11] In Glasgow, the Labour councillor Patrick Dollan later recalled 4 May being 'quieter than a Scottish Sabbath':

> Rail and dock traffic suspended. Only a few trams. Municipal tube closed. No newspapers. Bus services dislocated. Taxi cabs scarce. The population is surprised but pleased with the novel experience of having to walk more than usual. Good humour and civility prevail.[12]

On the east coast, not a single bus had left its Edinburgh garage and all 2,000 dockers in Leith had stopped work.[13] Around 200,000 trade unionists in Scotland added to the 2,500,000 striking workers in the rest of Great Britain. For the miners' leader Arthur Cook it was 'a wonderful response'. 'What loyalty!! What solidarity!!!,' he later wrote excitedly.[14] In Nottinghamshire, the Methodist preacher William Pickbourne was less elated. 'It is (cruel?) war declared on the Nation by its workers! All this because of the stupidity of Masters & Men.'[15]

The *Scotsman* and most other morning newspapers had appeared as normal. *The Times*, still of broadsheet size, reported hopefully that the door to a resolution was 'not finally closed' and that 'eleventh-hour efforts' continued in Parliament, at Downing Street and at the Trades Union Congress.[16] That day, the 'wireless' came into its own. The fledgling BBC, still a company rather than a corporation, had arranged additional bulletins to be broadcast from London and Daventry at 10 a.m., 1 p.m. and 4 p.m., which attracted crowds outside the doors of radio retailers. At 10 a.m., an announcer solemnly declared:

> The B.B.C. fully realises the gravity of its responsibility ... and will do its best to discharge it in the most impartial spirit that circumstances permit ... We will do our best to maintain our tradition of fairness and we ask for fair play in return.[17]

By the afternoon of 4 May, those in London who had made it to work noticed other dramatic changes. In the centre of Hyde Park were canteens, rest rooms and recreation spaces; on its periphery, thousands of lorries. Initially, these were to be used for the delivery of milk, the price of which had increased by 2d a quart.[18] Over at the Foreign Office on Whitehall there were four queues of volunteers waiting to enrol as special constables or volunteer drivers, dock workers and canteen assistants.

Several of those present that day remembered a feeling of urgent excitement:

> For the thousands of working men on strike it was a time of holiday; for office workers and others not directly affected by the strike there was the excitement of the unusual, the improvised, the broken routine; for those who volunteered to do the work of the strikers there was the exhilaration of adventure, of incongruity, the spirit of a 'lark'.[19]

'Everyone', noted the society diarist Henry 'Chips' Channon, 'is doing something.' He did rather less than others, taking tea with the Obolenskys (Russian nobility) and the Duchess of Rutland, while her husband drove 'people about in his Rolls-Royce'.[20] For another diarist, Beatrice Webb, the strike was 'a batch of compulsory Bank Holidays without any opportunities for recreation and a lot of dreary walking to and fro'.[21]

But this was only one side of the strike. Thousands of men and women at London's East India Dock Road held up vehicles and forced their occupants to continue their journeys on foot. Drivers who resisted were roughly handled and their vehicles wrecked. Police baton charges were made on crowds trying to stop vehicles from leaving the Blackwall Tunnel.[22] There were also battleships anchored off large ports like Liverpool, their guns trained on the harbourside. Even this passed some Londoners by. 'But that's nowhere near London,' a milkman told Mrs Hamilton Fyfe when she mentioned the strike. 'It's the miners. Nothing to do with us.'[23]

The socialist politician and activist Fenner Brockway called it the 'quietest ever revolution' with a 'philosophic calm' everywhere except Number 10 and the Eccleston Square headquarters of the Trades Union Congress.[24] At Downing Street an official found Prime Minister Stanley Baldwin 'obviously rested' and 'happier in mind' than he had been in some days.[25] He proceeded to an audience with King George V, who had hurried back to London the previous weekend. 'We had a long talk about the situation,' recorded the monarch in his diary, 'which of course is serious, but all the arrangements made by the Govt are working well.' He and 'May' (Queen Mary) also paid a visit to see 'Bertie & Elizabeth', the Duke and Duchess of York, and what the Queen called their 'precious baby', the future Queen Elizabeth II.[26]

Baldwin had just framed the general strike as imperilling 'the freedom of our very Constitution',[27] although it was not just Conservatives who fretted on that dramatic first day. Herbert Asquith, the veteran Liberal leader and former Prime Minister, wrote in his diary: 'We are plunged into the cataract of the strike and already London presents an abnormal aspect.'[28] Readers of the Labour-supporting *Daily Herald*, meanwhile, would have been struck by a forlorn quote from James Ramsay MacDonald, Leader of His Majesty's Opposition:

> As far as we can see we shall go on. I don't like General Strikes. I haven't changed my position. I have said so in the House of Commons. I don't like it; honestly I don't like it; but honestly, what can be done?'[29]

The Liberal statesman Sir Herbert Samuel believed something could be done. On 4 May he was attempting to write philosophy in the Italian town of Bergamo, but decided to head back to London on his 'own initiative', despite a less than enthusiastic telegram from the Prime Minister, confident that the Royal Commission he had chaired earlier that year could still form the basis of a settlement.[30]

At Eccleston Square, telegrams and reports were flooding in amid scenes of frenetic activity. The TUC's General Council had instructed only workers in 'first line' industries to come out: transport workers,

THE GREAT TREK

printers, some building workers and those in the iron and steel, heavy chemical and power industries.[31] The 'second line', shipyard workers et al., were to follow after a week. Only three trade unions refused to join the strike: the National Union of Journalists, Havelock Wilson's National Sailors' and Firemen's Union and the Electrical Power Engineers' Association.[32] The General Council gushed that the:

> response has exceeded all expectations ... The General Council is confident that if the Trade Union members carry out the instructions that are officially conveyed to them and maintain order, discipline and loyalty in all sections of the Movement, its plans will proceed without a hitch, and its objectives will be attained.[33]

But what exactly were those plans and objectives? 'We at the Trades Union Congress always called it the "national strike",' remarked acting secretary Walter Citrine. 'We regarded it as a large-scale sympathetic strike.'[34]

By early evening, what Jimmy Thomas called the 'same ceaseless ebb tide' of people and cars began to make its way out of London.[35] For some of those who remained in London, things were almost normal. 'I dined in terrific luxury ... Gold plates and gorgeous food,' recorded Chips Channon in his diary. 'Will it be for the last time?' He then drove to see the Gershwins' *Lady, Be Good* in the West End. 'Later we went to the stage dressing rooms to see the Astaires,' added Channon. 'Coming home we were foully insulted by a drunken woman, annoyed by the panache of the car and jewels.'[36]

Leo Amery, Secretary of State for the Colonies, dined at the Japanese Embassy with the Danish Minister and his wife, who recalled a local general in China dealing with unrest by adorning trees with 'decapitated heads looking like radishes'. 'I am not sure', mused Amery, 'whether she meant us to be equally drastic with [Jimmy] Thomas and his men.'[37] In Trafalgar Square the Conservative MP Duff Cooper bumped into the Chancellor of the Exchequer, Winston Churchill, looking 'young and carefree'. The future premier had just commandeered the premises of the *Morning Post* to produce a government-supporting 'newspaper' patriotically entitled the *British Gazette*.[38]

Although a few boat services continued to cross the English Channel, the Prince of Wales, 'breaking all orders against flying without the special authority of the King and Government', flew from Le Bourget aerodrome to Croydon and was greeted by a large crowd at 8.10 p.m. Edward had somehow arranged to requisition Imperial Airways' *City of Pretoria* aircraft. Although this was fully booked, the *Daily Mail* rather implausibly suggested passengers had 'willingly' given up their places to His Royal Highness and his 'suite' of five courtiers. 'It has been a wonderful trip,' the heir to the throne told reporters before motoring back to London. 'These machines are marvellous.' Remembering himself when asked about the strike, the Prince replied solemnly but blandly: 'Yes, it is very serious.'[39]

In the centre of London, meanwhile, illuminated signs were switched off in order to preserve electricity supplies, while thousands of people who had either been unable or unwilling to return home continued to throng the streets before returning to sleep in their offices or in hotel rooms arranged by their employers.[40] The South African journalist William Bolitho said he missed the 'usual and dominant' colour of the capital's streets, 'the ubiquitous red of the buses and the yellow of shop signs and boardings'. Instead, he added sadly, all was 'grey'.[41]

A century after that dramatic day, it is difficult to visualize a militarized Hyde Park, armoured cars, milk convoys and university students driving trains, still less an almost complete absence of reliable news and trade unions so powerful they could order millions of people to cease work. Other aspects are easier to grasp. Anyone who lived through the 2020–23 Covid-19 pandemic will recall its startling impact on the streets of the UK's major cities, the wild rumours, the close attention paid to the broadcasts of the Prime Minister and the disruption to everyday life.

Nevertheless, the challenge for the contemporary historian is to bring the world of 1926 to life, its personalities, politics and its atmosphere. Usefully, sources are plentiful. Those involved realized it was important, so preserved newspapers, correspondence, documents and memories. Bookshelves also burst with historical studies, which came in three waves: instant and usually partisan accounts published in the immediate wake of the strike; a batch of academic studies published to coincide with its fiftieth anniversary in 1976; and more recent studies of particular aspects of the general strike, its writers, women and volunteers.

This book follows the biographical approach of *The Wild Men: The Remarkable Story of Britain's First Labour Government* (2024), and indeed some of those wild and not-so-wild men – Jimmy Thomas, Ramsay MacDonald, King George V – feature alongside new but familiar figures, including Stanley Baldwin, Winston Churchill and John Reith. It introduces others, long forgotten and much maligned, for example the coal owners and Civil Commissioners who directed the UK's emergency machinery. An effort has been made to use fresh or less familiar sources, both primary and secondary, moving beyond London-based archives and the most ubiquitous publications to highlight fresh perspectives and insights. This has produced a largely unavoidable 'high politics' and middle-class emphasis, for politicians and volunteers were more inclined to record their experiences than striking railwaymen, printers and bus drivers.

It was also a 'national' strike, not one confined to London and the South East, so all parts of the United Kingdom are considered. Typically, previous studies have ignored Northern Ireland, Scotland less so. And given that the strike was depicted by opponents as an unprecedented assault on the uncodified British constitution, care has been taken to explain exactly what that was understood to mean a century ago. But before we get into 1926 and all that, we must explore the complex origins of the UK's first – and only – general strike.

2

THE ORIGINS OF THE GENERAL STRIKE

At root, the general strike was about coal. Before the First World War, coal mining had enjoyed unparalleled growth and prosperity, its product forming the basis of Victorian industrial enterprise as well as domestic consumption for heating, fuel and railway transport. It was also a major employer: around one in eleven working-age men were employed in the industry.[1] More than four million men, women and children were directly concerned with the fortunes of coal mining.[2]

Britain's coalfields were distributed over twenty-seven districts, twenty-one in England, four in Scotland and two in Wales.[3] In 1917 the Liberal-Conservative coalition took control of the mines and imposed a relatively generous 'national' wage agreement. In June 1919 a Coal Industry Commission chaired by Lord Sankey recommended full nationalization of the mines, although this was rejected by the government. Two years later, and in anticipation of reversion to private control, the mine owners proposed a return to lower 'district' wage rates. When this was rejected by the Miners' Federation of Great Britain (MFGB), on 1 April 1921 more than a million miners found themselves 'locked out' of their pits until they accepted lower rates of pay.[4]

The MFGB asked the other members of the so-called 'Triple Industrial Alliance' – the railwaymen and transport workers – to join in strike action to support the miners. This was agreed on 15 April 1921, the same day Prime Minister David Lloyd George offered to reopen negotiations with the MFGB. But when the miners refused to compromise on wages, the other unions withdrew their support and called off the strike. This became known as 'Black Friday'.

The idea of joint industrial action by several trade unions, usually out of 'sympathy' with the demands of just one, owed something to the 'syndicalist' ideas of the pre-war era, the ultimate aim of which was a worker-controlled economy, but was also what Henry Pelling called the 'logical conclusion of a constant broadening of the field of industrial conflict'.[5] The 'first' general strike, strongly aligned to the Chartist movement, had taken place in parts of Great Britain in 1842. In 1886, the International Working People's Association (IWPA) organized a nationwide general strike in the United States with the aim of securing an eight-hour day. Its epicentre was Chicago, where police repression of striking workers led to a riot and the execution of eight IWPA organizers.

Despite its failure, there followed general strikes – or attempted strikes – in Belgium, Sweden, Catalonia and particularly Italy. During 1919 there were significant general strikes back in North America, in Seattle and Winnipeg. Wherever they occurred, these were largely political strikes, their aim being economic reform rather than revolutionary action to overthrow capitalism. Since the late nineteenth century, the right to withhold labour had become accepted by successive Conservative and Liberal governments in the UK as 'an integral part of the British constitutional structure'.[6]

Legislation often rectified unfortunate decisions in the courts. The House of Lords' notorious Taff Vale judgment,[7] which held that unions could be liable for a loss of profits caused by strike action, was followed by the *Trade Disputes Act 1906*, section 4 of which provided that any 'action' against a trade union would 'not be entertained by any court'. The *Trade Union Act 1913* also reversed the 1910 *Osborne* judgment by permitting the use of union funds for certain political purposes.[8] Many Conservatives, however, came to believe a Liberal-dominated Parliament had placed trade unions 'above the law'.[9]

Indeed, the cumulative effect of this confusing mix of statute and case law had been to recognize the existence of trade unions but to exclude their activities from the purview of the courts. In practice, a strike – or, rather, action by an individual striker – only became illegal when accompanied by common law offences such as rioting, sedition or a breach of the peace.[10]

Developments in trade union theory and practice did not go unnoticed by the Conservative-Liberal coalition government. During the First World War, *The Times* warned of trade unions 'formally attempting to supersede constitutional government' and frightening 'Ministers of the Crown into doing its will'.[11] Following a 'general' strike on 'Red Clydeside' at the beginning of 1919 and a Britain-wide railway strike later that year, an Emergency Powers Bill was introduced to Parliament.

What became the *Emergency Powers Act 1920* contained just three short clauses. The first provided for declaration of a 'state of emergency' if:

> at any time it appears to his Majesty that there have occurred, or are about to occur, events of such a nature as to be calculated by interfering with the supply and distribution of food, water, fuel, or light, or with the means of locomotion, to deprive the community, or any substantial portion of the community, of the essentials of life.

Once an emergency had been proclaimed by the King, the government was empowered to make 'any regulations' necessary to secure the supply of services for 'purposes essential to the public safety and the life of the community'. The *Special Constables Act 1923* also enabled additional police officers to be sworn in during a disturbance.

These measures revealed the belief, shared by successive premiers (Lloyd George, Andrew Bonar Law and Stanley Baldwin) that the prospect of a general strike was very real. The government first assumed its new emergency powers prior to Black Friday, but for the next few years the miners did relatively well, benefitting from rising demand for British coal following the French occupation of the Ruhr in January 1923. Ironically, Ramsay MacDonald's diplomatic success during his first short-lived Labour government in persuading the French to quit Germany brought this advantage to an end.[12]

Another decisive event flowed from the Conservative government which took office in November 1924. Winston Churchill became Chancellor and in his first budget announced the restoration of the gold standard at its pre-war parity of $4.86 to the pound. Although this delighted the Bank of England, the Treasury and the Conservative Party, an overvalued pound negatively impacted the UK's export industries, including coal. As a consequence, the Liberal economist John Maynard Keynes prophesied an eventual 'war' between capital and workers.[13]

In order to remain profitable, the coal industry had to raise net proceeds by three shillings a ton, which could only be achieved through a combination of lower wages, economies of production and higher prices for domestic consumers. The coal owners, however, refused to touch often chaotic organization and instead insisted that miners work longer hours for less pay. It did not help that 'die-hard' Conservative MPs were also pushing for legislation to curtail what was known as the 'political levy', the means by which trade unions funded political activity from their members' subscriptions. But when a backbench Trade Union Levy Bill looked likely to attract majority support in March 1925, Prime Minister Stanley Baldwin made a celebrated plea for 'peace in our time' and the measure was withdrawn.[14]

On 30 June, meanwhile, the coal owners gave a month's notice to end the existing 1924 settlement regarding hours and wages. This was refused by the Miners' Federation and another lockout was threatened for 31 July. But on what became known as 'Red Friday', the Prime Minister conceded a nine-month Treasury subsidy to maintain existing wages and profits, something one Cabinet minister called 'a bribe which bought off the attack'.[15] The *quid pro quo* was another Royal Commission – the fifth since the end of the war and the third within two years – to investigate the industry and make recommendations. This became known as the Samuel Commission after its chairman, the Liberal statesman Sir Herbert Samuel. Asked why he had capitulated, Baldwin replied simply: 'We were not ready.'[16] At the same time, the premier bluntly informed the Miners' Federation that all British workers would ultimately have to 'face a reduction in wages' to 'help put industry on its feet'.[17]

Between 31 July 1925 and 30 April 1926, when the subsidy was due to run out, the Conservative government sought to 'examine, lubricate and tighten up' its emergency machinery.[18] Lloyd George had established the Supply and Transport Committee (STC) back in 1919 as well as a system of 'Civil Commissioners' responsible for administering different parts of Great Britain during a crisis.

THE ORIGINS OF THE GENERAL STRIKE

In December 1924 Sir William Mitchell-Thomson, the Edinburgh-born Postmaster General,[19] was appointed Chief Civil Commissioner, and by November 1925 the STC and Cabinet had approved a Ministry of Health circular which was to provide details of the emergency organization to local authorities. Issued as 'Circular 636', this was generally well received, although there was resistance from left-wing councils in east London.[20] In Scotland, the Lord Advocate (a law officer) was to direct five district commissioners based in Glasgow, Edinburgh, Inverness, Aberdeen and Dundee.[21] Finally, the devolved 'province' of Northern Ireland was to be administered by its Minister of Commerce, Milne Barbour, and five county 'controllers'. Given that it had only one major industrial centre (Belfast) and 'a hinterland from which supplies of agricultural produce can be drawn', it was confidently predicted that Northern Ireland's problems would be of a simpler nature 'than those which face the Imperial Government'.[22]

Operating in parallel to this official activity was the Organisation for the Maintenance of Supplies (OMS), ostensibly a private and voluntary body of concerned and patriotic citizens. Lord Hardinge, a former Viceroy of India, and the Earl of Stair, acted as presidents of the OMS in England and Wales and in Scotland respectively. Keen to be signed up were members of the British Fascists (BF), an organization formed in the aftermath of Benito Mussolini's 1923 March on Rome. Hardinge, however, stipulated that the BF could only enrol in the OMS if they 'abandoned their quasi-military formation'.[23] This resulted in a split between members of the BF who were willing to adapt and serve and those who were not.

By February 1926 Sir William Joynson-Hicks, the Home Secretary, felt able to inform the Cabinet that there was 'now very little remaining to be done before the actual occurrence of any emergency'.[24] By contrast, the General Council of the Trades Union Congress had done virtually nothing. Only in January 1926 did its acting secretary Walter Citrine compose a 'characteristically clear-headed memorandum'.[25] This identified increasing anti-trade union militancy among Conservative MPs and a depiction of the trade union movement 'as a menace to society and ordered government'. The result, warned

Citrine, might be a 'determination to wage a decisive struggle with Labour'.[26]

The Samuel Commission's report was published on 11 March 1926, a blue book of 300 pages which cost a shilling.[27] This tried hard to chart a middle way, neither recommending nationalization of the mines (as the Miners' Federation demanded) nor siding unequivocally with the coal owners. The Commissioners said they could not agree:

> with the view presented to us by the mineowners that little can be done to improve the organisation of the industry and that the only practicable course is to lengthen hours and lower wages. In our view large changes are necessary in other directions and large progress is possible.[28]

But while the Commissioners recommended a continuance of national (rather than local) wage agreements and extensive reorganization – including improvements in working conditions, pit amalgamations and the nationalization of mining royalties – in the interim wages would have to come down.

As Keith Laybourn has observed, these recommendations 'embarrassed the Government, offended the miners and aggrieved the mine owners'.[29] Only the Labour movement greeted them enthusiastically. Ramsay MacDonald thought it 'a conspicuous landmark in the history of political thought',[30] while Jimmy Thomas hailed it as 'a wonderful document'.[31] On 24 March 1926 the Conservative government said it would give effect to Samuel's recommendations only if both parties – the miners and mine owners – would agree. It is clear from the diary of Conservative MP Cuthbert Headlam, however, that Stanley Baldwin believed this was unlikely. 'He is determined to avert it [a general strike] if it is humanly possible to do so,' wrote Headlam on 14 April, 'but if the wild men force such a catastrophe, he means to fight them.'[32] The Prime Minister apparently threatened Jimmy Thomas with an 'immediate general election on the question of clipping the wings of the trades unions'.[33]

When agreement indeed proved elusive, on 16 April the coal owners posted lock-out notices at pitheads. These meant that if miners did not accept new (and worse) terms of employment, they would be locked out of their places of work on 30 April. The Labour MP Tom Griffiths called these a reversion to 'the most degrading, the most demoralising, and the most inhuman terms that had ever been submitted'.[34] Even the Prime Minister thought it 'not an offer but an ultimatum'. Privately, Sir Herbert Samuel – who had escaped to Italy as soon as his report was published – expressed irritation at the owners' stance.[35] The miners stuck doggedly to their three main demands, the first two of which had been endorsed by the Samuel Report: a national agreement, a seven-hour working day and, crucially, no reduction in wages.

When the miners again turned to the Triple Alliance for support, the Trades Union Congress now refused to bind itself in advance of negotiations, viewing as unhelpful the miners' now constantly repeated refrain, 'not a penny on the day, not a penny off the pay'.[36] Negotiations quickly became bogged down with debates about the minutia of wage arrangements. Ernest Bevin of the Transport and General Workers' Union confessed to Arthur Cook of the Miners' Federation that talk of 'quantums, minimums, percentages, etc' was difficult for an 'ordinary man' like him to understand.[37] The Prime Minister was similarly baffled. But the impression left on the public by the continuation of talks was generally optimistic. It was widely assumed a settlement would be reached before the miners' lockout took effect on 30 April 1926.

Only on 28 April were the TUC's plans in the event of a general strike presented to its General Council, and the following day the executive committees of 141 trade unions – a total of 828 delegates – met at the Memorial Hall on Farringdon Street in London.[38] Chairman Arthur Pugh presided as the oratory flowed. Ernest Bevin told delegates they were moving:

> to an extraordinary position. In twenty-four hours from now, you may have to cease being separate unions. For this purpose, you will have to become one union with no autonomy ... The miners will have to throw in their lot and come into the course of the general movement and the general movement will have to take the responsibility for seeing it through.[39]

Among the delegates were the president and secretary of the Scottish Trades Union Congress, which, although an autonomous body, had anxiously awaited a lead from London. 'Until a strike was decided on by the T.U.C.,' recalled a Scottish official, 'we did not know what to do.'[40]

William Bridgeman, the First Lord of the Admiralty, noted Stanley Baldwin's 'extreme reluctance to commit himself to one side or the other in a dispute until the last moment',[41] but, having now intervened, the Prime Minister managed to extract a compromise from the coal owners: a national wage agreement on the basis of the 1921 settlement, an eight-hour day and 'about three million pounds' to 'ease the situation' by way of 'temporary assistance'.[42] The Miners' Federation, however, would have none of it.

On the evening of 30 April, while the Prime Minister conferred with the TUC's negotiating committee at the House of Commons, King George V – who had detoured to Buckingham Palace from the races at Newmarket – signed a proclamation declaring a state of emergency under the *Emergency Powers Act 1920*. The General Council only learned of this when a print union refused to produce a poster announcing the move and instead showed a copy to the Labour MP (and railway union leader) Jimmy Thomas, who challenged an obviously uncomfortable Baldwin.[43] Amid the tension, an emotional Thomas spoke of being 'dragged' into a 'whirlpool':

> That is why I feel it is a desperate state, and if we are a bit over-anxious too, remember our knowledge of our people. Our love of our country and our anxiety for the future of our country, not our politics, is the driving force, the impelling motive, that makes us plead more than we otherwise would.

It was, recalled Walter Citrine, 'a dramatic statement and was not without its effect on Baldwin'.[44] Alluding to the government's emergency machinery, Thomas later remarked: 'They have got everything prepared, every bloody detail.'[45] The Prime Minister told Cuthbert Headlam that the position looked 'hopeless'. 'He was bitterly disappointed at his failure to bring about peace,' recorded Headlam in his diary, 'but he declared himself ready now to fight the extremists.'[46]

Back at Memorial Hall, Ernest Bevin described the proclamation as a 'declaration of war'. It now fell to delegates to vote on handing control of a general strike to the General Council, which they did by 3,653,529 to 49,911. With that, Ramsay MacDonald – hitherto an observer rather than a participant – was invited to address the gathering. Walter Citrine recalled delegates' faces as the Labour leader spoke of:

the miner's wife and her looking at her child with an aching heart because of her inability to manage on the paltry wage of the miner ... I do not remember seeing one man in that hall who did not seem moved.[47]

As delegates filed out of the Memorial Hall on, aptly, May Day, they sang 'The Red Flag'. Just a few hours later, telegrams were despatched by the Triple Alliance's respective executives instructing their members to cease work at the appointed time: 11.59 p.m. on Monday 3 May. 'So it has come,' wrote Cuthbert Headlam in his diary, 'and, on the whole, it is perhaps just as well – too long have the majority of sane people in this country doubted what these extremists are after — it is either Trade Union supremacy or that of Parliament.'[48]

Convinced a strike was imminent, members of the Miners' Federation executive quickly departed London for their districts. Later that Saturday (1 May) Walter Citrine sent two letters to Number 10, one offering cooperation to provide essential food supplies, a second announcing that the General Council would now be negotiating on the miners' behalf. The government rejected the first (William Bridgeman considered it 'impertinent') but responded to the second by inviting the TUC's negotiating committee back to Downing Street to see if a suitable 'formula' might be agreed.

The negotiating committee and members of the Cabinet subsequently worked towards what Bridgeman considered a 'nebulous' and 'unsatisfactory' formula, although Sir Horace Wilson, permanent secretary at the Ministry of Labour, believed that as the miners were sure to say no, this would put the government 'in a better strategic position'.[49] By early Sunday (2 May), the form of words was:

> The Prime Minister has satisfied himself ... that if negotiations are continued (it being understood that the [strike] notices cease to operate), the representatives of the T.U.C. are confident that a settlement can be reached on the lines of the [Samuel] Report within a fortnight.[50]

There then ensued what in any other context would have been a comic situation. When the TUC's General Council tried to consult the miners on the formula it discovered to its horror they had all gone home. Although they were hastily recalled, as a result the

Cabinet summoned to meet at noon on Sunday lasted virtually all day 'with intervals for food and individual discussion'.[51] Not until nine o'clock that evening did the TUC's negotiating committee again meet members of the Cabinet, some wearing dinner jackets, and immediately sensed the mood had changed. 'It seemed very incongruous to me to see these well-fed men complacently listening,' noted Walter Citrine in his diary, 'while we were pleading against a lowering of the standard of life of men forced to toil underground.'[52] Arthur Pugh got the impression the Cabinet believed the miners' absence from London to be some sort of delaying tactic.[53]

When the miners' representatives finally arrived at Number 10, the mood lightened as Lord Birkenhead, the Secretary of State for India, reminisced with Herbert Smith, a former boxer, about his great-grandfather, who had been a reputed prize-fighter. It then darkened again when Sir Horace Wilson asked the TUC's negotiating committee if they could provide some sort of assurance to the Cabinet. Jimmy Thomas, recalled Citrine, was 'rude in the extreme', not least because he suspected Wilson was acting as a block on any settlement:

> He first read a lecture to Wilson on his position. 'Don't forget you are a civil servant, a permanent official. Your business is to advise the Minister. You are not responsible for policy, and you want to keep that in mind.' 'But what the Prime Minister wants,' said Wilson, 'is just something to satisfy his own mind that there will be a settlement. You know that I have a difficult team to handle inside, and Baldwin wants to feel sure of his position.'[54]

The TUC's negotiating committee then broke off to meet the Miners' Federation executive in the Treasury Board Room. To complicate matters, Ernest Bevin had come up with his own proposals, which, with the exception of one word, the miners agreed to. This advocated a 'National Mining Board' comprising representatives of the government, miners and mine owners to examine the Samuel Report, first tackling reorganization before moving on to hours and wages.[55]

It was after midnight when an exhausted Baldwin reported back to the Cabinet on the outcome of earlier discussions regarding the government's formula, that if the subsidy was continued for a fortnight and the lockout suspended, the TUC would urge the miners to proceed on the basis of the Samuel Report, understanding that this might include some reduction of wages. As Leo Amery recorded in his diary:

> The Cabinet as a whole ... did not at all like this. They thought there was no real assurance that it would lead to anything nor did it take any notice of the general strike about which our feelings had stiffened considerably when we discovered during the course of the day from the Post Office that the actual telegrams to the different Unions telling them to cease work had gone out on Saturday evening.[56]

As the Cabinet considered an 'ultimatum' letter addressed to the TUC, the *Daily Mail* editor Thomas Marlowe (notorious for his publication of the Zinoviev Letter, a forged directive ordering a British revolution which had blown apart the 1924 general election campaign) telephoned Number 10 to say printers at his newspaper had refused to run a leading article which declared a general strike a 'revolutionary moment' rather than an industrial dispute.[57] 'They asked for a modification of that paragraph,' NATSOPA's George Isaacs told Labour leader Ramsay MacDonald, 'but were ordered to print it or get out, so they got out.'[58]

Neville Chamberlain, the Minister of Health, left a vivid account of what happened next:

> 'Thank God' shouted FE [Lord Birkenhead] & was immediately & hotly attacked by Winston [Churchill]. 'A great organ of the press is muzzled by strikers & you say "Thank God" ...' But Horace Wilson who has a cool head said 'This changes the whole situation & I think it gives you a way out'. FE instantly seized on the idea & reversed his attitude, the PM gave way & in a few minutes we were revising our ultimatum so as to make this 'overt act' the main reason for breaking off.

Although Amery agreed the incident had 'tipped the scales', and Air Secretary Samuel Hoare that it acted as a 'kind of spark',[59] as with so many key incidents in the run-up to the general strike, this one was subject to competing interpretations. The *New Statesman* later alleged that Churchill remarked that 'a little blood-letting' would be no bad thing,[60] while the historian Charles Mowat was clear Baldwin 'was over-ruled, partly by threats of resignations', with Churchill, Neville Chamberlain and Home Secretary Sir William Joynson-Hicks urging a robust response.[61]

A tired but relieved Cabinet finally dispersed at 12.30 a.m. leaving a beleaguered Baldwin to hand the ultimatum to the TUC's negotiating committee in the Cabinet room. Speaking with 'evident emotion', Jimmy Thomas recalled Baldwin saying:

> The task of the peacemaker is hard. Since we spoke to you an hour ago, an incident has happened upon which the British Cabinet takes such a serious view that they have instructed me to break off negotiations and convey their decision in this letter which I now hand to you; to all that you gentlemen have done to try and effect an honourable peace, courtesy demanded that I should tell you personally.[62]

Walter Citrine recalled making for the exit 'somewhat perplexed' while Baldwin exchanged pleasantries with his TUC colleagues. When Citrine remarked that it had been 'difficult for all of us', the Prime Minister replied:

> 'Well, I have been happy to meet you, and I believe if we live we shall meet again to settle it.' Then he added solemnly, 'If we live.' With that we went out.[63]

Back in the Treasury Board Room, the premier's letter was read aloud by a 'coolly unemotional' Arthur Pugh (the TUC chairman) and greeted with 'derisive laughter' and a 'menacing growl from some of the sterner spirits'.[64]

Eventually, Ernest Bevin suggested they draft a reply, but when Pugh and Walter Citrine tried to deliver this at 1.30 a.m., they were told by the office keeper at Number 10 that the Prime Minister was asleep. Later asked if he had retired to avoid receiving the TUC's 'surrender', Baldwin replied: 'No, I had done all I could and there was nowhere else to go.'[65] At 12.25 a.m. someone at Number 10 had also called Windsor Castle to ensure the King did 'not go off the deep end' when he read the morning papers. 'We don't take the "Daily Mail"', replied an assistant private secretary, 'or the "Daily Express".'[66]

Citrine eventually despatched the TUC's reply from Eccleston Square at 3.30 a.m. This expressed regret that it:

> was not given an opportunity to investigate and deal with the alleged incidents before the Government made them an excuse for breaking off the peace discussions which were proceeding. The public will judge the nature of the Government's intention by its precipitate and calamitous decision in this matter, and will deplore [that] an honourable settlement has been wrecked by the Government's unprecedented ultimatum.[67]

Outside the TUC's headquarters, Jimmy Thomas remarked to a journalist that the government had just 'declared war'. Turning to Arthur Cook, regarded as the most intransigent member of the Miners' Federation executive, Thomas added melodramatically: 'We must now, Cook, fight for our lives.'[68]

Writing in his diary in the wee small hours, Ramsay MacDonald lamented that:

> The Government has awfully mismanaged the whole business ... But the [trade unions] have been equally blameworthy ... It really looks tonight as though there was to be a General Strike to save Mr Cook's face. Important man! The election of this fool as miners' secretary looks as though it would be the most calamitous thing that ever happened to the T.U. movement. The chief criminal, however, is the Government.

'I am ill', concluded the exhausted Labour leader wearily, 'and my head is likely to burst.'[69]

Monday 3 May represented the calm before the storm. At a meeting of the women's section of the London Municipal Society, Lucy Baldwin, the Prime Minister's wife, recalled sympathizing with her husband, who had worked so hard 'for peace and a better understanding among people':

> He looked at me and said, 'Well, I'm sorry. It is rather like building a house of cards, going up storey by storey, putting a card here and a card there, and then something comes and brings the whole thing down flop. The only thing is that I must collect the cards, pick them up again and build again.'

'I thought to myself with pride,' added Lucy. 'He is a man.'[70] All Chips Channon could think about was Hubert, a 'beautiful, strong and nectar-like' guardsman he was infatuated with. 'Poor Hubert may be killed in the rioting,' he recorded sadly in his diary, 'as the Life Guards are certain to be called out. I promised to write a beautiful memoir of him if he is.'[71]

Quixotically, the Trades Union Congress was still at work, with Bevin, Pugh and the miners' leaders (Smith and Cook) having agreed another compromise formula they hoped to put to the government. But apparently encouraged by Cook, the Miners' Federation executive rejected this by twelve votes to six.[72] Ernest Bevin nevertheless gave a copy to the Ministry of Labour and another to Ramsay MacDonald. When the government failed to bite, Bevin hoped MacDonald might highlight the formula in his Commons speech later that day, but the Leader of the Opposition had already resolved 'to swallow his own misgivings' and 'concentrate on keeping his followers together'.[73] At a meeting of the Parliamentary Labour Party executive, the Labour leader told Walter Citrine his hair had 'gone greyer' with worry.[74] Cuthbert Headlam considered MacDonald 'a helpless passenger' in the whole 'wretched business'.[75]

A packed Commons convened at 2.45 p.m. and an hour later Walter Citrine found himself squeezed below the gallery between Arthur Cook of the Miners' Federation and William Lee of the Mining Association. The Prime Minister spoke first, claiming that by ordering a general strike the TUC had moved:

> nearer to proclaiming civil war than we have been for centuries past ... Perhaps they thought that there was nothing more at stake than bringing a certain amount of spectacular pressure to bear, which might suffice to persuade the Government to capitulate without serious damage to the liberties of the nation. But they have created a machine which they cannot control.

'It is not wages that are imperilled,' continued Baldwin, 'it is the freedom of our very Constitution.'[76] 'His speech,' wrote the Colonial Secretary Leo Amery in his diary, 'made a great impression and was listened to with hardly any interruption.'[77]

Other ministers then pressed home the constitutional point, which was furiously rebutted by Jimmy Thomas and Ramsay MacDonald. Thomas asked 'whether it is still too late to avert what I believe is not only the greatest calamity for this country',[78] while MacDonald, who to Ernest Bevin's surprise said nothing about the new formula, merely committed the Labour Party to 'further explorations' as well as a powerful defence of the miners' position:

> If you were dealing with a body of men like that [the miners], and dealing with wages like that, and if you were a trade union secretary, a national secretary, or a district secretary, and these figures were your incomes ... there is not a single one of you that would be very pliable if the proposition was made to reduce those wages.[79]

Arthur Cook later accused Thomas of the 'most humiliating crawling and pleading' and MacDonald of making 'one of the most sickening speeches in the history of the House of Commons'. He especially resented the Labour leader's 'superior tones' in admitting that with 'the discussion of general strikes and Bolshevism and all that kind of thing, I have nothing to do at all'.[80]

Afterwards, there were 'constant conferences' in the Prime Minister's room at the Commons.[81] In Walter Citrine's second-hand account, the former Labour Home Secretary Arthur Henderson got the impression Winston Churchill was determined to prove 'we could not dictate to the Government':

> 'You tried it in Italy and failed, and you are not going to be successful in Great Britain.' [Sir Arthur] Steel-Maitland [the Minister for Labour] had also got on his 'high horse' and had said to Henderson that 'it was about time we were put in our places'. Henderson retorted, 'It seems to me, Winston, that you are trying to give us a dose of Sidney Street.' Churchill replied, 'You will be better prepared to talk to us in two or three weeks.'[82]

Baldwin told the King that Labour leaders 'were sincerely anxious of finding an honourable way out of the position into which they had been led by their own folly',[83] while a wounded MacDonald recorded a 'bad rebuff' from the Cabinet in his diary. 'Just home by Tube,' he added, 'for the last time – for how long?'[84]

Meanwhile, a crowd in Parliament Square had grown to around 5,000 when the House of Commons finally rose at 11.15 p.m. Only with difficulty and the aid of dozens of extra policemen was a way cleared for the cars and taxis leaving New Palace Yard. Jimmy Thomas, 'tears streaming down his face', was collected by his wife Agnes in their Morris Oxford.[85] When Big Ben 'boomed' out the beginning of the general strike at midnight, one section of the crowd sang 'The Red Flag' while another responded with 'God Save the King', at which point there was a rush in the latter's direction. The police, noted Fenner Brockway, 'got the people away quietly; indeed, most of the people neither cheered nor sang, much in the mood of the eve of the Great War'.[86] For the government, noted Julian Symons in his 1957 history of these dramatic events, 'it was a threat to the Constitution; for the General Council a tiger to be ridden; for some alarmists (or optimists) the dawn of revolution.'[87]

3

'The road to anarchy and ruin'

Stanley Baldwin had long viewed himself as a 'peacemaker', almost above party politics, but the general strike – which came in the midst of his second premiership – represented the Conservative leader's greatest political challenge. With his broad shoulders, parted hair and trademark pipe, the Prime Minister gave the impression of an archetypal Englishman, equally at ease in the countryside or in the metropolis. The diplomat Lord Vansittart believed his face 'dispelled impropriety'.[1]

Baldwin's oratory, though not spectacular, was calculated to appeal to traditional and 'national' values. Vansittart reckoned the 'immense' hold this generated among his fellow countrymen was because Britons liked 'to feel good and he made them'.[2] To some of his contemporaries, however, the premier was something of an enigma. The future Conservative MP Harold Nicolson believed he regarded logical processes as 'un-English', preferring to 'rely upon instinct' and sniffing 'at problems like an elderly spaniel'.[3]

Born to a prosperous iron- and steel-making family in Bewdley, Worcestershire, Baldwin was educated at Harrow and Cambridge before joining the family firm and succeeding his father Alfred in the House of Commons. Then aged forty, his political career advanced quickly: he was a minister by 1917 and a member of the Cabinet four years later. In October 1922 he joined in the Tory revolt which brought down the Liberal-Conservative coalition and became Chancellor in Andrew Bonar Law's short-lived ministry. In May 1923, Baldwin succeeded Bonar Law as Conservative leader and premier.

Baldwin's landslide election victory in October 1924 had helped restore his standing in a party shocked by his decision to call a snap election the previous year, a move that had ushered in the first Labour government. During that period, he had modernized the party, creating a 'Shadow Cabinet' and dropping the now outdated 'Unionist' nomenclature, a party label intended to emphasize its opposition to Irish Home Rule. Now that the Irish Question had apparently been settled by the creation of the Irish Free State (later the Republic of Ireland) in 1922, Britain's main centre-right party reverted to its historic 'Conservative' brand.

Faced with the general strike, meanwhile, the Prime Minister's instinct was to show a combination of calmness and firmness, what one critic called a 'most curious mixture of the sentimental phrase and the hard act'.[4] This fitted neatly into a broader narrative Baldwin had been constructing since the subsidy capitulation of July 1925, identifying Conservatism with democratic constitutionalism and turning 'democracy' and 'progress' into weapons to be used against the Labour Party whose rise, paradoxically, he applauded on account of disdain for the Liberals. The Trades Union Congress was now framed as an anti-democratic force seeking to dictate to a government which indisputably commanded the confidence of Parliament.

That was the line Baldwin had taken in his Commons speech on 3 May, in a message to the public issued to newspapers (and printed as a flyer) on 6 May, and in the important broadcasts he made later in the strike on 8 and 12 May. 'His tone throughout was one of sorrow not anger,' judged the Conservative historian Stuart Ball, 'and the strikers were depicted as misled rather than dangerous.'[5] Modern communications greatly aided this strategy. 'The country must be taught to look to "Baldwin" all the time,' wrote the Bristol MP Freddie Guest to his cousin, Winston Churchill. 'He should be the one name in people's minds. It must be "Baldwin, the man of steel", and no other ministers must be got into public thought.'[6]

The first of Baldwin's messages opened dramatically with the declaration that constitutional government was 'being attacked':

> Stand behind the Government, who are doing their part confident that you will co-operate in the measures they have undertaken to preserve the liberties and privileges of the people of these islands. The laws of England are the people's birthright. The laws are in your keeping; you have made Parliament their guardian. The

general strike is a challenge to Parliament and is the road to anarchy and ruin.

This was hardly moderate, and indeed Baldwin's critics highlighted what they saw as 'hypocritical platitudes' from a holier-than-thou premier. The TUC's Walter Citrine wondered whether the Prime Minister was 'as honest, plain, and straight-forward as he appears, or whether he is a hypocrite and a humbug',[7] while the former Labour Chancellor Philip Snowden reminded banker Sir Charles Addis that 'Mr Honesty came from the town of Stupidity which liveth about three or four leagues on the other side of the City of Destruction'.[8] Even some ministerial colleagues felt their chief overdid it. Watching Baldwin in the Commons the day before the strike, William Bridgeman, the First Lord of the Admiralty, thought the Prime Minister sailed perilously close to 'cant'. 'It is no use repeating,' he observed, 'your love of peace on every occasion.'[9]

On Saturday 8 May Baldwin addressed an anxious nation once more, this time via the wireless. He spoke of the 'lamentable struggle' but took care to separate the 'stoppage' in the coal industry, to which he still hoped to find a solution, from the general strike, which he bluntly characterized as an attempt to 'starve us into submission'. Continuing, the Prime Minister said he wished:

> to make it as clear as I can that the Government is not fighting to lower the standard of living of the miners or of any other section of the workers. That suggestion is being spread about. It is not true. I do not believe that any honest person could doubt that my whole desire is to maintain the standard of living of every worker, and that I am ready to press the employers to make any sacrifice to this, and consistent with keeping the industry itself in working order. But there are many people who say: 'I do not hold with the general strike but I feel a good deal of sympathy with the miners'. So do I.

Baldwin concluded by repeating that a solution was 'within the grasp of the nation' if only the TUC would 'abandon' the strike:

> I am a man of peace. I am longing and working, and praying for peace, but I will not surrender the safety and the security of the British Constitution. You placed me in power 18 months ago, by the largest majority accorded to any Party for many, many years.

Have I done anything to forfeit that confidence? Cannot you trust me to insure a square deal for the Parties? To secure even justice between man and man?[10]

A second BBC bulletin later that day carried a further message from the premier, which was also printed and distributed as a leaflet:

Every man who does his duty by the country, and remains at work, or returns to work, during the present crisis, will be protected by the State from loss of Trade Union benefit, superannuation monies, or pensions. His Majesty's Government will take whatever steps are necessary in Parliament or otherwise, for this purpose.[11]

Beneath this confident public posture there was also no doubt that the 'completeness' of the general strike over the past few days had 'astonished' the government as well as the strike leaders.[12] While Lucy Baldwin organized a 'special convoy' of motor cars to assist suburban business women and girls to reach their places of work,[13] her fifty-eight-year-old husband was under what the Deputy Chief Civil Commissioner J. C. C. Davidson, perhaps Baldwin's closest political confidant, called 'severe strain'.[14]

This led to an extraordinary story in the Paris edition of the *New York Herald Tribune* on Saturday 8 May (the same day as Baldwin's first broadcast) to the effect that the Prime Minister was on the cusp of a breakdown. This was apparently the product of a conversation between a *Herald* correspondent and Sir Robert Horne, a womanizing bachelor Tory MP Baldwin regarded as a 'Scots cad'.[15] The Labour leader Ramsay MacDonald took this report seriously enough to ask the Prime Minister's PPS if it was true; Captain Herbert assured him it was not.[16] J. C. C. Davidson prepared a denial but the story had already 'been checked' by Baldwin's 'most effective' radio broadcast.[17] Reuters finally carried a rebuttal on 11 May, reporting that the Prime Minister was 'hard at work and in the best of health'.[18]

The day after the story first appeared, William Bridgeman took Baldwin to London Zoo to 'distract his mind'. 'He is standing the strain pretty well,' he told his mother on 9 May, 'but of course it is very tiring and trying to his nerves.'[19] That same day the civil servant Tom Jones, the Prime Minister and the latter's younger son 'squeezed' themselves:

into the little Bean car with the chauffeur and the detective in front, and at about 10.40 set out for Hampstead Heath, passing Regent's Park which was closed to the public. We got out at Whitestone Pond, walked to Ken Wood, and then over the Heath to Parliament Hill where after an hour or so the car met us. We talked hardly at all, except about the Heath, and I kept off the Strike. In the car the P.M. showed me an almost affectionate letter which the Prince of Wales had sent him last night about a quarter of an hour after listening to the P.M. broadcasting. The P.M. was obviously much moved at receiving so promptly so cordial a message from the Prince.[20]

Bridgeman later told the Prince of Wales his letter had pulled Baldwin back from the brink. 'I found that the words of sympathy he had received from you,' he wrote, 'had done more to keep him up than anything else during those two or three days of terrific anxiety.'[21]

'SERVANTS OF THE CROWN'

Supporting Baldwin and his government was a decade-old Cabinet Secretariat led by Sir Maurice Hankey, the first Cabinet Secretary and clerk to the Privy Council, and his Welsh-speaking deputy Thomas (or Tom) Jones, whose home renovations in Belsize Park were halted as a result of the strike.[22] 'It is going to be interesting seeing if we can beat these fellows,' Hankey told his wife on 3 May. 'I think we can, but it involves a big effort.'[23]

Some senior officials even felt able to criticize members of the Cabinet. Sir John Anderson, the permanent secretary at the Home Office, was by 1926 a Whitehall veteran with 'none of the hesitations and dubieties attributed ... to Civil Servants'.[24] He attended the Cabinet committee that met daily during the strike and, on one occasion, when Winston Churchill advocated sending armed troops to the London Docks to protect paper supplies, begged the Chancellor of the Exchequer 'to stop talking nonsense'.[25] It was Anderson, recalled the Secretary of State for Air Samuel Hoare, who:

> was mainly responsible for the successful working of the machine during the nine days. There he sat, next to Jix [the Home Secretary], quietly listening to the speeches of the Ministers, discounting foolish suggestions and going on with his work in spite of the talk.[26]

Also blurring the lines of civil service neutrality was the Ministry of Labour's Sir Horace Wilson. For him, the strike was a 'regrettable necessity which had to be faced and defeated before the pragmatists on both sides of industry could sit down together and agree practical solutions to mutual problems'.[27]

The situation as regards more junior-ranking Crown servants was complicated. The civil service was then regulated under the royal prerogative rather than an Act of Parliament, and individual civil servants did not really have contracts, more verbal undertakings not to take part in certain activity, political or industrial.[28] The main civil service unions had not been called out by the TUC, but the Air Ministry felt it necessary to warn established members of staff 'that any refusal of duty ... will entail the forfeiture of his pension rights'.[29] A Treasury missive dated 6 May stated that once existing staff had been reallocated within Whitehall then arrangements should be made 'for the registration of Civil Servants of every grade, men and women alike, who wish to volunteer for emergency duties'.[30]

The advice from the General Purposes Committee of the civil service unions, however, was not to volunteer and work only at regular duties. This led to bitter opposition, especially among higher-ranking officials,[31] and some clerks resigned from the Civil Service Clerical Association in protest at what they regarded as (left-wing) 'political' action.[32] Its general secretary William Brown had rashly put his union's membership and resources at the TUC's disposal on 1 May.[33] Staff at the Foreign Office protested that it was a matter for each as individuals, while 'as servants of the Crown, they take a wide view of their duties, amongst which they include all civil services necessary to ... perform during the existence of a state of emergency'.[34] The Secretary of State for the Colonies also felt it necessary to inform Colonial and Indian Service officers on leave that they were free to offer their services as volunteers.[35]

'LORD BURSTINGHEAD'

Among the key figures in the Cabinet during the strike was Frederick Edwin Smith, the 1st Earl of Birkenhead and Secretary of State for India. Tom Jones thought Birkenhead had 'all the ability required to grasp the situation, he only talks when he has something to say, and when he speaks does so with perfect lucidity', high praise from the Deputy Cabinet Secretary.[36] William Bridgeman noted his 'contemptuous manner' and often 'intolerably rude' speeches'.[37] Although only in his mid-fifties, by May 1926 'F. E.', as he continued to be known, cut a rather pompous figure – the cartoonist David Low caricatured him as 'Lord Burstinghead' – but in his prime Frederick Edwin Smith had been one of the most dazzling barristers and politicians of his generation.

Born and raised in Birkenhead, F. E. was a precocious child who modelled himself on his father, also Frederick, a robust Tory and skilful orator who had died just a month after being elected mayor of the city. Frederick junior made his name at Oxford but built his reputation as a highly paid lawyer in Liverpool before entering Parliament in 1906, retaining the working-class Conservative seat of Walton against the Liberal tide. F. E.'s maiden speech made him a star, as did his case against the legal immunity of trade unions during debates on the Trade Disputes Bill.[38]

By the 1910s, Smith was presenting himself as a progressive modern Conservative and heir to the Disraelian tradition of 'Tory Democracy'. He supported salaries for MPs, proportional representation, national insurance and a minimum wage. 'A contented proletariat,' he wrote in 1913, 'should be one of the first objects of enlightened Conservative policy.'[39] During the Ulster crisis of 1912–14, Smith adopted an apparently extreme Unionist position in opposition to Irish Home Rule, supporting Bonar Law's argument that there were 'things stronger than parliamentary majorities' and declaring that he would stand 'side by side' with Ulster Unionists in 'refusing to recognise any law, and prepared with you to risk the collapse of the whole body politic'.[40] Like most Conservatives, Smith appeared rather more comfortable with the creation of a paramilitary Ulster Volunteer Force and provisional government (both of which were illegal), than the passage of a Home Rule Bill backed by a large Commons majority.

This recent and uncomfortable history was naturally dragged up during the general strike to demonstrate Birkenhead's hypocrisy now that he and others railed against the defiance of Parliament and the TUC as an 'alternative' government. The miners' leader Arthur Cook not unreasonably asked:

Did Ireland obtain Home Rule by legal and constitutional means? And was it illegal for Ulster to take up arms against Home Rule? ... The claim that a general strike is unconstitutional may be met by a demand for a definition of the term. And the definition may be, that any notion of an opponent to which you take exception, is unconstitutional, even though you may have taken similar action yourself on some previous occasion.[41]

During the First World War, Smith – now Sir Frederick – was appointed Solicitor General for England and Wales and spent most of the rest of his life in office. In 1919 he became Lord Chancellor, despite opposition from the King, and took the title Baron Birkenhead (upgraded to viscount in 1921 and earl in 1922), while as Secretary of State for India from November 1924, Birkenhead was 'thoroughly reactionary', unwilling to believe that Indians would ever be fit for self-government.[42]

As the day-to-day government of India was the responsibility of its Viceroy, Birkenhead was free to apply himself to whatever political issues might arise, such was the lucidity of his judgement, legal knowledge and drafting skill. This included before, during and after the general strike, although by May 1926 he no longer had much desire for a 'contented proletariat'. Rather, Birkenhead had become as diehard as his great friend Winston Churchill. 'To whatever unhappy lengths this quarrel may be carried,' he told the House of Lords on 5 May, 'it will be ended only with the recognition, alike in fact and in law, that there is one Government and one Government only in this country.'[43]

'MUSSOLINI MINOR'

Also viewed as a diehard was Sir William Joynson-Hicks, who had served as Home Secretary since the Conservatives' return to government in 1924. Until the beginning of the strike, he had been known as 'Mussolini Minor' (Churchill was 'Mussolini Major'), but once it actually got under way he surprised many colleagues with his tact and moderation. More affectionately known as 'Jix', the Home Secretary was something of a fanatic, convinced there were Reds under every bed. His colleague William Bridgeman could not 'exonerate' him from 'an excessive love of popularity'.[44]

Born William Hicks in London to a prosperous merchant and evangelical family, he 'took the pledge' to become teetotal at fourteen and kept it the rest of his life. Hicks married in 1895 and added his wife Grace's maiden name Joynson to his own the following year. Joynson-Hicks worked as a solicitor specializing in copyright and motoring law, and entered Parliament following a memorable Manchester by-election in 1908, which was characterized by suffragette attacks on his then Liberal opponent Winston Churchill and Jewish hostility to Joynson-Hicks given his support for the controversial *Aliens Act*. Created a baronet in 1919, Sir William joined the short-lived government of Bonar Law and was thereafter rapidly promoted by Stanley Baldwin. Samuel Hoare considered him 'the very embodiment of a Victorian Home Secretary, frock-coated, eloquent, determined to rise to a historic occasion';[45] to others Jix was 'an exuberant exhibitionist with a taste for the limelight', his diehard views 'undeniably popular in the constituencies'.[46]

As Home Secretary, Sir William was in his puritanical element, cracking down on nightclubs and what he considered to be 'filthy' literature. But it was Communists he most despised and whom he regarded as responsible for growing industrial strife. Shortly after Red Friday and the granting of a temporary mining subsidy, Sir William warned that the 'danger' was not over. 'Sooner or later this question had got to be fought out by the people of the land,' he said. 'Was England to be governed by Parliament and by the Cabinet or by a handful of trade union leaders?'[47]

On 13 October 1925 the Cabinet decided to prosecute the leadership of the tiny Communist Party of Great Britain (CPGB, formed in 1920) for sedition under the *Incitement to Mutiny Act 1797*. Twelve were arrested, including Scot John Ross Campbell, whose activities and resulting 'Campbell Case' had helped bring down the first Labour government the previous year. Campbell conducted his own defence but was sentenced to six months' imprisonment, meaning he was released on 10 April 1926 – just in time to play an active part in Scotland during the general strike.[48] Robin Page Arnot, an early chronicler of the strike, was also out of prison in time to become an active Communist organizer in the north-east of England.[49]

In unpublished autobiographical notes, Jix was clear that a general strike was 'bound to come sooner or later', not least because of the 'great spread of Communism and foreign Bolshevik agitation'. His memoirs include a long and paranoid account of how the 'forces at work' in favour of a strike 'had their origin in Moscow'; to Sir William, it was 'perfectly clear there were forces working not only for an economic struggle, but actually for a revolutionary struggle'.[50]

It was therefore no surprise that when the general strike actually began, the authorities 'bore down' on Communists and, in Keith Laybourn's estimate, arrested around 2,500, roughly half the CPGB membership. This rather exaggerated their real influence, for few Communists dominated local strike committees or councils of action.[51] Nor was the TUC as awash with Reds as Jix fancied. On 5 May 1926 the Metropolitan Police raided the CPGB's London HQ but only found, according to John Murray, 'an old worn-out model of a Roneo duplicating machine which had not been used for years'.[52] They also discovered a list of names and addresses which were distributed to police forces around the country so that those producing seditious literature could be targeted.[53] One of those arrested was Isabel Brown in Castleford, who was sentenced to three months in prison. The press made much of her having given her 'last permanent address' as 'Moscow'.[54] She later recalled a bench 'composed entirely of coal owners' and refusing to have her fingerprints taken as she 'claimed to be a political prisoner'.[55] When premises being used by the Communist Bradford Strike Bulletin were raided, Vic Feather (a future general secretary of the TUC) narrowly avoided arrest by hiding in the toilets.[56]

A lengthy survey of Communist activity later produced by New Scotland Yard and MI5 worked hard to justify Jix's paranoia. The report simultaneously revelled in the number of Communists arrested during the strike while maligning them as 'cowards and amateur revolutionaries who have not the tendency towards violence which characterises the Russian'. MI5 also reported a 'considerable intensification' of Communist efforts to 'tamper with the loyalty of the Forces' in the ten months preceding the strike, not just the usual leaflets and slogans stencilled on barrack walls, but heightened 'underground' activity such as accosting marines near pubs. A number of men at Deptford's Foreign Cattle Market had been 'systematically lured' into nearby public houses 'where they were plied with drink and Red propaganda'. But MI5 noted this was 'without much result, apart from the consumption of an inordinate quantity of beer'.[57]

Several contemporaries, meanwhile, observed that the *Emergency Powers Act 1920* gave the Home Secretary the authority of a European autocrat. Joynson-Hicks chaired the main Cabinet committee (Supply and Transport) concerned with the general strike, which met almost daily at a conference room in the Home Office. Jix himself recalled that Emergency Regulations issued under the 1920 Act 'practically made the Government dictators. They had power thereby to take possession of land, public services, raw material and stores, to use for whatever purpose they saw fit.' In addition to ministers, also present at daily meetings were the technical head of the Royal Air Force, representatives of the Army and Navy, and the Metropolitan Police. As Sir William recalled:

> We sat as an executive council of war every morning. Reports were brought to us by telegram and telephone from all parts of the country; we were able to keep our finger on the very pulse of the nation, and the very mind and heart of the people. If disturbances arose the necessary protection was rushed to that place. No one knew how long it would last; no one knew to what extent the Strike would develop into revolution.[58]

J. C. C. Davidson, on the other hand, found the proceedings of the Supply and Transport Committee 'amazingly entertaining, for there was a distinct cleavage of view':

> Winston and [others] regarded the strikers as an enemy to be destroyed. Jix, who up till the beginning of the strike had been known as Mussolini Minor and about whose possible conduct of affairs many despondent Civil Servants had grave doubts, not only handled the Committee with supreme skill, but showed that he really understood his own countrymen. Jix was never rattled, was most businesslike and adopted a policy with regard to the Police which it is not too strong to say was superb.[59]

Joynson-Hicks even slept at the Home Office, while the police protection normally accorded to the Home Secretary was doubled.[60] The TUC's Walter Citrine recorded an exchange between the Labour MP and railway union leader Jimmy Thomas and Sir William on 6 May:

Hicks had said to him … 'I wish you had my job, J.T.,' to which Thomas replied – 'No you don't; you are as happy as hell.' 'No, I'm not, it is a very worrying time,' replied Joynson-Hicks, and Thomas certainly judged from his appearance that he was really worried. However, Jimmy retorted – 'Yes, and you see where your Mussolini is driving you.' This was a hint at Winston Churchill. Joynson-Hicks shook his head in doleful fashion, and it was evident to Thomas that he is carrying out his responsibilities with difficulty.[61]

One of the Home Secretary's main tasks was the enrolment of special constables made possible under a 1923 Act of Parliament. In a wireless broadcast on Wednesday 5 May, Jix appealed on behalf of the government:

> to all who are fit and strong to offer their services as Special Constables by going to the Police Station nearest to where they live, where they will find a Magistrate in attendance ready to swear them in … I am appealing to employers not to put any obstacles in the way but to do their utmost to make it easy for their employees to enlist.

Although his appeal related only to the capital, the Home Secretary made clear the same assistance was required in the 'counties and boroughs outside London', where chief constables stood ready to enrol willing volunteers. 'I am quite sure,' he concluded, 'that I shall receive the support of all loyal men in the work the Government is now doing.'[62]

Subsequent events demonstrated the power of a wireless even with limited reach. The number of special constables recruited in London rose from 3,035 on 4 May to 51,807 by 11 May (Jix had set a target of 50,000), but the call demonstrated that the actual and potential level of violence was the Home Secretary's principal source of anxiety during the first week of May. The Home Office urged police authorities to apply the most stringent interpretation of laws concerning 'peaceful picketing',[63] although a subsequent survey of chief constables found widespread cynicism as to the efficacy of the *Trade Disputes Act 1906* in this respect, not least because 'peaceful' picketing close to factories and offices often amounted to 'grave intimidation'. The chief constable of the Port of London Authority declared that the 'Act as it now stands and the way in which it is interpreted by pickets affords no protection to willing workers'.[64]

THE ROAD TO ANARCHY AND RUIN

On 6 May the Supply and Transport Committee also recommended the creation of a Civil Constabulary Reserve (CCR) recruited from Territorial Army (TA) units and other former soldiers, controlled by the War Office (through chief constables) and intended for crowd control. This flowed from a typically bellicose and unsuccessful demand by Winston Churchill to 'call up' TA reserves. 'If we start arguing about petty details,' stormed the Chancellor when asked who would pay, 'we will have a tired-out police force, a dissipated army and bloody revolution.'[65] The CCR was placed under the command of General Sir Nevil Macready, a former Metropolitan Police Commissioner who had also been Commander-in-Chief during what the *Daily Mail* called Ireland's 'troublous period'.[66] On 10 May Macready complained to the Air Secretary Samuel Hoare that his 'own little office consists practically of myself and a lady typist plus an orderly to answer the bell'.[67] Despite attracting 1,000 recruits in London and 7,000 more in the provinces, the CCR was never actually mobilised given the strike ended two days after enlistment began.[68]

In the Home Secretary's view it was better to be safe than sorry, and between 10 and 12 May his departmental reports suggested the danger of serious disturbances had lessened. Later, there was considerable criticism as to the behaviour of regular and special constables, what the academic Ralph Miliband called 'numerous instances of baton charges by mounted and foot police against strike pickets', not to mention 'a fair amount of licensed brutality on the part of volunteer special constables'. Large numbers of arrests were made during the strike, both under Emergency Regulations and the criminal law, often on what Miliband called the 'flimsiest of pretexts, and sentences ... freely handed down by magistrates little disposed to sympathy with those brought before them'.[69]

Despite encouragement from certain sections of the Cabinet, soldiers were given no special powers under the Emergency Regulations and the role of the Armed Forces in the general strike was deliberately kept to a minimum. Troop movements did take place between 1 and 12 May but were low-key, stimulating various rumours of mutiny and confinement to barracks.[70] More visible were the naval battleships or cruisers which were stationed at Hull, Belfast, Liverpool, Glasgow, Newport, Barrow and other strategic ports around the UK, including a total of twenty-four ships on the Thames. These inevitably provoked more speculation. 'A lot of people thought ... that if the strike got out of hand,' remembered one striker in Liverpool, 'they'd put the guns on the city.'[71]

Further rumours that the Army had run out of money or that troops had refused to obey an order to perform strike duties prompted the War Office to ask the BBC to make clear 'that with the exception of Guards for a few vulnerable points in Great Britain, no troops have yet been called up in aid of Civil power'.[72] The War Office later characterized the strike as having had three phases, what it called the 'Preliminary Period' (30 April–3 May), the 'First (Defensive) Period' (4–6 May) and a 'Second (Offensive) Period' (7–12 May).[73]

Where the Armed Forces did get involved was at the London Docks. There, the stoppage was complete. Between 4 and 6 May, trade union pickets had prevented any food leaving the docks, which led to concerns about shortages of flour and meat in the capital. Lord Ruthven, General Officer Commanding London District, opted for shock-and-awe tactics, and on 7 May a battalion of Coldstream Guards marched through the East End wearing, as Sir William Joynson-Hicks recalled:

> the tin helmets which they had worn in France, followed by tanks and armoured cars. Crowds of volunteers slept that night in improvised beds on the floors of the great dock buildings, and the next day the lorries left the East End loaded with provisions, and triumphantly entered Hyde Park without a stone being thrown or a shot fired.[74]

That first food convoy on 8 May was escorted by twenty armoured cars and consisted of 100 lorries each carrying two armed soldiers. Although this was watched by vast crowds of spectators, any jeering was balanced by many of those cheering 'as if it were a Lord Mayor's show'.[75] Ralph Miliband thought there was enough artillery to 'kill every living thing in every street in the neighbourhood of the mills'.[76] It was certainly provocative, but soon Hyde Park, which had been converted into a gigantic food storage depot, was overflowing with vital supplies. Tugs flying the White Ensign (by permission of the First Sea Lord, Earl Beatty) also carried 17,000 tonnes of food to London's wharves. The blockade, reflected J. C. C. Davidson, 'was completely broken'.[77]

On 10 May there was payback when the 'exceedingly Socialistic' local council gave notice that all power to the London Docks was to be cut off, imperilling both the water level and perishable foodstuffs being held in an enormous refrigeration plant. An official called E. T. Williams at the Admiralty had the ingenious idea of towing several submerged submarines into the King George V Dock. These, as Jix triumphantly recalled, 'transferred a cable to the shore, connected it with the Docks plant and manufactured the necessary electricity with her own engines'.[78] Within half an hour of the electricity shut down, the power supply had been restored. Naval ratings also manned more than half of London's generating stations to maintain the power supply in other parts of the capital.[79]

Even before the government's twin triumphs at the docks, several ministers had been urging Stanley Baldwin to introduce legislation declaring a general strike illegal and on 7 May a small (and rather diehard) committee comprising Lord Birkenhead, Lord Cave (the Lord Chancellor) and Sir Douglas Hogg (the Attorney General) was formed to draft an 'Illegal Strikes Bill'. This was presented to Cabinet the following day, Hogg having 'only just succeeded' in getting it on the agenda.[80] This three-clause bill declared as illegal any strike of 'a sympathetic character calculated to intimidate or coerce the Government or the community', authorized the restraint of trade union funds and prohibited the expulsion of members who refused to participate. The bill was to be fast-tracked through both Houses of Parliament on Monday 10 May.[81]

Baldwin had actually warned the Labour MP Jimmy Thomas back in April that in the event of a general strike the 'pressure' from Cabinet to 'restrict the powers of the Trade Unions would become irresistible',[82] while the Prime Minister himself floated the 'total repeal' of the *Trade Disputes Act 1906* with the Conservative MP Cuthbert Headlam on 14 April.[83] In the event, the government made its first move under Emergency Regulations, specifically Regulation 13A, which permitted the Home Secretary to halt bank transfers 'for any purpose prejudicial to the public safety of the community'. Jix used this several times during the strike to prevent monies transmitted from the State Bank of the Soviet Union from reaching the TUC,[84] although he grudgingly praised the General Council for refusing an initial payment on the grounds that it would be 'wilfully misinterpreted'.[85]

As for the bill, Gordon Phillips viewed this as largely performative, a way of reinforcing 'the impact of previous propaganda on the legal and constitutional status of the stoppage, and thereby to hasten a voluntary capitulation'.[86] But the bill's existence also provoked a backlash from ministers and civil servants. Deputy Cabinet Secretary Tom Jones told Baldwin:

> Eccleston Square was already beaten, and knew it was beaten, that it had taken some time to get the country to appreciate what the General Strike was, but this new Bill would come as a thunder-clap on the country which was utterly unprepared for it, and would greatly confuse its mind. It would be held to be an attack on Trade Unions, and would profoundly change the quite peaceful temper of the men now on strike.

Sensing the Prime Minister remained in two minds, Jones and Baldwin's private secretaries decided the only way left of 'influencing the P.M.' was 'through the King' and contacted the Palace. Sharing their 'view', Lord Cromer (the Lord Chamberlain) saw George V 'at once', and in time for the monarch to 'get a message through [the Colonial Secretary Leo] Amery to the Cabinet'.[87] Even the Cabinet Secretary Sir Maurice Hankey told Jones in 'his unemotional way' that 'he rather felt that the thing was being hurried'.[88]

At Cabinet on 10 May, the Prime Minister urged colleagues to pause for a few days and delay introduction of the bill for a week. Most ministers agreed only reluctantly, with Neville Chamberlain, Winston Churchill, Lord Cave, the Earl of Balfour (the Lord President) and Amery in opposition. Amery's view was:

> that the sooner we got the thing on the basis of legality the better knowing that as long as it was an issue between the Government and the strikers a great section of the public would always treat it as a party battle; the moment it became a matter for the strikers versus the law the position would be quite different.[89]

Matters came to a head on 11 May. Lord Stamfordham, the King's private secretary, came to Number 10 with messages from the monarch, while Bolton Eyres-Monsell, the Conservative Chief Whip, reported that a majority of Tory MPs were opposed to provocative legislation, and Walter Elliott, a moderate junior minister at the

THE ROAD TO ANARCHY AND RUIN

Scottish Office, suggested that any attempt to rush legislation through Parliament would give many Scottish MPs the impression the government was panicking.[90] After conferring for two and a half hours, Cabinet agreed to defer the bill but also resolved to announce their intention of introducing it. Meanwhile the press Lobby was informed, with several newspapers carrying full reports the following day. At an audience with the King, Leo Amery discovered him 'full of talk' and 'very glad to know that we were postponing legislation for the moment'.[91]

William Bridgeman found himself impressed at the Prime Minister's calm stewardship while J. C. C. Davidson later observed that in everything written about Baldwin and the general strike it had to be made 'absolutely clear' that 'his vision and his judgement were clear and decisive':

> The idea was always put about that he was under pressure. But there was no question of pressure; he saw the thing as clear as crystal ... There were many people ... running about the streets like dogs, trying to do something about it, but nothing deflected the simple man ... he just said 'No. I will not accept anything but the surrender of the TUC and the calling off of the strike.'[92]

4

'Anxious times'

'One rumour, much in the London spirit, that has got about,' reported the *Guardian* on 7 May, 'is that the King is going to ask both sides to tea at the Palace':

> It is said that the bishops of Winchester and of Southwark have approached the King with the proposal, the plan being that as neither side can ask to meet the other at this juncture without it being thought a sign of weakness, the King is the only one who could bring them together without prejudice to either side. A conciliation tea party at Buckingham Palace to end a national strike would indeed make history.[1]

John St Loe Strachey, a journalist who until the previous year had edited the *Spectator* and now a 'universal busybody', had begun bombarding Lord Stamfordham with a similar proposal, in essence a reprise of the sort of 'constitutional conference' convened in the wake of King Edward VII's accession to resolve an impasse over House of Lords reform.[2] Strachey suggested the King 'summon all the men available who had been Prime Ministers', something he believed 'would save face' on 'both sides'. And while he recognized that Ramsay MacDonald might see himself a 'minority of one' at such a gathering, Strachey reported that the Labour leader 'approved warmly' of the idea. The Leader of the Opposition had, however, added that 'nothing could, or ought to, be done without the advice of Mr. Baldwin, who was the King's constitutional adviser'.[3] Lord Stamfordham, who carefully annotated Strachey's letter, wrote '*cela va sans dire*' – that goes without saying.

Quite properly, Stamfordham at once informed Number 10, including the fact the King had read Strachey's letter 'and absolutely declines to entertain the idea of any intervention on his part except, of course, at the request of the Prime Minister'. Lord Oxford and Asquith, the former Liberal premier, had also made clear he 'deprecated' any repeat of the 1910 conference. 'No doubt Mr. Ramsay MacDonald would be very glad,' added Stamfordham caustically, 'if the King were to do anything to help him out of the very difficult position into which he has got himself.'[4]

What really annoyed the King's private secretary was MacDonald's suggestion (as quoted by Strachey) that the negotiations would not have broken down at all 'but for the perfectly local and accidental outbreak at the Daily Mail',[5] a reference to the incident seized upon by the Cabinet to call off negotiations. That, wrote Stamfordham, was 'hardly fair':

> On the contrary there was a conviction in the minds of the Government that the authority within which the T.U.C was negotiating was far too limited to make an agreement with the Government possible ... If Thomas and Ramsay MacDonald would only come out and express disapproval of the general strike and persuade the T.U.C. to recall the [strike] notices, negotiations for reconciliation would not be for a moment delayed.

Only once 'Messrs. Bevan [sic] and Co.' had hauled 'down their revolutionary flag', he stormed, would the Prime Minister consider further talks.[6]

Within a couple of days, Stamfordham appeared to have cooled down, particularly after a *Manchester Guardian* editorial caught his eye. This asked 'why should not the King take a hand and call the parties – all of them – together? He could do no greater service to the people of his Kingdom.'[7] The King's private secretary then wrote to one of Stanley Baldwin's officials saying that while he had 'stoutly refused' to listen to suggestions of intervention, he highlighted the 'circulation and influence' of that newspaper 'in the North of England'.[8] That was a pretty clear hint that the Prime Minister might consider offering his sovereign some advice to that effect.

King George V, then in the sixteenth year of his reign, and Queen Mary had returned to London from Windsor on 3 May and were to remain at Buckingham Palace throughout the nine days. 'By their excellent example and unfailing fortitude under conditions which closely approximated to those which beset us in 1914,' gushed *The Tatler*, 'Their Majesties have once more endeared themselves to the hearts of their loyal subjects.'[9] They did so amid the wild rumours which characterized the early stages of the strike. One had it that the government and Royal Family had fled to France,[10] and another that Stanley Baldwin had resigned and the King had 'sent for MacDonald' to form a new government.[11]

Strikes made the King-Emperor uneasy, although his instinctive sympathy for the underdog competed with impatience. When, at Newmarket, the coal-rich Lord Durham called the miners a 'damned lot of revolutionaries' the King retorted: 'Try living on their wages before you judge them.' Privately, however, he told Queen Mary that the 'hopeless' miners risked costing the realm 'many millions' and giving pleasure to 'our communists & the Russian Soviet'.[12]

As H. C. G. Matthew has observed, Lord Stamfordham was more of a diehard than the King, although the existence of this difference of views showed 'how far George V took his own line and stuck to it'.[13] The Prince of Wales, however, noted the confusion in his father's mind as to whether the strike was purely industrial or smacked of revolution.[14] During the strike, therefore, the King spoke with 'two voices', initially hawkish, later more moderate; a prisoner, in the perceptive judgement of his biographer Kenneth Rose, of his naval upbringing, which 'had implanted in him a lifelong antipathy to disorder'.[15]

Writing to Lord Derby on 12 April 1926, a rather complacent Stamfordham could not 'imagine that there would be anything like a general strike, as the country will be, I should think, all against the miners'.[16] Even on 29 April, he told the Home Secretary he hoped it would 'not be necessary to put in force what seem to be complete and admirable arrangements for dealing with the strike'.[17] Within twenty-four hours, however, the King had detoured from Newmarket to sign the proclamation declaring a state of emergency at a meeting of his Privy Council. 'I fear it is inevitable that there will be a coal stoppage tomorrow followed later by a general strike,' George wrote sadly in his diary, 'one never seems to be able to have any peace now for long.'[18]

The King's diary also captures his deepening gloom in the days that followed:

> Saturday 1 May: Had a talk with him [Lord Cave, the Lord Chancellor] about the situation which is not good ...
>
> Sunday 2 May: The Lord Chancellor went to London for a Cabinet & only returned at 7.30. with bad news & I fear the railways & transport will come out tomorrow at midnight.
>
> Monday 3 May: Our Engagement Day ... Held a Council at 2.30. Had talks with L[or]d Balfour & the Home Secretary; all arrangements have now been made by the Gov[ernmen]t to carry on when the general strike takes place tonight.

On 3 May, Stamfordham informed Sir Laming Worthington-Evans, the Secretary of State for War, that the King was 'rather surprised, and even a little hurt', that he had received 'no information whatever from the War Office about the very important movement of troops in connection with the present serious crisis'. 'Certainly in the old days,' he added sniffily, 'no movement of troops out of the ordinary roster would have taken place without communication with the Sovereign.' Sir Laming sent a grovelling reply two days later deploring what he called a 'misunderstanding'.[19]

Meanwhile, Stamfordham wrote to one of the Prime Minister's private secretaries to say:

> that so long as the General Strike lasts the King would like to see a Minister daily, who could report upon the situation. His Majesty would make the audience as short as possible, as he knows how busy everyone is.[20]

First up was the First Lord of the Treasury (Baldwin) on 5 May, who along with other Ministers of the Crown kept the sovereign fully briefed on developments. A minor courtier called Christopher Roundell also took it upon himself to include 'light and bright human touches' in his reports, which Stamfordham assured him would be 'welcomed by His Majesty and all here' during 'this lamentable crisis'. These were largely verbose and dull, although the King approvingly scribbled 'capital boys' next to a story about undergraduates at Oriel College defying university policy to volunteer with the London

General Omnibus Company. A few days later Roundell recounted that an aristocratic special constable had been told he would never become a porter at Paddington Station as 'they only take Earls'.[21] This ephemera did not completely expel the monarch's gloom. On 6 May, the day 'Dear Papa' (Edward VII) had died in 1910, the King spent all morning reading reports about the strike from around the country, including that taxi-cab drivers had just joined the stoppage. 'I have passed,' he wrote in his diary, 'through some anxious times during last 16 years.'[22]

Members of the Prince of Wales' and the Duke of York's households, meanwhile, gave voluntary service, with all their footmen enrolling as special constables or despatch riders.[23] Prince Edward, who had flown back to England on the first day of the strike, felt acutely the conflict between his 'natural desire' to get involved during the crisis and what he called 'constitutional constraints'. Within the limits of his father's 'counsel' to keep a low profile, the Prince of Wales spent the mornings gathering news from government departments, afternoons with 'Bertie' (the Duke of York and future George VI) listening with 'rapt' interest to 'acrimonious' debates in the House of Commons and evenings 'making the rounds' of London.[24] Towards the end of the strike, Edward spent a whole night touring voluntary canteens in the capital.[25]

Inevitably, long-planned engagements were disrupted. In early May the Home Secretary said he was 'quite sure' the Prince of Wales 'must not go to Yorkshire during the general strike', not least 'because of the question of Police, of whom we have none too many'.[26] The Prince reluctantly agreed, and it was later announced that a visit to Reading to open a new bridge over the Thames had been postponed and a trip to Hull and Halifax cancelled.[27] On 7 May, the Lord Chamberlain announced that the Courts arranged for the middle of May had been postponed until further notice, while the Jockey Club had already called off a hunt. 'Personally', remarked the King, 'I should have been inclined to go further and stop [the] racing at Chester.'[28]

The King followed closely the recruitment of special constables, whose enrolment included an oath of allegiance. A force was even arranged 'for duty in and around Windsor Park' so that the Crown Estate would be 'efficiently protected'.[29] On 10 May the King and Queen 'went to the Mews & saw the men & horses of 25 special mounted constables', whom he was 'putting up'.[30] The monarch's only gesture to normality came on Sunday 9 May when, following divine service in the chapel at Buckingham Palace ('the Head Master of Eton preached an excellent sermon & referred to the present situation') Their Majesties visited the Royal Academy of Arts at Burlington House, although the King 'thought the pictures there less good than usual'.[31]

On 8 May, the sentries at Buckingham Palace swapped their scarlet for khaki service dress with revolvers. This was not, the *Sunday Times* reported, intended to be 'provocative', but 'demonstrates the fact [it] is not a merely ceremonial observance'.[32] Nevertheless, noted the *Daily Herald* editor Hamilton Fyfe, the change caused 'comment' which was 'not very complimentary to the King':

> He is roughly criticised, too, because of the Royal Arms appearing on the British Gazette [a government-produced newspaper]; it is regarded as HIS paper by millions who don't know the ways of the Stationery Office. Many complained as well of HIS proclamation about the State of Emergency, which was signed by him as a matter of form. The impression that he is taking sides against the mass of working people is curiously widespread.[33]

All MI5 agents had picked up while monitoring the Aldershot military base on 4 May, however, were remarks from a grocer's wife and a chambermaid that there 'was a great deal of "anti-King" feeling in the town', although in 'conversation with various soldiers none were found with any disloyal feelings'.[34] With the Prince of Wales and Duke of York watching from the peers' gallery, meanwhile, the Independent Labour Party MP George Buchanan declared himself a republican. 'I would abolish the Monarchy to-morrow,' he said. 'It is not a crime to be a republican. I am proud of it.'[35] According to the Labour MP J. R. Clynes, a 'gravely disturbed' King even gestured towards his lavish surroundings and remarked to Jimmy Thomas: 'If the worst happens, I suppose all this ... will vanish?'[36]

And despite the perception that the government-run *British Gazette* was 'HIS' newspaper, the King was furious on learning that its 8 May edition had stated that the 'Armed Forces of the Crown would receive the full support of the Government in any action that they may find it necessary to take in an honest endeavour to aid the Civil

Power'.[37] 'His Majesty cannot help thinking that this is an unfortunate announcement', Stamfordham told General Milne tersely, 'and already it has received a good deal of adverse criticism.'[38] The Chief of the General Staff protested that the announcement had been made by the Cabinet and that 'the War Office had nothing to do with it'.[39] As John Murray remarked in his history of the general strike, to 'give the armed forces such carte blanche authority was ... something quite unique in modern history'.[40]

The King proved more directly interventionist when it came to 'so-called peaceful picketing' and other attempts by strikers to intimidate volunteers, interfere with transport and hold up food supplies. As early as 5 May, Lord Stamfordham had asked the Number 10 official Sir Ronald Waterhouse if it would be 'possible to introduce emergency legislation' to prevent picketing 'and at the same time relieve the police of the additional work imposed upon them in dealing with picket trouble'.[41] That this request came from the King was confirmed in another letter two days later, in which Stamfordham informed Waterhouse that the monarch was again 'concerned' to learn that vehicles were 'being held up and damaged'. The King even suggested that 'one Executive Officer' be made responsible 'for all Police control' – the Metropolitan Police Commissioner in London and the Home Secretary 'in the provinces'. Stamfordham continued:

> His Majesty does not wish to add in the slightest to the endless absorbing questions with which the Prime Minister is confronted: but he is gravely impressed that the moment has arrived for the adoption of the most effective of measures to ensure the fullest protection to those who are trying, under serious pressure and provocation, to do their duty by supporting the Government in their formidable task.[42]

Waterhouse immediately showed Stamfordham's letter to the Prime Minister, who cautioned that amending the *Trade Disputes Act 1906* (which covered peaceful picketing) would be 'highly controversial' since Labour and the trade unions regarded that Act 'as their more important charter'. He added:

> The practical difficulties confronting the Police are not caused so much by insufficient powers as by inadequate strength available at

a particular point to deal with sporadic crowds assembled at dock gates etc. for the purpose of intimidation.[43]

The following day, and stressing its great secrecy, Sir Maurice Hankey informed Stamfordham that the Cabinet intended to introduce its emergency bill to amend the law regarding illegal strikes and restrict trade union funds, but not outlaw peaceful picketing.[44] In the interim, the King was also expected to approve an Order in Council which, as we have already seen, the Home Secretary required to restrict the transfer of funds from the Soviet Union to the Trades Union Congress.

This, however, made both the King and his private secretary nervous. Stamfordham considered it 'dangerously akin to confiscation' which might 'provoke retaliation in the form of looting shops and even banks, which indeed spells Revolution, from which Heaven defend us'.[45] At a Privy Council meeting on Sunday 9 May, the King told both the Home Secretary and Sir Douglas Hogg, the Attorney General, he 'was not at all sure' the government would be acting 'wisely' in adopting either the measures authorized by the Order in Council or those in their intended bill. Echoing Stamfordham's words, he continued:

> So far the situation was better and more peaceful than might have been expected. The spirit of the miners was not unfriendly ... but any attempt to get hold of or control the Trades Union Funds might cause exasperation and provoke reprisals. If money were not forthcoming to buy food, there might be looting of shops, even of banks.

The following day (10 May) Stamfordham saw the King again, who asked his private secretary to see the Prime Minister 'at once' and repeat what he had already said to the Home Secretary and Attorney General, that:

> the King regarded with considerable apprehension the proposed step of the Government, which might be fraught with grave results, beginning with a storm in the House of Commons and a panic among the strikers, who would regard the action of the Government as little less than confiscation.

Stamfordham took this message to Stanley Baldwin, who pointed out that the Palace had misunderstood the object of the Order in Council, which was 'merely to prevent the banks paying out Foreign Monies' and that the proposed bill was an 'entirely separate' matter. The Prime Minister then took care to add that he 'understood and appreciated the expression of His Majesty's natural concern'.[46] When the King was asked to hold another Privy Council on the morning of Tuesday 11 May to strengthen the previous Order in Council, George again 'begged' the Home Secretary to 'impress upon the Prime Minister what a grave mistake His Majesty felt it would be'.[47] The King, of course, did as he was requested.

At an earlier audience on 8 May, William Bridgeman, the First Lord of the Admiralty, found the King 'very loquacious' and 'very angry' with what he called 'the lawless people'.[48] A few days later, the monarch carefully annotated his copy of the daily War Office Intelligence Survey, which included the following observations:

6. Mr. [John] Bromley [of the National Union of Railwaymen] said at Canning Town that the T.U.C. would call out its second line of defence to-night, thus adding 1 or 2 millions to the number of strikers.
7. Communists are reported to be endeavouring to find out the strength of guards at various depots and of the police and their reserves in the London District.
8. The Workers Defence Corps are reported to have set up a Central Advisory Committee ...

Next to all three the King scribbled in an agitated hand: 'Could these not be arrested?'[49] Lord Stamfordham diligently but hastily passed this on to the Secretary of State for War who, doubtlessly relieved, referred it to the Home Secretary. Jix responded at diplomatic but firm length on 12 May, saying he did not consider that the statement attributed to Bromley 'put him in any different category from that of other responsible Trade Union leaders who have called out their men or advocated a general extension of the strike'. As for the Communists, their activities were:

being most carefully watched and whenever any evidence can be obtained which would justify legal proceedings, such proceedings are immediately undertaken. Already there have been several arrests ... On the whole, however, I am impressed by the comparative lack of activity on the part of the Communists. I think the recent prosecutions have had a very salutary effect.

'I shall not, however,' Sir William told his sovereign, 'relax my vigilance.'[50]

5

'BLACKLEGS'

The timing of the general strike, observed the Conservative politician Harold Macmillan in his memoirs, was fortuitous. The weather at the beginning of May 1926 was fine and there was, he noted, a 'kind of holiday atmosphere' in which volunteers enjoyed undertaking 'new and rather exciting jobs':

> Members of Parliament became porters and guards; some even drove locomotives. Very large numbers of men and women of all classes acted as bus-conductors, drivers of lorries, helpers in canteens, and so forth. The essential services were thus carried on.[1]

To those on strike, such volunteers were 'blacklegs', a pejorative term which apparently originated in strike-breaking miners being given away by their coal dust-covered legs.

The description does not appear to have bothered those at which it was aimed. For Lieutenant Commander Murray of the Royal Navy, the general strike evoked G. K. Chesterton's poem 'The Secret People' – the people of England 'that never have spoken yet'. Although he was convalescing after a major operation, the Admiralty gave Murray permission to work as a bus conductor in London. In an unpublished memoir he described Hammersmith Broadway as 'a seething cauldron, with all bedlam howling in the scum'. But Murray also found himself questioning the government's claim that its 'authority' derived from the 'will of the people':

> It should have resigned a week earlier and invited the people to proclaim its will through the ballot box. If not – if it was still

convinced of its own standing as the august and legitimate servant of a sovereign people – why did it not govern without fear or favour, starting with the arrest of such as dared to challenge that sovereignty? Proclaiming that a conspiracy existed and yet leaving the conspirators free to go on conspiring ... was a dangerous advertisement, surely, of its lack of faith in its own powers.[2]

Also acting as a bus conductor for the London General Omnibus Company was E. L. Amies. He told a friend of two buses that had been 'very badly smashed':

> in one instance I had a full complement of passengers who were most brave. I issued an order for the women passengers to put up their umbrellas which they did and so saved glass hitting their eyes, but I must say seeing the people sitting on the floor of the bus holding up umbrellas and travelling at about 30 miles an hour was most comical!![3]

William Burton Stewart, meanwhile, volunteered at YMCA-run canteens in Hyde Park, which had been turned into a huge milk and lorry depot:

> At 12 o'clock midnight we were serving tea, buns and sausage rolls to the lorrymen, a process which went on till 7 a.m. the next morning. The staff consisted of 4 ladies, all veteran war workers ... and myself. I learnt a lot from these four ladies and humbly salute them as masters in the art of catering and in being tireless and resourceful workers.

Later, Stewart's responsibilities as furnaceman, policeman and washer-up were shared by a general, two colonels, two science professors at the University of London and some Boy Scouts.[4]

The Education Officer's Department at London County Council, meanwhile, praised the 'really splendid manner' in which East End teachers had 'overcome transport and other difficulties and "carried on" in the national emergency'. One teacher recorded starting from Reigate at 8.15 a.m., riding in a 'lorry from there to Redhill, walked to Mersham, motored to Croydon, took a "pirate" bus to Westminster, and then had a taxi to Jamaica Road'.[5] At Calais in France, hotels were crowded with British passengers held up by the strike, although the wealthiest opted to fly, with three times as many 'machines' transferring both passengers and mail across the English Channel than normal.[6] Back in Great Britain, many retailers sold out of bicycles within a few hours of the strike beginning, while the sale of motor bikes doubled. The *Daily Mail* even reported sightings of penny-farthings in Brixton.[7] Flo Jones recalled a family holiday to the Isle of Man being spoiled by the need to take a cattle boat back to the mainland.[8]

Volunteer-run transport, however, was concentrated in urban areas. Alan Lascelles, assistant private secretary to the Prince of Wales (and later private secretary to King George VI and Queen Elizabeth II) found himself stranded in the north of Scotland. He told his wife Joan:

> no trains are running north of Perth, which is a long way from here, & we have no means of reaching it. The only car for miles is the hotel Ford, which is their only link with civilisation & has only a limited supply of petrol, so we can't commandeer it ... if the worst comes to the worst, I'll start to walk to Perth.

Lascelles particularly feared acting on the rumour of a train to Inverness and then getting stranded for several days 'at some beastly place'. 'Probably motors are not to be had for love or money,' he observed in another letter, 'or at any rate a good deal more of the latter than I have got with me.'[9]

Back in the south of England, the 'Bentley Boys' – a team of motoring enthusiasts famous as racing drivers on the track and as playboys off it – formed the Brooklands Squad of crack drivers to assist the authorities.[10] To the relief of many Englishmen, transport difficulties merely reduced rather than cancelled much-loved spectator sport. On 8 May, Kingsley Game walked to Lords and back to see if there was going to be any cricket. 'There was quite a fair crowd outside Lords waiting to get in,' he told his wife. 'We are an extraordinary people. Imagine a general strike in France!'[11] The committee of Marylebone Cricket Club recommended that the counties carry on their programmes 'as well as circumstances permit':

> They suggest to cricketers that they should be guided by a sense of public duty rather than by affection for their counties, but they

strongly recommend that the best possible elevens should be put into the field against the Australians, as on those occasions cricketers may, out of courtesy to our guests, legitimately obtain leave from their public duties.[12]

The Jockey Club and the National Hunt Committee decided to abandon all meetings except at Chester.[13] This disruption to 'normal' life was widely felt. Henrietta Joseph (whose sister Beatrice was married to the Liberal grandee Sir Herbert Samuel) described a 'foreign world' where 'things were not done for us' and 'one had to do one's own arranging and fixing':

> Everyone was a pioneer. Life became an adventure ... As in the war, we all fraternised with one another. As days followed strange day, the resources of civilisation began to be foreshadowed rather than actually to appear as we got to know how things began. Gradually these young lords and varsity men became increasingly efficient at their jobs. The railways began to lose some of their amateurishness. One or two papers began to come out – almost life-like – in some cases there were 4 pages.[14]

Others were simply bored. 'How would you like it cut, sir?' ran the caption accompanying a *Punch* cartoon depicting a barber. 'Without,' was the customer's reply, 'the slightest reference to the strike.' Chancellor Winston Churchill observed that there were masses of people who felt 'quite detached from the conflict', waiting, 'as if they were spectators at a football match', to see 'whether the Government or the trades union is the stronger'.[15]

'VARSITY MEN'

Most university undergraduates had no doubt whose side they were on. Accounts of the general strike are awash with stories of 'varsity' volunteers at Britain's most famous seats of learning, which in 1926 were considerably fewer and less egalitarian than they would be a century later. At St Andrews in Scotland, virtually the entire body of 650 matriculated students together with many members of staff volunteered, while in Aberdeen and Glasgow the proportions were more modest. At Edinburgh University more than 2,000 of its near-4,000 students signed up, although only half those were given something to do. Jennie Lee, a miner's daughter at that time studying law, recalled that: 'Inside twenty-four hours I began to hear normally good-natured young fellows talk with unholy glee of the pleasure it would give them to run a tank through some of our mining villages.'[16]

Lee's future colleague Hugh Gaitskell was a hitherto apolitical undergraduate at Oxford. But the impact of the strike, he later wrote, 'was sharp and sudden, a little like a war ... which forced us to abandon plans for pleasure, to change our values and adjust our priorities'. When the future Labour leader sought leave from his college warden to volunteer for the Trades Union Congress it was refused. Undeterred, he and others gathered at the historian G. D. H. Cole's home in Holywell, which became the nucleus of a University Strike Committee. As Gaitskell recalled:

> What could I do? Precious little. Speak at meetings? God forbid! Organise? Absolutely no experience. Had I got a car? No. Could I by any chance drive a car? Yes, I had learnt the year before ... I went off to the Oxford Strike Committee headquarters, got myself enrolled as a driver and received my instructions.

Equipped with a paid-up trade union card as a papermaker, Gaitskell drove undergraduate speakers to village meetings around Oxford, carried messages to Didcot with the future poet John Betjeman ('who thought it all a great lark') and liaised with London by ferrying Margaret Cole (the historian's wife) and copies of the *British Worker* (a TUC-produced newspaper) to and from the capital. But while the general strike served as a memorable introduction to the Labour movement, Gaitskell's family were appalled. One cousin even accused him over dinner of 'betraying his class'. 'Henceforth,' Hugh wrote to a doubtlessly surprised aunt, 'my future is with the working classes.'[17]

The historian A. J. P. Taylor later remembered the strike as a welcome interruption to Oxford's cloistered existence:

> No one in Oxford discussed it beforehand. No one even among the rowing men had any feeling that the miners were wrong or the government right. But when the general strike started most undergraduates responded to the call of duty and went off as

strikebreakers. It was August 1914 all over again. One of the departing heroes even said to me, 'I wonder if I shall ever come back again', quite in the spirit of Rupert Brooke.[18]

The Oxford Trades and Labour Council's appeal for undergraduates to 'remain neutral ... and not to engage themselves provocatively against the striking workmen' was politely ignored.[19] Formally, the university itself took a neutral position, and students were ordered not to do 'blackleg' work in the city, although in practice examinations were postponed and volunteering tolerated in other parts of England.[20] They were usually conspicuous. At the Southampton docks, several Oxford undergraduates 'wearing plus fours and Oxford trousers' could be seen unloading foodstuffs,[21] while others helped unload ships at Hull. When a 'weary looking undergraduate' approached a Home Office official and asked if they could eat some of the supplies, he was told: 'Your orders were to come here and shift apples, and the method you employ to shift them does not in the least matter.'[22]

In Cambridge, meanwhile, the divisional Civil Commissioner Sir Philip Sassoon arranged for its undergraduates to be organized in gangs according to their capacity for various kinds of work. If led by 'suitable leaders', he observed, they make:

> a very high-spirited, efficient force which produces an excellent moral effect where it is employed. But if they are left unorganised they tend to rush eagerly about the country in search of work, which they sometimes find and sometimes not, perhaps behaving in an unfortunate way.[23]

Several Cambridge undergraduates achieved modest fame as the 'Dover Dockers'. Arguing that the 'lethargy' of the Cambridge authorities was incompatible 'with the duties incumbent on Youth in a time of such national crisis', around eighty volunteers, some of them chauffeur-driven, headed to the south-west of England where cross-Channel services and mail boats kept them busy. On Saturday 8 May they were disappointed not to be acknowledged by the Duke of Connaught and Strathearn (a son of Queen Victoria) despite giving him a 'specially loud cheer'. Even repeated rumours that hundreds of strikers were on their way to 'storm' or even 'murder' the Dover Dockers simply added to the novelty and excitement.[24]

Not all strikers were hostile to university undergraduates. J. C. C. Davidson recorded a story concerning the son of Home Secretary Sir William Joynson-Hicks, who had volunteered at Tooley Street:

> One lorry had been loaded with boxes of sugar and had gone away, and as some undergraduates were starting to load the second lorry, a picket pushed past young Jix who was just preparing to stop him when the fellow remarked: 'It's all right, Guvnor,' and went up to an undergraduate carrying a box of sugar and said to him: 'For Gawd's sake turn it over, Sir; you will find it much easier to carry with your fingers in those little runners.'

'There was the man who ought to have gloried in the inefficiency of the volunteer,' observed Davidson, 'but whose professional pride had so overcome him that he could not bear the sight of work which he himself was accustomed to do being done badly.'[25]

The Attorney General's son Quintin Hogg, 'determined to be in the thick of it', also helped fix up a fleet of decrepit Renault lorries to collect refuse in his father's St Marylebone constituency. When Hogg later contested the seat himself at a 1963 by-election, his activity during the general strike was used to describe him as 'an enemy of the working class'.[26] Stanley Baldwin's daughters Betty and Diana, meanwhile, volunteered as a driver and canteen worker respectively.[27] In one sense, the strike acted as a great leveller, giving the middle classes a taste of working-class life.

This was not unwelcome. As Julian Symons observed in his 1957 history of the general strike, the 'very finest opportunity' for 'fulfilling childhood dreams of adventure came in this chance of working on the railway'. The actual driving of a railway train, he noted, was not difficult, but to:

> distinguish the correct signal, to discern the proper line, to keep up steam on a gradient, requires a degree of skill and experience which very few of these volunteers possessed. It is extraordinary, not that there were some minor accidents and misadventures, but that so many trains reached their destinations without mishap.[28]

The historian of the National Union of Railwaymen later expressed scepticism at the then Minister of Transport's claim that between 4 and 14 May only six accidents occurred in which four people died and thirty-five were injured. Philip Bagwell cited a single issue of the *British Worker*, which reported five serious passenger train accidents within thirty-six hours of dawn on 10 May. At Bishop's Stortford a goods train coming from Cambridge crashed into a passenger train causing the death of one person and injury to three others,[29] while the most serious accident occurred near Edinburgh, when a 'blackleg' passenger train from Berwick smashed into refuse wagons at St Margaret's Tunnel just outside Waverley Station. Three people were killed and eight injured.[30] When an LNER inspector appealed to a breakdown squad 'in the name of humanity' to help with the rescue effort, one driver said it 'served the injured b—y well right for trusting themselves with a blackleg Driver'. An agricultural student on board was 'cursed' as he clambered out of the tunnel, his abusers mistakenly believing him to have been driving the train.[31]

Some volunteers were more skilled than others. R. J. Cogswell, who considered the general strike an act of 'supreme folly', had undergone a full apprenticeship in heavy engineering, including locomotive work. After being handed a Great Western Railwayman's cap 'new from the store', he and others helped transfer milk from Wiltshire to Paddington. Cogswell did not mind being called a 'blackleg', though he enjoyed the description 'mercenaries of the class war' more.[32] Thomas Elmhirst (later Sir Thomas) of the RAF also became a railway fireman at King's Cross on the basis that he had once taken charge of a battle cruiser boiler room. With a driver ('who I think was a bit of a blackleg') they ran one of London's few suburban trains to High Barnet, and on 11 May led a trial run of the *Flying Scotsman* as far as Grantham.[33]

Not everyone worked the trains. The Old Etonian Major Des Allhusen became a porter on the Great Western, which usually involved unloading milk at Paddington. As he told a friend:

> I am getting very handy with a milk can! In the interval between two milk trains I went to interview the peaceful picket ... Of course we intended to lay them out, but it was very disappointing, as the picket

were perfectly friendly & rather pathetic. Quite a crowd collected and I was having quite a good meeting when the police told me to stop – whereupon all the strikers I visited are shaking hands!

As far as Allhusen was concerned, 'the Strike has simply been a holiday'.[34]

The press was particularly interested in 'titled' railway workers. At Paddington, Lord Portarlington (who had also volunteered during the 1919 railway strike) was 'everywhere ... throwing milk churns about, now opening doors, always finding a new task and performing it willingly',[35] while Lord Weymouth watered railway horses. Elsewhere, Lord Raglan (the son of a former Lieutenant Governor of the Isle of Man) worked as a railway guard, the Earl of Caledon and Lord Monkswell occupied themselves at an LNER engine shed at Marylebone, and Lord Herschell drove a train on the Isle of Wight.[36]

The degree to which railway services were operating normally became the subject of some controversy. The Trades Union Congress grew irritated by several items on BBC bulletins and in the government-run *British Gazette* to this effect, which were often inaccurate. A flyer distributed by the TUC ('How the "Gentlemen of England" man the trains') said:

> The Government issue bulletins saying that the railway services are improving day by day. What does this improvement amount to? They boasted of 200 trains a day on the Southern Railway on Thursday but from the two big railway stations, Victoria and Waterloo alone, the number is normally 1880. At Victoria to-day (Saturday) the Company 'hopes' to run 20 trains. The Electric Railways of London carry about 1,300,000 passengers a day. At present there is a service on the Central London of only one train in about 16 minutes, though the Company announces a 4 minute service ... The position on other railways and in the provinces is much the same.

'How can the feeble little army of blacklegs deal with such a task as this?' concluded the TUC. 'Compare your broadcasting programme with these facts.'[37]

There was further misinformation when, on 11 May, it was widely reported that the engine and four coaches of the *Flying Scotsman* had been deliberately derailed at Cramlington, ten miles north of Newcastle upon Tyne. Although the wrecking attempt was very real – a length of rail had been removed – the *British Gazette* took advantage of the confusion between the *Flying Scotsman* 'service' and the record-breaking locomotive of the same name and claimed it was the latter, a national icon, that had been targeted. Amazingly, only one passenger was injured, a Ministry of Agriculture official on his way back to London.[38]

The most visible volunteers during the general strike were those who enrolled as additional police officers. 'I have joined up as a Special Constable,' recorded Chips Channon in his diary on 5 May, 'and begin dangerous duties tonight at six with terror in my heart. Only for England would I do this. I have a baton and a whistle.'[39] Recruits were required to swear a declaration of allegiance to 'serve our Sovereign Lord the King in the office of Special Constable'.[40]

The following day, Channon drilled men in a 'stinking room' at Scotland Yard:

> Terror grips my heart at the prospect of the unpleasant baton charges. I shan't know what to do. Fortunately, today was fairly quiet, although there was rioting at Hammersmith and they say machine guns had been called on. Pickets everywhere, nevertheless, have been unable to prevent trains running, buses going and services generally being maintained ... The revolution is a reality but the Kingdom has well sustained the first shock and will undoubtedly win.[41]

On 7 May Channon was despatched to put down a riot at King's Cross, confessing in his diary that he was 'terrified' and 'muttered a prayer', although he was relieved when they had 'no trouble and the crowd dispersed at once'. Fear also occasionally entered his heart when at the head of a patrol of fourteen men he 'sallied' into Whitechapel, Shoreditch and Hackney, which he considered 'well-known terror sections'. Channon thought the regular policemen 'marvellous in their loyalty, courage and manliness', but his sympathy, such as it was, with the 'downtrodden' vanished on seeing how they lived. 'The squalor,' he told his diary, 'is much exaggerated!'[42]

Unlike Channon, some acted as special constables while holding down a regular job. Lord Denning, a future Master of the Rolls, recalled many young barristers serving as special constables in the mornings and then returning to their law offices in the afternoons.[43] The Scottish judge Lord Macmillan, who had recently chaired a court of inquiry into miners' wages, was 'equipped with armlet, baton, and whistle' and assigned to the royal waiting room at Paddington.[44] The vicars of Seaview and St Helens on the Isle of Wight, meanwhile, were enrolled as 'clergy specials', as was the headmaster of Eton (Dr Alington) and about fifty of his assistant masters.[45]

By the end of the strike, almost 1,000 Stock Exchange 'specials' had signed up.[46] At Liberty & Co. on London's Regent Street, Captain Stewart-Liberty swore in some fifty men in an improvised orderly room. Such was the steady stream of volunteers, two magistrates had to be installed in the store's boardroom. After a few days, the 'London Business Houses No. 2' division had reached 450 men.[47] Even Lord Gorell, one of the few Labour members of the House of Lords, signed up and patrolled the streets of Kensington. 'It is war v. the country,' he explained, 'and I cannot put party before country.'[48]

At Toynbee Hall in London's East End, William Garnett was so appalled by the presence of 4,000 strikers that he at once went to the Guildhall to be sworn in as a special constable, later persuading four of his colleagues to join him. 'The public adapted themselves so rapidly & so wonderfully to the novel circumstances,' he told his mother, 'that it was quite clear that no strike could succeed.'[49] It seemed likely that others volunteered just for something to do. The eighty-five-year-old Earl of Meath was sworn in as a special at Chertsey, while Prince George of Russia joked to a journalist: 'Be careful how you address me, I am now a superior police officer.'[50]

The writer Evelyn Waugh volunteered during the general strike to 'escape boredom' and gather material for what he called 'sociological novels'.[51] In *Brideshead Revisited*, Charles Ryder returns to England from Paris and is almost disappointed to discover how normal everything is:

> We dined that night at the Café Royal. There things were a little more warlike, for the Café was full of undergraduates who had come down for 'National Service'. One group, from Cambridge,

had that afternoon signed on to run messages for Transport House, and their table backed on another group's who were enrolled as special constables. Now and then one or other party would shout provocatively over the shoulder, but it is hard to come into serious conflict back to back, and the affair ended with their giving each other tall glasses of lager beer.[52]

'It is tedious & depressing,' wrote Virginia Woolf early in the strike, 'rather like waiting in a train outside a station.'[53] The war poet Siegfried Sassoon, whose cousin was a Civil Commissioner, mischievously contemplated the possibility that Sir Philip's Park Lane house might be burned down, but lost his enthusiasm when it occurred to him that strikers might also destroy his beloved Reform Club.[54] 'Clubland' in general 'purred' its approval of the government.[55] The National Liberal Club offered honorary membership to government volunteers for the duration of the strike,[56] while at the Carlton Club, former Conservative Party chairman Viscount Younger of Leckie, the Earl of Kintore and the Marquess of Londonderry coordinated volunteering activities from the 'leading London Clubs'.[57]

Siegfried Sassoon's main preoccupation during the strike was the actor and director Glen Shaw, who he imagined rescuing 'with immense heroism' from 'some wild mob'. He sent Shaw a 'patriotic' song composed by Ivor Novello:

> Boys and Girls, we're out to win;
> Hooray, hooray, we won't give in;
> So let Bulgaria join the fray
> And shout with me ... (falsetto)
> Hurrah, hooray.
>
> Chorus.
> Down in the mines of love, dear,
> There isn't a seam of coal;
> And for every shift
> There's a red plus lift
> Going down to the depths of the soul etc[58]

Although aggrieved the strike had 'killed' a recent book (*Satirical Poems*) 'stone dead', Sassoon produced several poems during and after the unrest: 'The New "Black & Tans" (from White's)', a dramatic monologue from a member of that club regarding his desire to 'crack the craniums' of the strikers; 'Perch and State', about the 'frigid phrases' of the Lords Balfour, Oxford and Grey concerning 'revolution'; and 'Strike Me Pink', about blackleg enthusiasm for the general strike. Although typeset for the *New Statesman*, these were not published in Sassoon's lifetime.[59] More reactionary was Rudyard Kipling, a cousin of the Prime Minister, whose poems appeared in the pages of the anti-strike *British Gazette*.

Many writers and poets also volunteered. Cecil Day-Lewis and W. H. Auden worked for the Trades Union Congress (Christopher Isherwood wanted to but was too late), while the political theorist and author Leonard Woolf circulated a petition among writers and artists which called on the government to restart negotiations. Only Sir John Galsworthy and the editor of the *Observer*, J. L. Garvin, refused to sign. Woolf later declared that anyone writing about their life in the years 1924–39 had to answer the question: 'What did you do in the General Strike?' 'Of all public events in home politics during my life-time,' he reflected, 'the General Strike was the most painful, the most horrifying.'[60] A journal entry written by Arnold Bennett after lunching at the Reform Club was later much quoted: 'General opinion that the fight would be short but violent. Bloodshed anticipated next week.'[61]

In London's West End, Sir Alfred Butt, manager of the Palace Theatre and a Conservative MP, proposed that all theatres should close at once, although Dame Sybil Thorndike and her husband Sir Lewis Casson decided to press on with their production of *Saint Joan*. 'With considerable difficulties in getting the members of our company home after the show,' recalled Casson, 'we finished the first week.'[62] The opera season also opened as planned at Covent Garden with *The Marriage of Figaro*. 'In spite of the general strike the house was well filled,' noted the *British Gazette*. 'The Countess of Oxford and Asquith, accompanied by her son and Princess Bibesco was among those present. Some of those in the gallery had been waiting all day for admission.'[63] The Australian soprano Dame Nellie Melba was less lucky. Her farewell concert at the Royal Albert Hall on 6 May was postponed.

Most writers and artists were upper or at least upper middle class and, as Charles Ferrall and Dougal McNeill have observed, the 'vast majority' knew 'what side they were on'. Radclyffe Hall and her partner Una Troubridge 'began putting their jewellery and furs in storage', while Jessica Mitford remembered going to bed with a pet lamb to protect her from 'Bolshies'.[64] As the Prince of Wales observed, the people he 'knew' felt 'they were putting down something that was terribly wrong, something contrary to British traditions. And they put on a first-class show.'[65]

As with gentlemen railway drivers and firemen, the press was particularly interested in members of the upper classes who were 'doing their bit'. Widely photographed was Edwina Mountbatten, who worked at the *Daily Express* switchboard, while *The Tatler*'s 'Emergency Number' recorded Lady Betty Butler, the 'unmarried sister of the Duchess of Sutherland', volunteering at the Hyde Park canteens. The same magazine featured an article entitled 'REVOLUTION, INDEED! How England Carried On' by the Scottish travel writer Sir John Foster Fraser.[66]

Letters written to Lady Halifax during the strike captured a range of emotions from titled ladies. Alice, Marchioness of Salisbury, complained of 'how horrible everything' was; Lady Manners said her life consisted of 'waiting for the wireless bulletins'; Lady Iveagh was astonished at how 'dependent upon newspaper comment' she was 'for the formation of one's own opinion'; Mabel, Countess Gray, said the 'whole atmosphere' reminded her 'indescribably of the war without … the immediate danger, but also most emphatically without any of the glamour or glow of patriotic feelings'. Others were more upbeat. Lady Sybil Middleton felt 'immense pride for one's country & the English race', while the 'splendidly run affair' also made Lady Henry Bentinck 'feel very British & proud'.[67]

If most of the upper classes supported the government in an instinctive and uncomplicated way, others harboured doubts. Lady St Helier, a London County Council alderman, felt throughout the strike that 'we are suffering for our own sense of smugness & laziness & omission',[68] while the impeccably establishment banker Sir Charles Addis wrote:

> Violence springs from doubt of the justice of one's cause and soon exhausts itself, but this solidarity of all classes of labour, their unselfishness, and their readiness to sacrifice their own interests to those of others is to me singularly impressive. It is vain to say that the

great body of the hard-headed and, in their way, educated working men of this country ... have been intoxicated by the windy rhetoric of a few hot-headed lunatic enthusiasts. They are not emotional men, but they are convinced that under the capitalist system they are not getting what they call a square deal ... There is profound discontent with the present unequal distribution of wealth.

Although Sir Charles shared that 'discontent', he was not wholly convinced capitalism would not 'have to make way for some new experiment':

When the present strike peters out, as peter out it will, and we are faced with another shilling on the income tax and are forced another step along the road to Protection by the necessity of increasing the indirect taxation, shall we be any nearer a settlement with Labour? I fear not. Strikes in 1919! Strikes in 1921! They are following each other in an accelerated succession.[69]

Sir Charles's unusual degree of introspection was shared to a degree by the upper-middle-class economist John Maynard Keynes, whose 'feelings' as distinct from his 'judgement' were 'with the workers'. The strikers, he wrote, were:

caught in a coil, not entirely of their own weaving, in which behaviour, which is futile and may greatly injure themselves and their neighbours, is nevertheless the only way which seems to them to be open for expressing their feelings and sympathies and for maintaining comradeship and keeping faith. The strike is a protest, a demonstration, an expression ... it is inarticulate, unlogical, ill calculated.

Perhaps fortunately, Leonard Woolf (Virginia's husband) refused to run Keynes' analysis in his weekly political newspaper *The Nation* out of solidarity with the strikers.[70]

At the other end of the class spectrum, 'working women' clearly understood the crisis was 'one which affects the lives of each of them'. As speaker's notes issued by the TUC observed:

It is as though we watched a great revolving chain, each link contributed by a different section of the working class community ... How were the women linked together? First the women of the coalfields, wives, mothers and daughters; second the women folk of other workers and women wage earners themselves; third come the housewives.[71]

To the historian Keith Laybourn, there was a 'public schoolboy feel' to the general strike, and one he judged 'must have heightened class and industrial tensions'.[72] The Belfast-born Scottish miners' leader Robert Smillie later wrote that he could 'see them to this day':

> those fresh-faced boys and well scrubbed men delighting in their temporary roles as industrial workers. How exuberant they would have felt if faced by a lifetime of poorly paid, industrial labour is, of course, another matter.[73]

Rejecting the received wisdom that the general strike 'was all a bit of a lark', Frank McLynn has argued that by the weekend of 8–9 May 'something like a pre-revolutionary situation had been reached',[74] though this is difficult to reconcile with contemporary accounts, even from those on the left of the Parliamentary Labour Party. The Dumbarton MP David Kirkwood considered the challenge 'serious', but observed that it was 'accepted in a spirit of fun':

> A trifling inconvenience is resented because it usually only affects a few, but the dislocation caused by the General Strike was so universal that people laughed at each other's difficulties and their own. When I saw car-loads of girls driving through the streets of London looking upon the experience as if it were a picnic, I knew that we were beaten.[75]

To Harold Macmillan, it was 'fortunate' that the strike did not last for more than nine days. 'Tempers,' he concluded, 'would undoubtedly have worsened on both sides had the struggle been prolonged.'[76]

6

'Napoleon-Churchill'

Winston Spencer Churchill had long been preoccupied by the idea of a widespread sympathetic strike. 'Thirty years ago the "general strike" was a very shadowy proposal,' the then Liberal Home Secretary warned in 1911, 'now it is a definite objective deliberately advocated.'[1] By May 1926 Churchill was the Tory Chancellor of the Exchequer, and now that 'definite objective' had become a reality, he was widely regarded to be spoiling for a fight. One journalist dubbed him 'Napoleon-Churchill'.[2]

Churchill had only been a *bona fide* member of the Conservative Party for eighteen months, and there was a sense that his new colleagues did not quite know what to make of such a big personality. As even his wife Clementine observed, he lived largely in a wonderland of his own imagination:

> He knows nothing of the life of the ordinary people. He's never been on a bus, and only once on the Underground. This was during the General Strike, when I deposited him at South Kensington. He went round and round (on the Circle Line) not knowing where to get out and had to be rescued eventually.[3]

Among his contemporaries, Churchill's incredible energy, courage and eloquence were frequently acknowledged, although these brilliant qualities were offset by what Paul Addison called 'supreme egotism, an adventurer's love of daring but perilous courses of action, poor judgement of men, erratic changes of course, susceptibility to rhetoric and flights of the imagination'.[4] His fertile brain, recalled William Bridgeman, 'turned out ideas by the score on all subjects, very few of which bore the test of analysis'.[5] Observing Churchill's intervention in the Commons on 3 May, the day before the strike, Cuthbert Headlam observed: 'Winston spoke to the point: but he is a danger to our side.'[6]

Stanley Baldwin also sensed his Chancellor needed to be managed; his volcanic energy directed if not contained. 'Don't forget,' the Prime Minister later remarked to a biographer, 'the cleverest thing I ever did. I put Winston in a corner and told him to edit the British Gazette.'[7] It would 'keep him busy, stop him doing worse things,' Baldwin told J. C. C. Davidson, adding: 'I'm terrified of what Winston is going to be like.'[8]

'THE ENEMY PRESS'

The decision to include printers in the first wave of workers called out by the Trades Union Congress was one of the strike's most controversial. The Labour Party had long been aggrieved by what it perceived as the shameless bias of the printed press, something exacerbated by the Zinoviev Letter during the October 1924 general election. Although several newspapers, including the *Manchester Guardian* and even *The Times*, usually tried to be fair, only the *Daily Herald* ostentatiously promoted a Labour point of view.

As Walter Milne-Bailey of the TUC research department later recalled:

> To stop the daily newspaper is to hit the imagination of the average person more sharply than he is hit even by the stoppage of his transport. He is not unused to a strike in transport. On this occasion it was desirable to impress him in a new way.

Had the British press truly been 'free' and 'fair minded', added Milne-Bailey, then the TUC would 'not have dreamed of suppressing it'.[9] Once that decision had been taken, Eccleston Square (ironically, Churchill's former home) was rigorous in its implementation. When the *Manchester Guardian* telegrammed Walter Citrine (the TUC's acting general secretary) on the first day of the strike asking that 'sane newspapers' be allowed to continue, Citrine regretfully replied that 'it would have been impossible to discriminate'.[10] As Herbert Treacy put it, to have closed down 'the enemy Press' and allowed the Labour

Press to continue 'would have appeared to the public as arbitrary and unfair'.[11] The Labour MP Ellen Wilkinson, however, believed the move 'greatly added to the success of the Strike' as the 'workers, and in fact, the citizens in general had just got to think for themselves'.[12]

Nevertheless, it left a considerable vacuum when printed news was widely disseminated and the 'wireless' was yet to reach a wide audience. The National Union of Journalists upset many of its members with an instruction not to aid non-union newspaper production, while the Institute of Journalists was even more bellicose, protesting:

> against the attempt to extinguish the Newspaper Press of the country, with its consequent suppression of freedom of opinion and curtailment of the supply of authentic news to the public. The Institute in this emergency calls on its members to do all in their power to frustrate this attempt at the earliest possible moment.[13]

When an offer from the devolved Government of Northern Ireland to distribute Belfast-printed newspapers on the mainland was rejected as 'inadvisable',[14] the UK government had already begun to consider its approach to the propaganda war. 'The field of battle,' declared Winston Churchill, 'is no longer transport but news.'[15]

The *British Gazette*

Initially, the government wanted existing titles to run a special strike publication, but when it became clear 'mutual rivalries prevented any such combination',[16] the Newspaper Proprietors' Association suggested it publish a daily news bulletin itself. This Churchill envisaged as a:

> really powerful readable broadsheet not merely to contain news but in order to relieve the minds of the people. Something must be done to prevent alarming news from being spread about and there is no reason why it should not be done as well as possible. I do not contemplate violent partisanship, but fair, strong encouragement to the great mass of loyal people.

The problem was how to print it. J. C. C. Davidson quickly vetoed Churchill's assumption that he could make use of the government's own printers, while Sir Andrew Caird, managing director of the *Daily*

Mail, pointed out that printing presses were 'highly complicated and very difficult to handle'.[17] Editorial and distribution were, by comparison, relatively straightforward.

The title of the new journal evolved. Churchill had rather unthinkingly settled upon 'The London Gazette', although that was an existing publication which by law had to appear twice a week and carry 'official' state notices such as emergency proclamations.[18] The Chancellor then proposed 'London Gazette Extraordinary' to which Samuel Hoare responded with the more pleasingly patriotic 'British Gazette'.[19] At another meeting at the House of Commons on the evening of Monday 3 May, Sir Malcolm Fraser, a veteran editor and until 1923 the Conservative Party's principal agent, suggested commandeering an existing newspaper office. As it was 'close to the centre of Government and situated on an island site from which distribution could easily be organized and carried out', Davidson et al. proceeded directly to the *Morning Post* – then Britain's main conservative daily – and took possession on behalf of His Majesty's Government.[20]

Initially the paper's machine-room overseers agreed to stay on, but as a precaution it was arranged to have the paper set in duplicate while William Codling, Controller of His Majesty's Stationary Office (HMSO), arranged for the type to be set. By 6 a.m. on 4 May there was a skeleton staff, but at 3 p.m. – and after setting five columns of type – the *Post* staff ceased work on union instructions. Compositors working on the duplicate type also downed tools and destroyed their work. Sydney Long, the night superintendent of the *Daily Express*, completed the nine remaining columns with his own hands. Editorial staff also took over the mechanical side, which included handling massive paper rolls, oiling the machinery, clothing cylinders with plates and removing the printed sheets. A foundry accident meant a delay of another two hours, but finally, at nearly midnight, the last plate was locked into place. P. J. Grigg, Churchill's private secretary at the Treasury, discovered:

> the great man sitting in solitary contemplation by the rotary presses. With a wave of his arm he directed my attention to the inexorable mechanical power rolling out newspapers which would, a few hours later, be distributed all over the country.[21]

A fleet of motor vehicles owned by one of J. C. C. Davidson's constituents then oversaw distribution from a motor park in the quadrangle at Somerset House.[22] Published by HMSO and featuring the royal arms on either side of its masthead, the *British Gazette* cost 1d (one pence). Various difficulties meant the two inside pages of the first four-page edition were left blank. In an unsigned article, Churchill spoke of 'this great nation' being reduced 'to the level of African natives dependent only on the rumours which are carried from place to place'.[23]

Although billed as 'editor', Churchill was heavily constrained by J. C. C. Davidson, who as Deputy Chief Civil Commissioner had overall responsibility for broadcasting and publicity. He regarded Churchill as without any power 'except the power of a personality which is very difficult to deal with'.[24] A direct telephone line was installed between the editor's room at the *Morning Post* and Davidson's room at the Admiralty, while Howell Gwynne, the *Post*'s editor, accepted 'without question' that Davidson (or his representative David Caird) had the 'last say' on 'everything that goes into the paper'.[25] Churchill, however, could not resist the drama. Hamilton Fyfe of the *Daily Herald* joked that the Chancellor saw the 'whole affair as a film producer would' but with one difference: 'Film producers do not act; Winston intends to appear as the hero of the story himself. Thus he will first play the part of newspaper editor!'[26]

While Davidson broadly agreed with Churchill's 'line' regarding the strike's challenge to the British constitution, he 'laid it down as a rule – absolute and unchangeable – that no official news that was untrue should appear, and that propaganda should be no part of our activities'. He recalled:

> After a great fight, Winston agreed to be blue-pencilled, and from that moment my blue pencil was seldom idle. Caird, who exercised editorial supervision, submitted all copy to me where necessary, but, despite all our efforts, a good deal of Winston's pugnacious spirit penetrated the Gazette and brought storms of questions in the House of Commons.[27]

That debate took place on 7 May. Joseph Kenworthy, a veteran Liberal MP, charged that the *British Gazette* was not publishing a fair summary of proceedings in Parliament, adding that those in charge had to be 'extraordinarily careful really to speak the truth' and 'not put in anything of a nature to inflame passions at this time'.[28] Davidson recorded another incident in which Churchill wanted to exclude coverage of a football match between policemen and strikers in Plymouth. When this was raised in Cabinet, Davidson's arguments for publication (it was good propaganda) carried the day and Winston was overruled.[29]

Later, there was another row in the Commons about the paper's failure to cover a significant intervention by the Archbishop of Canterbury. David Lloyd George joked that if Jesus Christ had visited 'contemporary London his utterances would have been excluded' from the *British Gazette*.[30] Deputy Cabinet Secretary Tom Jones, who regarded it as 'a paper for suburbia not for the working man',[31] also arranged for more sober government flyers and pamphlets to be printed by HMSO. On one occasion, a draft publication reached J. C. C. Davidson's office at 5.20 p.m. and thirteen hours later 350,000 copies had been distributed all over the country.[32]

The *Morning Post* building, meanwhile, became 'a kind of fortress hotel', guarded and protected – no one was allowed inside without a special pass – while great 'piles of army blankets and mattresses' were provided 'for those who could not get home'.[33] In a secret memo addressed to the Prime Minister, J. C. C. Davidson painted a vivid picture of an 'anxious' Chancellor's attempt to 'force a scratch staff beyond its capacity' during constant visits to that fortress:

> I must depend on you, and the staff are relying on me, to find some means of preventing his coming. By all means let him put what pressure he can personally upon Sir Malcolm Fraser, who is in general control, and the Stationery Office, by interview or letter, but the technical staff should be left to do their job. He rattled them very badly last night. He thinks he is Napoleon, but curiously enough the men who have been printing all their life in the various processes happen to know more about their job than he does.[34]

Baldwin's private secretaries also tried to get Churchill put in charge of emergency transport arrangements, while Tom Jones noted that even Winston's own private secretary was 'entirely out of sympathy with his chief's wild ways'.[35]

Even beyond the *Gazette*, the Chancellor caused trouble. When Tom Jones shared a plan drafted by the Anglo-American Viscount Astor contrived to reopen negotiations between the TUC and government, the Chancellor 'overwhelmed' him 'with a cataract of boiling eloquence':

> We were at war ... We must go through with it. [Churchill said] 'You must have the nerve.' I shouted back 'I have plenty of moral nerve, but we want something besides nerve.' He retorted, 'You have a terrible responsibility in advising a man so sympathetic like the Prime Minister.' I tried to say that I stood absolutely firm on the constitutional issues, but that we at the centre failed to realise the importance of making the Government's position absolutely plain to every man and woman in the country.

And when Jones remarked that the TUC chairman Arthur Pugh and railway union leader Jimmy Thomas were 'as loyal as you are to the State', Churchill broke 'into a fresh tempest' which left Jones feeling 'tossed about like a small boat in an angry sea'. The Chancellor was convinced that three or four days of what he called 'firm handling' would bring the TUC to its senses, so was disgusted when Montagu Norman, the Governor of the Bank of England, refused his demand to arrest all trade union funds.[36]

When, early in the strike, it was rumoured that a Cabinet minister had been assassinated, this was generally assumed to be Churchill.[37] The mere mention of his name provoked extreme reactions. 'That man,' stormed the trade unionist Ben Tillett, has:

> neither soul, conscience, honour or anything else ... He has been responsible for greater loss in blood and treasure than any man in the country. More even than [the Duke of] Wellington. Look at his work at Gallipoli, at Antwerp, and now in this country. In this dispute he is doing the same.[38]

The *Gazette*, meanwhile, grew at an alarming rate. When 450 tonnes of newsprint obtained from Holland quickly proved insufficient, the government commandeered suitable supplies from the *Evening Standard*, the *Observer* and *The Times*.[39] In addition to the offices of the *Morning Post*, it also took control of the Argus Press on London's

Tudor Street, the Northfleet papermaking works, Phoenix Wharf (for paper storage) and W. H. Smith's despatching warehouse on Carey Street. Not for a hundred years, noted the staff magazine, had a 'Mr. Smith' personally 'delivered newspaper parcels to his customers', while few at Strand House recognized Sir William Acland and his brother, two partners, 'in their working garb and grime'.[40] The Prince of Wales even sent his Rolls-Royce to help distribute copies to his principality.[41]

Air Vice Marshal Hudson also told Samuel Hoare (the Secretary of State for Air) about dropping bundles of the *Gazette* on 'Red' towns by aeroplane, although in initial attempts they hit the tail and jammed the controls. A second sortie with the papers tied in packets of ten was more successful, and Hudson watched as they were 'eagerly seized' by 'a large proportion of the inhabitants'.[42] Every morning at dawn, the *Gazette* was taken by Numbers 9 and 58 Squadrons (Virginias) from RAF Northolt (dubbed 'the "newspaper" Aerodrome') to Catterick and Sealand for distribution in the Newcastle and Liverpool areas. On the first day 40,000 copies were distributed in this way, and by the end of the strike 426,000. When other newspapers demanded access to similar distribution, the government refused.[43]

The *British Worker*

The TUC's response to the *Gazette*, the *British Worker*, did not appear until Thursday 6 May – a day after its government rival – and its birth was perhaps even more dramatic. At nine o'clock the previous evening, the TUC's Walter Citrine took a telephone call from Robert Williams, the general manager of the Labour-supporting *Daily Herald* newspaper, who told him that three 'burly' police inspectors had turned up with a warrant (signed by the Home Secretary) to search the premises for anything contrary to Emergency Regulations. The TUC General Council's 'indignant' response was that they ought to publish and be damned. But when a further report came through that the *Herald* offices were surrounded by around 100 police officers, many of them mounted, Citrine and a couple of directors of the Victoria House Printing Company, which was jointly owned by the TUC and the Labour Party, decided to head there and see what was happening. In Citrine's account:

When we got inside a strange sight greeted our eyes. The Despatch Room was packed with members of the staff. There seemed to be at least a couple of hundred of them there. Most of them were in their shirt sleeves and lustily singing the 'Red Flag'. Outside in the streets we could hear the refrain being taken up by the people.[44]

A plainclothes inspector politely asked if some copies could be run off and shown to the City of London Police Commissioner. When this was done, the inspector took them away, leaving some of his men in charge. 'They were quite friendly,' recalled the *Herald* editor Hamilton Fyfe, indeed 'the whole staff [were] in very good humour.'[45] Eventually, and with a smile, the officer in charge told them they could go ahead. 'Then we heard a low rumble of the machines starting up in the basement,' recalled Citrine, 'and the crowd outside responded with a tremendous cheer.'[46] The Home Secretary's orders to stop the printing had actually been cancelled by the Prime Minister when he discovered the Attorney General had not been properly consulted.[47]

Although the *British Worker* proved no less propagandist than the *British Gazette*, in the circumstances it was, judged historian Gordon Phillips, 'less tempted to falsification'.[48] Sitting at the editor's table with Hamilton Fyfe, an Old Fettesian who had almost quadrupled the *Herald*'s circulation since taking the editor's chair in 1922,[49] were four censors from the TUC's press and publicity committee, one of whom was one of former Home Secretary Arthur Henderson's 'two clever, capable sons'. Their chief aim, recalled Fyfe, was:

> to prevent anything from getting into the paper which might cause uncontrollable irritation and violence. I am entirely at one with them in this. Our task is to keep strikers steady and quiet. We must be not provocative; our line is to be dignified, calm in our own strength; to make our Statements forcibly, but with moderation of language.[50]

And although the *Worker* could not match the *Gazette*'s ever-expanding circulation, it proved a modest success. 'We could sell to purchasers at the doors three times as many as we print,' declared Fyfe, 'and we are printing half a million.'[51] With this in mind, the *Herald*'s assistant editor later observed that, had the TUC's decision to stop the press been accompanied by 'a decision at once to proceed with the publication of a strike bulletin, much delay and confusion could have been avoided'.[52]

On the very day the *Worker* first appeared (6 May), William Codling at HMSO informed the *Herald* that the government had commandeered its paper supplies. Given Victoria House had no facilities for storing large quantities of newsprint and its stock was 'rapidly disappearing', this could have strangled the publication at birth.[53] As a result, the second edition of the *British Worker*, which appeared on 7 May, was only half the size of the first. Its leading article called the Prime Minister's action 'provocative' and 'bound to be angrily resented'.[54] The *Worker*, however, managed to obtain supplies from the *New Leader*, *Racing and Football Outlook*, the *People* and the Caledonian Press, which produced the popular *Lansbury's Weekly*.[55] On 11 May, the *Herald*'s general manager appealed in writing to the Prime Minister, saying he felt sure it was not the government's intention to 'hamper' a rival publication. Winston Churchill replied to say that the Law Officers of the Crown were 'being consulted on the question of whether paper even if available should be placed at the disposal of a newspaper engaged in advocating and sustaining' what he and others considered 'to be an illegal strike'.[56]

There were also challenges in Scotland, where neither the *Worker* nor the *Gazette* circulated. While the TUC's General Council insisted that the former be reprinted in Glasgow, the Scottish Trades Union Congress declared this 'utterly impracticable' given delays in road transport and, in a rare display of independence, pressed ahead with a completely different publication called, inevitably, the *Scottish Worker*, six issues of which were produced by voluntary labour at the trade union-controlled Civic Press.[57] Regional editions of the *British Worker* were successfully produced in other parts of England and Wales. A Manchester edition edited by Fenner Brockway – who thought the TUC's decision to halt the mainstream press 'a big tactical mistake' – reached a circulation of around 50,000 copies,[58] while in Cardiff the South Wales Miners' Federation placed its printing works, the Cymric Federation Press, 'at the service of the movement'.[59]

Despite these challenges, other newspapers – both national and provincial – managed to keep going during the nine days of the strike. Smaller presses in provincial towns were less affected for the simple reason that they were less unionized. In Northern Ireland, the *Belfast Telegraph* appeared throughout, as did the *Scotsman* and *Edinburgh Evening Dispatch* thanks to de-unionization following another strike half a century earlier. Although it also came close to running out of paper, the circulation of the *Scotsman* nearly doubled.[60] In Glasgow, highly paid strike breakers combined that city's usual six dailies (including the *Glasgow Herald* and *Daily Record*) in an 'Emergency Press'. Strikers tried to grab copies of this 'scab' paper and dump them in the River Clyde.[61] Particularly impressive was the Cardiff-based *Western Mail*, the 'defiant standard-bearer of the South Wales industrial middle class and mouthpiece of the coal-owners', which managed to publish an eight-page daily throughout the strike, copies of which were eagerly snapped up in London at 8.30 each morning.[62] On 7 May the generally anti-strike Newspaper Society declared it 'evident that, viewing the country as a whole, the heart of the printing and newspaper workers is not in this strike'.[63]

There were some ingenious moves. A small party of staff at the *Daily Mail* 'smuggled' themselves across to Paris on the first day of the strike 'to make the continental edition look like the London edition'.[64] Despite attempts by the TUC to prevent this being shipped to England,[65] by 11 May around half the copies of the *Mail* in circulation were being printed in Paris. Some were also flown. When Imperial Airways refused to transport copies from Paris, the *Mail* contacted the Air Union and secured twenty-four private aircraft.[66] Those aiding its distribution on the ground included Betty Baldwin, daughter of the premier.[67] Domestically, special editions of the *Mail* were also printed in four south-western cities as well as in Manchester. On Sunday 9 May it claimed triumphantly that 'the North had no other newspaper but the "Daily Mail"'.[68]

Apart from what one reader called a 'funny little Times about ½ the usual size' which was printed on 4 May,[69] and a single sheet measuring 13 inches by 8 the following day, *The Times* appeared in its usual form. This was despite one notable act of sabotage. On the afternoon of Wednesday 5 May, a stream of petrol was poured through a loading port in the newspaper's machine room and ignited. The novelist Graham Greene (a volunteer sub-editor) was relaxing after a tiring night of loading and packing that morning's edition when the fire alarm sounded:

The bell rang once, twice, three times. Someone asked with mild curiosity, 'A fire?' After a while the assistant chief sub-editor, Colonel Maude, rose and moved with his usual elegant and leisurely gait into the corridor ... when he returned to the room and sat down, it took quite a time to realise that The Times – so he was telling us – had been set on fire.[70]

Greene was one of several enthusiastic volunteers who had descended on Printing House Square. Among those who drove lorries were the Duchess of Westminster and the Duchess of Sutherland, as well as Lady Maureen Stanley, daughter of the Marquess and Marchioness of Londonderry.[71] Before heading to his northern constituency, Harold Macmillan also helped with packing and despatching.[72] These celebrity volunteers were supervised by a group of proprietors and editorial staff who later produced a light-hearted souvenir volume, *Strike Nights in Printing House Square*, for private circulation.[73]

There were also tensions. By 9 May, the *Daily Mail* threatened to withdraw staff loaned to the *British Gazette* as its owners felt they were 'placing themselves at a disadvantage'.[74] Also increasingly aggrieved was *The Times*, whose paper supplies had been requisitioned by the government. Although Major Astor (the newspaper's chairman and a Conservative MP) had promised to limit each day's edition to 80,000 copies, in fact *The Times* produced 'somewhere about three times that quantity',[75] which irritated the irascible Chancellor of the Exchequer. *The Times*' editor Geoffrey Dawson, who had just returned to London from Greece, nevertheless held Churchill responsible for the paper shortage and penned a critical editorial.[76] Lord Beaverbrook, the Canadian owner of the *Daily Express*, also complained to the Chancellor of having 'made immense sacrifices' in terms of staff. Churchill pleaded with him to 'defer' production of the *Daily Express* 'in the public interest', by which he meant continued production of his beloved *Gazette*.[77] Some parliamentary colleagues despaired. Cuthbert Headlam believed that now 'the ordinary press' was 'beginning to work again this rather futile Government production should cease'.[78]

At an evening Cabinet on 11 May, the Colonial Secretary Leo Amery suggested that while the *British Gazette* had been 'an excellent emergency newspaper', they 'ought to get back to normal newspaper publication as soon as we could'. This, he recalled in his diary:

> let loose Winston in a munificent tirade on the wonders achieved, the selfishness of The Times in wishing to increase its circulation at expense of others during the crisis, the impossibility of letting go at the moment without unfairness to one or other newspaper and ended with his determination to suppress the Daily Express, if, as they intended, they started an evening paper in the next few days. Against his vigour and enthusiasm nobody except Eustace Percy [President of the Board of Education] had the courage to say anything and most of those who for days had been going round and complaining rather left me alone when I belled the cat.[79]

Even J. C. C. Davidson was clear, however, that Churchill's 'drive' had been one of the 'major factors' in the *Gazette*'s success. But for Davidson and Baldwin's control, judged Robert Rhodes James, 'it would have been far more bellicose and partisan', though, equally, 'but for Churchill's energy and imagination, it would have been sadly deficient in vigour and spirit'.[80] Hamilton Fyfe, meanwhile, looked back upon the *British Worker*'s 'short life' with satisfaction, content that he and his colleagues at the *Daily Herald* had 'not fought unfairly or lowered the standards of decent journalism'.[81]

7

'RAISED PASSIONS AND FRAYED TEMPERS'

On Saturday 1 May 1926 Shapurji Saklatvala, the Indian-born Communist MP for North Battersea, made a speech which landed him in jail. In its coverage of an unusually large May Day procession in Hyde Park, the *Guardian* reported that:

> He is, one imagines, the most powerful mob orator of his day. This sallow Indian, with a face worn by fanatical passion, dominated the whole scene as, with outstretched, claw-like hands, he harangued for a good half hour. With a sort of sombre joy, he acclaimed the General Strike as the definite rising of Labour against their oppressors, to a chorus of 'Good old Saklatvala!'[1]

But the crucial line in Saklatvala's speech was:

> We tell the Government that the young men in the forces whether [the Home Secretary] likes it or not; whether he calls it sedition or not to soothe the financiers and his rich friends, we have a duty towards those men to say to them that they must lay down their arms.[2]

No immediate action was taken, indeed on Monday 3 May Saklatvala was heckling the Prime Minister in the House of Commons over the *Daily Mail* stoppage, interjecting that it 'was not part of the general strike at all'.[3] But on 4 May, the MP was arrested at his home and charged with incitement and breach of the peace. Although the Director of Public Prosecutions had advised postponing the arrest 'pending further consideration', a messenger did not get there in time.[4] It was doubly premature in that the Emergency Regulations had yet to take effect. According to his daughter, Saklatvala graciously agreed to make himself available for arrest once they had.[5]

The first person of Indian heritage elected to the UK Parliament, Shapurji Dorabji Saklatvala was born in Bombay (later Mumbai) in 1874 to a merchant and his wife Jerbai, a sister of Jamsetji Tata, the owner of India's largest commercial and industrial empire. After working for Tata as an iron and coal prospector, Saklatvala moved to the UK to run the firm's Manchester office. He later joined the English Bar and the Independent Labour Party (ILP). When the ILP refused to admit Communists, Saklatvala instead transferred his allegiance to the newly founded Communist Party of Great Britain.

In October 1922 Saklatvala was elected in North Battersea with the Labour Party's endorsement, and although he lost his seat the following year, he returned to the Commons, this time without Labour support, at the October 1924 general election. Winston Churchill referred to 'a foreign element in Socialism' which ought 'to awaken a sense of repulsion in every British breast',[6] while the National Fascisti (later the British Fascists) attacked Saklatvala for claiming that most British Imperial subjects had 'no traditional sentiment in regard to the Union Jack'. It is difficult to tell if they hated him more for being a Communist or an Indian.[7]

At first, Saklatvala was released on bail, which gave him a chance to explain to his daughter Sehri 'at bewildering length and detail' about the miners 'being asked to accept less money ... what a strike was, and ... his speech in Hyde Park and why he had made it'.[8] On 6 May a packed Bow Street Police Court listened as Sir Chartres Biron, the same chief magistrate who had approved warrants to arrest eleven prominent Communists in October 1925, told the MP his speech had been seditious and 'calculated to promote public disorder'. 'It is the more mischievous considering the circumstances under which it was delivered,' he added solemnly. 'At such a moment as this, to inflame public opinion by such speeches is an act of criminal folly.'

Saklatvala was bound over to keep the peace for the sum of £500, which meant he was required to find two further sureties of £250 or go to prison. Conducting his own defence, he denied any intention to incite disorder, although he admitted the 'fairness and accuracy' of the police report of his speech. Having 'regard to the present propaganda and political outlook', Saklatvala added that he should not be bound over 'any more than the prime minister should be bound over for his speeches against a section of the community'.[9] When he declared that in his 'honour and conscience' he could not 'accept the decision to be bound over', his wife called out 'Hear! Hear!' Unimpressed, Sir Chartres sentenced Saklatvala to two months in prison.[10]

On his arrival at Wormwood Scrubs, a prison officer advised Saklatvala to state his religion as 'Church of England' so he would qualify for church services on Sunday mornings, giving him a chance to mix with other prisoners. Sure enough, visits to the prison chapel gave him some comfort and he came to find his time in prison interesting as well as restful.[11] Prisoner 4472 also fired off letters to the Home Secretary, Sir William Joynson-Hicks, cheekily appealing for day release so he could speak in Parliament, and to Speaker Whitley, although the latter quite properly refused to intervene in what was a judicial matter.[12]

As was his duty, the Speaker informed MPs of Saklatvala's arrest and imprisonment when the Commons met on 7 May. The Independent Labour Party MP David Kirkwood asked if he was not protected under 'privilege' and implored 'this all-powerful House' to 'step in and say that this Member of it is not to be interfered with in this manner'. The Speaker, again quite properly, replied that parliamentary privilege did not extend to a breach of criminal law.[13]

There was a certain irony in John Henry Whitley occupying the Speaker's Chair during the general strike, for in 1917 he had chaired a committee (as Deputy Speaker) on relations between employers and employees in the wake of the Shop Stewards Movement. Whitley proposed a system of regular consultative meetings dealing with pay, conditions and arbitration which became known as 'Whitley Councils'. Although this progressive proposal quickly became a feature of the public sector, it failed to gain ground in coal, cotton, engineering and other heavy industries which generally experienced the most disruption.[14]

J. H. Whitley was the last Liberal to serve as Speaker of the House of Commons. Born in Halifax in 1866, he joined his uncle's cotton spinning business and was elected to represent his home town in Parliament in 1900, holding it until his resignation almost three decades later. Whitley was a junior Treasury minister in Asquith's government but in 1910 was appointed Deputy Chairman of Ways and Means. Thus began his journey to the Speaker's Chair, which he assumed in succession to James Lowther on 27 April 1921. This coincided with a disturbed and anxious period in British politics. Whitley was re-elected no fewer than three times on account of frequent elections and experienced five different governments, including Labour's first in 1924.[15] In a later tribute, Ramsay MacDonald said the Speaker had shown 'how to be patient and courteous without being lax, how to be strict and severe without being mechanical and formal'.[16]

Confronted with the general strike, Whitley demonstrated great resourcefulness in ensuring the House of Commons could continue to function without interruption. While rumours spread that 'armed blue-jackets' were guarding its corridors,[17] or that Baldwin intended to adjourn Parliament until the strike was over,[18] on 7 May the Speaker defiantly declared that if it became necessary he 'would conduct the business of the House without any printing, or without any electric light'. Nothing, he added, should 'be allowed to prevent us from doing the duties with which we are charged'.[19] These duties were made more challenging by the fact that men engaged in several of 'the principal services of the House' had been withdrawn as a consequence of strike notices issued by the Trades Union Congress.

Most problematic was the cessation of printing work, on which Parliament depended for the distribution of the daily Votes and Proceedings (the Order Paper) and, following each sitting, its Official Report (Hansard). On the first day of the strike (4 May) the BBC reported that no Order Papers had been delivered for the 'first time in the history of the House of Commons',[20] while only twenty copies of Hansard were circulated throughout its lobbies.[21] After that dated 5 May it was suspended indefinitely.[22] This meant important interventions were only available in truncated newspaper reports.[23] When Sir Gerald Strickland suggested that 'extraordinary efforts' be taken to 'accelerate' publication of particular speeches, the Rev. James Barr (a Labour MP) opposed the 'singling out of a single speech', which he feared 'would not be exactly impartial or balanced'.[24]

The daily Order Paper was also only 'partially distributed' on 6 May, with the Vote Office operating a policy of 'first come, first served'. When Sir Francis Lowe (a Conservative) demanded that a sufficient number be made available to all MPs, the Speaker wearily replied that as Parliament was 'without the assistance of our usual printers ... we have to do the best we can by other means'. On being bombarded with unhelpful suggestions regarding manual duplication, Whitley remarked that he did 'not think that hon. Members can appreciate the difficulties more than I do', to which the Labour MP Martin Connolly made it known that if any papers were to be printed by 'blacklegs', then those on the opposition benches 'would sooner be without them'.[25]

As the Speaker protested, he had done his best, including a desperate appeal to Nichols & Son, Parliament's usual printers on Victoria Street:

> I feel that considerable importance attaches to the printing and circulation of the proceedings of this House ... If you can make any arrangement that would enable the proceedings of the House to be published and circulated in the ordinary way, it would let the public know what is taking place in the House of Commons and would be, I feel, for the public's advantage.

When this was forwarded to the secretary of the Machine Managers' Union, the TUC replied that it had made an offer on 1 May 'to deal with essential services' but that the government had 'absolutely refused to allow any action and we therefore regret we are unable to make any exception in this case'.[26] Instead, the Order Paper was typewritten and duplicated between 10 and 17 May,[27] while Hansard finally resumed on 10 May 'with the help of men from the Foreign Office Press and Harrow'.[28] Copies were even sent to Shapurji Saklatvala at Wormwood Scrubs.[29]

Meanwhile, the Ministry of Transport arranged for cars to bring Members of Parliament 'from their homes and take them home in the evening' at no cost to the Exchequer.[30] Twenty-six MPs volunteered to act as drivers, twenty-two Conservative and four Liberals but no Labour Members. An official told Winston Churchill the House of Commons was undoubtedly 'an essential service' and the presence of Members and officials 'necessary to enable work to carry on'.[31] Shortly before the strike began, parliamentary clerks had fretted over a requirement for the King formally to respond to 'humble' Addresses from both Houses thanking him for declaring a state of emergency.[32] Sir Arthur Thring, the Clerk of the Parliaments, believed a reply had to be communicated to the Lords by the Lord Chamberlain and to the Commons by members of the Royal Household. But Sir Lonsdale Webster, the somewhat shrewder Clerk of the House of Commons, noted 'a strong feeling that in a time of crisis like this, it was quite inappropriate that the Vice-Chamberlain should appear in full uniform and carry out such a pure formality'. Sir Arthur promptly changed his tune and the usual ceremonial was dispensed with.[33]

The 117-strong parliamentary branch of the National Union of Journalists (NUJ) was also in uproar after receiving instructions to stop work on account of its affiliation with the Printing and Kindred Trades Federation. It protested that:

> the effect of the instructions would be that in a short time the Gallery of the House of Commons would be practically empty and Parliament deprived of its link with the nation at a time of unexampled national emergency. Members absolutely refused to bring about such a state of affairs.[34]

The NUJ executive protested that it had not anticipated 'when issuing their telegram of instructions, that any member of the press gallery would have to withdraw his labour'.[35] Other NUJ branches were swift to congratulate the parliamentary branch on its 'stand for the freedom of the press'.[36] Keen to manage the flow of news, the government despatched Lord Eustace Percy – President of the Board of Education and the youngest son of the coal-owning Duke of Northumberland – to brief Lobby journalists at the Palace of Westminster. Indeed, it was during the general strike that they began to be treated as a favoured subset within the press gallery.[37] The Lord Great Chamberlain also arranged for transcripts of BBC news bulletins to be circulated to members of both Houses of Parliament.[38]

The nine days in Parliament were those of almost continuous debate, either on the Emergency Regulations or on the adjournment. 'The general tone and temper of the House of Commons was responsible and impressive,' recalled the young Conservative backbencher Harold Macmillan. 'Except for the extreme Left wing of the Labour Party, speakers tried hard to be fair and moderate.'[39] The historian John Murray believed while that was true of the first day of the strike, when MPs 'seemed glad to get away from the Commons', it was very different on the second, when the 'old ferocity returned: raised passions and frayed tempers bandied about their harsh words'.[40]

Proceedings certainly drew distinguished spectators. Sitting above the clock in the peers' gallery on 7 May was the Prince of Wales, looking:

> tanned, vivacious and obviously keenly interested in every detail of the strange scene set out before him. With him was his brother, the Duke of York. Every now and then they exchanged comments, and not a detail escaped them. A few yards away was Mr. Herbert Smith, the President of the Miners' Federation — dour, glum, heavy-jowled, unsmiling. Occasionally some one leaned forward to speak to him. He sat apparently unhearing and unheeding, refraining from reply and refusing to relax the Sphinx-like set of his heavy features.[41]

On another occasion, when the House debated regulations concerning the right of the police to arrest a person of 'known character', the ILP MP George Buchanan joked that Lloyd George might be a 'known character' if near a landlord, or Lady Astor if near a brewery. From the peers' gallery, the King's sons 'roared with laughter'.[42]

On 8 May, Princess Bibesco, otherwise known as Elizabeth Asquith, a daughter of the former Liberal premier, wrote to Speaker Whitley thanking him for securing her and her cousin, the Duchess of Rutland, seats in the Commons Gallery, although she expressed herself 'surprised at the complete emptiness of the Labour benches'.[43] This was due in part to a decision of the Parliamentary Labour Party (PLP) not to participate in any debates other than those concerning the general strike. As a result, there was no debate on the report stage of the Finance Bill (which implemented the Budget), with Labour MPs merely voting on each resolution.[44]

On 7 May, the 'spectacled and grey-haired Socialist' Susan Lawrence returned to the Commons after winning the East Ham by-election on an increased Labour poll. She was introduced by Arthur Henderson, previously Home Secretary in the first Labour government, and George Lansbury, a future Labour leader, although their party's joy was punctured just moments later when the result of another by-election in the agricultural constituency of Buckrose spread around the Chamber.[45] This was a Conservative hold, although the Labour candidate had taken votes from both the government and Liberal candidates. 'The declaration of the strike left you without the ghost of a chance,' was Ramsay MacDonald's rather blunt message of commiseration to

Herbert Laycock, 'and under the circumstances your poll was quite good.'[46]

Following the 1924 general election, there were 412 Conservative MPs in the House, including the newly elected Harold Macmillan in the largely working-class constituency of Stockton-on-Tees. On 4 May, the first day of the strike, Stanley Baldwin addressed his parliamentary party in a large committee room and suggested that Members representing industrial constituencies 'might do well to go there at the end of the week and see how things were going'. 'This advice,' recalled Macmillan in his memoirs, 'I followed.'

The thirty-two-year-old scion of the Macmillan publishing empire left for Teeside that Friday, driven by his friend and neighbouring MP Leonard Ropner (Sedgefield) in 'an open car at great speed'. He spent two days in Stockton, where he found the mayor and voluntary organizations hard at work. There was a rather tenser atmosphere in the mining communities, where some people were naturally very 'windy' and 'thought that the revolution was about to begin'. Macmillan then drove to Newcastle to see Sir Kingsley Wood, the Civil Commissioner for the Northern Division. 'Electricity was in difficulties,' he recalled, 'but the crew of a submarine was arriving. Otherwise, things seemed reasonably calm throughout the North-east area.'

Macmillan was amused to eavesdrop on a local superintendent who was juggling matters both serious and frivolous during a telephone call to a colleague in Durham:

> 'Oh, they have stopped a train, at —, and thrown some carriages over the embankment. Now about the police concert next Thursday. I am very anxious that that girl who was put at No. 2 last time should have a better place – in the second half I would say – she's very good. Oh, they have overturned a tram and stopped some buses at —. Yes, I expect we will deal with that all right. But about the concert. I've sold nearly all our tickets and could do with some more if you can spare them.'

Macmillan listened to their conversion with 'growing admiration', for it gave him 'great confidence'.[47]

Partly on account of his constituency, Macmillan was on what his friend Noel Skelton termed the 'constructive' wing of the Conservative Party, impatient to match Labour's electoral offer with progressive policies on welfare and unemployment.[48] During the strike, however, more 'diehard' voices were in the ascendancy. In a letter to *The Times*, Hugh Cecil, an MP and younger son of Lord Salisbury, stormed that the purpose of the strike was 'revolutionary, and the method is revolutionary ... The wars of the sixteenth and seventeenth century arose out of religious disagreements, but they were not theological controversies — they were wars.'[49]

Building on this historical analogy was the Earl of Balfour, a cousin of Cecil and a former Conservative premier who had returned to the government in 1925 as Lord President of the Council:

> Two hundred and thirty-eight years have passed since a revolution occurred in this country, whose object was to secure the supremacy of Parliamentary Government, and the traditional liberties of our people. Through eight generations it has proved successful. But we are now threatened, it seems, with a revolution of a very different kind; and it behoves us seriously to consider what are its practical methods, what are its avowed objects, what would be its actual results were it unhappily to succeed.[50]

When the House debated an extension of the Emergency Regulations, the Labour MP and railway union leader Jimmy Thomas riled the Conservative benches by claiming the government had taken advantage of the *Daily Mail* incident to break off negotiations while he and his colleagues were still attempting to find a formula for peace. Thomas then said he had in his possession – and in the Prime Minister's handwriting – a means of arriving at a settlement which he had accepted on behalf of the TUC. Baldwin, who had just consumed a hurried meal 'with a pint of fizz',[51] was alerted and entered the Commons while Thomas was still on his feet. Ramsay MacDonald waded in to support his colleague and a furious argument developed about the exact meaning and nature of the formula, which frustrated backbenchers who had only heard about it for the first time. Baldwin later told the King that Thomas's account of events had been deliberately 'incomplete and misleading'.[52]

Nevertheless, another young Conservative backbencher, Anthony Eden, noted some 'restiveness' among his colleagues. Duff Cooper, for example, believed the government had been 'over hasty in breaking off negotiations'.[53] As Eden recorded in his diary:

Slesser [Solicitor General in first Labour Government] came and saw one or two of us in the lobby and suggested that, even now, if we could get the P.M. to say 'We will negotiate again at once if you call the General Strike off' instead of 'Call off the General Strike first and then I will negotiate', Thomas might be able to get the General Strike recalled. Conferred accordingly with Sidney [Mr Sidney Herbert – Parliamentary Private Secretary to the Prime Minister], Hugh Cecil and [Sir Alfred] Mond. Cecil maintained there was no distinction, Mond and Sidney that it might prove a trap.

Ultimately, Baldwin made a statement later that evening 'which at least made the government position clear'. It had been, noted Eden, 'an anxious and topsy-turvy day'.[54]

The *Daily Telegraph*'s parliamentary correspondent, meanwhile, had detected a more conciliatory 'atmosphere'. Herbert Smith and Arthur Cook of the Miners' Federation were in the House and conferred with the Leader of the Opposition, while Arthur Pugh of the TUC was also seen in Central Lobby.[55] But, as usual, it all came to nothing. 'At one minute to 12 on Monday night I would have grovelled for peace,' Jimmy Thomas told the House shortly before midnight, 'I would have grovelled to the Chancellor of the Exchequer, because I hated war. Unfortunately, it was refused.'[56]

Also less than united was the Labour movement's 151-strong parliamentary contingent. At least three of its most 'influential men', noted Margaret Bondfield, who had become the first female government minister in 1924, were against the general strike: Ramsay MacDonald, Jimmy Thomas and the former Chancellor Philip Snowden. 'The cause in each case was the same,' she explained, 'they did not like any step that depended upon the demonstration of force.'[57] Beatrice Webb also believed 'JRM' and Thomas were 'depressed at their powerlessness to bring about a settlement ... The inner circle hates the General Strike and sees no good coming out of it.'[58] Snowden even claimed to be ill, although Roy Jenkins judged this more 'diplomatic than clinical'.[59] When Ethel, Snowden's wife and herself a political figure, urged everyone to stand 'quietly behind the Government – any Government – for it would have been the same if a Labour Party had been in power', the resulting furore compelled her to clarify that her sympathies were 'entirely' with the miners.[60]

For MacDonald, meanwhile, the outbreak of the strike was indeed what his biographer called 'a black moment'. 'He had fought the idea of a general strike since its reappearance in labour politics before the war,' observed David Marquand, 'and he had fought the attitudes behind it since his twenties.'[61] Like many Labour parliamentarians, the Leader of the Opposition felt caught between the miners, who provided many of the party's safest seats, and concern that too close an attachment to the Miners' Federation might limit the construction of a broader electoral coalition.[62] But ever the realist – not to mention a loyalist – once the strike began MacDonald's main objectives were to keep his party together and maintain its morale: 'He pleaded for negotiations, defended the miners, and kept his criticisms of the unions to himself.'[63] Unhelpfully, the Labour leader's 1912 observation that a general strike 'empties markets ... raises prices [and] stifles consumption' was dusted off by Conservative opponents and much quoted.[64]

Privately, however, the nearly sixty-year-old Leader of His Majesty's Opposition was less discreet, telling several correspondents that the general strike was a 'colossal mistake', albeit pursued with 'the best of intentions and without any idea of raising a constitutional issue'.[65] At the same time, MacDonald was consistent – privately and publicly – in holding the government primarily responsible. Not only did he believe constant talk of an 'unconstitutional challenge' was beginning to create 'something like a revolutionary feeling ... amongst those who were being worked up into the belief that the constitution was in danger and that the Soviets were in our midst', but that Baldwin was the prisoner of a divided Cabinet. 'The Prime Minister, like King James IV of Scotland at the Battle of Sauchieburn,' he later wrote, 'was in the hands of the nobles and was being used for their purposes.'[66]

When the diplomat James Young Simpson wrote to MacDonald ('as an old friend') to warn that 'momentum will carry away you moderate men and your control will be gone', the Labour leader replied:

> There never was the slightest idea of this general strike being against any body or anything, it was a great moral gesture in support of the miners. I warned them of what might happen but the moral momentum was too strong. The quiet state of the country indicates the spirit of the strike and if a few mischievous persons were not in the Cabinet there would be no danger.[67]

Another correspondent was Oliver Baldwin, the Prime Minister's estranged gay son and a Labour Party activist. Observing that the 'majority of people are in favour of the miners' claims, but against the general strike', he suggested MacDonald say publicly: 'We have just shown what we can do. We will now call the general strike off.' Baldwin argued this would give the miners better terms while showing 'the mass of the people' to be with the Labour Party. MacDonald replied rather vaguely on 10 May:

> You speak of the majority of the people. All I need say is please assume that I belong to them and quite agree with what you say. I am working every hour of the day trying to get the situation changed.[68]

The Labour leader certainly did not rest, even if he was necessarily on the fringes of the dispute. In the Members' Lobby, MacDonald told the *Evening News* he was 'not letting a moment pass unused for some attempt to devise ways of peace and accommodation'.[69] His only formal press statement during the strike was directed to the European and North American media. 'No one party can claim the right to be the sole supporter of parliamentary institutions and representative Government,' declared MacDonald. 'I hope that the people of foreign countries will not be misled and that the constitutional traditions of my country will not be damaged by Government propaganda.'[70]

MacDonald also recorded in his diary some 'straight talk' to the Miners' Federation of Great Britain (MFGB) that other:

> unions were sacrificing much to help them, that they were not considerate of this, that the T.U.C. would have to come to a decision itself if the strike was or was not to continue. Miners stiff ... Was asked to speak but contented myself with reading what I had written: that the settlement would be in three stages (1) withdrawal of [strike] notices made possible by renewal of subsidy for very short period; (2) [coal industry] reorganisation where it was proposed miners would have to accept temporary adjustment of wages (this is where our present difficulties lay); (3) working of final settlement ... during (2) ... If agreement on this programme the general strike could terminate.

At a joint meeting of the MFGB executive and the TUC, Jack Bromley of the National Union of Railwaymen bluntly told the former: 'If you insist we shall go on until we are bled white but you will kill us.' MacDonald thought this split 'serious', not least because the miners' position could be summed up as: 'If you order us to accept reduction, we shall, but the miners will revolt.' If such division persisted, added the Labour leader presciently, then the 'only way out is that miners ask [the] T.U.C. to cry off general strike, carry on lock out with finance assistance, clear decks of everything except miners' claims, & wait for events'. Whatever his frustrations, MacDonald clearly found it stimulating. 'Should like to write history of [the] strike,' his diary concluded, 'when all is over.'[71]

'Popular disgust with the loss and inconvenience of a General Strike will considerably check the growth of the Labour Party in the country,' predicted Beatrice Webb in her own diary, 'but will lead to a rehabilitation of political methods and strengthen J. R. McDonald's leadership within the party itself.'[72] She was only half right. The Independent Labour Party organizer John Paton, meanwhile, fumed that the 'gigantic machine' of the Labour Party 'with its organisation in every constituency in the country' was as 'immobilised' as that of the ILP and the 'magnificent machine of the London Labour Party', all of which were left 'with all the principals, with their highly specialised skill, high and dry above the battle'. 'The General Council,' added Paton, 'had made up its mind that this was an industrial fight and the "politicians" were to be kept out.'[73]

At the time, Paton's ILP colleague David Kirkwood was 'heartily in favour' of a strike in theory, believing it would result in 'such an uprising of the people that the Government would be forced to grant our demands'. But when the general strike actually came, it was 'so tremendous that there was no one big enough to control it'. When he came to write his memoirs almost a decade later, Kirkwood's revolutionary spirit had dimmed. It had become clear, he observed, that:

> the nation would not allow any section of the community to supersede Parliament. Trained through centuries to regard Parliament as the instrument of redress, they disapproved of actions which seemed to reduce the stature of Parliament.[74]

The Liberal Party, meanwhile, was a much-diminished force in the House of Commons with only forty MPs, although it continued to be taken seriously as a once formidable party of government led by two former premiers, the Earl of Oxford and Asquith in the Lords and David Lloyd George in the Commons. They were not exactly happy warriors. At the beginning of the strike, the Liberal shadow cabinet agreed to take up a middle position in the crisis, supporting the necessary emergency measures to protect the authority of the government, but declining to endorse its handling of the dispute. Asquith's speech in a Lords debate on 4 May was accordingly moderate in tone, though thereafter most leading Liberal spokesmen moved, 'apparently without forethought or collusion, into a strongly anti-union position'.[75]

By 8 May, Asquith was fulminating in the *British Gazette* about acquiescing in the 'substitution for Free Government of a Dictatorship',[76] a 'pretence' which annoyed three Liberals of journalist Hamilton Fyfe's acquaintance. 'They each said the Liberals had a great opportunity to act as mediators and have thrown it away,' recorded Fyfe in his strike diary. 'Instead of pitching into the Cabinet, they are backing it up.'[77] Viscount Grey of Fallodon, a former Liberal Foreign Secretary, also wrote in the *Gazette* that the alternatives to 'democratic Parliamentary Government' were 'Fascism or Communism'.[78]

As one of Lloyd George's many biographers has observed, his 'pose of studied moderation' during the strike was one of those things, 'like the première of an Ibsen play, which aroused in contemporaries a degree of shock and outrage incomprehensible fifty years later'.[79] Indeed, Hamilton Fyfe sneered that the Welsh Wizard had been 'making a great effort to get into the limelight':

> He seems to have fancied that he would be called to the Premiership by the voice of the people. He still thinks of himself as a man of destiny. He can't realise that nobody trusts him or believes in him.[80]

On the first day of the strike, Lloyd George called it 'an ordinary trade dispute' but displeased the House with what Conservative Harold Macmillan called 'a rather casuistical distinction between a sympathetic industrial strike and a general strike intended to coerce the Government'.[81] Prime Minister Stanley Baldwin also complained to the King of Lloyd George's 'vague and indeterminate vacillations, his niggling criticisms of the Government, and his insincere fraternisation with the Labour Party',[82] an allusion to rumours that he had offered to put his substantial political fund at the disposal of the main opposition party. Although this was later vehemently denied by Lloyd George and Ramsay MacDonald, it was almost certainly true.[83]

At the same time, there was a degree of opportunism on Lloyd George's part. When Baldwin conceded a temporary subsidy for the miners in July 1925, he had mocked the government for 'running away from the Reds'. Now, almost a year later, Lloyd George was accusing Baldwin of inflexibility for refusing to negotiate with the TUC. A more charitable view (as posited by biographer John Campbell) was that, given the former premier had moved steadily leftward since leaving Downing Street in 1922, there was actually a 'perfect internal consistency'. Lloyd George had published detailed proposals for the industry in a 1924 paper entitled *Coal and Power*, while the emergency machinery now in place was a legacy of his time in office.[84]

By the time the Liberal shadow cabinet was due to meet again on 10 May, Lloyd George had grown weary of his colleagues' more extreme statements and made a point of refusing to attend, telling the party's chief whip Sir Godfrey Collins that these committed 'us, without previous consultation, to a point of view from which I feel obliged most regretfully to dissent'. 'I prefer the Liberal policy,' he added pointedly, 'of trusting to conciliation rather than to force.'[85] The significance of his absence seemed greater to Asquith et al. than it did to the absentee. Asquith remarked that Lloyd George had 'cast in his lot' with 'the clericals', by which he meant the Archbishop of Canterbury and other Church leaders whom he regarded as 'a hopeless lot' for urging a resumption of negotiations. And, sensing an opportunity to rid themselves of their turbulent priest, Asquith's supporters seized upon an article by Lloyd George in an American newspaper. In retrospect, this, too, was relatively innocuous, with the *Manchester Guardian* calling it 'such an article as any sensible and moderately-minded man might have written'.[86] The Liberal-supporting *Daily Chronicle* loyally declared that 'talk about a great row in the party was sheer nonsense',[87] but divisions over the general strike meant that another Liberal storm was brewing.

8

'THE BIG THREE'

On the morning of Wednesday 5 May, Fenner Brockway found the Trades Union Congress headquarters at Eccleston Square 'in chaos':

> Nothing seems to have been thought out. The Committee appointed some time ago to prepare plans reported that no plans could be prepared until the emergency arose. The result is that nothing has been arranged – not even a panel of despatch riders to take and report news about the country![1]

Ernest Bevin's biographer Alan Bullock also described the scene:

> The T.U.C. organisation, a handful of officials and office staff, was totally inadequate to cope with an operation which would have strained the resources of a fully-equipped army command. Committees could find nowhere to meet; the telephone line was jammed with calls; deputations, dispatch-riders, trade-union leaders, Labour M.P.s, journalists, cameramen tramped up and down stairs looking for someone to speak to, while in the midst of this bedlam, the General Council in full session attempted to discuss policy, listen to the reports of the committees, make decisions, answer questions and issue instructions.[2]

Things were not much better in Glasgow, where the National Union of Railwaymen refused to move foodstuffs despite instructions to do so from the Scottish Trades Union Congress (STUC).[3] The situation was at least calm in Northern Ireland, where representatives from thirteen trade unions had formed an Emergency Council despite the strike having not reached that part of the United Kingdom.[4]

Back in London, Ernest Bevin, although a relative newcomer to the TUC's General Council, suggested that he take personal control of a small 'Strike Organization Committee'. Acting general secretary Walter Citrine recalled the 'storm' which greeted Bevin's offer 'and a good deal of straight speaking', with Jimmy Thomas and others resorting to sarcasm. Bevin was unfussed. 'We must not,' he remarked, 'have too many generals in this business.'[5] Prime Minister Stanley Baldwin shrewdly suspected that Bevin viewed himself as 'the Napoleon of the Trade Union movement'.[6]

Bevin nevertheless assumed central control of the strike, which served to diminish if not completely eliminate the organizational confusion.[7] The STUC also moved to a similar system for the distribution of daily bulletins and transport permits throughout Scotland.[8] Meanwhile, in all Great Britain's major towns and cities local strike committees – often with the militant title of 'Councils of Action' – sprang into life and communicated with Eccleston Square via despatch riders. Walter Citrine had pushed for the already-extant Trades Councils (local groups of trade unionists) to form the 'nucleus' of local strike organization, but Bevin vetoed it.[9]

Councils of Action often comprised Labour councillors, magistrates and other local officials, which led the Home Office to believe they were 'illegally' attempting 'to arrogate to themselves functions of Local Government and of the Police'.[10] As with the Communist Party of Great Britain (formed in 1920), these Councils found themselves targeted for breaches of Emergency Regulations and of the ordinary law. Although most senior trade union leaders considered the government's claim that the TUC was trying to usurp democratic government absurd, they were sufficiently concerned to deny it. One flyer stated that:

> The General Council of the Trades Union Congress does NOT challenge the Constitution. It is not seeking to substitute unconstitutional government. Nor is it desirous of undermining our Parliamentary institutions ... The sole aim of the Council is to secure for the miners a decent standard of life. The Council is engaged in an Industrial dispute.[11]

Yet as David Howell has observed, the 'close and complex' relationship between the TUC and the Labour Party meant such a thorough demarcation was both 'implausible and typically unsustainable'.[12]

It was also undeniably the case that the General Council of the TUC was an incredibly powerful body. Its most influential union leaders were known as 'The Big Three' – the Miners' Federation of Great Britain, the National Union of Railwaymen and the Transport and General Workers' Union – which we shall now meet in turn.

'A QUIVERING MASS OF EMOTIONS'

If the general strike had a bogeyman, it was Arthur James Cook, the forty-two-year-old general secretary of the Miners' Federation. The wounding pen of Beatrice Webb depicted him as 'a loosely-built, ugly-featured man' but nevertheless one:

> you watch with a certain admiring curiosity ... he is a quivering mass of emotions, a mediumistic magnetic sort of creature – not without personal attractiveness – an inspired idiot, drunk with his own words, dominated by his slogans. I doubt whether he even knows what he is going to say or what he has just said.[13]

Although born in Wookey, Somerset, Cook's formative years were spent in the coalfields of South Wales, to which he had moved in 1901. A talented boy preacher, he joined the Independent Labour Party (ILP) and took part in the Tonypandy riots of 1910–11. In 1912 Cook co-authored *The Miners' Next Step*, the central themes of which were class struggle and the need for rank-and-file control. By 1918 he was advocating the use of a 'general strike' to achieve revolutionary change.

In 1918 Cook was charged with sedition under the *Defence of the Realm Act 1914* (a forerunner to the *Emergency Powers Act 1920*) and served two months in prison. He joined the executive of the South Wales Miners' Federation in 1919 and the national Miners' Federation executive a few months before Black Friday, after which he was again imprisoned, this time with two months' hard labour for incitement and unlawful assembly. He later told Walter Citrine that the memory of being handcuffed and led in chains from one end of a Swansea–Cardiff train to the other was seared in his memory.

Cook was briefly a founder member of the Communist Party of Great Britain but resigned in 1921 and instead promoted the radical 'National Minority Movement' in South Wales, which provided important backing for his successful bid to become general secretary of the MFGB in April 1924. He was committed to nationalization, the overthrow of capitalism and the 'Triple Alliance', which extracted a subsidy from the government on Red Friday. 'Why the hell should I want to go to see the King,' Cook said after being invited to Buckingham Palace at the height of the crisis. 'Bugger him. Who is he?'[14] Cook was also deeply suspicious of Ramsay MacDonald. 'It appears to me ... that the greatest enemies of the working-class movement are some of its supposed leaders,' he stormed after taking umbrage at a speech by the Labour leader in August 1925. 'It is only to abuse the English language and the accurate use of it,' MacDonald replied coolly, 'to put upon my words the meaning which you say you see in them.'[15] Although the Leader of the Opposition liked Cook 'in a sort of way', he despaired that he could not 'keep his mouth shut'.[16]

When the negotiations of April/May 1926 failed, Cook toured the coalfields to deploy his magnetic, emotional oratory. The ILP MP David Kirkwood likened him to 'a Salvation Army preacher' who swept 'over the industrial districts like a hurricane'.[17] It took the Welsh trade unionist Arthur Horner a while to figure out why Cook's 'sometimes almost inarticulate' oratory could 'electrify' a meeting while his did not. 'I was speaking to the meeting. Cook was speaking for the meeting,' he recalled. 'He was expressing the thoughts of his audience, I was trying to persuade them. He was the burning expression of their anger at the iniquities which they were suffering.'[18] As Fenner Brockway observed, while most trade union leaders could not wait to elevate themselves, 'Arthur Cook never left the rank and file. He had their thoughts, their language, their habits, their simple trusting comradeship and good fellowship.'[19] He would arrive at public meetings the 'suited official' but, as he spoke, remove his jacket, collar and tie while rolling up his sleeves. 'The barrier between leaders and led was removed,' judged David Howell, 'he became a miner once again.'[20]

But as Hywel Francis has observed, Cook's public 'obduracy' masked a genuine desire to negotiate a settlement which would mitigate suffering among his members.[21] At the end of April 1926, for example, he remained 'convinced that a settlement can be reached by a straight return to the [Samuel] Commission's proposals, and from them to a discussion on the basis of a national agreement'.[22] Cook held what his biographer called 'a realistic – some might say pessimistic' view of the Miners' Federation's position, although he kept this private through fear of damaging the 'solidarity and morale' of the miners.[23]

Publicly, therefore, most of Cook's pronouncements during the general strike were models of moderation and firm determination. 'Is peace possible?' he asked rhetorically on the evening of Sunday 9 May:

> 'Yes, yes,' I repeat. We are not fighting the Constitution. This is a fight for bread. What are the terms of peace? A living wage. We are not asking the impossible. We are not chasing the moon.[24]

Although this was not the received wisdom during the strike, it came to be acknowledged that it was not Cook who represented the real obstacle to a negotiated compromise but Herbert Smith, the sixty-three-year-old President of the Miners' Federation. An orphan raised by miners in West Yorkshire, Smith's brevity was in stark contrast to Cook's emotional outpourings. 'My motto,' he once remarked in broad Yorkshire, 'is to say nowt.'[25] During the final negotiations, Stanley Baldwin even amused the Conservative MP Cuthbert Headlam with an impersonation, recounting that all Smith had said throughout their conferences was: 'Government 'as got us into the mess: Government 'as got to get us out.'[26]

The socialist economist R. H. Tawney remarked that Smith seemed to perceive 'England as a coal-pit with some grass growing on top', while Sir William Beveridge, who had served on the Samuel Commission, thought his mind like 'granite'. The TUC's Walter Citrine, however, was rather fond of Smith, considering him 'calm' and 'straight as a die'. He recalled him sitting at meetings 'in his blue suit and soft collar, with his little moustache turning grey and his high balding forehead, with his spectacles resting on the end of his nose'.[27] The press did not differentiate, vilifying both Cook and Smith for their intransigence and poor leadership. MI5 kept them under surveillance and extracted gossip from chambermaids at their hotel.[28] While Cook was 'low caste', Beatrice Webb dismissed Smith as 'senile'.[29]

'LET'S BLAME THOMAS!'

Another of the Big Three who attracted opprobrium was James Henry Thomas, the Welsh-born general secretary of the National Union of Railwaymen and lately Colonial Secretary in the first Labour government. With his stocky figure, chubby face, moustache and round-lensed spectacles, 'he was a cartoonist's delight'.[30]

An early historian of the general strike considered 'Jimmy', as he was generally known, the:

> greatest buffoon the Labour movement has known, a man who dropped his aitches as eagerly as he put on a dinner jacket, the personification of the beery, cheery, plain-speaking man that music hall comedians felt the British working man to be.[31]

Egon Wertheimer observed that Thomas had created round him 'an atmosphere of vulgar cordiality and a hail-fellow-well-met manner which appears to have taken in the whole of the British Empire with the exception of about a dozen Communists'.[32]

Unlike Cook, Thomas was not worshipped by his rank-and-file members, many of whom blamed him for Black Friday in 1921. There was significant suspicion of Thomas's apparent 'capture' by the British establishment: his eagerness to dress up and ingratiate himself with the great and the good. He could not care less. Thomas later mused on:

> the persistency with which I am picked out as the villain of all the industrial moves that go wrong in this country. 'We're in a fix; let's blame Thomas!' seems for some years to have been the stand-by of certain types of people in our own movement. This is highly flattering to me, but ... what about the other fellows? [What] About men like Ramsay MacDonald, like Arthur Pugh ... Am I the ringleader ... Have I got them all in my pocket? Am I a sort of Machiavellian superman of the entire Labour movement?[33]

Like most trade union leaders in the 1920s, Thomas had reached his exalted position following decades of hard graft, opportunism and not a bit of luck. Born in Newport, Monmouthshire, the illegitimate son of a servant, he joined the Great Western Railway in 1889 and advanced via the Amalgamated Society of Railway Servants (ASRS), the Newport Trades Council and later Swindon Council. In 1906 Thomas became organizing secretary of the ASRS and in January 1910 the Labour MP for Derby. The Conservative Lord Birkenhead considered him 'unquestionably the cleverest politician hitherto produced by the Socialist Party'.[34]

But what made many contemporaries suspicious was Thomas's lack of socialist politics. Rather, he was a centre-right progressive, keen that his members improve their prospects within existing constitutional and economic structures. And while this left room for strike action – Thomas led a spate of unofficial strikes during 1911 and helped organize the first national railway strike – he did not approve of syndicalism and its goal of a wider, more overly 'political', strike. In 1913 the amalgamated National Union of Railwaymen (NUR) was formed, of which Thomas became general secretary in 1916 and thereafter a member of the TUC's parliamentary committee, a forerunner of the General Council.

Thomas's establishment capture can perhaps be dated to 1917, when he was sworn a member of the Privy Council despite not being a member of the government. Notwithstanding their shared roots in Baptist South Wales, he regarded Arthur Cook of the Miners' Federation as 'mad'. In one oft-repeated anecdote, Thomas recalled Cook suggesting that poor families stockpile food in anticipation of a general strike. This, he noted, took:

> our breath away, but we got it back again with a gulp when [Cook] continued – 'My own mother-in-law has been taking an extra tin of salmon for weeks past!' I could not refrain from ejaculating: 'My God, the British Revolution on a tin of salmon!'[35]

Thomas also delighted in baiting the notoriously short-tempered Ernest Bevin and he often swallowed the hook, on one occasion 'erupting and charging from the room to the accompaniment of rude noises' from Jimmy.[36]

But in spite of it all, when the TUC endorsed a general strike at the Memorial Hall, Thomas did not demur. The *Daily Herald* editor Hamilton Fyfe recalled him making 'a stirring, thrilling speech':[37]

> Do not lose your heads. We have striven, we have pleaded, we have begged for peace because we want peace. We still want peace.

THE EDGE OF REVOLUTION

> The nation wants peace. Those who want war must take the responsibility.[38]

Later challenged as to why he had not argued against a general strike, Thomas was contemptuous:

> I could have warned all the Trade Unionists in the country that they were likely to be bled to death by a General Strike. I could have told the world that my own Union, for which I have proudly worked for so many years, and which I had seen rise to power and financial resources of wonderful magnitude, would, in a few brief weeks be reduced to borrowing money upon its own buildings and properties! I could have done all this. What a sensation Jim Thomas could have caused! what a nine-days' 'marvel' he would have been! ... But would I have done any good by adopting such an attitude? Is it not likely that I would have done more harm than good?[39]

That was certainly Thomas's attitude during the nine days, which he spent in constant conference with ministers, civil servants and potential intermediaries in an attempt to bring it to an orderly and early end. Initially, he even surprised TUC colleagues with his bullishness. 'Up to the evening of the strike the Government thought they knew our power,' Walter Citrine recalled Thomas saying, 'but the strike exceeded their greatest expectation.'[40]

Only halfway through did Thomas break ranks, telling a crowd in Hammersmith that he had 'never been in favour of a general strike', although he was careful to add that just as workers had no right to demand that an employer 'must negotiate under the threat of a strike', equally 'workers should not be asked to negotiate under the threat of a lock out'. He also criticized Stanley Baldwin raising 'the constitutional issue'. 'The only way we can replace this Government,' concluded Thomas, 'is by the exercise of our rights at the ballot-box.'[41]

'THE DICTATOR OF ECCLESTON SQUARE'

The last of the Big Three was Ernest Bevin of the mighty Transport and General Workers' Union. Broad-shouldered, heavily built and possessing a strong West Country accent, Bevin's:

physical appearance, powerful and emphatic, was an inseparable part of his personality. It expressed in his look, his stance and walk the qualities which attracted attention the moment he entered a room or climbed on to a platform: energy, force and determination.[42]

A considerably less divisive figure than Arthur Cook or Jimmy Thomas, Bevin immediately became the 'big man' of the strike. As one eyewitness account judged:

> It was his quick brain and natural genius for organisation that saved the strike from being a complete fiasco ... All through the first week, cool and unfurled by anybody or anything, he kept the machine of his making smoothly at work. He could be called 'The Dictator of Eccleston Square', to whom all applied and sought advice. His word was absolute.[43]

Born in Somerset in March 1881, like Thomas and MacDonald Bevin was an illegitimate child with a frugal upbringing. His early working life was itinerant, including stints as a van driver, waiter and horse tram conductor. Like Cook and Thomas, Bevin was a Baptist, and he was active in several Bristol missions as a preacher. His long association with the Bristol dockers began in 1910 and the following year he became a paid official of the Dockers' Union. Less than a year after Black Friday (at which he was criticized for not supporting the miners), Bevin helped create the 300,000-strong Transport and General Workers' Union (TGWU) in January 1922 and became its overwhelming choice as general secretary.

The post-war years also brought Bevin into close contact with the leaders of the Parliamentary Labour Party. During the first Labour government, however, Ramsay MacDonald accused him of 'disloyalty' when the TGWU threatened a London-wide transport stoppage in early 1924. In turn, Bevin criticized the Labour premier's lack of consultation with the TUC and readiness to invoke the *Emergency Powers Act 1920*. His wariness increased over MacDonald's handling of the Zinoviev Letter during the 1924 election campaign and he unsuccessfully urged Arthur Henderson to stand for the Labour leadership. At the 1925 Labour Party conference, Bevin's attempt to make a parliamentary majority a condition of a second Labour government was defeated.[44]

The ILP's John Paton felt that the pressure of the strike led Bevin to adopt one of Ramsay MacDonald's 'favourite devices in times of difficulty' – withdrawal from 'all contact with his fellow-men':

> It was whispered in the office that he was tearing his hair in a secret fastness somewhere in the building behind a securely locked door; the door was guarded on the inside by a familiar dragon in the person of his faithful secretary. The barriers, I was assured, were impenetrable. Communication with the beleaguered garrison was maintained by notes slipped under the door.[45]

Bevin, however, never pretended he made no mistakes during the nine days, among them the decision to call out printers (thus closing down most newspapers), the failure to mobilize postal workers and only issuing strike orders to engineers and shipyard workers when it was too late. From start to finish, observed Bevin's biographer, 'it was a feat of improvisation which left far too much to chance and local initiative'.[46] But the extent to which it worked at all was thanks to the Dictator of Eccleston Square.

Bevin was also a realist. By the first (and as it turned out only) weekend of the general strike, his Strike Organisation Committee decided the time had come to reopen negotiations with the government and mine owners. In Bevin's recollection:

> You could not sit in the Strike Organisation room, with deputations and committees coming in all the time from all over the country, without sensing pretty clearly how long we could carry it. I felt and said that we would reach the maximum of strength about the following Tuesday [12 May] – then it would be a case of 'holding out' and I thought approximately three weeks would be necessary after that to clean up.

The problem was that Stanley Baldwin and his colleagues would not budge from their position that the strike had to be called off *before* talks could resume. This put the TUC's General Council between a rock and a hard place, either committed to a prolonged stoppage or capitulating in a way which could split the trade union movement from top to bottom.[47]

'A HYGIENIC PURITAN'

Beyond the Big Three, Walter Citrine and Arthur Pugh were key figures in the smooth running of Eccleston Square. As ever, Beatrice Webb provided a vivid (and caustic) portrait of Citrine:

> Tall, broad-shouldered, with the manners and clothes and way of speaking of a superior bank clerk, black hair growing low on his forehead, large pointed ears, bright grey eyes set close together, big nose, long chin and tiny, rather 'pretty', mouth, it is difficult to say whether or not he is good looking. In profile he is; in full face he is not ... He is a non-smoker, non-drinker, small, slow eater, takes a daily cold bath, sleeps with his windows open—altogether a hygienic puritan in daily life.[48]

Only thirty-eight years old, Citrine was born in Liverpool in 1887, the third of five children to a sailor and a nurse, although the name (originally Citrini) suggested Italian heritage. An autodidact, Citrine left school at twelve but taught himself economics, accountancy and socialism. Originally an apprentice electrician, in 1914 he joined the Electrical Trades Union as an official, moving to its Manchester headquarters in 1920 and then to London four years later on becoming assistant secretary of the Trades Union Congress. When Fred Bramley died in October 1925, Citrine was recalled from a visit to the Soviet Union to serve as acting secretary.[49]

Clear-sighted and methodical, it was Citrine who had warned the General Council in January 1926 that it should prepare for the inevitability of a general strike. During the nine days, he also kept a diary. As early as 6 May, Citrine recorded the Strike Organisation Committee giving consideration to 'alternative arrangements for carrying on the strike in the event of the General Council being arrested', while on Friday 7 May, Bevin, 'in a state of considerable perturbation', even demanded that Citrine stop taking notes of proceedings to deprive the police of evidence in the event of a raid.[50]

Arthur Pugh, meanwhile, hailed from a moderately more prosperous background than his contemporaries – his father was a civil engineer – although both parents had died when he was an infant. Pugh was apprenticed to a farmer and butcher at thirteen before moving from Herefordshire to Wales to work as a steel smelter. By 1917 he was the first general secretary of the Iron and Steel Trades Confederation (ISTC) and in 1925 was elected chairman of the TUC's General Council.[51] Although Jimmy Thomas admired Pugh for never once losing 'control of himself or of his associates' during 'long and weary' debates concerning the strike,[52] he was a reluctant participant. As John Hodge, who had vainly attempted to persuade the ISTC not to participate in the general strike, wryly remarked: 'I have never heard him say that he was in favour of it, but I have never heard him say that he was against it.'[53]

What of the general strike beyond Eccleston Square? The Marxist Plebs' League (an educational and political organization founded in 1908) later divided British towns into four classes. Those in Class I had 'unexpectedly and amazingly' a response of between 90 and 100 per cent to the strike call; in Class II the strike was 'wholly effective' but a 'lack of information' or 'a weakening in some section' prevented it being classed any higher; Class III covered towns where 'there was a weakness in one section or another of a quite serious character' while in Class IV the strike had completely broken down.[54]

Tredegar in the Welsh Valleys doubtlessly belonged in Class I. There, the twenty-eight-year-old Aneurin Bevan was the 'effective ruler of the town' as chairman of its Council of Action.[55] Over in Stepney in the East End of London, the borough council had hoisted the red flag over its town hall and restricted non-essential use of its electricity supply.[56] Chairing its electricity committee was the forty-three-year-old Clement Attlee, and when a local engineering firm took legal action against the future Prime Minister for loss of earnings, a £300 court penalty threatened him with bankruptcy.[57] The Ministry of Health, meanwhile, feared left-wing Boards of Guardians in east London were granting Poor Law relief in a 'political' way.[58] The Labour group on London County Council refused to participate in its emergency committee and instead urged cooperation with trade unions.[59]

During the strike, the TUC's General Council despatched two of its most popular female propagandists to report on activity in different parts of England. 'Red' Ellen Wilkinson motored:

> about two thousand miles; through the West of England, back to London, and then to the North, addressing forty-seven mass

meetings, both in country towns and in the big industrial areas, attending strike committees in sessions, and meeting every kind of person on the job, from town clerks and chief constables running the Government machinery, to harassed trade union secretaries and enthusiastic pickets.

She recalled a 'huge' meeting cheering for several minutes when a miner said: 'If the British Constitution makes a miner work underground for less than £2 a week, it is about time that constitution was challenged!' At Crewe, Wilkinson joined others in addressing a massive crowd at its local football stadium. 'The Strike Committee in Crewe simply ran the town,' she recalled. 'No food could enter or leave without its permission. Every worker on light (gas or electric) worked under their permit.'[60]

Meanwhile, Margaret Bondfield, who had become the UK's first female minister in 1924, drove around south-west England in a car and driver loaned by the Labour-sympathizing aristocrat Lady de la Warr. Although Bondfield was in 'no doubt' public opinion was 'definitely on the side of the miners', when she reached Yeovil she began to detect an 'anxiety to end the strike'.[61] If Yeovil was in Class II, then Leeds was probably Class III, possessing no fewer than 'four rival Strike Committees, mutually jealous ... the worst conducted town in England'.[62]

The press, especially American newspaper correspondents, made much of the local strike committees arranging football matches, concerts and other distractions. At Plymouth the chief constable suggested a game of football which was kicked off by his wife. Watched by a crowd of more than 10,000, the strikers won by two goals to one. Half-time was enlivened by the Tramway Band.[63] A Frenchman who saw newsreel footage apparently remarked that England was not a nation but 'a circus'.[64] At Lewes in Sussex the police and strikers arranged a public billiards match, while Cardiff's strike committee advised: 'Keep smiling. Refuse to be provoked. Get into your garden. Look after the wife and kiddies. If you have not got a garden, get into the country, the parks and the playgrounds.'[65]

When New Scotland Yard surveyed chief constables after the strike, it received a surprising number of positive reports. In Bedfordshire, the local police chief expressed 'great admiration for [the] behaviour of strikers' and noted that two cricket matches had been played between them and the police. In Oldham, the chief constable said the conduct of miners was 'excellent' and that 'local Labour leaders fell in with all requests'. And considering that Glamorganshire had 'long been the scene of grave disorders in industrial disputes, the conduct of strikers was remarkable', due in part to trade union advice and police preparation. In Merthyr Tydfil, the strike committee was 'in daily consultation with [the] Chief Constable and [had] assisted in organisation of sports and concerts, thus keeping strikers off the streets'.[66]

Susan Lawrence, the Labour MP for East Ham, addressed a dozen meetings in London's East End during the strike. 'A glorious spirit,' she gushed to Beatrice Webb. 'Never again will the workers be trodden under foot as they are now – we are living in momentous times – a revolutionary reaction.' Webb was contemptuous. 'There is no earthly use in it all except to get rid of a proletarian distemper,' she informed Lawrence. 'There will not even be a revolutionary reaction. Thomas and Baldwin will see to that – they will broadcast messages of Peace and Goodwill every few hours until we are all hypnotized into loving one another!'[67]

Not everywhere was so convivial. On 9 May several Labour councillors on the Birmingham Watch Committee were charged under Emergency Regulations, one for calling special constables 'nothing more than a body of traitors',[68] while in London Noah Ablett of the South Wales Miners' Federation was charged with making a speech likely to cause disaffection among the civil population.[69] Permits for vehicles transporting food also led to confusion and a degree of abuse. According to one of his clerks, Hugh Lyon of the Scottish Horse and Motormen's Association was 'in his element' as a 'stream of employers' was ushered into his presence: 'Hughie sat there smoking a cigar; sometimes he would not give a permit. It depended on whether he thought the employer would be co-operative in future.' Lyon also classified whisky as a 'staple food stuff'.[70]

On the whole, however, and 'despite manifest errors and omissions', Gordon Phillips judged the TUC's handling of the general strike to have been a success:

> The wish of the General Council to avoid a widespread stoppage in the food and retailing industries, their initial willingness to create

some kind of permit system, their reluctance to bring about a total stoppage in the power industries, indicate a tentativeness, even an anxiety, about the use of the weapon of the general strike. But to say that the TUC did not wish to cause severe food shortages or to bring about a cessation of all normal processes of life, is merely to repeat the obvious. The general strike had never been regarded as a revolutionary weapon. Its lineaments were moulded by its confined and modest purposes.[71]

The strike was also confined to Great Britain until dockers in Northern Ireland were called out on 10 May.[72] Attempts to attract continental support failed. The government-produced *British Gazette* made much of the 'fiasco at Ostend', where Frank Hodges of the Miners' Federation launched 'a dramatic appeal ... in favour of a general international strike'. Despite some support from Belgium and France, opposition from Germany – now growing fat on exports of Ruhr Valley coal – meant such a dramatic expansion did not stand a chance.[73]

A week into the general strike, there was a noticeable defensiveness regarding its constitutionality. A TUC bulletin protested that the British constitution included the 'right to strike',[74] while the *Scottish Worker* declared that 'loyalty' to the constitution was not 'associated in their minds with starvation wages to the British worker'.[75] But to the ILP's John Paton, the General Council's repeated restatement of the 'legal correctitude of its conduct' was 'so much moonshine':

> The only purpose of the strike was to coerce a constitutionally elected government into doing what it did not want to do. If, by its direction of the strike, the General Council had succeeded in compelling the Government to do its will, then in fact the General Council would have been the actual governing body – an extra-constitutional governing body – imposing its dictates on a puppet government. And if it could impose its will on this matter, why not on others?[76]

9

'THE STUPIDEST MEN IN ENGLAND'

The other distinct group at the heart of the general strike were the coal owners. Lord Birkenhead, the Conservative Secretary of State for India, spoke for many of his Cabinet colleagues when he caustically remarked that 'it would be possible to say without exaggeration of the miners' leaders that they were the stupidest men in England if we had not had frequent occasion to meet the owners'.[1]

This was most likely a reference to Sir Adam Nimmo, a London-based Scot, and perhaps Evan Williams, a Welshman, both doyens of the powerful Mining Association of Great Britain, a representative body for wealthy mine owners. Beatrice Webb wondered why the 'capitalists of the coalfields' were so 'dreary and incompetent a lot':

> but the verdict that they have been and are wholly unable to run their business with decent efficiency has been given over and over again and by all parties in the state ... Each successive court of enquiry, whatever its composition, has declared against them.[2]

To the historian G. D. H. Cole, miners and mine owners alike were 'stubborn folk, tenacious and unadaptable, and therefore out of their element in a world of rapid change needing above all the constant application of new methods and new ideas'.[3] Of the coal industry's entire leadership, despaired one senior civil servant, there was 'hardly an outstanding personality'.[4]

It was ironic that the coal owners – individuals who straddled politics, industry and the media – came to be viewed in Whitehall as little better than the miners' leadership. But while Prime Minister Stanley

Baldwin was always friendly and sympathetic towards the latter, Deputy Cabinet Secretary Tom Jones observed that it was:

> impossible not to feel the contrast between the reception which Ministers give to a body of owners and a body of miners. Ministers are at ease with the former, they are friends, jointly exploring a situation. There was hardly any indication of opposition or censure.[5]

One member of the Cabinet, President of the Board of Trade Philip Cunliffe-Lister, was even married to a coal owner and offered his resignation on that basis. This was not accepted, and though generally regarded as a diehard, Cunliffe-Lister was also prepared for the government to impose a solution if the coal owners and miners could not come to an agreement.[6]

Figures quoted by Arthur Cook of the Miners' Federation in March 1926 highlighted the great profits yielded by Britain's coalfields as well as a degree of volatility. In 1922 there had been a loss of £1,800,000 and in 1923 a profit of £15,800,000. In 1924 this had risen to £28,800,000 but fell back in 1925 to £6,900,000,[7] a decline which perhaps explained the owners' determination to impose wage cuts and longer hours. The 1919 Sankey Commission had also highlighted the annual royalties drawn by certain aristocrats, the wealthiest of whom were the Marquess of Bute, who had grown rich on the South Wales coalfields, and the Duke of Hamilton from those in Lanarkshire. Even the established Church of England benefited from royalties to the extent of £370,000 a year.[8] For this reason, among others, John Maynard Keynes considered coal a 'decadent, third-generation industry'.[9]

At the same time, many mining areas were in a 'parlous' state by the end of 1925 and had been artificially sustained by the government's subsidy. Without it, the Prime Minister pointed to figures suggesting that 'practically 100%' of the Northumberland pits would 'go out of action', 97 per cent in Durham, 90 per cent in South Wales and 88 per cent in Scotland. When Baldwin asked the taciturn Herbert Smith of the Miners' Federation if he realized that meant at least 200,000 miners being thrown out of work, Tom Jones noted his reaction: 'Yes, Mr. Smith was perfectly prepared to face unemployment on this scale, and preferred to do so to any variation from the present standard of wages and hours.'[10]

THE STUPIDEST MEN IN ENGLAND

But if the miners were blind to the economic realities of falling exports, the owners took the equally stubborn view that there was nothing wrong with the coal industry that could not be rectified by 'free, individualistic and unaided' management. They also indulged the reductive view that the generally prosperous record of the industry before the First World War spoke to the effectiveness of private enterprise, while increasing state intervention after 1914 explained falling productivity and incessant concessions to what they regarded as unreasonable demands from the miners.[11]

By March 1925, the owners were prepared to face down a coal stoppage so were appalled when Baldwin preached peace and promised a nine-month bailout. 'If you have a General Strike with public opinion on your side I think the struggle will be probably short and sharp,' the Prime Minister warned the Miners' Association. 'If you have public opinion against you it might be long, and it would be difficult.'[12] In the event, the owners accepted yet another Royal Commission and, when this looked likely to recommend widespread reorganization, became even more determined to preserve the status quo.[13] The Samuel Report in March 1926 noted that the employers resented:

> the accusations levelled against them, which, in the main they feel to be unjust. The abuses of a bygone day, which have long disappeared, have nothing to do, they consider, with the affairs of the present ... The grievances, they are convinced, are often deliberately exaggerated, in order to support the political case for a fundamental change.

The Mining Association told the Samuel Commission that the Miners' Federation did 'not desire to come to agreements with the employers, but to destroy them – to secure their elimination from the industry altogether'. Furthermore, it claimed:

> the men do not do their best to produce a satisfactory output, even during the short hours when they are at work ... They point to the frequent absences from work of the miners, and especially of the hewers, on whom the whole working depends ... They instance the not less serious disorganisation and loss occasioned from time to time by unauthorised stoppages of a whole mine, in order to secure the remedy of some trifling grievance, which could have been easily disposed of by discussion.[14]

But who constituted the Mining Association of Great Britain? Between 1919 and 1926 its leadership had been remarkably stable, with the same small group of individuals representing it in frequent negotiations. Its main public face on such occasions was Association president Evan Williams, though just as influential were the foremost members of its Central Council, Sir Adam Nimmo and Lord Gainford, also chairmen, respectively, of the Scottish and Durham mine owners.

'AN INSIGNIFICANT LITTLE MAN'

Tom Jones, the Deputy Cabinet Secretary, considered Evan Williams 'an insignificant little man',[15] although his colleague William Lee admired his 'patience ... clear thinking and sound judgement'.[16] Balding, moustachioed and with a kindly face, coal was in Williams' blood. Born at Llwynhendy, Carmarthenshire, in 1871, he was the eldest son of coal owner Thomas Williams and his wife Mary. Unusually for Welsh coal owners of this period, he was educated privately (Christ College, Brecon) and then at Clare College, Cambridge. In 1903 Williams married Charlotte, the youngest daughter of the Scottish coal owner David Lackie. Proudly Welsh, his Carmarthenshire home was named after the fourteenth-century patriot Owain Glyndŵr.

Williams presided over the conciliation board of the South Wales Coal Owners' Association from 1918 to 1944 and acted as President of the Mining Association of Great Britain (MAGB) for almost as long.[17] His presidency coincided with the Sankey Commission of 1919, whose interim report famously concluded that:

> Even upon the evidence already given, the present system of ownership and working in the coal industry stands condemned, and some other system must be substituted for it, either nationalisation or a method of unification by national purchase and/or by joint control.[18]

Conscious this verdict had attracted widespread public sympathy, the MAGB reorganized: making the hitherto temporary and honorary post of president permanent, acquiring a full-time staff and four standing committees, including one charged with 'propaganda'. The target was state control, and with the events of 1921 – the aversion of a national strike on Black Friday and the return to private ownership – the MAGB felt that fight was being won. Williams was even credited for 'putting nationalization to sleep'.[19]

Williams' two hymn sheets were 'no national settlements, especially on wages, for the coal industry; and – even more vehemently – no interference (by state, miners, or anyone else) with the sole prerogative of the owners to manage the collieries'.[20] Unsurprisingly, he despised the emotional Miners' Federation secretary Arthur Cook. 'Do you know what ought to be done with you Cook?' Williams said at one meeting in early 1925. 'You should be fastened to a chair and three-inch nails run into you.'[21]

When Stanley Baldwin announced a nine-month subsidy in 1925, Williams was 'shocked and thrown off balance' at what he saw as a needless sell-out to union militancy.[22] But he was evidently not as 'insignificant' as some Whitehall mandarins liked to believe. Even the Communist Robin Page Arnot described Williams as 'ever-polite and courteous' in expressing his admittedly inflexible views with 'a singular tenacity ... precision and in exactly formulated phrases'.[23]

'ONE OF THE GREATEST STUMBLING-BLOCKS ON THE PATH TO PEACE'

While Tom Jones considered Sir Adam Nimmo to be more significant than Evan Williams, the Deputy Cabinet Secretary found him just as exasperating:

> He is powerfully built and lays down the law in stern tones. His Company pays [a dividend of] 10%, but the Coal Owners [according to Nimmo] have always gone to the utmost limit of self-sacrifice, the question in debate (whatever it be) is always fundamental and always involves a vital principle on which the Owners cannot possibly carry compromise an inch further. He is one of the greatest stumbling-blocks on the path to peace.[24]

Like Williams, Nimmo was the son of a coal master. Born in Stirlingshire in November 1866 he received a gentleman's education at Edinburgh's Royal High School and the University of Edinburgh. In 1908 Nimmo's wife Isabella died aged thirty-two and he never remarried. By then his father's ten collieries in Stirlingshire and Lanarkshire employed 2,700 men and boys. James Nimmo passed the managing directorship to his son when he was widowed, and it provided a useful distraction.[25]

With a strong sense of noblesse oblige, Nimmo devoted himself to the Lanarkshire Coal Masters' Association (LCMA) and later to the Mining Association of Great Britain. Although moderately wealthy, he showed little personal interest in accumulating money, caring more about safeguarding coal as one of the foundations of national wealth. To William Lee, secretary of the MAGB, he was 'a man of broad views and of progressive outlook' who 'combined great intellectual powers with a very warm heart'.[26] In 1916 Nimmo was elected President of the Mining Association and emerged alongside Evan Williams as one of the public faces of the mining industry. Knighted in 1918, Sir Adam joined the Sankey Commission the following year and worked hard to temper the critical tone of its later reports.[27]

When in 1924 Ramsay MacDonald's first Labour government floated nationalization of the mines, Nimmo warned darkly that it would not only 'destroy' the coal industry but 'the structure of British industry as a whole'.[28] By January 1925 he was telling the National Liberal Club:

> The wages of those engaged in the industry cannot permanently rest upon considerations of cost of living, or what the men may call a living wage. So long as British coal has to compete with the coal produced in other countries it must meet competition by providing similar conditions in respect of the production of coal as obtained in competing countries. It is of no avail to suggest that the wages received do not permit of the miners having a proper standard of living.[29]

In response, the Scottish miners' leader Robert Smillie asked rhetorically if their 'womenfolk' and children were also 'to go to the mines to make fortunes for Sir Adam Nimmo and his friends?'[30]

By April 1926, judged Tom Jones, the majority of coal owners, including Nimmo, 'clearly wanted a strike'.[31] The government even attempted (unsuccessfully) to encourage a coup within the Mining Association and replace the Williams–Nimmo duopoly with more moderate leadership epitomized by the Earl of Crawford, chairman of the Wigan Coal and Iron Company. It did not succeed.

LORD GAINFORD

Balancing the Celtic duo of Sir Adam Nimmo and Evan Williams was Lord Gainford. With his centre-parted hair, drooping moustache and winged collar, Jack Pease (as he was until 1917) was a prominent Liberal politician as well as a Durham coal owner. Born in Darlington in January 1860, he was the younger son of the Quaker industrialist and banker Sir Joseph Whitwell Pease, Baronet. A talented sportsman and actor, he was drawn into the exclusive social circles of the Liberal Party via his Cambridge University friend Eddie Tennant and his sister Margot, who later married H. H. Asquith.

After a career in local Durham and Darlington politics, Pease was elected the MP for Tynemouth in 1892 and became a minister at the Treasury in 1908, joining the Cabinet two years later as Chancellor of the Duchy of Lancaster.[32] After serving briefly as Postmaster General, in 1917 Pease was elevated to the House of Lords as Lord Gainford. Thereafter he became a leading figure in the industrial world, speaking on behalf of the Mining Association of Great Britain before the Sankey Commission in 1919. He suggested coal owners would prefer outright nationalization to any scheme of joint control with their workers.[33] Gainford was also asked to chair the fledgling British Broadcasting Company in 1922, and quickly became an enthusiast for the 'wireless' medium which would prove so important during the general strike.

By early 1926 Gainford's party loyalties had been strained by infighting between Lord Oxford (Asquith) and David Lloyd George. Although he liked Stanley Baldwin, he told the industrialist and Liberal MP Sir Alfred Mond he 'could never be a Tory'. 'I want to see some alternative government to a Conservative one and other than a socialist one if possible,' Gainford mused in January that year. 'It may be a dream but I believe in the innate Liberalism of my country men.'[34]

And while Gainford resented government interference in 'economic laws and with trade affairs', by March he believed it was up to the Conservatives to find a solution to a 'difficult position' largely of their own creation. 'It must be apparent that it is impossible to carry on indefinitely an industry without a profit,' he wrote to a newspaper. 'Speaking after experience of over forty-five years in the coal trade,

I can say that I think almost everything has been done in our County in this direction which is possible to do with a view to the reduction of costs.'[35]

On the first day of the strike, Gainford used a speech in the House of Lords to appeal for miners to 'come down from their pedestal' so that there might be the possibility of a settlement. Generously, he added that he was willing to adopt a 'conciliatory attitude'.[36]

'A NATURAL AND SPECIAL SHREWDNESS'

The 7th Marquess of Londonderry's Ulster estate and provenance neatly complemented the three parts of Great Britain from which Williams, Nimmo and Gainford hailed. Given the paucity of coalfields in that part of the United Kingdom, however, Londonderry's interests were, like Gainford's, situated in the north-east of England. The writer Osbert Sitwell recalled his:

> accustomed air of Irish grandee and sportsman who has strayed into politics, with a certain nonchalance, combined with geniality, but also with, under this façade, a natural and special shrewdness that it would be easy to misinterpret and underrate.[37]

Unlike Lord Gainford, Londonderry was regarded by the government as one of the more enlightened coal owners, although this was relative. In a letter to Londonderry written on the eve of the general strike, Malcolm Dillon, his chief agent, observed:

> The men are quite docile and taking very little interest in the situation. They have little idea of the merits of the dispute and say that everything is done in London. They will draw ... pay on Friday and they are quite happy. They will keep all ready cash for their amusement and beer ... After next Saturday they will be feeling the pinch a little and then I suppose we shall have to go through the same wearisome performance of feeding the children.[38]

In a letter to Stanley Baldwin at around the same time, Londonderry noted that he could sell every ton of coal produced in Durham, which was not universally the case. And although he remained 'purposely' aloof from the broader negotiations, Londonderry expressed 'humility' on the basis that:

> we collectively, owners and men, have failed to do what I earnestly hoped and prayed we could do, which was to join together and work out a solution of the problem. If our failure is due to deeper reasons than those which appear on the surface, it is for those outside the industry to diagnose the causes which are nullifying the best elements in the representatives of each side.[39]

Charles Stewart Henry Vane-Tempest-Stewart was born at London's Eaton Place in 1878, the eldest son of the sixth marquess and his wife Theresa, daughter of the 19th Earl of Shrewsbury. Educated at Eton and Sandhurst, Viscount Castlereagh (a courtesy title) enjoyed a military career before his father persuaded him to stand for the House of Commons as a Unionist (or Conservative) in 1906. Bucking the national trend, he defeated the incumbent Liberal MP and survived a subsequent legal challenge. In 1915 Castlereagh succeeded as the seventh marquess and took his seat in the House of Lords.

Having failed to shine in opposition, Londonderry had a 'good' war before being appointed secretary to the Ulster Unionist delegation at the 1917 Irish Convention, a cross-party initiative intended to end the impasse between Ulster and Catholic Ireland over Home Rule. Although the Convention collapsed in 1918, it led Londonderry to flirt with the idea of a federal United Kingdom with 'Home Rule' (or devolved) parliaments in England, Scotland, Wales and Ireland. This was at odds with mainstream Ulster Unionist thinking, but Londonderry's political career finally took flight, first in London – his second cousin Winston Churchill helped him become junior air minister in 1920 – and more fruitfully in Northern Ireland.

When in May 1921 Ireland was partitioned and its six northern counties granted a devolved parliament and executive, Londonderry quit the UK government and instead became leader of its Senate and Minister of Education in the first Government of Northern Ireland. Although he was committed to an entirely secular system of state education, Londonderry's *Education Act (Northern Ireland) 1923* was resisted by vested religious and political interests. He resigned as education minister in January 1926 but remained a senator until 1929. 'I wanted the Province governed in quite a different way,' Londonderry later wrote, 'but I was a voice crying in the wilderness.'[40]

A handsome and rather vain individual – Bassano's photographic portrait from 1920 shows off his magnificent nose – Londonderry was politically well connected, and not just within his own party. His wife Edith (a granddaughter of Scottish landowner the Duke of Sutherland) was a noted socialite and Ramsay MacDonald her close friend. And although Lady Londonderry's relationship with the Labour leader was purely platonic, it gave rise to persistent gossip. Lord Londonderry shared MacDonald's view of the emotional miners' leader Arthur Cook, warning in a 1925 speech that:

> if it became an issue between Mr Cook and the British Government and the British nation they would find every right-thinking Labour man – and a great majority were right-thinking men – ranged on the side of the Government – not the Conservative Government, not the Liberal Government, but the Government of the country under his Majesty the King.[41]

Cook retorted that Londonderry was the last person 'to charge our people with fomenting revolution' given that he had been the 'greatest fomenter of revolution in Great Britain', a reference to his pre-war support for militant Ulster Unionist opposition to Home Rule.[42]

'The question which must be answered soon,' Lord Londonderry told Stanley Baldwin towards the end of 1925:

> is how the cost of the production of coal can be reduced and the way it can be reduced is by a greater freedom from restrictions and by a larger output. In my opinion, there is no need to reduce wages, in fact I should be very sorry to see that happen. It would merely mean a reduction of purchasing capacity throughout a large section of the community.[43]

On the first day of the strike itself, and while Lady Londonderry mobilized the full wartime strength of the Women's Legion to drive lorries,[44] Lord Londonderry was among those who visited the Archbishop of Canterbury, then planning an intervention. Randall Davidson was surprised when Londonderry encouraged this, writing that 'the one mine owner whom I have found to possess suggestiveness or resource is Londonderry, of whom I myself should hardly have expected it'.[45] Finally, on 7 May, Londonderry was among a deputation of ten major colliery owners who secretly met the Prime Minister to propose a compromise based on the recommendations of the Samuel Commission.[46] Stanley Baldwin was unmoved: there were to be no negotiations until the general strike was called off unconditionally.

10

THE ARCHBISHOP, THE CARDINAL AND THE MODERATOR

A 'shrewd septuagenarian' who disliked dramatic gestures and felt out of his depth on economic questions,[1] Randall Davidson had nevertheless been a key figure in a series of political crises since his enthronement as Archbishop of Canterbury twenty-three years earlier: reform of the House of Lords, Irish independence and the First World War. The events of May 1926 invited another opportunity to make his voice heard.

Paradoxically, Randall Thomas Davidson began his life in April 1848 not as an Anglican but as the member of a prosperous Church of Scotland family in Edinburgh. This, however, was sufficiently casual that when he converted to the Church of England as a schoolboy at Harrow, there were no repercussions. Ordained in 1874, Davidson became, successively, chaplain and secretary to Archbishop Tait (another Edinburgh-born Anglican convert), Dean of Windsor and chaplain to Queen Victoria, Bishop of Rochester and finally Bishop of Winchester. In 1903 he succeeded Frederick Temple as Archbishop of Canterbury, the recognized leader of England's established Church.

During the final week of April 1926, Davidson had discussed the prospect of a general strike 'very fully' with the Prime Minister, the King, Lord Oxford and Asquith and the Conservative MP Hugh Cecil.[2] His first personal statement came during a House of Lords debate on the Emergency Regulations, in which the Archbishop referred to the 'unwisdom' and 'mischievousness' of a strike so 'intolerable' that it ought to be brought as 'speedily as possible' to an end. The Primate also pressed for renewed efforts at a settlement given the real fear among industrial workers that their 'standard of living' would be further eroded.[3] He did not declare that the Ecclesiastical Commissioners, which managed the Church's property assets, earned hundreds of thousands a year from coal royalties, although they had no objection to these being acquired by the state.[4]

The following day the Archbishops of Canterbury and York announced that they were considering ways of 'bringing Christian opinion' to bear on the strike, while the Bishop of London offered Lambeth Palace as a neutral meeting ground for the railwaymen's leader Jimmy Thomas and other negotiators.[5] Only on Friday 7 May, and after rejecting a proposal from the Bishop of Liverpool for a special fund to replace the government's temporary subsidy ('it would be regarded as a capitalist dodge or bribe'[6]), Davidson had a long meeting with a group of Anglican churchmen and nonconformists about issuing a conciliatory appeal. In mind was Bishop Westcott's apparently decisive role in settling the Durham miners' strike of 1893, not to mention the more recent Lambeth Conference of 1920 on 'Industrial and Social Problems'.[7]

Prompted by the Free Church Council and Prebendary P. T. R. Kirk of the Industrial Christian Fellowship, the three points which formed the basis of the appeal were suggested by Luke Thompson, a Wesleyan coal merchant and the Conservative MP for Sunderland. The wording was considered carefully by the Bishop of Ripon, Henry Carter, a Wesleyan and Christian Socialist, and Dr John Lidgett, another Wesleyan and the anti-socialist Progressive leader on London County Council.[8] The Marquess of Londonderry, who as we have seen called on Davidson during the meeting, also had some input.

Once agreed, the Archbishop of Canterbury telephoned John Reith, the British Broadcasting Company's general manager, to request a broadcast slot that evening. When Davidson took the draft appeal to the House of Commons, meanwhile, he found Ramsay MacDonald enthusiastic, although the Labour leader suggested making the ending of the strike the first rather than the third of the appeal's action points. As the Cabinet was meeting in the Prime Minister's room at the Commons, Davidson could only communicate with Stanley Baldwin in an 'awkward' series of exchanges via one of his private secretaries. He nevertheless managed to glean that the premier 'entirely approved' of the appeal except for the words 'simultaneously and concurrently'.[9]

The final 'expression of considered opinion' stated:

> Representatives of the Christian Churches in England are convinced that a real settlement will only be achieved in a spirit of fellowship and co-operation for the common good, and not as a result of war ... If it should seem to be incumbent on us to suggest a definite line of approach, we would submit, as the basis of a possible Concordat, a return to the status quo of Friday last ... Our proposal should be interpreted as involving simultaneously and concurrently—
>
> 1. The cancellation on the part of the T.U.C. of the General Strike;
> 2. Renewal by the Government of its offer of assistance to the Coal industry for a short definite period;
> 3. The withdrawal on the part of the mine owners of the new wages scales recently issued.[10]

This appeal was issued with the 'full knowledge and concurrence' of the Archbishop of York,[11] but not the Bishops of Gloucester and Durham, the latter of whom believed class-consciousness was 'un-Christian'.[12] The political response was immediate. Colonel Lane Fox, the Conservative Secretary for Mines, told Davidson his 'utterance' was 'harmful and might be gravely detrimental to the cause of peace',[13] while William Bridgeman, the First Lord of the Admiralty, told his mother he would be boycotting the Archbishop's garden party. 'I wish our Church could be a little more clear in discerning fundamental right from fundamental wrong,' he added, '& not always trying to condone the unchristian behaviour of the mob, because they are poor.'[14]

The Archbishop of Canterbury, meanwhile, had not unreasonably assumed his request to broadcast the appeal would be granted. The BBC's John Reith, to be fair, had not agreed outright but asked to see what he proposed to say. 'When it came I found it was a suggestion that the Strike should be called off and negotiations opened concurrently,' Reith recorded in his diary. 'As the PM had said he would not negotiate until the Strike was called off, I was sure the manifesto should not be broadcast.' He continued:

> The Archbishop had sent a copy to the PM so I phoned [Ronald] Waterhouse to find out what the PM thought. He got on to Fry [Baldwin's personal private secretary] who said that the PM had

told the Archbishop that he would not stop it being broadcast, but would prefer not. In view of what Fry said, I said I would turn it down on my own ... The BBC is in a very awkward position. [J. C. C.] Davidson told me later in the evening categorically that the Archbishop's statement should not be broadcast.[15]

The first indication of pushback came in the form of a letter from the BBC chairman and coal owner Lord Gainford, which contained points on the appeal he considered 'worthy of notice' as well as a lengthy defence of the Mining Association's position. Gainford closed by saying that he was leaving it 'entirely' up to 'Mr. Reith' to 'decide what should be broadcast'.[16]

Reith maintained this fiction when he called the Archbishop and, putting it as 'nicely' as he could, said he believed broadcasting the appeal would 'run counter to his tacit arrangement with the Government about such things'. Detecting the dead hand of Number 10, Davidson asked if a 'hint' had come from Downing Street, which Reith rejected along with the idea Lord Gainford's letter had contributed to the sudden refusal. This, he wrote in his diary, he did 'out of loyalty' to the government.[17]

The following day (8 May), the Archbishop wrote to Reith expressing puzzlement as to what the position actually was:

> Are we to understand that if the Churches desire to put something forth their grave utterance must be subject to the approval of its wording by the [British] Broadcasting [Company], and that without such approval we are confined, as we were yesterday, to utilising the scraps of publicity available by means of the few newspapers which have their limited circulation?

Davidson closed in the 'friendliest way' by tentatively asking whether his forthcoming address at St Martin-in-the-Fields (which *was* to be broadcast) could make any reference to the Churches' 'Joint Message'. Reith annotated this letter rather tersely, noting that he had made it 'quite clear' a broadcast was conditional on 'what the message was'. As for the St Martin's address, he was of the view that this 'must not embarrass the Gov[ernmen]t'. 'The greater the authority', he added, 'the more the embarrassment.'[18] An 'evidently distressed' Reith came to see the Archbishop later that day and argued that broadcasting the appeal would have 'accentuated' the Churchill–Birkenhead axis in Cabinet, making a government takeover of the Company more likely.[19] 'A nice position for me to be in between Premier and Primate,' he reflected in his memoirs, 'bound mightily to vex one or other; at thirty-six years of age.'[20] Nevertheless, judged the broadcaster's historian Asa Briggs, this moment represented the 'low-water mark of the power and influence of the BBC': 'The Company existed on 8 May by sufferance, and Reith realized this.'[21]

Given that the Churches' appeal was printed in *The Times* and the *British Worker* (if not in the *British Gazette*) on 8 May,[22] and news of its 'suppression' by the BBC quickly spread, if anything the 'immense excitement' claimed by Davidson's biographer was probably greater than might have been expected.[23] Letters and telegrams poured into Lambeth Palace while the Archbishop contented himself that his 'spiritual' objective had reached a wide audience. Leonard Woolf remarked to his wife Virginia that if the Archbishop succeeded in restarting negotiations between ministers and miners then he would be baptized.[24]

Less fruitful was a gathering in the Bishop's Room at the House of Lords initiated by the Anglo-Catholic Labour MP and former law officer Sir Henry Slesser. This 'little gathering' of peers and MPs expected by the Archbishop turned out to be a meeting of twenty-eight people who made speeches for nearly two hours, very few of which, he later noted, 'struck really a religious note'. The Marquess of Londonderry even made a swift exit, pleading that he had 'come there under some misapprehension'.[25] In Sir Henry Slesser's account:

> Lord Phillimore said that as one breach of contract was a sin, a million such, simultaneously committed, crushed him with the enormity of the offence. This mathematical method of assessing wrong did not help to bring about agreement. A Liberal apologised for the absence of a very eminent statesman, then in opposition: 'I never asked him to come,' answered the Archbishop. One Labour member present tactlessly said that there was little food left in the docks; this statement was condemned by a Conservative fellow-churchman as seditious. The poor Archbishop was attacked, rudely, I thought, for his efforts to introduce Christian charity into the affair, and the meeting broke up in discord.[26]

'On the whole the Meeting did not I think do much good,' observed Davidson diplomatically, 'but it cannot have done any harm.'[27]

That same day in the House of Commons, the embattled Liberal MP David Lloyd George twice raised the appeal's non-coverage by the *British Gazette* and BBC. In his parliamentary report to the King, Baldwin conceded that its omission from the *Gazette* was 'probably a mistake of policy' which had required Churchill to 'draw fully on his inherent ingenuity in order to justify his action'. This was an oblique reference to the Chancellor's commitment to include the 'declarations' of both Archbishop Davidson and Cardinal Bourne in a later edition of his newssheet.[28]

This incensed J. C. C. Davidson, who believed publication 'might attract the unthinking quarters of the population that were for peace at any price'. Nevertheless, a compromise was reached whereby his namesake's 'weak and waffly' message was printed on the back page without comment, while Cardinal Bourne's sermon was given considerable prominence.[29] As Frank McLynn has observed, if the Archbishop's words were really so pathetic then it is not clear why the government did not allow him to broadcast and therefore discredit himself.[30] When two Conservative MPs, Sir Joseph Nall (also a member of the Church Assembly) and Major Kindersley compared the Archbishop's comments unfavourably with the Cardinal's, Davidson took great delight in pointing out to them that Bourne had also endorsed the Churches' appeal. 'This,' wrote the Archbishop, 'staggered them and amazed them.'[31]

The reaction from those in the Labour movement was inevitably more positive. *Daily Herald* editor Hamilton Fyfe gushed that for the 'first time in history' the Church of England had 'put itself on the side of the People against the Privileged Class'. Meanwhile on Rogation Sunday (9 May), a day on which God was beseeched to protect mortals from calamities, church attendance in Britain's industrial towns appeared larger than normal.[32] At St Albans Cathedral the previous day, 1,500 strikers attended a service of intercession, after which the bishop discussed the crisis with another group of workers outside.[33]

Davidson's intervention was embarrassing for the government given its framing of the general strike as an attack on the British constitution. Yet here was a core part of that constitution – the leader of the established Church – refusing to toe the 'revolutionary' line. 'He takes precedence constitutionally even of the Prime Minister and the Lord Chancellor,' noted the *New Statesman* editor Clifford Sharp. 'Yet he was suppressed by the Constitutionalist party!'[34] And while the Archbishop's earlier speech in the Lords suggested he was at one with the Prime Minister as regards the strike's challenge to 'the community', Davidson was attempting to chart a middle way in which the dispute would not be settled by 'victory' or 'defeat'. To that end, he saw Baldwin on Tuesday 11 May:

> I was afraid that he might be drifting into the same position as other people and regard me as hostile to him and his whole policy and as having raised an antagonistic flag which I was prepared to nail to the mast, and to regard him as stupidly hostile that he did not conform to what our Appeal on behalf of the Churches had said. I told him that was not my position and that we had very deliberately come to the conclusion we had formulated as a suggestion for the Government to consider.

The Prime Minister surprised the Archbishop by informing him that his appeal was finally to be broadcast later that day. After Davidson expressed 'distrust' in the 'truculent and fighting attitude' of some members of the Cabinet (he presumably meant Churchill), premier and primate 'parted in the friendliest way'.[35] The Archbishop later expressed his 'utmost respect' for Baldwin's 'honest and public-spirited endeavour to handle right one of the most difficult questions which have ever confronted a minister'.[36] Modestly, Davidson believed the 'direct' importance of his appeal had been 'somewhat exaggerated' but accepted that its 'indirect' impact had 'evidently been very great'.[37]

'A SIN AGAINST THE OBEDIENCE WHICH WE OWE TO GOD'

Davidson's spiritual nemesis during the nine days was Francis Alphonsus Bourne. Born in London in 1861, educated in France and ordained a priest in 1884, he became the domestic prelate to Pope Leo XIII in 1895 and was appointed the Roman Catholic Bishop of Southwark two years later. In 1903, Bourne was elevated to the archdiocese of Westminster, where he was to remain for a remarkable thirty-two years, becoming a cardinal in 1911 and forging a close relationship with Pope Pius XI (1922–39). Irish politics brought Bourne national attention, although his support for self-government under Crown and Empire irritated some Catholic adherents in the not-so United Kingdom.[38]

The genesis of Bourne's sermon during the general strike is harder to identify than that of his Anglican counterpart, although the Cardinal had in 1912–13 expressed opposition to sympathetic strikes. In other respects, his intervention was surprising. At the end of the First World War Bourne had written a pastoral letter entitled 'The Nation's Crisis' in which he appeared to sympathize with working-class discontent. And when the Labour Party added a 'common ownership' clause to its constitution (clause 4) in 1918, the Cardinal joined those who defended it.[39]

Among Cardinal Bourne's papers is a letter from a Joseph B. Curran, who wrote from Edinburgh on 5 May 1926, the second day of the strike. With 'humility and respect' Curran begged that he 'intervene in the present Labour troubles', suggesting that Bourne offer to act as an 'intermediary' between the government and trade union leaders if the latter called off the strike. Curran added:

> With good effect your Eminence with others intervened in the railway strike of 1919, and there is also the notable example of Cardinal Manning settling the doctors' strike. It is a terribly heavy task for a man of your venerable years to undertake, but you may save the country.[40]

Two days later, the Archbishop of Canterbury's chaplain (the Rev. F. D. V. Narborough) visited Cardinal Bourne with an advance copy of the Churches' appeal. In a covering note (Bourne was out), Narborough said:

> It will be noticed that His Grace is saying 'Leaders' not 'the Leaders', and he does not expect His Eminence will necessarily make any statement about the document. If His Eminence felt disposed, however, to share his approval to the Archbishop, it would be welcomed, as he expects to be asked after the broadcasting – in private conversations – with which [leaders] he had consulted.[41]

Upon receiving the note and the appeal, Bourne sent a message which:

> expressed his general agreement with the document, and said that the Archbishop of Canterbury might mention his name if questioned as to who were the leaders of the Churches with whom he had taken consultation.[42]

Like Ramsay MacDonald, Bourne suggested that the withdrawal of the strike should be the first of the appeal's three suggestions. Having made this change, the Archbishop of Canterbury naturally believed the two Church leaders were at one.

But on Sunday 9 May, two days after that exchange, Cardinal Bourne made the following declaration regarding the general strike during High Mass at Westminster Cathedral:

> It is a direct challenge to a lawfully-constituted authority, and inflicts without adequate reason, immense discomfort and injury on millions of our fellow-countrymen. It is therefore a sin against the obedience which we owe to God, who is the source of that authority; and against the charity and brotherly love which are due to our brethren.[43]

It is no exaggeration to say that Downing Street was delighted. 'My dear Cardinal,' wrote the Prime Minister. 'Your clear and strong pronouncement will be of the greatest value to the Government in the present crisis, and I am most grateful to you for your support.'[44] On Monday 10 May, *The Times*' leading article urged the nation to act on Bourne's words, while even the staunchly Protestant *Belfast Telegraph* promoted the Cardinal's views.

The Archbishop of Canterbury, who in 1920 had sponsored Bourne's membership of the Athenaeum, truly believed he had associated the Cardinal with the Churches' more moderate appeal. The *Daily News* even erroneously suggested the Cardinal's declaration had followed consultation with the Archbishop.[45] His surprise perhaps turned to anger when Anglican opponents of the general strike began to berate Davidson for having allowed the Cardinal to outflank him. Dean Inge, the right-wing Dean of St Paul's, later wrote that while Bourne saw the issue 'clearly' and issued a 'manly and straightforward order to all Catholics to support the lawful authorities', his own Church's prelates had published:

> only flabby and feeble exhortations to compromise – while the nation was at death-grips with a mad dog. I cannot count the number of men who have declared that they are seriously considering the question of joining the Church of Rome, in consequence of this illuminating and melancholy contrast. Nothing in our time has done so much injury to the Church of England.[46]

The Cardinal's own mail bag attracted mixed views. On the one hand there was praise, not just from Stanley Baldwin but Dorothy F. Gordon, the stepdaughter of former Conservative MP Lord Danesfort, who claimed 'Jix' (the Home Secretary) had told her mother that he considered it 'one of the best speeches on the strike'. 'They are proportionately angry with their own Archbishop whom however they excuse on account of his age,' she added, 'but they are furious with the B[isho]p of Winchester and the Archbishop of York.'[47] Another correspondent passed on the unlikely claim that Bourne's 'manifesto' had 'absolutely stopped the strike of some 500 men' at a mill in north Liverpool.[48]

On the other hand there was genuine anger, including from working-class Catholics who asked why Bourne had not mentioned the miners' poor pay and conditions. One correspondent contrasted the 'tolerant and humane spirit' of the Protestant Churches' appeal with his Eminence's 'cold, hard message'; another wrote of his apparent 'desire to toady to the aristocracy of this Country'; while a 'Catholic working man' implored the Cardinal to 'go down to the mining districts in Wales and see the white pinched faces of the women & little children' or, even better:

> go down into the coal mines start at 70/- [shillings] in the morning on bread and margarine ... work in a black hole for 7 hours & often in water up to the waist and facing death every minute you are down there. I wonder if you would then consider it a sin to try to maintain the already miserable standard of living the miners have ... you are a parasite murderer supporting the starving to death of the workers by the employers of this country ... you are trying to make Catholic workers scab and blackleg on their fellow workers – the lowest of all things.[49]

More considered was an anonymous correspondent from the English Bar, who said it was for the Cardinal to judge the 'desirability' of using the pulpit of the Catholic Church 'to interfere in a partisan fashion in political or industrial controversy'. He also took exception to Bourne's suggestion the government was somehow divinely appointed, pointing out that the same must therefore have been true of that in revolutionary France or Henry VIII's when it separated England from Rome.[50]

The Catholic Social Guild later attempted to lend some intellectual ballast to this aspect of Bourne's argument, and not entirely successfully:

> An English [sic] 'Government' or Ministry is always doing two works: (1) carrying on the King's government, *i.e.*, the work appointed by God [and] (2) political work, *i.e.*, choosing methods of mending or marring, managing or mismanaging, the machinery of Government. It is right to obstruct them in (2), but not in (1).[51]

Kathleen Chambers, a Catholic Labour alderman on Bradford City Council, pointedly asked what the Cardinal's attitude would be if a 'lawfully constituted authority' was to 'attack the position of the Catholic schools' in the UK. She added:

> Of course I do not know whether Your Eminence is endeavouring to force all Catholics out of the Labour movement, or to force all Catholic Socialists out of the Church; but whatever may be the object of Your Eminence in the statement that you have issued I can only say that, knowing that we have every right to do so, we shall remain loyal to our principles and to the Labour Party of which we are proud to be members.[52]

A letter from five 'seriously perturbed' Catholic Labour MPs also underlined these points:

> We have striven for peace and peace has been denied us by the Government. We therefore hold that our fellow-workers are doing what is right, and with all respect, yet with emphasis, we protest against a high dignitary of [the] Holy Church making a statement which neither the morality nor the theology of our faith justifies.[53]

It was indeed curious that the leader of the Christian community in the UK with the greatest working-class support had ended up denouncing the strike, while the Archbishop of Canterbury, the leader of what was often described as the 'Conservative Party at prayer', stood accused of undermining a Tory government. But while condemning the strike in such categorical terms risked alienating Catholic supporters of the strike, Cardinal Bourne had spotted an opportunity to 'demonstrate the loyalty of the church to English law'.[54] It was also, judged Stuart Mews, 'an attempt to reassert clerical control before things got out of hand' and prevent a further radicalization of the Catholic working class in a socialistic direction.[55]

'A COWARDLY WEAPON'

While most historical accounts of the general strike have covered the ecclesiastical battle between Archbishop Davidson and Cardinal Bourne, almost none have highlighted the role of the UK's other established Church.[56] At the beginning of the strike, the Christian Socialist and Master of Balliol College, A. D. Lindsay, sent a telegram to Professor Archibald Main asking if he could 'mobilise Scottish churches to hold religious meetings asking for peace and resumption of negotiations'.[57] Although Lindsay hailed from a Scots Presbyterian background and had many friends within Scotland's religious and educational establishment, this invitation was angrily rejected by John White, the then Moderator of the General Assembly of the Church of Scotland. A paternalistic Tory, White disliked Lindsay's left-wing politics, while there was also a hint of nationalism: those in England did not tell Scotland's churches what to do.[58]

White had become Moderator in 1925 largely on account of his leadership of the Church Union movement, which sought reconciliation with the 'Free' Church of Scotland which had split from the 'Kirk' during the 'Great Disruption' of 1843. Born in 1867, the son of a West of Scotland flour merchant, White was educated at Glasgow University and later served as a chaplain on the Western Front. In 1919, he became co-convener of the Church of Scotland's new Church and Nation Committee, which gave voice to the Kirk's thinking on social issues. In 1923 this infamously published a report entitled *The Menace of the Irish Race to our Scottish Nationality*, which demanded an end to Irish Catholic immigration and even the deportation of those convicted of a criminal offence or living on state benefits.[59] By the mid-1920s, however, White's overriding concern was completing the unification of the Presbyterian churches alongside the Aberdeen-born Dr James Harvey, Moderator of the General Assembly of the United Free Church (UFC).[60]

Having rejected A. D. Lindsay's missive, meanwhile, White and Harvey – who between them spoke for the majority of churchgoing Scots – issued a joint statement exhorting their followers 'to labour and pray for the healing of the wounds of the nation'. They continued:

> With the political and economic aspects of the present dispute we do not intermeddle: but it is manifest to every thinking man who loves his country that industrial disputes should never be allowed to become a menace to the very existence of the community, and that the new world we long for cannot be built upon a promise of mutual frustration and class conflict.[61]

Almost as if to ensure this was not misinterpreted as a moral criticism of both strikers *and* the government, Dr Harvey preached the same day that although the miners deserved adequate wages and better working conditions, the general strike was a 'cowardly weapon'.[62] Another UFC luminary, Principal Alexander Martin of New College, Edinburgh, criticized the Archbishop of Canterbury's three-point appeal in an angry letter to the *Scotsman*. 'We are faced,' he asserted, 'with the attempt of a self-constituted minority to impose its will upon the community by sheer weight of *force majeure*.' There could be no negotiating with such an evil, added Martin, and the general strike had to be broken 'at whatever cost'.[63] The Scottish Conservative MP Sir Henry Craik later expressed his 'deep admiration' for what he considered this 'courageous letter'.[64]

On the day the Moderators' joint statement was issued – Sunday 9 May – church attendance in Edinburgh was reportedly twice its average size, although Scotland's clergy was divided – as in other parts of Great Britain – in its response to the crisis. Some ministers used their pulpits to condemn the strike, others like the Rev. D. Bruce Nicol of St Mark's in Dundee resisted congregational pressure and remarked that 'sympathy with the poorly paid wage-earners, and some experience and understanding of their lot' had persuaded him to 'keep silence'. Meanwhile, and in an unprecedented action, the meetings of the General Assemblies of the Church of Scotland and the United Free

Church which had been scheduled to begin on 18 May were postponed. As in Parliament, the general strike had disrupted the normal printing and mailing of the Assemblies' reports and papers, and two further weeks were deemed necessary to complete preparations.[65]

In his account of Scotland's churches and the general strike, Stewart J. Brown was sharply critical of what he viewed as their neglect of the huge social, economic and political issues raised by the crisis. The Church of Scotland, he concluded, had chosen to:

> restrict itself to preaching the gospel of personal salvation and individual self-help, while leaving social welfare largely to the impersonal forces of the market-place. The ideal commonwealth would exclude Roman Catholics and would relegate labouring people to the role of a permanent proletariat in a hierarchical social order.[66]

The general strike, therefore, had a definite spiritual dimension. In England, it found Anglicans and Catholics competing over the moral high ground, while in Scotland the dispute proved an unwelcome distraction from Presbyterian unity.

11

'THAT WUTHERING HEIGHT'

On 16 January 1926 a broadcast by Father Ronald Knox in Edinburgh was relayed from London and heard throughout the British Isles, including in Dublin. This included the dramatic news that the National Gallery in Trafalgar Square had been reduced to rubble by an army of the unemployed and that the interior of the House of Commons had been bombed. In the capital of the Irish Free State, newspaper offices were bombarded with telephone calls from listeners anxious for verification of the terrifying news.

Crucially, at least part of the Dublin audience had tuned in too late to hear a preliminary announcement warning listeners not to take Father Knox's 'news items' seriously, for they were part of a 'burlesque', a simulated live report of a revolution in London entitled *Broadcasting the Barricades*. The British Broadcasting Company was even forced to release a statement expressing regret that anyone 'should have been perturbed by this purely fantastic picture'.[1] The American actor and broadcaster Orson Welles later claimed Knox had inspired his 1938 dramatization of H. G. Wells' *The War of the Worlds*, which ignited a similar panic among its audience.[2]

This incident, which took place just a few months before the general strike, vividly illustrated the power of the infant 'wireless'. The BBC's Daventry transmitting station – the world's first longwave radio transmitter – had opened only in July 1925 and brought about 80 per cent of the UK's population within its reception area. By 31 March 1926, 1,965,000 licences were in force, meaning one in five households had a set. It also demonstrated what Winston Churchill recognized as the power of news during a crisis. In May 1923 the Mexican-born

Peter Eckersley had written a memorandum identifying the BBC's 'unique facilities for the purposes of communication during a state of emergency'. It would now be possible, he added, 'for the highest authorities to speak over the Broadcast, and to use their influence to quell panic'.[3] As the TUC's Walter Milne-Bailey noted in his unpublished study of the general strike, that the radio 'might broadcast to millions of people the only news they would get of a strike' would have seemed in 1919 'like the romance of a Jules Verne'.[4]

As is the case with all new technology, radio was regarded with suspicion by certain 'superior' individuals. 'Lots of people to lunch today,' recorded John Reith in his diary during this period, 'including a freak professor from Oxford, who did not like telephones or wireless. I soon disposed of him.'[5] By May 1926, the thirty-six-year-old Reith *was* the BBC. In 1922, and while looking for a job in London, an advertisement for 'The British Broadcasting Company (in formation)' caught his eye. Although the serious Scot had little concept of what 'broadcasting' involved, he applied and was appointed the Company's first general manager.

John Charles Walsham Reith was born in July 1889 in the northeast of Scotland, the youngest of seven children to a minister in the Free Church of Scotland and his English wife Adah, the daughter of a prosperous London stockbroker. In October 1915, during the Battle of Loos, Reith was struck on his left cheek by a sniper's bullet, the anniversary of which he marked for the rest of his life. Following an intense, though most likely platonic, relationship with a younger friend called Charlie Bowser, Reith fell in love with his colonel's driver, Muriel Odhams, and they were married the year before he took control of the fledgling BBC.[6]

Reith's craggy face and huge frame – he was more than 6 feet 6 inches tall – served to emphasize his intellectual confidence. Winston Churchill called him 'that Wuthering Height',[7] and he became a familiar presence in Parliament and Whitehall as the Postmaster General pondered whether to accept the recommendations of the Crawford Committee. Here Reith encountered prominent coal owners, for the 27th Earl of Crawford was both the premier Scots earl and a Lancashire coal merchant, while Lord Gainford had served as BBC chairman since 1922. The Crawford Report urged the transformation of the BBC into a corporation governed by a Royal Charter, which neatly dovetailed with Reith's belief that broadcasting should be conducted as a 'public service'. In this respect, the occurrence of the general strike was fortuitous.

In common with many others, Reith had little sympathy either with the coal owners or with organized labour and disliked the very idea of a general strike. On 23 April 1926 he noted in his diary that unrest was brewing and made preliminary contact with J. C. C. Davidson at the Admiralty, doubtless aware of his role in the government's emergency machinery. It helped that they were near neighbours on London's Barton Street, and it was there on the evening of 30 April that Reith received a request from Number 10 for an immediate announcement about the coal stoppage. At midnight, Jack Payne's orchestra was cut off and Reith – who had asked for all transmitters to be connected to his private telephone line – made the announcement. 'Very impressive performance,' he noted immodestly in his diary.[8]

The next few days was a blizzard of activity. On 1 May the Prime Minister suggested a message – 'Keep steady; remember that peace on earth comes to men of goodwill' – which Reith again broadcast personally; at 1.10 a.m. the following day he announced from his study that negotiations between the unions and the government had broken down; while on Monday 3 May Reith again saw the Deputy Chief Civil Commissioner J. C. C. Davidson:

> His special job is the control of all news. Things were very mixed up at the Admiralty and Davidson with no clear ideas of what he wants me to do, nor what he is supposed to be doing himself. A government newspaper, called the British Gazette, is to be produced ... He apparently thought that the BBC news was to be regarded as a kind of off-shoot to that. I told him I was not going to have that at all.

Reith then encountered Stanley Baldwin having lunch at the Travellers' Club:

> He said we had the key situation now and everyone depended on us. He asked if we were properly protected and I said we were everywhere. Savoy Hill is hotching with policemen and special constables. He said the government had no alternative but to break off negotiations. I said he ought to broadcast soon. Home at 8.00.

Davidson came in at 1.00 a.m. with a first copy of the British Gazette. He was pleased with it, but I told him I did not think much of it.

Reith's contemporaneous diary then ceased, although he filled in the blanks two weeks later. 'I was most happy throughout,' he observed in a contextual note. 'I do not say that I welcome crises, but I do welcome the opportunities which they bring.'[9]

Given the BBC's evolving status, there was no clear policy regarding its output during an unprecedented industrial and, according to the government, constitutional crisis. Under the Company's licence, however, it was clear that if the Postmaster General believed an emergency to have arisen then His Majesty's Government should 'have control over the transmission of messages' and any authorized person 'may enter upon the stations, offices and works of the Company ... and take possession'.[10]

If the legal position was clear, what Asa Briggs called the 'diplomatic' position was much more complicated. The Cabinet and its Supply and Transport Committee (the 'strike committee'), encompassed two distinct positions:

> One, led by Winston Churchill ... was ready and willing completely to take over the BBC and to mobilize broadcasting as a direct agent of government. The other section ... who included [the Air Secretary] Samuel Hoare (later Lord Templewood), believed – doubtless for reasons of temperament as much as of policy – that it would be wiser to leave the BBC a measure of independence or at least of 'semi-independence'.[11]

Usefully from Reith's point of view, both Davidson and the Prime Minister also fell into the latter camp. On the third day of the strike (6 May), he accompanied J. C. C. Davidson to see Baldwin immediately after breakfast:

> He [Baldwin] walked up and down the Cabinet Room while Davidson and I leaned against the mantelpiece and explained our views – at least I said what I thought and Davidson joined in. Every time I made a point the PM stopped in his perambulations and faced us. He said he entirely agreed with us that it would be far better to leave the BBC with a considerable measure of autonomy and independence.

'The Great Trek' as seen by the Italian weekly magazine *La Domenica del Corriere*. Thousands of office workers walked, cycled or hitched a lift to central London as the general strike got under way. *The Sphere*, a British illustrated newspaper, devoted its cover to a traffic jam on London's Embankment. © *Mary Evans Picture Library*; © *Illustrated London News Ltd/Mary Evans*

Prime Minister Stanley Baldwin outside Number 10 Downing Street during the general strike. Although the crisis challenged his preferred image as a 'peacemaker', he cynically but successfully framed it as a violent assault on the British constitution. Sir William Joynson-Hicks, Baldwin's Home Secretary since late 1924, saw Reds under every bed but surprised Cabinet colleagues with his moderation. © *Central Press/Getty Images*; © *Topical Press Agency/Getty Images*

King George V and Queen Mary photographed in 1926. Strikes made the King-Emperor uneasy, while his sympathies fluctuated between empathy for the underdog (the miners) and what one biographer called a 'lifelong antipathy to disorder'. The Prince of Wales (later King Edward VIII), meanwhile, felt conflicted between a 'natural desire' to get involved and what he called 'constitutional constraints'. © *Universal History Archive/Universal Images Group via Getty Images;* © *Fox Photos/Getty Images*

Special constables swearing an oath of allegiance to the King. Thousands answered the Home Secretary's call to aid the government during the crisis. Not all of them had enough to do, and others proved overzealous. © *Central Press/Getty Images*

The deliberately derailed *Flying Scotsman* service at Cramlington, ten miles north of Newcastle. Only one passenger was injured, but the incident received extensive press coverage. © *SSPL/Getty Images*

Another prominent story was a memorable football match between policemen and strikers in Plymouth. Watched by a crowd of more than 10,000, the strikers won by two goals to one. © *Illustrated London News Ltd/Mary Evans*

The Chancellor of the Exchequer – or 'Napoleon-Churchill' – took charge of the government's propaganda sheet, the *British Gazette*. Hamilton Fyfe, who edited the rival *British Worker*, joked that the theatrical Churchill could not resist playing the 'part of newspaper editor'. The *Worker* was editorially superior, but the *Gazette* sold more copies. © Charles E. Brown/Royal Air Force Museum/Getty Images; © Illustrated London News Ltd/Mary Evans

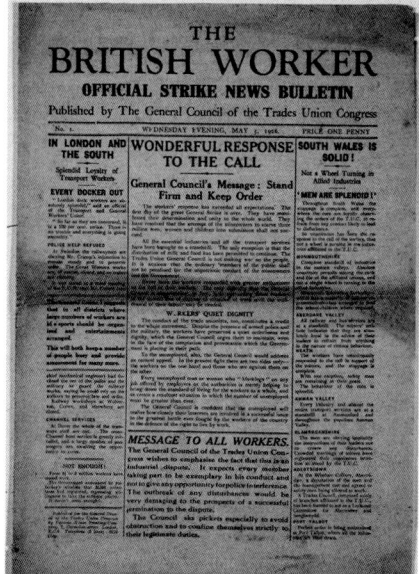 

John Reith, the general manager of the British Broadcasting Company, held the *Gazette* in low regard but relished the strike. 'I do not say that I welcome crises,' he later reflected, 'but I do welcome the opportunities which they bring.' © Photo12/Universal Images Group via Getty Images; © Hulton-Deutsch Collection/CORBIS/Corbis via Getty Images

The Indian-born Communist MP for Battersea North, Shapurji Saklatvala, pictured with Walton Newbold, the Communist MP for Motherwell, in November 1922. Saklatvala was imprisoned early in the strike for making a seditious speech in Hyde Park. John Henry Whitley, Speaker of the House of Commons since 1921, declared that he would, if necessary, 'conduct the business of the House without any printing, or without any electric light'. © *Topical Press Agency/Hulton Archive/ Getty Images*; © *National Portrait Gallery*

The Labour leaders Arthur Henderson (left), Ramsay MacDonald (centre) and 'Jimmy' Thomas (right) did not agree with the general strike but did their best to appear supportive of their trade union colleagues. David Lloyd George (depicted on a 1926 Player's cigarette card) led the Liberals in the House of Commons but annoyed his party colleagues by refusing unequivocally to condemn the strike. © *H. F. Davis/Topical Press Agency/Getty Images*; © *Universal History Archive/ Universal Images Group via Getty Images*

Ernest Bevin, the imposing general secretary of the Transport and General Workers' Union, photographed in 1926; he was dubbed the 'dictator of Eccleston Square'. The executive of the Miners' Federation of Great Britain (left to right), Thomas Richards, A. J. Cook (secretary), Herbert Smith (president) and W. R. Richardson (treasurer), often exasperated Bevin and others on the General Council of the Trades Union Congress. © *Worger/Topical Press Agency/Getty Images*; © *Bettman/Getty Images*

Sir Adam Nimmo (centre) at a coal-owners conference in 1920. Tom Jones, the Deputy Cabinet Secretary, considered him 'one of the greatest stumbling-blocks on the path to peace'. The Liberal politician Lord Gainford was a Durham coal owner as well as chairman of the fledgling British Broadcasting Company. Lord Birkenhead, the Conservative Secretary of State for India, mused that they were the 'stupidest men in England'. © *Shutterstock*; © *National Portrait Gallery*

Randall Davidson, the Archbishop of Canterbury, at work in Lambeth Palace; his intervention on behalf of Anglican and non-conformist churches infuriated the Conservative government. By contrast, Cardinal Bourne's declaration that the general strike was 'a sin against the obedience which we owe to God' delighted them. © *Keystone/Getty Images;* © *National Portrait Gallery*

Government leaders during the general strike – 1. The Chief Civil Commissioner: Sir William Mitchell-Thomson, 2. Principal Chief Assistant Commissioner: A. B. Lowry, 3. Civil Commissioner, London and Home Counties Division: Major William Cope, 4. Civil Commissioner, Eastern Division: Major Sir Philip Sassoon, 5. Coal-owners' representatives leaving Downing Street (left to right): Messrs W. A. Lee, Evan Williams, Edward Mann and Guthrie, 6. Civil Commissioner, North Midland Division: Captain H. Douglas King, 7. Members of the Coal Commission (left to right): Kenneth Lee, Sir William Beveridge, Sir Herbert Samuel, (chairman) and Sir Herbert Lawrence, 8. Minister for Labour: Sir Arthur Steel-Maitland, 9. Civil Commissioner, Northern Division: Kingsley Wood, 10. Civil Commissioner, Midland Division: Lt Col G. F. Stanley, 11. Civil Commissioner, North Eastern Division: Captain D. H. Hacking. 12. Parliamentary Secretary to the Department for Mines: Colonel G. R. Lane-Fox, 13. Civil Commissioner, South Midland Division: Major Earl Winterton, 14. The Home Secretary: Sir William Joynson-Hicks. Edward Wood, the Viceroy of India, likened the Civil Commissioners to colonial governors. © *Illustrated London News Ltd/ Mary Evans*

The Liberal statesman Sir John Simon provoked a storm by branding the general strike an 'utterly illegal proceeding' during a House of Commons debate. In obiter remarks at the High Court, Mr Justice Astbury concurred, although their interpretation of complex trade union law attracted widespread criticism. © *Central Press/Hulton Archive/Getty Images;* © *Universal History Archive/UIG via Getty Images*

The Liberal statesman Sir Herbert Samuel interrupted his philosophical writing to try and broker an end to the general strike. Fatally, he had no authority to negotiate on behalf of the government. Sullen members of the TUC General Council leave Number 10 Downing Street after informing the Prime Minister of an unconditional end to the general strike. The government wasted little time in declaring victory. © *Universal History Archive/Universal Images Group via Getty Images;* © *Mary Evans/Sueddeutsche Zeitung Photo*

The Prime Minister then suggested Reith attend a meeting of the strike committee, which he did. But while the Home Secretary, who was in the chair, concurred with Baldwin, Churchill:

> emphatically objected, said it was monstrous not to use such an instrument to the best possible advantage. Jix then weakly said he would have it discussed at a Cabinet meeting if anybody felt strongly about it. Churchill then launched out on other matters without asking the chairman to say anything, and at this stage I thought I better clear out as they had apparently finished with broadcasting.[12]

Back at home, Reith marshalled his arguments with what one of his biographers called 'remarkable assurance and authority':

> The BBC has secured and holds the goodwill and affection of the people. It has been trusted to do the right thing at all times. Its influence is wide-spread. It is a national institution and a national asset. If it be commandeered or unduly hampered or manipulated now, the immediate purpose of such action is not only unserved but prejudiced. This is not a time for dope [false information], even if the people could be doped. The hostile would be made more hostile from resentment. As to suppression, from the panic of ignorance comes far greater danger than from the knowledge of facts. If the government be strong and their cause right they need not adopt such measures.[13]

Reith's memorandum might be contrasted with 'suggestions' for broadcasting policy written by BBC chairman Lord Gainford, who as a coal owner was hardly in a neutral position. The Company, he wrote, should try:

> to convey to the minds of people generally that the prolongation of the general stoppage is the one sure process calculated to reduce wages and the standard of living which it is the avowed endeavour of the Trade Unions to maintain and improve; and to try to make it clear that the sooner the general strike is satisfactorily terminated the better for wage earners in all parts of the country.

In a more balanced section, Gainford noted that the Company was 'already suspected of being partisan' as strikers had 'interfered' with motor transport labelled 'BBC'. 'If we pursue a policy calculated to exacerbate this irritation,' he warned, 'there are many ways in which the strikers can interfere and perhaps paralyse our whole service.'[14]

In the event, the Cabinet of 7 May did not get around to discussing the status of the BBC. J. C. C. Davidson believed this was deliberate, the Prime Minister having played a 'very skilful game' in postponing any decision to fend off Churchill and Lord Birkenhead's demand that it be run 'as a Governmental propaganda agency'.[15] At the same time, Davidson's 'unofficial control was complete', with two direct telephone lines connecting the Admiralty with the BBC's Savoy Hill HQ. And although the Deputy Chief Civil Commissioner found Reith 'a little stiff-necked', on the whole relations between the near neighbours were amicable.[16]

As it had been declared an 'essential service', BBC employees could not volunteer for other duties during the strike. Of its central staff, 247 men and women lived near enough to Savoy Hill or had private transport facilities allowing them to reach their place of work. Forty-six others, it was decided, were to be provided with special transport, while forty-two were given leave of absence. A special transport system was organized with two charabancs (open-topped coaches) and two motor cars. Station directors were warned to take extra care in the scrutiny of visitors and to cease the practice of showing people around the studios.[17]

Throughout the strike, Reith 'vetted almost every item of every bulletin' personally,[18] while by 10 May he even read some himself following complaints that the BBC's full-time announcers 'had been sounding panicky'.[19] Restrictions on how often the BBC could broadcast were temporarily lifted and five bulletins made daily at 10 a.m., 1 p.m., 4 p.m., 7 p.m. and 9.30 p.m. An emergency news staff worked in three shifts from a single room measuring 15 x 20 feet with five telephone lines and four typewriters. Most of the news came from Reuters and J. C. C. Davidson's office at the Admiralty, where two BBC staff (Miss Shields and W. Fuller) had also been installed. They were later joined by Gladstone Murray, who 'received, filtered, and passed on' news material, including his own 'appreciation of the situation', which was broadcast as a leading item each day. One or two employees even left Savoy Hill to collect their own news, something expressly forbidden under normal conditions.[20]

Stanley Baldwin had made his first wireless speech during the 1924 general election campaign and immediately recognized the potential of the new medium.[21] Initially, his officials decided to 'reserve him for the moments of greatest crisis',[22] but on Saturday 8 May he contacted the BBC to say he would like to broadcast personally that evening, the first instance, noted Reith, 'of a Prime Minister talking to the nation in a crisis'.[23] The text was a product of several drafts by two civil servants (Sir Horace Wilson and Tom Jones) and, oddly, a former secretary to David Lloyd George, Philip Kerr.[24] Reith recalled collecting:

> the PM, a police tender with about a dozen policemen close behind us all the way. Muriel [Reith's wife] talked to him for a bit after he arrived, then he had a voice test, then gave me his manuscript asking me what I thought of 'this tripe' and to make any comments. He said he thought of ending with something personal, and I said yes, something about trusting him. Then I said, 'What about this – I am a man of peace; I am longing and working and praying for peace; but I will not compromise the dignity of the British constitution.' He said, 'Excellent; write it down if you have a legible hand.'

With J. C. C. Davidson (who had earlier thwarted a suspected 'Communist' attempt to interfere with the broadcast[25]) sitting in a nearby armchair, the Prime Minister spoke for just under ten minutes. As he reached the penultimate page of his text, Reith took the last 'from under his hand' and substituted 'safety and security' for 'dignity'. 'When he came to this,' recalled Reith, 'he paused but almost imperceptibly.'[26] Listening at Downing Street, Tom Jones thought the speech had been delivered with 'great vigour and determination'.[27] Virginia Woolf was less enamoured. 'Impressive as it is to hear the very voice of the Prime Minister, descendant of Pitt & Chatham,' she wrote in her diary, 'still I can't heat up my reverence to the right pitch.'[28]

Reith's mother had been listening outside her son's study and afterwards was taken in and introduced to the Prime Minister. She said she was proud to be the first to see him after his broadcast.[29] Anxious that Mrs Baldwin might be 'worrying' about him, the premier hurried back to Number 10 with the BBC's general manager in tow. 'In the car going back,' Reith wrote in his diary, 'he indicated quite clearly that his anxieties were not lessened by some of his colleagues.'[30]

This was undoubtedly a reference to Winston Churchill, who Reith met for the first time shortly after the Prime Minister's speech, although the Chancellor had earlier asked for 'the noises of the production of the British Gazette' to be broadcast on the wireless.[31] Asked to collect Viscount Grey of Fallodon from Number 11 Downing Street before the former Liberal Foreign Secretary made his own broadcast, Reith recalled that Churchill:

> came out and asked me in to have coffee. He asked me if I were connected with the BBC. I said I was the managing director. He swung round with 'Are you Mr Reith?' – almost shouted out. I said I was. He said he had been hunting for me all the week. I said I was on the job all the time and he could have asked me to come along, and that he ought to do so when he was feeling indignant with us. He was really very stupid; his wife backed him up but Lord Grey approved the idea of keeping the BBC to some extent impartial. [Churchill] was quite polite throughout, but I certainly kept our end up.

On accompanying Grey to a waiting car, Churchill said he had heard that Reith had been badly wounded in the war. 'I said that was so but that had no bearing on my actions at present,' recalled Reith, 'which embarrassed him.'[32]

The impact of the broadcasts by Baldwin and Grey was naturally limited to the minority of Britons who possessed wireless sets. Churchill's son Randolph later told his mother of having defied instructions at Sandroyd School in Wiltshire to install a 'secret' radio in the bottom of his armchair, which worked 'extraordinarily well'.[33] But beyond such rarified circles, radio 'was non-existent as far as the working class was concerned'.[34] As Asa Briggs diplomatically observed, there was also 'no doubt that the straight facts of working-class life were not well known to most members of the early BBC'.[35]

There was, however, a degree of 'communal' listening and crowds even formed outside wireless retailers in order to hear news bulletins. The cartoonist David Low depicted a group of people (including Low and his dog) listening to an imagined broadcast from a loudspeaker: 'Mr Baldwin has eaten a good lunch and is hopeful ... it is denied that the Albert Memorial has been wrecked. There will be several trains tomorrow and the other six million of you can walk.'[36]

There was also a degree of cynicism even among more middle-class listeners. 'It was clear that the BBC had been commandeered by the Government,' noted Beatrice Webb in her diary, 'and that the main purpose was to recruit blacklegs for the closed services.'[37] Unlike the *British Gazette*, however, the BBC *did* broadcast messages from the General Council of the TUC and summarize the speeches of trade union leaders and other critics of the government. But it did not help that misleading items were broadcast, most likely due to failures in news collection and verification rather than deliberate distortion. Among these were accounts of railwaymen returning to work at Oxford, the apparent breakdown of the strike at Salisbury and the discharge of food ships near Grimsby. Each of these reports was corrected by the unions in the areas concerned, but went unacknowledged by the BBC.[38] This naturally led to accusations of bias. The Company itself learned that the nickname 'BFC' (British Falsehood Company) was employed in some parts of the country,[39] while the *Furness Strike Bulletin* for 10 May included a cartoon in which 'BBC' stood for 'BOSSES BUNKUM CENTRE'.[40]

Most damaging in this respect was the failure to allow any Labour politician to broadcast, although as with the Archbishop of Canterbury this was the government's doing rather than the BBC's.[41] On 5 May, the second day of the strike, Reith met a delegation from the Parliamentary Labour Party with such a request, while, on 7 May, William Graham, a former Labour minister and a member of the Crawford Committee on the future of the BBC, requested that 'one of their people' be allowed to address the nation. J. C. C. Davidson made clear his opposition, but when the Liberal Viscount Grey broadcast on 9 May, Graham again pressed the point:

> In Labour circles many of us who are most anxious for peace believe that it is utterly unfair, and certainly thoroughly undesirable, that no opportunity is given to any representative Labour or Trade Union leader to state the case for the miners and other workers in this crisis. Knowing what Governments can do under emergency regulations we fully appreciate how you are placed, but we trust you will appeal to the Government not to prejudice broadcasting, now and in future, by using it now merely as an agency for Government propaganda.[42]

Ramsay MacDonald, the Leader of the Opposition, then piled on the pressure by telephone the following day. As Reith wrote:

> He was reasonable enough. He said he was anxious to give a talk. I said that we were not entirely a free agent, but that he might send the manuscript along.[1] I got it at No. 6 with a friendly note offering to make any alterations which I wanted ... I sent it at once to Davidson for him to ask the Prime Minister, strongly recommending that they should allow it to be done. I do not think that they treat me altogether fairly. They will not say we are to a certain extent controlled and they make me take the onus of turning people down. They were quite against MacDonald broadcasting, but I am certain it would have done no harm to the Government. Of course it puts me in a very awkward and unfair position. I imagine it comes chiefly from the PM's difficulties with the Winston lot.[43]

In his diary, MacDonald noted that Reith had told him 'in confidence' that he was 'dissatisfied with the Government's attitude to the Company and was trying to get some understanding'.[44]

The Labour leader's request was even discussed at Cabinet on 11 May, although the Colonial Secretary Leo Amery found himself 'quite alone' in supporting it:

> My efforts were successful in getting a decision that no political speeches were to be allowed to be Broadcasted [sic] except statements by the Prime Minister himself, and also that this should be done by the Broadcasting Company on their own and that there should be no taking over and running the BBC purely as propaganda which is what Winston and F.E. [Lord Birkenhead] had been trying to bring about.[45]

Given that by this point Baldwin, Grey and Sir William Joynson-Hicks had already broadcast such statements, this was moot. Reith was, however, relieved that Cabinet had finally reached a decision as regards the BBC's position. As he observed in his diary:

> The Cabinet decision is really a negative one. They want to be able to say that they did not commandeer us, but they know that they

---

[1] This text is reproduced in full in the Appendix (p. 235).

can trust us not to be really impartial. Davidson came round again at 8.15 and we were supposed to draft a notice defining the BBC position. I wanted the inconsistencies in our acts so far squared up, setting us right with the other side. Davidson, however, thought the Cabinet would only agree to a statement that we could do nothing to help the Strike since it had been declared illegal. This does not seem to me straight.[46]

Reith's justified qualms regarding Lord Astbury's *obiter* remarks[47] indicated his discomfort at having been reduced to a messenger between a government jealously guarding its broadcasting privileges and an opposition frustrated by its relative inability to get across its point of view. As he later reflected in a confidential letter to senior BBC staff, the strike was a period of 'unprecedented strain, with the situation changing several times a day'. Reith was satisfied, however, that the outcome he most feared, 'namely that BBC prestige and tradition might suffer', had not come to pass.[48] He also believed the Company had calmed the situation and dispelled the wildest rumours. 'If there had been broadcasting at the time of the French Revolution,' Reith remarked in his memoirs, 'there might have been no French Revolution.'[49]

Listeners appeared to concur. During the strike the BBC received 3,696 'appreciations' of its special strike coverage and just 176 criticisms, together with 1,477 regarding its announcers and a mere sixteen negative comments.[50] Although even a single complaint pained the conscientious Reith, these were not bad proportions. When it was all over, he often wondered if it would have been better had the BBC been commandeered after all. Reith's conclusion was that it would have been 'better' for him but 'worse for the BBC and for the country'.[51]

12

THE CIVIL COMMISSIONERS

In a letter to Edward Wood, the recently appointed Viceroy of India, the 6th Earl Winterton observed that the 'ultimate powers' invested in him and his fellow Civil Commissioners were 'as comprehensive as those of any head of a Province in India'.[1] The colonial simile was probably intended to tickle Wood at the vice-regal lodge in New Delhi, but it also spoke to the dramatic changes in domestic governance: for almost two weeks the normally highly centralized UK was divided into twelve 'divisions' administered by junior government ministers temporarily equipped with powers, as Winterton put it, akin to those of provincial Indian governors.

This emergency structure – ten Civil Commissioners in England and Wales and one each in Scotland and Northern Ireland[2] – had been developed by successive governments since 1919 and by October 1925 each of the divisions had its own headquarters with a staff of eight. While the government in London grappled with the strike's 'high politics', the Civil Commissioners were supposed – in the sombre language of the *Emergency Powers Act 1920* – to secure 'the essentials of life to the community'. Although individuals with similar powers had existed during the First World War and would again during the Second, their peacetime activation was a first.

For the duration of the general strike, the Civil Commissioners were to exercise all the powers of the government in their respective divisions and act on their own initiative except on 'decisions of great importance'.[3] In his memoirs, Earl Winterton recalled the Civil Commissioners having been given further instructions 'in the event of a complete breakdown' to take 'drastic action of a comprehensive character'. But as there had been no need to carry these out, he pleaded the *Official Secrets Act* and did not elaborate.[4] To return to the colonial analogy, one can only assume Winterton was alluding to matters of life and death.

Standing 6 feet 4 inches tall, quick-tempered and often 'exceptionally offensive',[5] Winterton certainly administered the South Midland Division as if it were an unruly Indian province. In his letter to Edward Wood (later Lord Halifax), he recounted with glee how one assistant to an 'old woman' (by which he meant a local voluntary service chairman) had been transformed – under his guidance – into 'a complete local Mussolini':

> He reduced the Mayor and Town Clerk, who were very frightened of the strikers, to a condition (after 24 hours of his rule) in which they were much more frightened of him than they were of the strikers and ate out of his hand; the result was that serious trouble was averted in that particular town.

Winterton also claimed to have succeeded in mobilizing the 'natural leaders' in all the country districts and in most of the major towns, what he called the local 'big man' ('if and where he was popular; I didn't use him where he wasn't') with 'a title or some distinction gained in the Army, in India, etc'. In a 'rather sketchy and unofficial manner', Winterton also organized a local intelligence network as he was 'anxious to know what the ordinary working man was saying in the street, in the public house or in his club'.[6]

The South Midland Division headquarters were located in Reading Gaol, which had once been used to hold Irish prisoners involved in the 1916 Easter Rising and later foreign internees during the Great War. It had also been made famous by Oscar Wilde's residence and poetry, which was apt given that Winterton, like Oscar, was of Irish provenance. Born Edward Turnour in London in 1883, he was educated at Eton and New College, Oxford, where his legal studies were interrupted by the 1904 Horsham by-election. Viscount Turnour (a courtesy title) became the Baby of the House and, three years later, also became the 6th Earl Winterton following his father's death.[7] During the First World War, he served alongside T. E. Lawrence in the Hejaz operations which culminated in the fall of Damascus,[8] while by May 1926 Winterton was Lord Birkenhead's Commons deputy as parliamentary under-secretary for India.

THE CIVIL COMMISSIONERS

Never short of self-confidence, Winterton thought nothing of asserting himself in relation to his superiors in London. When the Home Office refused to allow provincial police forces from his division to cross the Metropolitan Police boundary to protect lorries collecting food supplies, the resulting obstruction by strikers and threats of violence led to warnings that the South Midlands was running dangerously low on provisions. 'Some of the food lorry drivers,' Winterton noted in his diary, 'are afraid to go to London.'[9] He sent an urgent message to Sir William Mitchell-Thomson, the Chief Civil Commissioner, basically threatening to resign. Immediately realizing this had been couched in characteristic but 'unnecessarily strong terms', Winterton was relieved when Sir William replied saying he was not alone in his complaints and promising that a 'showdown' was imminent.[10]

Winterton also visited his alma mater and found the headmaster, provost, vice-provost and housemasters of Eton waiting patiently with notebooks and pencils ready to receive his 'instructions and advice'. Being 'desperately tired' after a trying day, he 'made a speech of an appalling character (deficient alike in diction and coherence) which I am sure gave to the assembled beaks [teachers] the impression that I was still as great a half-wit as I was when at Eton'.[11] At Oxford University, meanwhile, Winterton's car was surrounded by undergraduates not only 'begging' to be made special constables but allowed to 'kidnap' the then Master of Balliol, the left-wing A. D. Lindsay, who they claimed ('without any solid evidence') was trying to impede the government's emergency operations in that part of England.[12] While Winterton had heard 'disquieting rumours of the effeminacy and of the perverted political views of Oxford undergraduates', to his relief he saw 'no signs of either during the Strike'.[13]

By the last day of the strike, Winterton found himself with a surplus of 10,000 volunteers. 'One lot of young wage-earners from a certain village asked to be sent as special constables to Glasgow,' he recalled in his memoirs. 'When I asked why, their spokesman replied, "To have a crack at them dirty bolshies on the Clyde".'[14]

Like Winterton, the other Civil Commissioners were junior Ministers of the Crown, although Scotland's was a law officer and Northern Ireland's a member of its devolved government. Those in England and Wales were supported by a senior Ministry of Health official familiar with the area, as well as representatives from the Ministry of Transport and Board of Trade. Each Commissioner directed what appeared to be a mini-Cabinet, with officers for food, the railways, the Post Office, coal, finance and, where necessary, shipping, harbours and docks. There were also liaison officers for the police and the Armed Forces. Perhaps most important was each division's roads commissioner, who was to relieve haulage contractors of existing contracts and grant legal priority to the transport of essential commodities.[15] 'Elaborate arrangements' were also made to insure motor transport against the risk of sabotage.[16]

Each Civil Commissioner's division was subdivided into a number of areas, where existing local authorities were expected to cooperate in the event of a stoppage. There had been a plan to involve Lord-Lieutenants, but this was abandoned in July 1925 given their connection with the Crown and the need to 'preserve' the King from 'any contact, actual or implied, with the emergency organisation'. Their ability to remain discreet was also considered doubtful, and instead they were to 'smooth over any friction between self-important Lord Mayors and Mayors and Chairmen of Volunteer Service Committees'.[17] During the strike itself, the Transport and General Workers' Union derided what it called the 'comic opera display' of Civil Commissioners and the 'hopelessly inadequate' Organisation for the Maintenance of Supplies (OMS),[18] the latter having merged with the government organization on 4 May.

LONDON AND HOME COUNTIES

The Civil Commissioner for London and the Home Counties was Major William Cope, a junior Treasury minister. A former international rugby union player for his native Wales, Cope's father had been 'a pioneer of the South Wales coal trade'. After a career at the English Bar, William became the Conservative MP for Llandaff and Barry at the 1918 general election.

The capital proved more of a challenge for Major Cope than the Home Counties. Early on 6 May, Elephant and Castle witnessed some of the worst violence of the strike when a crowd stopped a private bus on St George's Road, ordered the passengers, driver and conductor off and then set it on fire. This was quickly extinguished and the local police force augmented with a large detachment of mounted police. In Hackney, meanwhile, huge crowds of tramway workers gathered close to a London County Council depot and forced the occupants of several motor vehicles to alight.[19]

Perhaps the most notorious incident outside London was the 'Battle of Lewes Road' in Brighton. On 11 May, a group of volunteers (including some students) attempted to remove trams from the Lewes Road depot. They were blocked by strikers while local residents looked on, including mothers who had just collected their children from school. Chief Constable Charles Griffin ordered the strikers and crowd to disperse, but when they failed to do so:

> A mixed force of some 300 foot police and about 50 mounted specials advanced in wedge formation, the latter led by 'Sergeant' Harry Preston, proprietor of the Royal Albion and Royal York hotels and a friend of the Prince of Wales, with Harry Mason, a well-known professional boxer acting as his second-in-command. This motley collection of ex-cavalry men, ex-black and tans, and ex-yeomanry, gradually forced the strikers back ... Someone in the crowd threw a bottle at a constable; blows were exchanged between officers and civilians; stones and bricks began to fly through the air; and the police came to a standstill.[20]

'They came through as if they were mad,' claimed another eyewitness, 'one special on horseback jumped over the wall into the recreation park where women and children were for safety and others went into the park and frightened the little children to death.' One man of seventy who was in the park said to a young mounted constable: 'I am old enough to be your grandfather.' The special backed his horse into the seventy-year-old, who fell on his back before being hit with a truncheon.[21] There were seventeen arrests and two cases of serious injury.

As this died down, there was a fresh disturbance at the Brighton Labour Institute. 'Car after car, laden with police and specials, raced to the scene of action,' wrote Ernie Trory, 'followed by the hard-faced mounted men, their batons swinging from their saddles. Those at the end of the procession were met by cars returning with fresh victims of police brutality.' This resulted in another five arrests, and all twenty-two were brought before the bench at an emergency magistrates' court the following morning. On being charged with incitement to riot under the Emergency Regulations, seventeen were sentenced to hard labour for up to six months, three received fines, an eighteen-year-old youth was remanded in custody for eight days while the remaining striker, said to be 'abnormal mentally', was simply handed over to his father.[22]

EASTERN DIVISION

The Civil Commissioner for England's Eastern Division was Sir Philip Albert Gustave David Sassoon, a denizen of the prominent Jewish Sassoon and Rothschild families. Born at his mother's mansion in Paris and educated at Eton and Oxford, Philip was elected to Parliament as the Unionist Member for Hythe in 1912 and served as private secretary to Field Marshal Sir Douglas Haig during the First World War. Willowy and attractive (something captured in John Singer Sargent's 1923 portrait), Sassoon had 'fickle, moody fascinations with young men with whom he soon grew bored'.[23]

In 1920 Sassoon became Parliamentary Private Secretary to Prime Minister David Lloyd George and, having long championed aviation, was a natural choice as under-secretary for air in Stanley Baldwin's second government. 'An atmosphere of luxury and mystery surrounds him,' mused the Labour MP Ellen Wilkinson:

> Sir Philip makes one want a revolution just to see him for once in an environment that had not been planned with perfect taste, but alas! Even if the Westminster Soviet made him carry coals, he would do it with a delicate air.[24]

Two days after the general strike began, Sassoon wrote to Samuel Hoare, his superior at the Air Ministry, to say he had:

> got my organisation working all right & everything is very quiet in the area except for the electricians coming out at Bedford & Yarmouth ... I am really amazed at the little trouble there seems to be in the country as a whole up to now & it seems certainly fortunate that, if we were to have a general strike, it sh[oul]d have come out so speedily. It must mean a shorter strike. Everyone is glad that the Gov[ernmen]t are being so firm. Winston [Churchill] must be in his element – we sent you some would be printers yesterday & the university has been an invaluable reservoir for providing parties of men for very special work.

THE CIVIL COMMISSIONERS

On 9 May he wrote again to say he was 'sending up' to London 'large detachments of undergraduates for special constable work', and asking that:

> it be made quite clear on the wireless & in the [British] Gazette that the [Organisation for the Maintenance of Supplies] have ceased to exist. This is [not well] understood & makes for confusion – it is quite clear that the O.M.S. haven't helped & that it w[oul]d have been just as good in fact much better to start fair with the [Volunteer Service] Committees. This having caused a certain amount of friction & discontent.[25]

Sassoon was not alone in his negative assessment of the OMS, long planned as a voluntary ballast to the emergency machinery of government. Indeed, in other parts of England, the failure of the OMS risked causing London considerable embarrassment.

NORTHERN DIVISION

In the Northern Division, for example, it led Sir Kingsley Wood to cooperate more closely with the strikers than the government would probably have liked. Born in 1881 to a Methodist minister, Howard Kingsley Wood flourished as a solicitor before masterminding the establishment of the UK's first Ministry of Health in 1918. Wood was knighted the same year and subsequently elected the Unionist MP for West Woolwich. After serving successive Ministers of Health as their Parliamentary Private Secretary, in 1924 he became Neville Chamberlain's deputy at the same department.[26]

It was Sir Kingsley's growing reputation within government which led him to be appointed Civil Commissioner for the Northern Division, although he was a last-minute replacement, John Moore-Brabazon (the first person to qualify as a pilot in the UK) having been recalled to handle the London Docks.[27] Wood took control of a division with a well-organized local Communist party. At the beginning of the strike, its local organizer Robin Page Arnot suggested that:

> no time be spent discussing the purpose of the Strike, its national or international implications, but attention be concentrated on the immediate objective, i.e. defeat the Civil Commissioner (Sir Kingsley

Wood) appointed by the Government to control the North East area of the country ... Those who control the movement of food supplies and transport generally, will have control of the situation.[28]

A few days later, Martin Connolly, the Labour MP for Newcastle East, created a stir in the House of Commons when he claimed that in Newcastle:

> the [Organisation for the Maintenance of Supplies] has entirely broken down, that the authorities have approached the trade unions and asked them to take over the vital services, and that the trade unions have consented to do so on condition that all extra police, all troops, and all OMS services shall be withdrawn. This has been done, and the city is going on all right.[29]

An hour later, Sir Douglas Hogg (the Attorney General) said he had spoken to the chief constable in Newcastle who had assured him this report was untrue. When, a few days later, the question was raised again and another minister claimed the OMS in Newcastle was working satisfactorily, Martin Connolly read a statement from the Newcastle Trades Council:

> He [Sir Kingsley Wood] admitted that he had lost control of the situation, and asked the Transport Union to co-operate in maintaining supplies. The position was so desperate that provided the unions would come to his help he was prepared to ask the Government to withdraw the troops and marines.[30]

Piecing together what actually happened has challenged several historians of the general strike. What is clear is that on Wednesday 6 May, members of the OMS were brought to the Newcastle quayside to unload food supplies which had arrived the previous day. Trade union members there (with permission from the TUC) stopped work, partly on account of the OMS volunteers but also what they regarded as the provocative presence of two destroyers and a submarine, which were moored close by.

This stoppage prompted Sir Kingsley to interview members of the Newcastle Strike Committee before visiting its headquarters at Burt Hall. Julian Symons takes up the story:

> Wood said that the outside labour imported on to the quay was there without his knowledge or authority. The Committee asked that only

food cargoes should be unloaded, and also said that 'it was impossible for us to agree that our men should be forced to work under the shadow of guns'. Wood said that the boats were kept there to deal with possible riots or attacks on power stations, 'but appeared to indicate that a suggestion from him to the Commanders of the vessels might have the desired effect'. With regard to the unloading, Wood ... suggested a system of dual control, with two officers appointed to deal with any trouble, one from the Government and the other from the [Strike] Committee.[31]

The Strike Committee responded by refusing 'dual control' and withdrawing all permits for trade union labour.

Sensing an opportunity to embarrass the government given its strict line of no cooperation before the general strike was called off, Robin Page Arnot (who had been hiding in another room at Burt Hall) picked up a telephone and:

> got on to the Daily Herald in London, on to W. N. Ewer who was then the Foreign section ... and told him what had happened. I then got on to Arthur Greenwood at the House of Commons and told him what was happening. In each case I said, 'Well, it means they're negotiating, they're suing for peace. So far we've got to the stage of winning, we've broken their ultimatum.'[32]

This was one version of events. In his own account to the Commons after the strike, Sir Kingsley denied that any form of dual control had been offered and that 'from that day to the end of the strike the whole of the work of the food supplies in that district was carried out by voluntary labour under police protection'. Less convincingly, Wood claimed not to have realized that the three men he met were connected with the local strike committee, believing them to be representatives of the dock workers.[33] As Tony Mason has pointed out, this was undermined by the fact at least one of Wood's staff referred to a 'conference between the Civil Commissioner and the Strike Committee' in a Board of Trade bulletin.[34] Robin Page Arnot dismissed Sir Kingsley's Commons performance as a 'very whimpering explanation'.[35]

Whatever the truth, the incident clearly rattled Wood, who had hopes for political advancement. A Home Office memo from the last day of the strike recorded Sir Kingsley telling an official that 'the local people needed "gingering up"', a reference to the Communist-influenced *Workers' Chronicle* in Newcastle. 'It was said in confidence,' added the official, 'that this appeared to be on account of the paper containing criticisms of Sir Kingsley Wood.'[36]

NORTH WESTERN DIVISION

Major George Hennessy in the North Western Division (which included North Wales) was another of the more colourful Civil Commissioners. A Franco-Irish aristocrat and vice-chamberlain of the Royal Household (a government whip), even before the strike began he kept the local press fully briefed. 'The Government,' he told the *Manchester Guardian* chirpily, 'are not taking sides in the dispute but are merely, as it were, keeping the ring.'[37]

When the strike began on 4 May, Major Hennessy said:

> The sands have run out, and in the grave emergency which has arisen the Government, acting on behalf of the whole nation, must ensure that those services which are essential to the national wellbeing continue in operation. I therefore appeal with every confidence to all citizens to do their utmost to support the authority of the King's Government. This can best be done by offering their services at the local recruiting station, by refraining from hasty judgment or action, and by doing everything in their power to promote goodwill and a just settlement of the present trouble.

The tone was markedly less truculent than that of most of his colleagues. Hennessy even permitted a *Guardian* journalist a 'glimpse' inside his Liverpool headquarters:

> In each of many rooms in a building guarded by police officers is a map of the British Isles with the area under the control of the Commissioner (extending from Cumberland to Merionethshire) minutely divided into sub-districts. There are comprehensive lists of traders and all those concerned in the provision of essential supplies; and in the hands of the Road Commissioner is the name of the owner of every vehicle which could possibly be used for road transport. This afternoon a workman was busy fixing additional telephone communication – the last touch which completed the organisation.

Everyone the journalist spoke to confidently predicted almost 'normal services' while the emollient Major Hennessy was 'especially anxious' to emphasise that his emergency machinery was 'in no sense a strike-breaking organisation'.[38]

Hennessy's strategy appeared to work. Liverpool was at that time the second most important seaport in Britain and handled about one-fifth of its total imports, making the city a vital distribution centre. But while the railway stoppage in Merseyside was almost total, by 8 May 80 per cent of Liverpool's trams appeared to be running while the Mersey ferries never ceased operation as they were deemed 'essential to the movement of food'. Large numbers of ships also managed to clear the Merseyside ports during the nine days, while two battleships helped land food supplies. The response to Major Hennessy's call for volunteers was also considerable, with 20,000 – more than three times the national average – offering their services by the strike's end. Remarkably, there were only seven arrests under the Emergency Regulations.[39]

SOUTH WALES DIVISION

The Civil Commissioner for the other half of Wales was the 6th Earl of Clarendon. A grandson of a three-times Foreign Secretary, the Old Etonian George Villiers was installed at the Dominions Building in central Cardiff, then the largest coal-exporting port in the world. The historian Hywel Francis considered the strike in South Wales more akin to that in the Home Counties than in the other coalfields, for Cardiff, Swansea and Newport had a substantial 'loyal' middle class, 'eager for the jape of playing at being workers or enlisting as special constables'.[40] In all, 12,000 volunteered, including just under 7,000 in Cardiff. Many of the near-700 special constables enrolled were students at University College, the Welsh School of Medicine or a local divinity school.[41]

An infantry battalion (the Cheshires) arrived in Cardiff on 2 May, a submarine docked on 4 May and a cruiser was anchored off the city on 5 May. Clarendon insisted the soldiers were not used as strike-breakers, although rather provocatively they were marched through the streets of Cardiff each day 'for exercise'.[42] The key area of confrontation between volunteers and strikers was in the operation of Cardiff's trams. Initially, there was a complete stoppage, but when the Lord Mayor called on tram workers to come back or be sacked, within days a limited bus and tram service had been restored to parts of the city run by volunteers dubbed by strikers as the 'Lord Mayor's Own'. This resulted in attacks on buses and trams and large crowds blocking their progress in the centre of the city. A path was only cleared after hundreds of police, including some on horseback, broke up the crowds with a baton charge.[43] A Welsh Liberal noted that as the Cardiff Corporation services passed by, the crowds were 'mixed', 'for immediately a shout is set up against the volunteers, there are numbers of others who are cheering them'.[44]

During the only weekend of the general strike, Cathays Park hosted one of the largest open-air demonstrations Cardiff had ever seen, with between 15,000 and 20,000 strikers listening to seventeen speakers. At the mass meeting, James Edwards, President of the Cardiff Trades and Labour Council, emphasized that disorder was treachery to the cause. This clearly had an impact, for no further disturbances against vehicles or their crews were recorded for the remainder of the strike.[45]

NORTHERN IRELAND

Northern Ireland has been curiously absent from accounts of the general strike, and with some justification. To a degree, its outbreak caught the devolved Government of Northern Ireland on the hop. Although its version of the UK government's emergency organization had been dusted off towards the end of 1925, only on 5 May 1926 – the second day of the strike – was an Emergency Powers Bill given a second reading in the Northern Ireland House of Commons.[46] This basically adapted the provisions of the *Emergency Powers Act 1920* to the six counties.

Sir James Craig, Prime Minister of Northern Ireland since 1921, said the bill was necessary to 'prevent any panic or greed' and ensure the public ('especially poor people') were not 'deprived of their fair share of food, coal and the other amenities of life'. The Northern Ireland Labour Party promoted an amendment preventing regulations outlawing strikes or picketing, as was the case in the 1920 Act. Sir Milne Barbour, who was Northern Ireland's Chief Civil Commissioner as well as Minister of Commerce, said sources of coal and some imported food had been 'seriously interrupted' by events on the mainland.[47] On 11 May the Minister of Labour also estimated that around 5,500 people in Northern Ireland had lost employment 'either wholly or partly, as a result of the situation in Great Britain'.[48]

The bill passed the Commons and Senate in a day and on 6 May Lords Justices acting on behalf of the vice-regal Governor of Northern Ireland belatedly proclaimed a state of emergency under the *Emergency Powers Act (Northern Ireland) 1926*. A coal-rationing order was made the same day, which extended to the whole of Northern Ireland except Derry/Londonderry.[49] Orders made under the *Constabulary (Ireland) Act 1922* stationed an additional force of the Royal Ulster Constabulary (RUC) in Belfast and Derry.[50] The people of 'Ulster', Sir Milne Barbour told a group of Northern Irish journalists, 'were very anxious to avoid being drawn into the struggle. This was a question that is being fought out on the other side of the Channel.'[51]

John Milne Barbour was born in County Antrim in 1868 to John Dougherty Barbour, the chairman of one of Ulster's biggest flax-spinning firms. Educated at Harrow and Oxford, he succeeded his father as chairman in 1904 and in 1921 was elected to the newly created Parliament of Northern Ireland as the Ulster Unionist MP for Antrim. Barbour immediately became parliamentary and financial secretary at the Ministry of Finance, to which he added Minister of Commerce in 1925. Also active in the general synod of the Church of Ireland and the Royal Ulster Agricultural Society, it was suggested that 'his accumulation of ... offices verged on the obsessive' on account of his American wife's death in 1910.[52]

'The people in Belfast are not anxious for a strike,' reported the RUC to the Northern Ireland Ministry of Home Affairs on 7 May, 'and even though a demand is made on the Unions to come out it is thought a large number, probably the majority, will not respond.' The RUC, which had been on heightened alert since 1921, also surreptitiously attended public meetings. This did not yield much, though on 9 May the Labour councillor Harry Midgley (a future Stormont MP and minister) was recorded saying that 'any soldier or sailor who would take up arms against those engaged in this strike were dogs' and that 'a more manly and Christian thing to do would be to turn the guns on those that gave the orders'. It was submitted to the Attorney General for Northern Ireland that Midgley be prosecuted for sedition.[53]

Archives at the Public Record Office of Northern Ireland give the impression that relations between London and Belfast were somewhat confused. Wires from Stormont Castle to Sir John Anderson at the Home Office went unanswered, and when strike notices were issued to Belfast dockers on 10 May, delayed communications with the Admiralty in London made it hard for the devolved government to protect the city's ports. Even the Prime Minister of Northern Ireland seemed unclear as to his remit. On 11 May he telegrammed his counterpart at 10 Downing Street asking about the guarantee that 'loyal' workers would be protected from trade union retaliation, to which Baldwin replied:

> any legislation is not within competence of [the] Imperial Parliament but lies within competence of [the] Government and Parliament of Northern Ireland. If therefore you think it advisable to give assurance on lines of that given here you should give it as Prime Minister of Northern Ireland.[54]

There was similar confusion at Eccleston Square and in Dublin. Goods bound for the Irish Free State were piled high at Fishguard and Holyhead, while in the port town of Drogheda, which depended heavily on imports of British coal, all sailings were cancelled.[55]

On 6 May 1926, James Larkin of the Workers' Union of Ireland told the TUC's acting general secretary Walter Citrine that railway workers were divided, with seventy Irish members of the TGWU having sailed for Liverpool 'to offer their services as scabs on your side'. 'Owing to the disunity here,' he added, 'the position is not as safe as it might be.'[56] By 11 May, Tom Johnson of the Irish Trades Union Congress was sufficiently 'anxious' regarding an 'extension of the strike to Ireland' that the Dáil (the Irish parliament) introduced its own emergency legislation.[57]

The Chief Civil Commissioner in London, meanwhile, revelled in having received 'numerous offers of services from men and women' in Northern Ireland and the Irish Free State, although Sir William Mitchell-Thomson made clear that given the 'splendid response' to the government's appeal for volunteers in the 'home country', it seemed 'improbable that the occasion will arise for taking advantage of these offers from Overseas'.[58]

SCOTLAND

Since 1885 Scotland had enjoyed a degree of 'administrative' devolution rather than the legislative sort granted to Northern Ireland in 1921. Beyond this constitutional distinction, the Scottish Emergency Organisation (SEO) in Edinburgh was run along parallel lines to that in the rest of Great Britain. The 'Minister in Charge' was William Watson, KC, the Lord Advocate, while the Chief Civil Commissioner was James Peck, a civil servant. Scotland was divided into five regions, each the responsibility of district commissioners based in Edinburgh, Glasgow, Dundee, Aberdeen and Inverness. The SEO was housed at the Board of Agriculture for Scotland building in the heart of Edinburgh's New Town.

William Watson was born in Edinburgh in December 1873, the third son of Lord Watson of Thankerton. In 1899 he was admitted to the Faculty of Advocates in Edinburgh, took silk in 1914 and became an advocate depute in 1919. Watson also entered Parliament, although largely with the goal of advancement to the Scottish Bench. In 1922 Watson was appointed Solicitor General for Scotland and became Lord Advocate later the same year. Tall and youthful in appearance given he was in his early sixties, Watson had considerable energy, walking long distances, playing golf and shooting. Indoors, his hobby was knitting at which, noted his biographer, 'he was very skilful'.[59]

The most prominent district commissioners were James Peck in Edinburgh and Sir Arthur Rose in Glasgow, Scotland's two main urban centres.[60] The latter infuriated William Whitelaw, chairman of the London and North Eastern Railway and grandfather of Willie,[61] by refusing to post military guards on the railways (Rose said he would rather resign) and attempting to reverse the firm's decision not to pay striking staff. Whitelaw alleged a conflict of interest given that Sir Arthur was a local director of the London, Midland and Scottish Railway in Glasgow.[62]

In a melodramatic message to 'the people of Scotland' on 10 May, the Lord Advocate thanked them for their response to the government's appeal for volunteers. 'We are fighting,' he declared, 'for freedom, for democratic Government, for the breaking of a type of tyranny which has reached its culmination in Russia.'[63] Events in the normally genteel Scottish capital must have convinced Watson that this was a good analogy. Early in the strike, thousands of women and some children had gathered in the heart of the city's Old Town. In one newspaper account:

> The crowd threw bottles and stones, shop windows were broken, and their contents looted. Five arrests were made, and five constables and a number of civilians were injured. One police sergeant was slashed on the back with a razor, by an unknown assailant. A policeman's horse, taking fright, crashed into a railing and was killed, while the constable was seriously injured. An attack was made by roughs on a tram, a cart loaded with stones providing a plentiful supply of missiles, wherewith to smash all the glass in the car.[64]

The police burst through the crowds and swept some of them down the Canongate and the ancient closes off the Royal Mile. One group of police charged down as far as the Palace of Holyroodhouse, the King's official residence in Scotland, turned, reformed, charged back up to the Tron and then down North Bridge, 'scattering the hundreds who were still loitering on the pavements'. Twenty people were arrested.[65]

Edinburgh was Britain's eighth largest city. Surrounded by coalfields, the city itself was a major centre for books, beer and biscuits. Long regarded as a weak spot in trade union activity, during the strike the city's printing trade ceased (apart from the *Scotsman* and *Edinburgh Evening Dispatch*), its docks were at a standstill, and its transport moribund apart from a few trams and buses operated by students.[66] This impacted Edinburgh's brewing industry, which produced 70 per cent of Scotland's beer, and on 8 May the city's magistrates ordered all pubs to close at three o'clock.[67]

Despite being at the heart of 'Red Clydeside', meanwhile, Glasgow was comparatively quiet, mainly on account of the TUC's decision not to call out engineers and shipbuilders in the 'first wave' of the strike.[68] The Glasgow Labour leader Patrick Dollan later criticized this as 'an error in tactics', as those workers' 'militant qualities would have strengthened the strike movement in the Clyde area'. He wryly observed that the events of May 1926 had caused less disruption than the forty hours' strike of early 1919. 'The milk and the breakfast rolls were delivered each morning at the regular time,' Dollan recalled one Glaswegian remarking. 'How then could it be a General Strike?'[69]

13

'An utterly illegal proceeding'

For a parliament full of lawyers, it took until the third day of the general strike – Thursday 6 May – before any of them addressed its legality. At eleven o'clock that evening, during a long debate on the Emergency Regulations, the Liberal MP and former Attorney General Sir John Simon rose to make what the Conservative backbencher Duff Cooper considered 'a most important and impressive speech'.[1] Indeed, it would come to dominate the last phase of the crisis.

Sir John began by ruminating on the word 'general', which he said was being used in a similar context as the 'great war', indicating something of 'exceptional gravity and importance and suffering'. But as far as Simon was concerned, the present crisis was 'not a strike at all', for that, properly understood, was 'perfectly lawful' – a right of workmen 'in combination, by pre-arrangement, to ... withhold their labour'. The decision of the Trades Union Congress 'to call out everybody', however, was 'not a lawful act at all', for every workman 'bound by a contract to give notice before he left work' had 'broken the law'. Sir John protested that he spoke without 'the slightest desire to blame or praise', but continued:

> it would be lamentable if the working classes of this country go on with this business without understanding that they are taking part in a novel and an utterly illegal proceeding. It is this feature of the general strike that constitutes its novelty. There may have been sporadic cases before, but this time it is part of a system. We have had serious strikes before, as we all know, but a general strike proclaimed by leaders of organised labour which disregards all contracts of employment is a wholly different matter.

Simon had another 'serious' point to share with the House. Every trade union leader, he declared, who had 'advised and promoted that course of action is liable [for] damages to the uttermost farthing of his personal possessions'. As for the *Trade Disputes Act 1906* (a measure introduced by a Liberal government), Sir John said it was 'quite certain' that what Parliament had in mind when it spoke of a 'trade dispute' and guaranteed immunity for trade union funds was a strike 'of a lawful character'[2] – not a *general* strike.

Most Labour MPs, noted Duff Cooper, left the Chamber before Sir John rose to speak, but all Liberal MPs were there except David Lloyd George and 'they were solidly behind him'. Simon's speech, he added, 'may prove the way to his supplanting Lloyd George as their leader'.[3] Cooper's colleague Harold Macmillan concurred, recalling in his memoirs that the intervention 'had a profound effect, both inside and outside the House of Commons'.[4] As Roy Jenkins later reflected in his biographical sketch of Simon, this provoked at least three reflections: first, that in 1926 a backbench speech could have such an impact; second, that this impact was a 'tribute' to Simon's legal authority; and third, that it 'illuminated the ambiguity of the position of most trades union leaders'.[5]

John Allsebrook Simon was one of the grand old men of the once mighty Liberal Party. To Labour MP Ellen Wilkinson, he was 'always decorative', 'his fine white head supported on the slender stem of his tall body' rather like 'an arum lily'.[6] Born in 1873 in a terraced house on Manchester's Moss Side, he was the eldest child and only son of a Congregationalist minister and a farmer's daughter, although his mother was a descendant of Sir Richard Pole and his wife Margaret, Countess of Salisbury. At Oxford Simon won many legal prizes and jousted intellectually with F. E. Smith, later Lord Birkenhead.

Smith was called to the English Bar in 1899. Widowed three years later, he entered the House of Commons as the MP for Walthamstow in the Liberal landslide of 1906. Four years later and aged only thirty-seven, Simon, now Sir John, became the youngest Solicitor General for England and Wales since the 1830s. In 1913 he was promoted to Attorney General and, in 1915, Home Secretary, but resigned the following year in protest at the conscription of single men, something he believed was a breach of Liberal principles. Sir John later became deputy Liberal leader and in October 1924 moved the amendment which brought down the first Labour government.[7]

By May 1926, Sir John Simon was one of just forty Liberal MPs in the House of Commons, and more respected as a lawyer than he was as a politician. The newspaper editor C. P. Scott, who had briefly trained Simon as a leader writer on the *Manchester Guardian*, was 'slightly repelled' by him. This was on account of an:

> affection of cordiality which hasn't much behind it, great volubility in talking about what interests him and no attempt to talk about what interests you. An appearance of deference with no real desire to consult, except in so far as may be needful to find out what line you mean to take.[8]

Lloyd George remarked caustically that Sir John had 'sat so long on the fence' that iron had 'entered his soul'.[9] There were also ideological objections. Since the 1924 general election, Simon had moved increasingly in a Conservative, or at least in an anti-socialist, direction. His pronouncement on the general strike, therefore, had to be viewed in a political as well as a legal context.

Baldwin's government nevertheless responded to Sir John's speech on 6 May with considerable caution, not least because it complicated its planned bill declaring the general strike illegal. On 8 May the *British Gazette* said it was 'understood that the law officers of the Crown do not dissent in general principle from [Simon's] conclusions',[10] hardly a ringing endorsement. This perhaps owed something to personal as well as legal misgivings among Conservative ministers. Like C. P. Scott, J. C. C. Davidson believed Simon 'spread around him an atmosphere of insincerity'.[11] Air Secretary Samuel Hoare also found the speech 'irritating', believing Sir John had overstated his case. 'My advice,' he noted, 'would always be to keep lawyers out of great occasions when emotions are deeply stirred.'[12]

When Sir Henry Slesser, a KC who had served as Solicitor General in the first Labour government, heard about Simon's speech on 7 May, he told Ramsay MacDonald it ought to be rebutted by His Majesty's Opposition. 'Without waiting to hear what I intended to say,' Slesser recalled in his memoirs, 'he replied that I was not to speak ... apparently he was contented that it should go unanswered.'[13] Sir Henry also had a personal reason for wanting to respond to Sir John, for not only had his speech been given 'the maximum advertisement of which the Government were capable', but a passage from Slesser's own textbook on trade union law, stating that a strike to coerce the government was probably not covered by the *Trade Disputes Act 1906*, had been 'widely advertised on posters'.[14]

What Slesser does not mention in his memoirs was his opinion regarding the legality of the strike, which was written with Arthur Henderson and sent to MacDonald on 10 May. This concluded that the *Trade Disputes Act* could not 'be pleaded to justify' individual trade unionists' breaches of contract. It continued:

> We have, therefore, to advise that the common law applies and that the only manner in which the liability of Trade Union officials or others of any sort who have taken part in the procuring of the breaches of contracts can be secured is by legislation ... nothing short of legislation can deprive an individual employer of his right to sue for damages unless an agreement can be entered into with him or some one on his behalf whereby he waives his rights.[15]

In other words, Slesser and Henderson believed Simon had a point. But with his professional reputation at stake, Sir Henry rose to speak on Monday 10 May, four days after Sir John's original intervention and a few minutes after he (Simon) had left the Chamber. His speech was rather opaque. Although Slesser privately 'deplored' the strike while feeling 'deep sympathy' for the miners,[16] he believed Simon had 'confused two entirely different matters', for section 3 of the *Trade Disputes Act 1906* conferred an 'express immunity' on 'anybody' who procured 'a breach of contract in contemplation or furtherance of a trade dispute'. He continued:

> The width, the size and the extension of the dispute will not in itself make illegal that which is not illegal if done in a smaller dispute. It has been decided over and over again in common law that, certainly where there is no breach of contract, a mere combination to cease labour, however great the extension, is not in itself an unlawful act. Whether it be an unlawful act or not must depend in the last resort on whether you have here a trade dispute within the definition of the Trade Disputes Act. That is a point that may or may not be decided in the future by a judge or jury.

AN UTTERLY ILLEGAL PROCEEDING

In that context, Sir Henry said it was 'in the highest degree unfortunate' that Parliament, although in truth he meant Sir John, should have prejudiced future judicial decisions. Westminster, he added, makes laws, it:

> does not interpret them. The proper place for the interpretation of laws is at the Royal Courts of Justice. That is the place where it will be decided what is legal and what not, and it is for that reason only that I have intervened.[17]

Sir Henry's speech was 'greeted with prolonged cheers', evidence, he believed, of 'uneasiness' at the pusillanimity of Labour's front bench in not replying to Simon sooner. His 'courage in standing up to the great lawyer' had won the approval of Labour MPs, although Ramsay MacDonald never mentioned the matter again.[18]

After some grumbling about Slesser not having given Sir John notice of his intervention, the Attorney General Sir Douglas Hogg defended Simon's original speech as a 'signal contribution to the knowledge of the public' but did not think it would be 'useful' to state his own view on the matter. 'Which hon. and learned Member has the greater weight in the legal profession the House must form its own opinion,' he said. 'Who is more likely to be right the House must decide.'[19]

Others, however, shared Slesser's doubts. Writing in the *Scottish Worker*, Craigie Aitchison KC, a former Labour parliamentary candidate and future Lord Advocate in Scotland, said he was 'quite unable to follow' the argument that 'because a strike is on a scale of unusual magnitude, therefore it loses its character as the exercise of a legal right, and thereby becomes unconstitutional'. The 'right to enforce an industrial demand by a strike,' he added, 'was part of Statute Law and of Common Law'.[20]

Although his critique has not survived, it seems Sir Owen Seaman, the editor of *Punch* and himself a barrister, also privately critiqued Simon's argument. 'I am not surprised at your feeling a little puzzled,' was Sir John's revealing reply to Seaman's letter, 'for the truth is that I spoke on the first occasion very late at night, and without full preparation, and am myself the cause of some misunderstanding.' He continued:

> I deliberately chose to put the breach of contract in the foreground when I <u>first</u> spoke because the only thing that mattered was to <u>stop</u> the strike by making clear to all concerned the alarming liability

173

in damages which they were rolling up against themselves. (And I have the strongest reason for knowing that my remark about the 'uttermost farthing' was the sentence that brought the opossum down the gum tree.) But the fundamental reason why the general strike is illegal goes deeper.[21]

This was a clear indication that Simon realized his initial argument, however dramatic its impact, had been intellectually weak, something he at once set about bolstering with a little help from Havelock Wilson and Mr Justice Astbury.

Joseph Havelock Wilson led one of the few trade unions to have voted against the general strike. Born in Sunderland in 1859, he went to sea as a boy and only settled ashore in 1882 upon opening a temperance hotel in his hometown. He became involved with the local seaman's union and in 1887 established the National Sailors' and Firemen's Union (NSFU), of which he was president until his death in 1929. Wilson was also politically ambitious. In 1892 he was elected an independent labour MP but thereafter aligned himself with the Liberals, whose whip he took until leaving Parliament in 1922.[22]

Wilson was a moderate, committed to working with shipowners and the government in pursuit of patriotic objectives (most prominently during the First World War) as well as the best interests of his members. Although often successful, this approach made him unpopular within the broader Labour movement. When the NSFU executive failed to support the general strike, its Liverpool branch nevertheless came out. Under the union's constitution this required a ballot, and this was ongoing as the strike progressed, albeit hindered by postal delays. On 6 May – the same day Sir John Simon made his dramatic speech – Mr Justice Astbury granted Wilson a temporary injunction to prevent union officials in Liverpool striking without executive sanction.

Like Sir John Simon, John Meir Astbury hailed from Manchester. After studying law at Trinity College, Oxford, he was called to the English Bar in 1884, took silk in 1895 and, along with several other Liberal lawyers, won a Commons seat (Southport) at the 1906 general election. According to *The Times*, Astbury made 'no mark' in Parliament and returned to his lucrative practice in January 1910. In 1913 Lord Haldane (while Lord Chancellor) appointed Astbury to the Chancery Division, although again he was not a conspicuous success. From the bench, he dealt with several trade union cases later described as 'unfortunate' by his critics, for at least a couple were overturned on appeal.[23]

On Tuesday 11 May, Mr Justice Astbury ruled in Havelock Wilson's favour. In doing so, he made some *obiter dicta*, remarks made in passing which did not form part of his judgment. These were that:

> The so-called general strike called by the Trades Union Congress ... is illegal and contrary to law, and those persons inciting or taking part in it are not protected by the Trade Disputes Act of 1906. No trade dispute has been alleged or shown to exist in any of the Unions affected, except in the miners' case, and no trade dispute does or can exist between the Trades Union Congress on the one hand and the Government and the nation on the other.[24]

Astbury then proceeded to pass binding judgment on the case before him, that the Liverpool branch had breached the constitution of the National Sailors' and Firemen's Union rather than that of the United Kingdom. Its secretary was immediately suspended, and eighteen further officials later dismissed for their action.

As Ellen Wilkinson observed in her 'workers' history' of the general strike, Sir John Simon now 'plumed himself on the Astbury judgment'.[25] Rising in the Commons just hours after his explosive remarks from the bench, Simon said he had no complaints about the criticisms made by his 'old professional and private friend' (Sir Henry Slesser) and joked about the 'kind of general strike proclaimed on the Labour Benches' when he had first spoken on 6 May. Sir John then subtly altered his original argument, saying that while he was 'quite willing to believe' the crisis 'had its origin in a trade dispute', once a general strike was declared it had started 'a movement of a perfectly different and a wholly unconstitutional and unlawful character'.

Then came Simon's *coup de grâce*. Alluding to Sir Henry's observation that such arguments could only 'be finally decided by judges', Sir John told the House he had within the last hour seen a judgment by Mr Justice Astbury he believed vindicated his argument. He then quoted three short extracts, 'because if the hon. and learned member for S. E. Leeds [Slesser] wants judicial authority, there is the judicial authority'. Twisting his knife, Sir John quoted from Sir Henry's 'very good' textbook on trade union law and, for good measure, other historic and apparently incriminating remarks from Labour MPs regarding the nature of a general strike. This, added Simon, had been a 'tragic blunder':

> It is not that the people who did it were a set of revolutionaries who wanted to break the country to pieces. It is that it has been done under some, I think confused, but at any rate quite mistaken impression, that this was a lawful exercise of the rights of organised labour. It is nothing of the sort, and until there are people who will say that openly and loudly and firmly in another quarter of the House, I feel it my duty to do my best to say it from this quarter.

Sir John closed with something more constructive, three conditions on which he believed the whole 'frightful business' could be brought to an end: 'an immediate and an unqualified calling off' of the strike, government legislation to carry out the recommendations of the Samuel Commission, and that the Miners' Federation and Mining Association 'give a definite undertaking that they will forthwith negotiate on the basis of the contents of that Report'.[26]

It is impossible to believe that a former Attorney General for England and Wales was unaware that *obiter dicta* were not the same as a legally binding judgment. As A. L. Goodhart, the American-born editor of *Law Quarterly Review*, later observed in an authoritative demolition job, Astbury's was:

> an offhand judgment given in a case where the defendants were not represented by counsel. Not a single authority is cited to support a view which would revolutionise the law relating to strikes if carried to its logical extent. Moreover ... the comment on the illegality of the General Strike was really extra-judicial. It was unnecessary for the learned Judge to consider this point as the defendants were clearly acting contrary to the rules of their own union.[27]

In his memoirs, Sir Henry Slesser, too, was politely scathing about both Simon's second parliamentary speech and the Astbury 'judgment'. On the former, he noted that Sir John had extended his 'doctrine of illegality' beyond breach of contract to encompass the 'degree of discomfort it inflicts upon the community', something that 'had never been suggested before'. As for Astbury, his:

judgment received the honour of a place in the Law Reports; unique, I think, in the case of unargued interlocutory proceedings, and has the further distinction of being irreconcilable with all other judgments ever pronounced on the Trade Disputes Act.[28]

Almost every other aspect of Sir John Simon's ever-evolving argument was subsequently neutralized.[29] To speculate about what was in the mind of Parliament when it passed the *Trade Disputes Act* was 'quite foreign to the accepted canons of statutory construction';[30] there was no need to prove that a general strike was a 'trade dispute' in accordance with the 1906 Act, for it was 'sufficient that it was called in furtherance of the dispute in the coal-mining industry';[31] and, finally, calling the strike 'an offence against the State' was meaningless in that it did not involve either treason, seditious conspiracy or criminal conspiracy.[32]

Mr Justice Astbury thus joined the pantheon of Labour bogeymen alongside Thomas Marlowe, the newspaper editor who had published the Zinoviev Letter during the 1924 general election. Ramsay MacDonald accused Astbury of abusing his office and reminding everyone 'that he has never tried to take a trade union fence without coming a cropper',[33] while the Labour MP Ellen Wilkinson spoke of judges finding law 'in the background of their unconscious economic prejudices'. 'The lawyers showed in the General Strike,' she added, 'that they will use every legal weapon they can discover to prevent a challenge being made to the divine rights of property.'[34]

But most of this learned analysis and political denigration lay in the future. At the time, Sir John Simon's second Commons speech and its weaponization of the Astbury judgment had an even more electric effect than his first. John Reith drafted but did not deliver an announcement to the effect that the BBC, 'an organisation within the Constitution', would be 'unable to permit anything which is contrary to the spirit of this judgement *[sic]*, and ... which might justify or prolong the General Strike'.[35]

'DISSOLVE THE T.U.C.!' screamed a typical headline in the *Daily Mail*:

It being now admitted definitely and clearly that the T.U.C. has no legal sanction ... why is the T.U.C. permitted to function any longer? Why is it not dissolved? Why is it allowed to sit in London issuing orders, directing what public services shall be carried on and what public services shall be forbidden, issuing 'permits,' pretending to the position of an alternative Government, and seeking to impose its will on the lawful, duly elected, and properly-constituted Government of the nation?[36]

The Independent Labour Party organizer John Paton recalled working:

> all that day in an atmosphere of increasing uncertainty; rumours multiplied and swirled around. There was talk that the judge's decision meant that the funds of the unions were liable to forfeiture; some even contended, with a hopeful gleam in their eyes, that the General Council would be arrested and thrown into prison.[37]

In a clear attempt to calm the General Council's nerves, Holford Knight, a criminal barrister and former Labour parliamentary candidate, left the following telephone message at the TUC's Eccleston Square HQ:

> Mr. Justice Astbury has not decided anything about a general strike ... The only question was whether a strike could be called without the authority of the Executive of the Union. All the rest of the judge's remarks are merely personal opinions which have no effect in law. It is sheer bluff to pretend otherwise, so this is the special bluff for today. I hope the Council are having continuous legal assistance on these matters, which are having a very prejudicial effect on the public mind.

'I despair,' Knight later told Walter Citrine, 'of getting the Labour Movement to pick their lawyers, in and out of Parl[iament], with greater care.'[38]

But even if there were understandable nerves, neither Simon nor Astbury had a direct impact on the TUC's decision-making. The Labour MP and railwaymen's leader Jimmy Thomas later recalled:

> Sir John Simon's statement was never once considered by the General Council, neither was all that balderdash about them being arrested, and all that kind of humbug. Nothing of that kind influenced anybody, or was even debated for a solitary moment. We concentrated on the single issue of an industrial dispute, how to do the best for the miners.[39]

The Astbury judgment, however, *was* considered by the Cabinet when it gathered at the House of Commons on the evening of 11 May. Having resolved to postpone its planned trades union legislation, premier Stanley Baldwin had also arranged for a question and answer in the House that evening:

> QUESTION. Does the Government intend to deal with the position of Trades Unions?
>
> PROPOSED ANSWER. The Government are not now contemplating any modification in existing trades union legislation, but they are considering the desirability of making clear what they believe to be now the law namely that a general strike is illegal.

Although clearly influenced by Sir John Simon's speech on 6 May, indeed the Attorney General had shown him a copy of the draft bill which Simon agreed to support provided it *declared* rather than *amended* existing strike law,[40] the Prime Minister now informed his colleagues that 'following the receipt of certain information' he had decided not to proceed with the planned Q&A.[41] Mr Justice Astbury had rendered it unnecessary.

14

THE JUDGEMENT OF SAMUEL

As soon as the Royal Commission on the Coal Industry published its report on 10 March 1926, its principal author and chairman, the Liberal statesman Sir Herbert Samuel, fled back to Italy with a boxful of books on philosophy. To 'settle down in solitude,' as he wrote to a friend, 'and get on with the writing which I had very happily begun when I was sent down my coal mine'.[1]

Sir Herbert was not allowed long to enjoy the Italian spring. During April he had followed events from Lake Garda with growing concern and, when the general strike began on 4 May, immediately made his way back to the UK. He travelled back via Paris, where he lunched with Chaim Weizmann (a future President of Israel), and arrived at Dover on the afternoon of 6 May. He had telegraphed ahead to Sir William Mitchell-Thomson, the Chief Civil Commissioner, who arranged for a driver. This turned out to be Major Henry Segrave, the 'most famous racing motorist of that day' with his 'powerful Sunbeam car'. After a quick stop to visit Sir Herbert's sister in Folkestone, they sped along a relatively new motorway and reached central London in just seventy minutes.[2]

Samuel took lodgings at the aptly named Reform Club and telephoned Jimmy Thomas, with whom he had established good relations during 1924, when the boisterous railwaymen's leader was Colonial Secretary in the first Labour government and Sir Herbert was approaching the end of his tenure as the UK's High Commissioner in Palestine. The timing for fortuitous. Never comfortable with the general strike, Thomas – one of the 'Big Three' at the Trades Union Congress – was increasingly open to any means of bringing it to a conclusion. As a result, he readily agreed to ask the TUC's negotiating committee if it would meet Sir Herbert. This, Thomas believed, was the escape route he and others had been waiting for.

With his moustache, side-parted hair and matinee idol looks, Herbert Louis Samuel cut a striking figure during the dramatic events of May 1926. Born in Liverpool in 1870, the youngest of five children, his German-Jewish ancestors had settled in England during the eighteenth century and became bankers: Edwin Samuel, Herbert's father, was a partner with his younger brother Montagu in the City firm of Samuel Montagu & Co. A year after Herbert's birth, the family moved from Liverpool to London as the firm prospered. When Edwin died suddenly in 1877, his accumulated wealth meant his wife and children did not even have to think about work.

Herbert Samuel thereafter enjoyed what his biographer called an 'untroubled, pampered childhood'. Raised in South Kensington and educated in Bloomsbury, he subsequently read modern history at Balliol College, Oxford. A significant influence was the first London County Council election of 1889, when Samuel campaigned on behalf of his older brother Stuart in Whitechapel, a working-class area with a significant Jewish migrant population. This encounter with grinding poverty – which was in stark contrast with his own privileged existence – led him to the Liberal Party, then the UK's main progressive force. Greatly influenced by the social thinking of Sidney and Beatrice Webb, what Samuel called the 'new Liberalism' emerged from a radical discussion group whose members included Ramsay MacDonald. Herbert's publication, *Liberalism: Its Principles and Proposals*, provided an 'intellectual foundation' for many of the social reforms subsequently enacted by Liberal governments during the early twentieth century.

In 1902 Samuel joined the House of Commons as the Liberal MP for Cleveland, an ironstone-mining constituency where he developed a strong following among the local workers. Never universally popular in Parliament, his alleged involvement with the insider-trading Marconi affair was pursued with 'a virulent edge of antisemitism'. Nevertheless, Samuel became Home Secretary in 1916 but lost his seat at the 1918 election.

An active Zionist, in 1920 Sir Herbert (he was knighted that year) visited Palestine for the first time and in April David Lloyd George approved his appointment as the UK's first High Commissioner under a League of Nations mandate. Samuel's main task was implementation of the 1917 Balfour Declaration, although none of his initiatives in support of Arab representation initiatives were taken up. By mid-1925, however, the Jewish 'national homeland' was firmly established and Arab nationalism relatively dormant. Although Sir Herbert wished to remain in Palestine to write philosophy, his successor as High Commissioner objected. He found himself back in the UK and tasked with chairing yet another Royal Commission on the coal industry.[3]

No one doubted Sir Herbert's motivation in returning to London under his own volition as the general strike got under way. Indeed, this was part of his appeal to the TUC as a prospective mediator. As well as Jimmy Thomas, Sir Herbert also reached out to his old colleagues on the Royal Commission, including Sir William Beveridge. They, however, believed even an 'informal intervention' could do no good, and, 'in the existing situation, might even do harm'. Samuel therefore decided to press on alone.[4]

A day after his return to London, Samuel met with Prime Minister Stanley Baldwin, Minister of Labour Sir Arthur Steel-Maitland, and the latter's permanent secretary, Sir Horace Wilson. At this meeting, he sketched out his proposals: an immediate end to the strike, agreement on reorganization of the coal industry, a TUC assurance that the coal dispute would be settled along the lines of the Samuel Commission report, continuation of a subsidy until the end of May and, finally, the reopening of the mines on the terms (wages and hours) in place prior to 30 April 1926. If this sounded pragmatic and practical, Baldwin and Steel-Maitland – in consultation with Neville Chamberlain and Lord Birkenhead – swiftly agreed (once Samuel had departed) that it would be inconceivable for the government to give this any sort of official blessing.[5]

In what even Winston Churchill considered 'too stiff and final' a letter to Samuel despatched the following day,[6] Steel-Maitland stated the government's position:

> They hold that the General Strike is unconstitutional and illegal ... In these circumstances I am sure that the Government will take the view that while they are bound most carefully and most

sympathetically to consider the form of any arrangement which a public man of your responsibility and experience may propose, it is imperative to make it plain that any discussion which you think proper to initiate is not clothed in even a vestige of official character.

In response, Sir Herbert put:

on record the assurance I gave you in conversation, that, in the discussions which I have had on the present situation, I have made it perfectly clear that I have been acting entirely on my initiative and without any kind of authorisation from the Government ... In any further conversations that may take place, I shall, of course, maintain the same attitude.[7]

While Steel-Maitland's declaration of illegality bore the unmistakable imprint of Sir John Simon's recent parliamentary intervention, this exchange hobbled the Samuel initiative from the start. Not only was there no departure from the government's consistent line on no negotiation without unconditional surrender, but all any subsequent proposals would receive was sympathetic consideration rather than executive action. Nevertheless, as Ellen Wilkinson observed, Sir Herbert remained 'perfectly willing to accept the diplomat's role', even if that meant allowing himself to be 'officially repudiated if that became more convenient to the Government'.[8]

Fresh from his conference with Baldwin et al., Samuel met the General Council's negotiating committee for the first time. To maintain discretion, Jimmy Thomas had arranged for this to take place at the grand Bryanston Square home of his friend Sir Abe Bailey, a South African mining magnate who had ties to Cecil Rhodes. Walter Citrine remembered marching up a 'fine marble staircase' and noticing paintings by Gainsborough, Reynolds and Lawrence. Waiting for him near the fireplace was Sir Herbert, 'standing with his hands behind his back and looking over his pince-nez'. When he mentioned the book on which he had been working in Italy, Thomas jokingly asked if it was about Palestine. No, replied Samuel, it was:

about the effect of religion on morality. It is about what is wrong with the world. The world is out of joint and I am trying to get down to fundamentals. I want to make it a short book and it is much harder to write a short book than a long one.

After recounting the work of his Royal Commission, Sir Herbert explained his thinking, chiefly that any revision of miners' wages ought to operate in parallel with reorganization of the coal industry. He readily agreed with TUC chairman Arthur Pugh's suggestion of a National Wages Board. Crucially, at this stage the TUC believed Samuel possessed authority to negotiate on the government's behalf. He and the negotiating committee then parted, with the latter returning to Eccleston Square separately to avoid giving 'press sleuths' a story.[9]

It was now the weekend. When the General Council met on the Saturday morning (8 May), Arthur Cook and Herbert Smith of the Miners' Federation of Great Britain (MFGB) demanded to be included in the talks they now understood to be taking place, although they were unaware that Sir Herbert Samuel was involved. Jack Bromley of the railwaymen's union, however, was unenthusiastic, exclaiming:

> By God, we are all in this now and I want to say to the miners, in a brotherly, comradely spirit, but straight ... that this is not a miners' fight now. I am willing to fight right along with them and to suffer as a consequence, but I am not going to be strangled by my friends.

Exasperated by this, the famously taciturn Herbert Smith retorted: 'If he wants to get out of this fight, well, I am not stopping him.' Things eventually cooled down and Smith said the MFGB would only insist on being present at 'definite negotiations' rather than mere 'conversations'.[10] The Labour leaders Ramsay MacDonald and Arthur Henderson also met with the miners separately and found Smith and Cook 'unimaginative but reasonable'.[11]

At three o'clock on the Saturday afternoon, the General Council's negotiating committee returned to the home of Sir Abe Bailey for another meeting with Samuel. Having now received Sir Arthur Steel-Maitland's missive, Sir Herbert reiterated his lack of government sanction. Samuel had therefore concluded that the only remaining option was to make a public statement regarding the terms on which he considered the strike might be settled, but only once he had agreement from the TUC. He also expressed frustration at both the government's response to the Royal Commission and the coal owners' inflexibility. 'There is only one epithet I can apply to the present position,' he concluded. 'It is a silly business.'[12]

The General Council's negotiating committee also had to decide whether to tell the Miners' Federation that Sir Herbert was involved. This they considered risky given Smith and Cook might insist on consulting their union's full executive or, worse, a full delegate conference. Later, there was a full meeting of the General Council at which MacDonald and Henderson were also present. In his diary, the Labour leader noted that Samuel's name was mentioned 'for the first time' and that the negotiating committee believed his proposals 'might be effective', albeit hampered by the fact that Stanley Baldwin had made clear he 'could hold neither direct nor indirect negotiations with anyone whilst [the] general strike lasted'. Rather indiscreetly, MacDonald then telephoned this news to the industrialist Sir Allan Smith and the former *Spectator* editor John St Loe Strachey.[13] The Leader of the Opposition also reached out to Conservative MP Sidney Herbert, the Prime Minister's PPS, who assured MacDonald of his willingness to receive constructive 'suggestions ... in a purely private & confidential way'.[14]

At Eccleston Square the following morning (Sunday 9 May), the General Council was clearly getting nervous. 'Unless the miners are prepared to accept a [wage] reduction in some form or other, it is no use going on,' Jimmy Thomas told Walter Citrine. As Citrine wrote in his diary, it was 'evident':

> that the General Council were coming to the conclusion that it was simply hopeless to continue the strike if the intention was that in no circumstances and in no conditions would the miners accept any reductions ... It will be said that the General Council have deserted them, but the position the miners are taking up is that while the direction of matters is in the hands of the General Council, the miners must be the people to decide as to whether they will return to work or not with a prospective reduction facing them. It will be a repetition of Black Friday, with the difference that we will have had the General Strike, and we will have realized either our strength or our impotence.

Citrine believed the 'logical thing' was to make the 'best conditions' while their members were 'solid'. 'We must retreat,' he added, 'if we have to retreat under compulsion, [we must do it] as an army and not as a rabble.' The General Council's acting secretary then lightened his mood by ruminating on his colleagues: Ernest Bevin, 'brawny of chest and broad of brow, swarthy of countenance', and of course Jimmy Thomas:

> always discovering new situations, with mysterious side glances and knowing looks endowed with facile entry into the innermost circles of Government. If we only knew what he knew! He had seen a Cabinet Minister that day in the House of Commons, looking very worried ... Or perhaps a well-known capitalist, whose name he withheld for reasons which we would all understand, had winked at him, whereupon the said James requires an urgent meeting of the Industrial Committee to debate the significance of the wink.

Other members of the General Council were 'somewhat bored, worried but far from rattled, almost in a state of coma'. Citrine also recalled a bizarre incident in which a man with 'rather sharp hawk-like features' turned up at Eccleston Square claiming to be called Rivett Carnac. In return for the princely sum of £1,000, he had a simple proposal:

> I want 100 trusted men and if you cannot find them, I can. I will arm them, take them along to Downing Street, shoot the members of the Cabinet and hold Princess Mary's children as hostages.

Smiling incredulously, Arthur Pugh said, 'but we don't do those things in the British trade union movement'. The interview then ended, after which Citrine and Pugh decided not to inform the police. Carnac (who went by several names) turned out to be a fraudster, drug addict and former felon who was, some weeks after the general strike, arrested for obtaining money under false pretences.[15]

Not content with one set of negotiations, the mercurial Jimmy Thomas then became involved in another. Lord Wimborne, like Sir Herbert Samuel a Liberal and former vice-regal appointee (in Ireland rather than Palestine), was so disturbed by the division arising from the general strike that he arranged a weekend lunch party at Wimborne House near the Ritz. In attendance were 'representatives' from each side, the coal owners Lord Gainford and the Marquess of Londonderry, as well as Ethel Snowden (deputizing for her apparently sick husband Philip, the former Chancellor) and Osbert Sitwell, whose brainchild the gathering had been.

According to his biographer, the normally ebullient Jimmy Thomas arrived last, looking 'worried and tired almost beyond bearing'. He ranted about Sir John Simon's recent speech on the legality of the strike but emerged from the luncheon party with renewed optimism regarding the Samuel initiative. This was artificially fortified when Selwyn Davies, Lord Wimborne's secretary, passed word of the gathering to his fellow Welshman Tom Jones, the Deputy Cabinet Secretary. With the assistance of Lord Reading (a former Viceroy of India), Thomas and Davies prepared yet another 'formula'. Even after Baldwin tossed this aside 'with some impatience',[16] Thomas nevertheless convinced himself the Samuel plan would, after all, prove acceptable to the government. All that remained, therefore, was to obtain the agreement of the miners.[17] At a weekend rally in Hammersmith, Thomas also sent a coded signal to the government, stating:

> The responsibility is indeed a heavy one. But there will be a graver responsibility on whichever sides fail to recognise the moment when an honourable settlement can be arrived at. That moment must be accepted and everyone must work to that end.[18]

Osbert Sitwell recalled Wimborne and Reading pressing Thomas with 'extreme urgency' to call off the strike either on Tuesday evening or Wednesday morning, ostensibly because the government had decided to arrest members of the General Council. This can safely be dismissed as a product of Sitwell's overactive imagination,[19] although Chips Channon picked up the same rumour on 10 May.[20] Walter Citrine recalled witnessing Thomas 'in a high state of excitement', convinced the strike had to be called off because he had received the 'fullest assurances' that whatever was agreed 'would be carried into effect'. Citrine got the impression Thomas had been in direct conference with Baldwin or even His Majesty the King.[21]

After writing 'hard for about 2½ hours' on the morning of Sunday 9 May, Sir Herbert Samuel completed a full draft of his proposals. 'The strike is intensely unpopular and was a most foolish undertaking on the part of the Labour leaders,' he told his wife wearily. 'They know that it must necessarily fail, and are grateful to me for trying to find a way out for them.'[22] What became known as the 'Samuel Memorandum' was placed before the General Council of the TUC that same day. This was the first time Herbert Smith and Arthur Cook of the Miners' Federation had been asked for their opinion of a definite proposition, but it merely served to reawaken their suspicions regarding the whole exercise. 'The Miners had had plenty of Sir Herbert Samuel,' Smith later observed grumpily, 'we knew him quite well and did not want any further dealings with him.'[23] Sir Herbert then held further meetings with Jimmy Thomas, Sir William Beveridge (one of his Royal Commissioners) and leaders of employers' organizations, but there was a growing sense of futility.

On the afternoon of Monday 10 May, Arthur Pugh and Walter Citrine attempted to break the logjam by taking Herbert Smith and Arthur Cook to meet Sir Herbert personally. After being 'badgered' by Smith over aspects of the Royal Commission's report, Citrine recalled Samuel saying:

> I hate this business. I was content in Italy writing on philosophy, and I have come here not at anyone's invitation, but merely to try to do my best as a good citizen, and as chairman of the Coal Commission, to see whether I can put things straight. No one else is doing anything at all. The Government has closed the door and you have done the same. I am not at all happy. I was brought into this business of the Commission against my own inclinations and I had to record the facts. It is not that I want to see miners' wages reduced. I think they are too horribly low altogether.

'Grim old Herbert [Smith],' recalled Citrine, 'not the slightest bit impressed by this, returned, "If I could have gone to the same school as you, I would have had it up here," tapping his forehead'. This at least lightened the mood:

> Samuel smiled approvingly. 'Oh, you need not be afraid of that,' he said, 'if everyone had the same capacity for argument as you, Herbert, no one would ever get anything done in this world. They would have too many arguments against it.' Old Herbert [Smith] lay back on the expensive couch, luxuriantly up-holstered, and rocked with laughter ... Samuel shook his head, 'No, but when it is a case of Herbert against Herbert, then there is bound to be a tug of war.'[24]

However convivial, this latest meeting had achieved nothing. 'Three hours of argument in our conference,' recalled Samuel, 'left Herbert

Smith's attitude on every point precisely what it had been at the beginning.'[25] As far as the emotional – and increasingly suspicious – Arthur Cook was concerned, Sir Herbert's involvement was nothing more than the creation of 'some pretext to justify calling off the General Strike'.[26]

Herbert Smith remained as 'dour and as dogged' when the General Council met the full executive of the Miners' Federation that evening. One miner after another got up and, 'speaking with intensity of feeling', affirmed that the miners could not countenance another wage reduction. Throwing 'out his hands imploringly', Cook said he realized the 'sacrifice' other trade unionists had made. 'You do not want to bring the miners down,' he said. 'Gentlemen, don't do it.' Walter Citrine recalled glancing round at:

> the hard-set faces of the miners, and I could not see the slightest sign of any compromise on any one of them. [Jimmy] Thomas sat beside me at the table with his head resting on his hands. He tells me he cannot sleep at night, and has the exhausted look of a man completely worn out. Old Herbert sat unmoved, stolid, leaning over his papers with his glasses on the end of his nose, not in the least influenced.

Arthur Pugh then made what Citrine considered 'one of the most intense statements he has ever made'. While the strike had once 'primarily been a miners' question', he said, it had 'now ceased to be a matter exclusively for them, and every trade union representative in the room had to face up to his own responsibility'. If, continued Pugh, they were going forward on the assumption that the miners were to look at the matter 'entirely from their own standpoint' then they must bring proceedings to a close. 'It is no use talking,' he added. 'We must go on with this struggle until the process of attrition has brought the whole trade union movement to its knees.'[27]

In response, Herbert Smith asked what guarantees the General Council had that the government or coal owners would actually implement Samuel's proposals. This made the others angry, but the much-maligned Smith had shrewdly identified the plan's central weakness. In his diary, Ramsay MacDonald recorded what he called the latest 'struggle' with the miners:

Their stiffness arises from various circumstances (a) they trust neither the Government nor the coal owners (b) they have been bound by words & slogans & will not face the objective facts.[28]

As the miners continued to deliberate in private, the General Council fretted about the likely recriminations if they decided to act unilaterally. 'Some would say we had sold the pass,' recalled Citrine, that 'we had betrayed the movement.'[29] The fruitless discussion ended at 1.10 a.m. with another 'no' from the Miners' Federation. 'The end comes & a sorry one it is,' MacDonald told his diary:

> The T.U.C. is to get its own views in draft for the morning. They have little appreciation yet of the difficulties they have to surmount in declaring the strike off & returning to work. [Jimmy] Thomas on the verge of a collapse & was worrying about railway accidents & a detective being put into his house to guard him.[30]

Walter Citrine remarked bitterly that the miners had failed to 'rise above their restricted vision of their own coal-fields'.[31]

Tuesday 11 May was what MacDonald called 'the final day', the point at which the TUC's General Council realized 'there was no end to the road on which it was travelling'.[32] That morning a 'very depressed' Jimmy Thomas rang Sir Herbert to say things did not look good. He (Thomas) was 'wearing down' and lacked what Citrine called his 'customary forceful driving manner', while Ernest Bevin was now determined to press on without the miners.[33] At 10 a.m. Samuel went to the Ministry of Labour to dictate a long letter to the Prime Minister. In this, he placed the blame squarely on the miners. After correctly identifying Herbert Smith (rather than Arthur Cook) as the 'dominating' and most 'immovable' influence, Sir Herbert concluded that the TUC had been 'deceiving themselves when they informed me that there was no longer an absolute [miners'] veto upon any kind of [wage] reduction'.[34]

The letter was never sent, for that afternoon Samuel was told of a decisive breach between the General Council's negotiating committee and the Miners' Federation of Great Britain. Arthur Pugh, 'tired, worn and a little bit sick of things', told the miners 'they had to have it or leave it'.[35] Herbert Smith asked if that constituted the

General Council's 'unanimous decision' and Pugh affirmed that it was. 'I appealed to them,' Smith later recalled, 'as I never appealed to anybody in my life to consider it.'[36] When Sir Herbert met the General Council's negotiating committee again at 3 p.m., he found:

> they had finally decided (so they said) to settle the matter, and if the miners did not agree, to require them to do so. The basis was to be a letter from me conveying a memorandum of the points we had agreed in our conversations. They wanted a few points added, mostly in order to make things easier for the miners. I was able to accept all but one, in the form they proposed, or an amended form. They did not improve the memorandum, but there was no harm in them, and it was necessary. The one I rejected was a paragraph about no victimisation after the strike was over. I said that was not my business. They agreed and did not press it.[37]

Importantly, Walter Citrine's understanding was that once Sir Herbert's letter was despatched and the General Council had formally called off the general strike, the government would then 'arrange for a withdrawal of the lock-outs'. Samuel, he wrote in his diary, 'appeared to be speaking with knowledge of the Government's attitude'.[38] Ernest Bevin also appeared under the impression that Samuel's proposals would be accepted, the notices withdrawn and negotiations resumed.[39] As Gordon Phillips concluded in his study of the general strike, the TUC had developed a 'psychological need' to believe this was so.[40] Only the Labour MP Arthur Henderson was more realistic, believing that if Samuel's memorandum was published but not implemented then public opinion would perhaps turn in their favour.[41]

Sir Herbert then returned to his brother Stuart's Mayfair home to draft a final version of his memorandum. Ever conscientious, he also summoned his fellow Royal Commissioners one final time. 'They were very lukewarm, and indeed timid, about the whole undertaking,' he recalled sadly, 'but made one or two important suggestions as to form.'[42] Back at Eccleston Square, exasperation with the miners jostled with admiration. As the Fabian intellectual Harold Laski wrote to a friend:

> The miners were impossible. They never budged an inch throughout. They have no plans, and, if they had their way, the T.U.C. would

be out until Domesday. Even now, they have nothing to say except that they won't budge. I have certainly never seen more hopeless (tho' more courageous) leadership than theirs.[43]

Throughout that final day, Arthur Cook – who generally dealt with reporters given Herbert Smith's unhelpful brevity – did his best to keep up a cheerful demeanour. When the executive of the Miners' Federation finally adjourned at 6.30 p.m., he said that 'whatever bridge was found it must be one that would secure the status quo at least for the miners'.[44] The General Council's publicity committee was also asked to take 'immediate steps' to 'counter the rumour which has spread round the East End of London … to the effect that the strike is ended'.[45]

It had been arranged for Sir Herbert Samuel to send his final memorandum to the General Council by 8 p.m., at which point the TUC would appeal once more to the Miners' Federation for its concurrence in the termination of the general strike. The final document called for a renewal of the government's subsidy for a 'reasonable period', a National Wages Board and 'sufficient assurances' that reorganization would accompany any 'revision' of wages. A covering letter reiterated that Samuel could 'give no assurances' of action by the government.[46]

The Miners' Federation and General Council then had their final joint meeting. Ramsay MacDonald's diary records the exhaustion and tetchiness on both sides, so much so that 'silent instants in speeches' proved 'painful'.[47] After three hours, the miners retired to consider the Samuel Memorandum for the last time. As he left Eccleston Square, Arthur Cook 'came out whistling cheerfully' and misled reporters by telling them everyone was heading home for the night.[48] Herbert Smith, recalled MacDonald, had been so 'brutal in his contempt and opposition' that once he and other members of the Miners' Federation had departed, members of the General Council made 'angry speeches upon their stupidity [and] ingratitude':

> The [General Council] was absolutely unanimous & angry & determined. We waited long & the miners returned at 12.45[a.m.] with a rude rejection. Smith also said that as they had not been consulted in the latter stages of the negotiation they might not consider themselves bound by their promise to continue to act with the T.U.C. what ever its decision may be.[49]

This provoked even more angry remarks about the miners not accepting their responsibilities to the broader trade union movement. 'I shall take my share of the blame,' declared Jimmy Thomas, 'but when the time comes for me to explain, I will neither excuse nor apologize. I will justify my part. I will remember that 455,000 railwaymen are on the streets.' When Herbert Smith and Arthur Cook once again demanded to know what guarantees there were that Samuel's proposals would be put into effect, Thomas replied with typical (but incorrect) flourish: 'You may not trust my word, but will you not accept the word of a British gentleman who has been Governor of Jerusalem?'[50] The former High Commissioner was at that moment waiting impatiently at his brother's home for confirmation that his memorandum had been accepted as a basis for calling off the strike. No such message arrived.[51]

At that moment, Patrick Gower (one of Stanley Baldwin's private secretaries), apparently aware something was afoot, called to ask if Walter Citrine had any 'news' for the Prime Minister. 'He has been sitting up for you,' he remarked almost sweetly. 'Do you want to see him this evening?' Although there was not much of the evening left, Citrine asked Gower to hold while he conferred with the General Council. After a few minutes' consultation, Citrine was told he 'should say we would see him [Baldwin] tomorrow at twelve noon, and that was a firm decision'. 'All right,' replied Gower, 'we may take that as fixed.' 'Our fate was decided in those few seconds,' Citrine later wrote in his diary. 'Our decision to see the Prime Minister meant plainly to them the calling-off of the General Strike.'[52]

After leaving Eccleston Square at 1.40 a.m., Ramsay MacDonald bleakly reflected on 'one of the most lamentable adventures in ... our labour history':

> There will be a mess & I am sure the men will not understand their leaders. The return to work will be dangerous, the Churchill gang will shout & yell, provocation will be rampant, our troubles may be beginning ... The Samuel document may not be worth the paper it is written upon, but it has enabled the [General Council] to face the inevitable. My task now is to protect the political party from the same crowd rush of emotion which has brought the [General Council] to this sorry pass.[53]

15

'A GROTESQUE TRAGEDY'

While the Trades Union Congress and Labour leadership resigned themselves to their fates, if anything the mood at Downing Street had brightened. 'Without being unduly optimistic, I think we may say that the tide has turned,' a government spokesman told reporters on the morning of Tuesday 11 May. 'There is a tendency all over the country for the strikers to drift back to work.'[1]

There were certainly reports to that effect, although these only began to reach the General Council's intelligence committee the following day.[2] So inevitable did the end appear, members of the Cabinet began to press their views upon the Prime Minister. There must, warned Winston Churchill, the excitable Chancellor of the Exchequer, 'be a clear interval between the calling off of the General Strike and the resumption of the coal negotiations':

> The first tonight – the second to-morrow. But nothing simultaneous and concurrent. That will I am sure be fatal. No question of subsidy even for a fortnight can be mixed with the withdrawal of the General Strike. To-night surrender. Tomorrow magnanimity. On the interval between these two depends the whole result of this deep national conflict.[3]

Churchill had jumped the gun, but only just. A buoyant London Stock Exchange shared his optimism; that day Wall Street bought so much sterling that it appreciated to $4.86 for the first time since the beginning of the crisis.[4]

At 9.30 a.m. on Wednesday 12 May, meanwhile, Walter Citrine was perturbed when Sir Herbert Samuel's memorandum failed to arrive after another 'little misunderstanding'.[5] At ten o'clock, however, the prearranged letters were finally exchanged. The Prime Minister and Sir Arthur Steel-Maitland (the Minister of Labour) received copies at eleven o'clock and the press an hour after that. Sir Herbert's was addressed to Arthur Pugh:

> I have made it clear to your committee from the outset that I have been acting entirely on my own initiative, have received no authority from the Government, and can give no assurances on their behalf. I am of opinion that the proposals embodied in the memorandum are suitable for adoption, and are likely to promote a settlement of the differences in the coal industry. I shall strongly recommend their acceptance by the Government when the negotiations are renewed.

A reply in the names of Pugh and Walter Citrine was full of similarly empty assumptions:

> The General Council having carefully considered your letter of to-day and the memorandum attached to it, concurred in your opinion that it offers a basis on which the negotiations upon the conditions in the coal industry can be renewed. They are taking measures to terminate the general strike, relying upon the public assurances of the Prime Minister as to the steps that would follow. They assume that during the resumed negotiations the subsidy will be renewed, and that the lock-out notices to the miners will be immediately withdrawn.

Meanwhile, Arthur Cook issued an 'emphatic denial' that the Miners' Federation also desired the strike be called off,[6] while rudely rebuffing Ramsay MacDonald's request to attend its executive meeting at 10 a.m.[7]

Some members of the Cabinet were also on edge. On learning the Prime Minister was to meet the General Council's negotiating committee at noon, the Home Secretary, Sir William Joynson-Hicks, wrote with the 'concurrence' of Samuel Hoare (Secretary of State for Air), Sir John Gilmour (Secretary for Scotland) and Philip Cunliffe-Lister (President of the Board of Trade) 'to say that we are very nervous as to the risk of even appearing to enter into any negotiations with the T.U.C. until there has been an unconditional withdrawal of the

General Strike'.[8] The General Council, meanwhile, was having 'an unpleasant time' in joint session with the Miners' Federation. Only at 11.45 a.m. did the latter deliver their final rejection of the Samuel Memorandum, which left Ernest Bevin just enough time to grab a taxi and join his colleagues at Number 10. Walter Citrine, who drove there with Jimmy Thomas, noticed troops being drilled – some with machine guns and gas masks – at Wellington Barracks. 'You know, Walter, this is a terrible business,' Thomas remarked darkly. 'We shall have awful recriminations now.'[9]

After making their way through a battery of photographers, reporters and sightseers, Citrine and Thomas met a 'fed up' Arthur Pugh and a gloomy Bevin, who told them the miners had refused to resume work. When Sir Horace Wilson, permanent secretary at the Ministry of Labour, sought an assurance the strike was definitely being terminated before allowing them to see the Prime Minister, Bevin exploded: 'For Christ's sake let's call it on again if this is the position.' Thomas briskly confirmed they had 'come to call the strike off' and Wilson let them proceed.[10]

In the Cabinet room at 12.20 p.m., a 'haggard and drawn' Prime Minister, flanked by colleagues including Sir Arthur Steel-Maitland, Lord Birkenhead and Colonel Lane-Fox (the Secretary for Mines), welcomed them with 'obvious anxiety'.[11] 'In came 30 very sorry looking dogs,' noted William Bridgeman, 'very different from the rather truculent & self-satisfied men we had seen a fortnight ago.'[12] 'It was so humiliating,' added Lord Birkenhead in his own account, 'that some instinctive breeding made one unwilling even to look at them.'[13]

Stanley Baldwin asked if Arthur Pugh would be 'good enough to make a statement', in response to which the TUC chairman rambled for several minutes. When the Prime Minister asked if this meant the general strike was to be called off 'forthwith', Pugh replied: 'Forthwith. That means immediately. There is just a point about the actual arrangement, but that is in effect what it means.' Walter Citrine noticed the palpable 'relief' of the premier and his colleagues. Baldwin thanked God for their decision, adding that although it was not 'a moment for lengthy discussion' he intended to summon his Cabinet and 'lose no time in using every endeavour to … ensure a just and lasting settlement'. Anxious to extract some concrete assurances, Jimmy Thomas hoped the TUC's 'big thing' (the decision to call off the strike) would be responded to in 'a big way', while Bevin, irritated at Thomas's vagueness and speaking in a 'confident, almost aggressive tone', asked the Prime Minister if he would make a 'general request' for immediate 'reinstatement' of the strikers and a withdrawal of the miners' lock-out notices. Baldwin was noncommittal, merely saying: 'I shall do my part and I have no doubt you will do yours.' He then tried to bring the meeting to a close, only for a 'persistent' Bevin to ask if they would meet again soon. An obviously impatient premier said he thought it 'may be that whatever decision I come to the House of Commons may be the best place in which to say it'.[14]

The General Council's uneasiness increased as they left the Cabinet room. While Citrine agreed a press statement with Tom Jones, the Deputy Cabinet Secretary, he got the 'uncomfortable feeling' ministers wanted 'to snatch the appearance of a victory'. The War Secretary Sir Laming Worthington-Evans demanded the statement include the word 'forthwith', but Citrine argued for 'today'. Citrine's discomfort increased further when he overhead Bolton Eyres-Monsell, the Conservative Chief Whip, itching to broadcast the statement, to which was hastily added a line 'saying men must not resume work except on the instructions of their unions'.[15]

Citrine then found Arthur Pugh in the garden between Numbers 10 and 11 Downing Street talking to Stanley Baldwin and Sir Arthur Steel-Maitland, the latter looking 'like a petulant schoolboy'. There was, however, 'no sign of jubilation' among the animated Cabinet members. Winston Churchill simply remarked: 'Thank God it is over, Mr. Pugh.'[16] Only it was not over. Sir Herbert Samuel later encountered an exhausted Jimmy Thomas 'almost weeping' because the government had not given a 'definite promise' regarding the withdrawal of lock-out notices.[17]

The normally publicity hungry Thomas ignored reporters as he left Downing Street, and at 1.10 p.m. a government official and Walter Citrine emerged to read the statement that the strike was at an end. 'Is it unconditional?' asked an 'excited' foreign journalist, but the TUC's acting secretary did not immediately reply. As journalists sped off to file their copy, Citrine added the feeble qualification 'in order to resume negotiations'. Churchill, meanwhile, disappeared into Number 11 'with a cheerful smile'.[18]

At the BBC's Savoy Hill studios John Reith was reading a bulletin when his colleague Stuart Hibberd received a 'tape' message with the breaking news. As the BBC historian Asa Briggs recounted:

> He ran down to the studio with it, exactly as it had come through, and after Reith had reached the end of the paragraph he was reading, pushed it in front of him at the microphone. Reith paused, read it through and reflected, then signed to Hibberd for a pencil. Quickly he scribbled on the paper 'Get this confirmed by 10 Downing Street'. Some ten minutes later Hibberd obtained the necessary confirmation, and Reith announced the end of the strike to the whole country.[19]

'It was rather wonderful to have been the first to give the news,' Reith recorded in his diary. 'I cannot pretend that I am not disappointed in some ways, and I have no doubt this is wrong. It is, however, great fun running a crisis.'[20] *The Times* produced its only ever afternoon edition while, aptly, a cartoon in that day's *British Gazette* was captioned 'Under Which Flag?' John Bull was depicted in front of a Union Jack, arms defiantly folded and looking at a trade unionist holding a 'general strike' banner. 'One of these flags has got to come down,' he was saying, 'and it won't be mine.'[21]

Number 10 had also telephoned Lord Stamfordham, the King's private secretary, to inform him that the 'whole position has changed'.[22] In his diary, George recorded:

> At 1.0 got the good news that the T.U.C. had been to the Prime Minister & informed him that the general strike was forthwith called off unconditionally. It is indeed a great relief to me as I have been very anxious about the situation. Our old country can well be proud of itself, as during the last 9 days there has been a strike in which 4 million men have been affected, not a shot has been fired & no one killed, it shows what wonderful people we are.

A contented King-Emperor then passed the good news to Queen Mary, arranged some stamps and received the Air Secretary Samuel Hoare, who told him 'the Gov[ernment]t. have remained firm, &

backed up by the people, have won a great victory for law & order'.[23] Cryptically, Hoare's diary notes also recorded the sovereign speaking of 'letters to him (abdication)' and about the prospect of the Prince of Wales arbitrating in the dispute.[24] With all his 'heart', the King later congratulated his Prime Minister and government:

> on having terminated the dangerous crisis we have experienced during the past ten days. This success is largely due to your own untiring patience and wise determination to abide by what you believed to be in the best and truest interests of the people by whose sufferings you have been elected to govern. These sentiments will, I feel sure, be shared by the country at large.

Added in the monarch's own hand was the postscript: 'I trust you are not feeling the strain too much, after all you have gone through.'[25] Baldwin replied in rather platitudinous terms, saying he was 'touched ... beyond measure' and 'inspired with renewed confidence' to face the challenge of restoring 'peace in the coal industry'.[26]

There was also a message for the King's subjects, drafted by Lord Birkenhead and revised by Lord Stamfordham:

> The nation has just passed through a period of great anxiety ... At such a moment it is supremely important to bring together all my people to confront the difficult situation which still remains ... Let us forget whatever elements of bitterness the events of the past few days may have created, only remembering how steady and orderly the country has remained, though severely tested, and forthwith address ourselves to the task of bringing into being a peace which will be lasting, because, forgetting the past, it looks only to the future with the hopefulness of a united people. GEORGE, R.I.[27]

When Baldwin emerged from Number 10 following lunch, he exclaimed 'I say' at the sight of hundreds of press and cameramen. As he made for his car, Clementine Churchill emerged from Number 11 and shouted 'Hooray!' To shouts of 'Good old Baldwin', the premier then made his way to Parliament with some well-wishers running after his car 'shouting and waving all the way down to the House'.[28]

When the Commons met at 2.45 p.m., the Prime Minister was cheered as he appeared from behind the Speaker's Chair and, watched by the Prince of Wales, Duke of York and Archbishop of Canterbury from the peers' gallery, declared:

> The peace that I believe has come – the victory that has been won, is a victory of the common sense, not of any one part of the country, but the common sense of the best part of the whole of the United Kingdom, and it is of the utmost importance at a moment like this that the whole British people should not look backwards, but forwards – that we should resume our work in a spirit of co-operation, putting behind us all malice and all vindictiveness.

Clearly sharing the TUC's concerns, Ramsay MacDonald asked if Baldwin could 'do many things of a practical and detailed nature to promote that good feeling'. The Prime Minister dissembled and insisted a further statement that day would be 'impossible'.[29] Angry at the premier for omitting a 'generous gesture or recognition of those who had borne the burden of making peace in the midst of war', MacDonald later (and privately) gave him 'a bit of my mind'. The Leader of the Opposition clearly realized the strike's termination had not been well handled. 'What is the value of the Samuel document?' he later ruminated in his diary. 'That troubles me.'[30]

Back at Eccleston Square, Ernest Bevin had also belatedly realized the TUC had placed too great an emphasis on Sir Herbert's mediatory role. He wondered if they had just 'committed suicide' and whether thousands of strikers would now be victimized 'as a result of this day's work'.[31] Telegrams poured in from districts wanting to know the terms of the settlement. 'The irony,' wrote a depressed Walter Citrine, 'is that we could not tell them.'[32] The South Wales Miners' Federation expressed its 'disgust' at the General Council's 'treacherous action'; Croydon's Council of Action called it 'a great betrayal of the whole working class'; and the Rhondda's as the 'blackest betrayal in history'.[33] At about five o'clock, several motor cars, some 'filled with young fellows ... in Fascist outfit', drove rapidly in procession outside the TUC's headquarters. When a crowd tried to stop them, Citrine feared a 'very ugly clash' before some police officers succeeded in clearing them away.[34]

At Edinburgh's central strike committee, the student and miner's daughter Jennie Lee recalled being 'huddled together' in a corner of their improvised office, 'stunned and listless, demoralised by the utter absolute fiasco of it all'. She and others 'ended the day with a cursing competition. I was shocked by the language I suddenly discovered I knew.'[35] Also downcast were the 'Dover Dockers'. An 'air of depression' settled upon the undergraduate volunteers as rumours of the strike's termination spread, news confirmed by the continental edition of the *Daily Mail* when it arrived from Calais. The words 'General Strike Ended' had been stamped on the edge of its front page just before it crossed the channel.[36] In his memoirs, Sir Herbert Samuel recalled watching newspaper sellers 'running down the streets calling out the news, and groups of people hurrying from the houses and shops to buy the little broadsheets'.[37]

That evening, John Reith was at the BBC studios again, this time contriving 'to invest the proceedings with an air of pure theatre'. After reading messages from the King and the Prime Minister, the craggy Scot followed with 'a little thing of our own':

> As for the BBC we hope your confidence in and goodwill to us have not suffered. We have laboured under certain difficulties, the full story of which may be told some day ... In going to work tomorrow or the next day, could we not all go as fellow-craftsmen, united in a determination to pick up the broken pieces, to repair the gaps and build up the walls of a more enduring city – the city revealed to the mystic eyes of William Blake.

Reith then recited Blake's 'Jerusalem' while an orchestra initially played quietly in the background. As he concluded, it 'came in with full orchestra and chorus'.[38]

The next day – Thursday 13 May – the situation seemed, if anything, worse. Not only did newspaper headlines drive home the strike's unconditional end ('Surrender of the Revolutionaries,' stormed the *Daily Mail*; 'Revolution Routed') but at Eccleston Square there was what Ramsay MacDonald called 'utter confusion'.[39] Strikers trying to return to work found themselves refused or admitted only if they accepted a wage reduction, other new terms of service, and in some cases even an undertaking to leave their union.[40] In response, Ernest Bevin sent instructions to his Transport and General Workers' Union that its members were to remain on strike. Not every employer, to be fair, took such advantages. At the Sunningend Aircraft Works in

Cheltenham, for example, management reinstated all employees who had struck on the same pay and conditions.[41]

While weakly protesting about certain employers 'deliberately and maliciously defying his Majesty's appeal for peace',[42] the TUC's General Council issued a statement via the *British Worker* which, unhelpfully, gave the impression the government had accepted the Samual Memorandum:

> The General Strike has ended. It has not failed. It has made possible the resumption of negotiations in the coal industry, and the continuance, during negotiations, of the financial assistance given by the Government. You came out together, in accordance with the instructions of the executives of your unions. Return together on their instructions, as and when they are given.[43]

An 'anxious' King fretted about workers having 'practically struck' a second time,[44] while Kingsley Game told his wife that London felt 'rattled', the 'general atmosphere of the streets' appearing 'angry and depressed'. 'One felt,' he added, 'that anything might happen.'[45] At a meeting of the Parliamentary Labour Party, Ramsay MacDonald found his MPs 'dismayed and unhappy' and urged them to 'refuse rigidly to take responsibility for anything' but instead use the House of Commons to secure a settlement. 'Everyone,' he added, was 'disturbed by [the] position in which [the] miners [have been] left.'[46] Perhaps feeling some good news was in order, Buckingham Palace announced that the 'fourth lady in the land', the Duke and Duchess of York's recent arrival, was to be named Elizabeth Alexandra Mary.[47] The King also decided to cancel that year's Trooping the Colour, the strike having prevented erection of the necessary terracing at Horse Guards.[48]

When the House of Commons adjourned on the evening of 13 May, the Labour frontbencher Arthur Henderson wanted to press for a vote of censure in the government, but the Leader of the Opposition's object was to extract from Baldwin 'some more pieties about peace and to make it plain [the] unions [were] not beaten'.[49] MacDonald did not pull his punches:

> The Prime Minister spoke yesterday. There is, unfortunately, a great contrast between what he said yesterday and what is in the

'British Gazette' this morning. I think it is a great pity that that should be so, a profound pity ... If there is any attempt to smash up trade unionism, if any section of the country, or any foolish person in the country thinks that after the events of last week and yesterday he can scrape the faces of trade unionists in the dust, he is very much mistaken. We want a settlement.

This clearly had an effect. In reply, Stanley Baldwin said he would:

not countenance any attack on the part of any employers to use this present occasion for trying in any way to get reductions in wages below those in force before the strike commenced or any increase of hours ... It would be impossible, in our highly organised and highly developed system of industry, to carry on unless you had organisations which could speak for and bind the parties on both sides.[50]

Cabinet had met earlier that day to discuss – and swiftly reject – the Samuel Memorandum. Herbert Smith of the Miners' Federation of Great Britain told Baldwin he was 'finished' with Sir Herbert Samuel, who Evan Williams of the Mining Association said had done a 'very great disservice' by 'butting in'.[51] The TUC's General Council, meanwhile, continued to delude itself, arguing that Sir Herbert's 'mediatorial intervention' had 'saved the Government from the fruits of its own reckless folly'.[52] Already depressed at his failure, that morning Samuel had discovered his brother Stuart's lifeless body. He had died in his sleep.[53]

By Friday 14 May, Ramsay MacDonald's mood had brightened, and he felt the unions were 'getting out of this all right':

Party very pleased with way the business in the House has been handled. It was doubtful & critical but it now sees after the event that handling was all right. Some of the doubtful ones have been to tell me. [Jimmy] Thomas rung me & spoke through tears. He had been photographed with the railway managers & feels that the old happy world has returned. He would sing Hallelujah![54]

At 4 p.m. the Prime Minister announced to the House of Commons that the railways had arrived at an agreement, negotiations with the dockers were proceeding and that he himself had prepared proposals for settling the coal stoppage which would be submitted to both parties later that day. 'It was the final culminating scene,' gushed the Conservative MP Duff Cooper, 'in the greatest personal and public triumph that any Prime Minister has ever had.'[55] To the socialist activist Fenner Brockway, however, the railway agreement was an 'utter humiliation', the railwaymen's representatives, led by Jimmy Thomas, having acknowledged 'wrongful action' and 'promising, like naughty schoolboys, never to do it again'.[56]

The government's proposals amounted to an immediate wage cut for the miners but mitigated for a short period by a further subsidy of £3 million, district rather than national pay agreements, and compulsory arbitration rather than collective bargaining to settle any disputes.[57] Predictably, neither the miners nor coal owners responded enthusiastically. The King, although now considerably more relaxed, correctly feared a coal settlement would 'take some time'.[58]

By the weekend of 15/16 May there had been a general resumption of work. As soon as the strike was called off on the 12th, the recruitment of special constables had ceased, and the Supply and Transport Committee had been wound down. Food convoys continued until Saturday 15 May, but two days after that both troops and volunteers vacated the London Docks. Writing in her diary, Beatrice Webb reflected that the failure of the strike had shown what 'a sane people the British are ... hopelessly good-natured and [full of] common sense, to which the British workman adds pigheadedness, jealousy and stupidity'. The nine days, she added, had been 'a grotesque tragedy'.[59]

16

Afterlives

Although the 'song' of the general strike had ended, its melody lingered on for several decades. Indeed, the strains could still be heard within this author's lifetime. The dramatic events of May 1926 also impacted its main protagonists in different and often surprising ways. The tempo of politics – industrial, parliamentary, cultural – had been changed.

Although Beatrice Webb fretted about the 'thoroughly unwholesome life' led by senior members of the Trades Union Congress during the nine days,[1] Jimmy Thomas lived until he was seventy-four, remaining general secretary of the National Union of Railwaymen until 1931 and returning to government as Colonial and Dominions Secretary on and off until 1936. He wrote to Ramsay MacDonald towards the end of May 1926 saying he was 'feeling very sad, as recent events are a nightmare to me', but adding wryly that some TUC leaders were already endeavouring to 'shelve their responsibility'.[2] Widely blamed for the strike's sudden end, Thomas relished the opportunity to defend his actions. Early in 1927 he penned a series of 'frank and trenchant articles' for the popular weekly magazine *Answers*, with headlines like 'How the Miners Were Led to Disaster', 'Why the T.U.C. Threw Up the Sponge' and, finally, 'A Plea for the Ballot-Box and for a New Spirit in British Industry'.[3]

Ernest Bevin also angrily rejected myriad criticisms. The historian Keith Laybourn distilled these to three main charges: that the TUC's General Council had betrayed the miners, that it was not committed to the struggle, and that the strike was winnable. He judged that the first was 'debatable', the second 'correct' and the third 'clearly wrong'.

At the General Council's own private 'inquest' in January 1927, its statement that it had 'no excuses to offer and no apologies to make for the conduct of the strike or for its termination' was endorsed by 2,840,000 votes to 1,095,000.[4]

Later that year Bevin was surprised to find himself part of a government delegation which toured industrial sites in Canada and the United States.[5] Sir Arthur Steel-Maitland had suggested his inclusion as 'the ablest leader in the Trade Union movement'.[6] Together with Walter Citrine, who was confirmed as secretary of the TUC in September 1926, Bevin nudged the General Council towards pragmatic collective bargaining rather than sympathetic strikes. And while the Mond–Turner talks of 1928 ultimately failed, the Labour Party, TUC and TGWU were bound more closely together both fraternally and even under the same roof at Transport House in Westminster's Smith Square.

For Citrine, the 'outstanding lesson' of the general strike was that 'authority must be invested exclusively and entirely in the directing body'.[7] He remained at the TUC until 1946 and later flourished as chairman of the British Electricity Authority. Knighted in 1935, appointed a Privy Counsellor in 1940 and a member of the House of Lords six years later, Citrine even ended up sharing anti-appeasement platforms with Winston Churchill. His long-standing colleague Arthur Pugh remained a diligent general secretary of the Iron and Steel Trades Confederation until 1935.[8]

Arthur Cook, by contrast, did not thrive. As the miners' lockout dragged on, the general secretary of the Miners' Federation was increasingly vilified for poor leadership even as he privately pursued compromise.[9] His incendiary account of the general strike, *The Nine Days*, increased Cook's isolation within the TUC, while his failure to seek medical attention for a leg injury, aggravated by a kick from a demonstrator during 1926, resulted in its amputation in early 1931. Cook died later that year with Walter Citrine and the New Party (and future Fascist) leader Oswald Mosley by his bedside.[10]

With the Miners' Federation and Mining Association deadlocked, the government responded legislatively. The *Coal Mines Act 1926* restored an eight-hour day – Ramsay MacDonald called it 'equipping the owners with knuckle-dusters' – while the *Mining Industry Act*

1926 implemented a Samuel Commission recommendation by using a 5 per cent levy on coal royalties to finance pithead baths.

The mine owners found themselves rapidly losing favour. In July 1926 Stanley Baldwin took the unusual step of naming (and shaming) Sir Adam Nimmo during a rally in Norwich:

> He seems to see two raw alternatives – nationalization and private enterprise. They are not simply alternatives. There is an indefinite series of intermediate positions between Socialism and laissez faire. Like the North and South poles of our children's geography books, those two Poles do not exist.[11]

When the Marquess of Londonderry told Churchill that he supported Nimmo and Evan Williams in their fight against 'socialism', his cousin impatiently replied that there would be:

> no worse way of combating Bolshevism than to identify the Conservative Party and His Majesty's Government with the [coal] employers, and particularly with a body of employers like those headed by Mr Evan Williams and Sir Adam Nimmo.[12]

Over champagne and oysters with miners and mine owners at the Savoy, meanwhile, 'Mussolini Major' found himself morphing into a moderate.[13]

When a deputation of Anglican churchmen lobbied Baldwin in July 1926, he dismissed both sides as 'equally stupid and equally bigoted'.[14] The bishops' proposals for ending the coal stoppage were accepted by the Miners' Federation executive but rejected in a ballot by the rank and file. In October, George Spencer, a Labour MP and Nottinghamshire Miners' Association official, negotiated a deal with local mine owners which resulted in that district returning to work.[15] On 29 November most Miners' Federation members voted to remain out but with less than the necessary two-thirds majority.[16] By Christmas 1926, several local agreements were in place and around one million miners, to quote the Colonial Secretary Leo Amery, 'struggled back to the pits on the owners' terms, including longer hours, a beaten and resentful army'.[17]

The weekend after the general strike, Stanley Baldwin retreated to Chequers for 'the first smell of fresh air', as he told the Earl of Derby, he had 'had for three weeks'. The Prime Minister later told Kathleen Hilton Young that 'a new state of affairs was coming' and 'altogether he was very hopeful'.[18] This optimism found fuller expression in a speech at Chippenham on 12 June:

> in spite of all the depression, in spite of all our troubles, never before has the wealth of this country, through the taxes and the rates, been so distributed to those less fortunate and for the provision of those thrown out of work. We carry in our hearts what is the innermost core of the British Constitution. We have the widest franchise. We have a party system highly susceptible to public opinion in the country, and we legislate in accordance with that opinion.[19]

Baldwin was indisputably the man of the hour. Letters from the public, overwhelmingly positive, fill five bound volumes among his personal papers.[20] But the progressive Conservative MP Harold Macmillan was not alone in recalling 'a strange lethargy', something he believed was almost a 'physical consequence' of the premier's 'special mental and moral strain'.[21]

Sir William Joynson-Hicks, the Home Secretary, showed no signs of flagging. On 10 June 1926 he annoyed Walter Citrine and the King by stating in the Commons that 'some money from the Russian Government' had been received by the strikers. Citrine thought it 'regrettable' that Jix had 'given credence to unwarranted allegations',[22] while the King was anxious to 'differentiate between money sent in aid of the General Strike ... and that contributed on behalf of those suffering from the Coal Strike'.[23]

Publicly, Jix provocatively claimed that volunteers had 'gone a long way to destroying the supposed necessity for ... skilled workmen',[24] while privately he was surprisingly diligent in remitting the sentences of some trade unionists imprisoned under Emergency Regulations. At one meeting on 9 July 1926, docker Ben Tillett said he 'refused to believe the Home Secretary to be a monster ... and was prepared to leave the whole issue to his good sense and judgment'.[25] Between May and December 1926, 7,960 people were charged with offences connected with the coal stoppage and the general strike – 4,656 of them for offences against the ordinary law and 3,304 for breaches of the Emergency Regulations.[26] And despite sixty-one complaints against Labour-aligned magistrates for improper conduct during the strike, only nine were removed from the bench.[27] Boards of guardians, which the government believed had politicized the distribution of poor law relief, were abolished a few years later.[28]

The Home Secretary continued to see Reds under every bed. Writing to his constituency party in August 1926, he warned of Moscow and its 'Communist tools' working 'underground' to 'effect revolution' in the UK.[29] The Communist Party of Great Britain, meanwhile, denounced the TUC for the 'greatest crime' ever committed 'against the working class of Great Britain and the whole world',[30] and in May 1927 – following agitation from Conservative backbenchers – the UK severed diplomatic relations with the USSR only three years after it had been recognized by the first Labour government.

The Civil Commissioners were stood down on 17 May 1926. Earl Winterton, who believed the 'resentment' of wives at their striking husbands spending too much time at home had contributed to the collapse of the strike, was presented with a copy of Oscar Wilde's 'The Ballad of Reading Gaol', a nod to his headquarters during the crisis.[31] As he told the Indian Viceroy Edward Wood:

> The day after the Civil Commissioners were allowed to return to London and resume their ordinary ministerial Duties, Philip Sassoon, himself a Civil Commissioner, invited several of us to lunch. All the Civil Commissioners present with one accord, guiltily confessed that they were sorry their period of active service as Governors of British Provinces was over and contrasted the glories of a ten days Proconsulship with the dullness of subordinate Ministerial Office.[32]

Most of Winterton's colleagues returned to relative obscurity, although Sir Kingsley Wood went on to serve as Chancellor of the Exchequer during the Second World War and the 6th Earl of Clarendon became Governor-General of the Union of South Africa in 1931. Sir Philip Sassoon's career never really took flight and in 1937 he was still the under-secretary for air. In Scotland, Lord Advocate William Watson made the unusual move straight from the Scottish Bar to Westminster as a Law Lord in 1929, while in Northern Ireland Sir Milne Barbour continued his duties as Minister of Commerce until 1941.

In the Chief Civil Commissioner's July 1926 report on the 'lessons' of the general strike, Sir William Mitchell-Thomson (who in 1932 became Baron Selsdon) identified too 'narrow' an interpretation of 'essential services' and recommended 'greater use' of Emergency Regulations in future disputes.[33] At the Scottish Office, Sir Arthur Rose stressed the 'vital necessity' for the Scottish Secretary to have 'overriding powers' as regards departments 'controlled direct from England'.[34] Instead of boosting the British Fascists, meanwhile, the splits provoked by the general strike led to its dissolution in 1935.[35]

In an intriguing fragment of a letter to Lord Halifax from June 1927, Stanley Baldwin faced both his past and future:

> I still think we were right in buying off the strike of 1925 though it proved once more the cost of teaching democracy. Democracy has arrived at a gallop in England, and I feel all the time that it is a race for life: can we educate them before the crash comes?[36]

The Prime Minister was probably alluding to the twin characteristics of parliamentary politics during that turbulent decade: an ever-expanding franchise – the vote was extended to all women in 1928 – as well as a dramatic realignment of Britain's two-party system.

With a ringside seat was John Whitley, who retired as Commons Speaker in June 1928 after ensuring Parliament could mitigate the effect of another general strike.[37] He declined the customary peerage and instead chaired the BBC's board of governors until his death in 1935.[38] Just two hours after his release from Wormwood Scrubs on 25 June 1926, meanwhile, the Communist MP Shapurji Saklatvala joked in the Commons of his return from 'a semi-Socialistic institution' in which he had been taken care of 'on a much better scale than the poor miners'.[39] In early 1927 he toured his native India to a rapturous reception.[40] 'Comrade Sak' lost his seat in 1929 and died seven years later.

In June 1926, Beatrice Webb wondered where the Labour movement would be 'a year hence':

> The Labour Party will prosper; the Baldwin government is going to become hideously unpopular ... There will be no revolution, either Communist or Fascist. If the Labour Party comes in [to government] it will move to the right and not to the left, whilst the Tory Party will move to the left and not to the right. Both parties will be mildly collectivist.[41]

Webb was not wide of the mark. After two months spectating events largely beyond his control, Ramsay MacDonald now had an opportunity to go on the offensive. Gradually, 'the dismayed and unhappy' Labour Party of May 1926 recovered its unity and 'little by little, one of the strongest Conservative Governments of the century was forced on to the defensive'.[42] The Labour leader quickly grew 'perfectly sick' of all the adulation of Baldwin ('one of the most incompetent and blundering men who has ever held an important position'). As he told A. W. Groundwater, a Congregationalist minister:

> The strike was a great demonstration of human emotion. As soon as it had started it changed the issue from the miners to Government propaganda. Its existence undoubtedly hampered negotiations; to have continued it many days longer would have been to completely smash Trade Unionism for our generation (it is very badly hit as it is) and no victory was possible.[43]

Although a hint of 'I told you so' crept into MacDonald's public analysis of the general strike, he tended to bury this beneath praise for the miners' struggle as a 'glowing point in the history of British Labour'.[44] His first major survey of the strike for the *Socialist Review*, in which he blamed 'those who preached it without considering it and induced the workers to blunder into it',[45] infuriated Ernest Bevin, who complained to Arthur Henderson about MacDonald 'wantonly ... stabbing us in the back at the moment when we had the whole forces of capital unleashed against us'.[46] The ever-diplomatic Leader of the Opposition 'smoothed Bevin down'[47] and together they helped facilitate the rapprochement between the industrial and political wings of the Labour movement.[48]

MacDonald also believed the Hammersmith North by-election of 20 May 'very amply demonstrated that we are suffering no set-back as a result of the strike'.[49] Labour's vote increased by 7.5 per cent following a lively campaign in which the Labour leader praised the strike's 'extraordinary manifestation of human solidarity'.[50] There was a similar pattern in subsequent by-elections,[51] while Herbert Morrison, the London Labour leader and a future Cabinet minister, agreed the strike had 'assisted in developing political solidarity'.[52]

Even those on the Labour left did not cause MacDonald much trouble. The Independent Labour Party's Patrick Dollan observed that:

> Thousands who voted Liberal or Tory at the last election were enthusiastic strikers. Once they have been arrayed against the Government in a wages fight they are unlikely to return to its support in politics.[53]

A few days after the strike ended, Arthur Henderson told MacDonald that Lloyd George had floated cooperation with Labour in return for adoption of his radical land policy. Never a fan, the Labour leader could 'see nothing but trouble'. 'The General Strike seems to have struck another sad blow at the poor Liberal Party,' observed MacDonald in his diary. 'No decent Liberal can do anything but resent Simon's mischievous speech.'[54]

Sir John Simon published his two parliamentary interventions and a third address to his constituents as *Three Speeches on the General Strike*,[55] a book Lord Birkenhead considered 'one of capital importance' and which served to 'enhance his reputation as a lawyer and as a statesman'.[56] But when the Liberal leader Lord Oxford and Asquith used the aftermath of the strike to move against Lloyd George, a grassroots and media backlash forced his resignation while the progressive Liberalism of the 'Welsh Wizard' triumphed over Sir John Simon's increasingly Conservative-aligned ideology.[57] 'The hopes of Liberal reunion,' reflected Simon in his memoirs, 'were thus again cast down.'[58] At his farewell speech in Greenock, Asquith pompously railed against the general strike as 'an offence of the gravest kind against both law and morals'.[59] He died in February 1928.

That same year, John Maynard Keynes and Sir Herbert Samuel helped draft the Liberal Yellow Book on 'Britain's Industrial Future', which called for rationalization of the coal industry. This followed *Industry and the State: A Conservative View* by a group of centrist Tory MPs including Harold Macmillan, which urged the state to reorganize not just coal but British industry in general.[60] In June 1926 H. E. Blain, the Conservative Party's principal agent, consulted constituency associations on the general strike and its consequences. This exercise identified an 'opportunity' for the party to remedy 'abuses' relating to picketing and the political levy. At the party's Scarborough conference that autumn, delegates made it clear they expected action.[61]

The Trade Disputes and Trade Unions Bill was introduced to Parliament in February 1927. Its principal clause made illegal a sympathetic strike or any action 'designed or calculated to coerce the government'. Conservative ministers also inserted other provisions close to Tory hearts. Civil servants were forbidden to join a union affiliated to the TUC, while union members who wished to pay the political levy now had to 'contract in' rather than 'contract out', thereby jeopardizing a substantial source of Labour Party income.[62] Not only did this legislation reveal the general strike to have been perfectly legal, but its provisions arguably dented Baldwin's conciliatory image.[63] When the devolved Parliament of Northern Ireland debated equivalent legislation later that year, Sam Kyle denounced it as a 'wicked attack' on his Northern Ireland Labour Party, which he believed had succeeded in 'keeping the peace' in that part of the United Kingdom.[64]

At the 1929 general election, Conservative candidates worked hard to remind voters of the 'deplorable and costly business' sponsored by 'most of the Socialist Leaders' three years earlier.[65] Labour's vote, however, grew from 5.5 million votes in October 1924 to 8.4 million, enough for an additional 138 MPs. In Barnard Castle, the incumbent Conservative Cuthbert Headlam lost to Will Lawther, who hailed from Durham's 'Little Moscow' and had been arrested during the strike for organizing a stone-throwing gang. Headlam had wondered in 1926 if this would 'interfere with his [Lawther's] parliamentary ambition or make him a hero and a martyr in the cause?'[66] He now had his answer.

With a plurality if not a majority of seats, Ramsay MacDonald's second government reduced the miners' eight-hour day by thirty minutes, although an attempt to amend the hated *Trade Disputes and Trade Unions Act 1927* was abandoned amid a blizzard of wrecking amendments from the Liberals.[67] Thereafter MacDonald and Stanley Baldwin shared the premiership until the accession of George VI in December 1936 established Princess Elizabeth, born shortly before the general strike, as heir presumptive. MacDonald declined the usual honours and died later that year; Baldwin accepted a peerage and passed away a decade later.

Among volunteers or 'blacklegs', the end of the general strike brought disappointment, boredom and even apathy. Chips Channon, who had enrolled as a special constable in London, 'enjoyed the strike, the hours, the air, the discipline' and mourned its end.[68] A *Punch* cartoon depicted an undergraduate standing listlessly in a doorway. 'Your son is looking very bored,' said a visitor, to which his 'Fond Mother' replied: 'Yes. You see, he misses the strike so dreadfully.' Manicurists reported a significant spike in business as 'members of society and professional people' endeavoured to 'remove traces of the grime of industrial warfare',[69] while one colonial official believed the strike had energized Britain's middle classes, 'on whom so much depends', and might 'prove a blessing in disguise'.[70]

There was a great urge to commemorate what had been for many a novel, exciting experience. Special constables received a certificate signed by the Prime Minister and Home Secretary, while at Cardiff City Hall there was a grand civic reception for volunteer drivers and conductors who were presented with souvenir albums and danced until two in the morning.[71] Railway companies also struck handsome medals, inscribed silver ashtrays and organized thanksgiving banquets.[72]

Some of those who had attempted to obstruct volunteers suffered the consequences. A campaign to free the 'Cramlington Miners' who had been sentenced to penal servitude for their role in the *Flying Scotsman* derailment lasted years. A deputation of Labour MPs finally convinced the Home Secretary to use the royal prerogative to reduce some of the sentences in August 1928.[73] There were some efforts at reconciliation. At East London's Toynbee Hall the warden arranged a meeting between striking dockers and undergraduate constables. It was a great success, with the dockers demanding a reunion in Cambridge.[74] William Garnett, a Toynbee Hall special, told his mother he was 'quite sorry when it all fizzled out ... I feel we shall never have such stirring times again.'[75]

Winston Churchill was so 'delighted' with the task of managing a paper with the 'largest circulation in the world' that he was most reluctant to 'abandon his charge'.[76] Nevertheless, the final *British Gazette* of 13 May observed, with Churchillian flourish, that the general strike 'becomes a memory; but it remains a monument'.[77] A year later, the Chancellor told the *Morning Post* editor Howell Gwynne that an 'extraordinary ten days' had formed 'one of the most vivid experiences' of his 'somewhat variegated life'.[78] Miniature copies of the *Gazette* were bound and distributed to members of the government as souvenirs, while on 2 June its union chapel held a commemorative luncheon at the Savoy.[79]

During a memorable Commons debate on 7 July 1926, Churchill mounted a robust defence of the *Gazette*'s editorial approach – 'I decline utterly to be impartial as between the fire brigade and the fire' – but also delighted the House with his self-deprecation. 'Make your minds perfectly clear that if ever you let loose upon us again a general strike,' declared the Chancellor, 'we will loose upon you – another "British Gazette".'[80] 'Our boys could not resist the ridicule and joined in the laughter,' recalled the ILP MP David Kirkwood. 'That astonishing performance made another General Strike impossible. No one can be serious when the victims treat their victimizers as a joke.'[81]

Hamilton Fyfe, meanwhile, proposed that the Labour-supporting *Daily Herald* be renamed the 'British Worker' to keep hold of hundreds of thousands of new readers, but this was rejected by its directors.[82] He subsequently resigned and joined the Liberal-supporting *Daily Chronicle*. In Manchester, the *Guardian* used the general strike to found a 'company' union,[83] while in Scotland, Glasgow's Outram Press, Dundee's DC Thomson and Aberdeen's Associated Press all completely de-unionized, provoking a bitter row which dragged on for several years.[84] The proprietors of the *Scotsman* and *Edinburgh Evening Dispatch* presented a bound copy of their general strike numbers – 'the only papers in the United Kingdom continuously produced and published as in normal times' – to the House of Commons Library.[85] The papers' Edinburgh staff received a bonus of one week's wages.[86] The Press Association, meanwhile, complained to Downing Street about having been expected to crib information from the BBC during the strike, an early indication that the printed press would gradually be displaced by radio and television news.[87]

Although Sir William Mitchell-Thomson, the Chief Civil Commissioner, considered John Reith's behaviour 'intolerable',[88] the Prime Minister thanked him for the 'help and service' the British Broadcasting Company had rendered to the 'Government and the Country during the emergency'. In reply, Reith spoke of his 'particular satisfaction in having been able to help you',[89] although he valued more the memorandum signed by thirteen senior BBC staff praising his 'magnificent leadership'.[90]

Less impressed was His Majesty's Opposition. Reith engaged in 'fatuous correspondence' with Ramsay MacDonald and the Edinburgh MP William Graham, who had served on the Crawford Committee,[91] for several months. Although Jimmy Thomas was allowed to broadcast on 14 May ('Both sides in the conflict have shewn themselves warriors'[92]), it was the exclusion of Labour spokesmen *during* the strike that continued to rankle. 'We have been so accustomed to unfair play in publicity that we are beginning to take it as an ordinary experience,' wrote MacDonald, 'but I regret that this new form of publicity seems to have already yielded to tendentious propaganda.'[93] Only in November 1926 was William Graham willing to appreciate the 'great difficulty' with which Reith had been faced, adding that 'not one trace' of ill feeling remained.[94]

The *Radio Times* also fuelled the row by providing a platform for the Labour MP 'Red' Ellen Wilkinson, who said she felt like asking the Postmaster General to refund her licence fee as she could 'hear enough fairy tales in the House of Commons without paying ten shillings a year to hear more'.[95] Internally, the BBC chairman and coal owner Lord Gainford was content the general strike had 'demonstrated to a remarkable extent the great national value of the B.B.C.', while another staffer believed its news had been 'doped' only 'by suppressions, not by fabrications', and the Company would likely benefit from 'forget and forgive' among listeners during what he called the 'reconstruction period'.[96]

The strike clearly did neither the BBC nor its general manager any long-term harm. There were 2,178,259 licensed wireless sets at the end of 1926 compared with 1,645,207 at its beginning. A dedicated BBC News section was formed for the first time, while in July 1926 the government accepted the Crawford Committee's recommendations and on 1 January 1927 established the British Broadcasting Corporation under a Royal Charter with Reith – now Sir John – its first director-general.

Perhaps as penance for his exclusion from the airwaves, a message from the Archbishop of Canterbury was broadcast during a rather curious 'service of reconciliation' held at the BBC's Savoy Hill studio on 20 May 1926. Cardinal Bourne also sent a statement, while the Chief Rabbi read his in person. The Bishop of Southwark preached from the text 'Be ye kind one to another, tender-hearted, forgiving each other, even as God in Christ forgave you'.[97]

Privately, the Bishop of Durham complained to Randall Davidson about the 'grotesque' way in which Cardinal Bourne had 'become the mouthpiece of national sentiment and civic duty', a role he believed belonged 'pre-eminently to the National Church, and therein conspicuously to the Primate', whom he believed ought to have 'placed' his weight behind 'patriotic' statesmen.[98] Nevertheless, the Archbishop's appeal helped overcome long-standing suspicion among trade unionists.[99] The then Bishop of Manchester, William Temple, thought it 'brought a new hope', a 'renewal' of the Church's 'power in relation to the life of the people'.[100] In November 1928 Davidson became the first Archbishop of Canterbury to retire and died two years later. Cardinal Bourne remained the Catholic Archbishop of Westminster until his death in 1935.

The strike also had a curious afterlife in Presbyterian Scotland. The delayed General Assemblies of the Church of Scotland and United Free Church (UFC) met briefly on 18 May 1926 before adjourning until early June. In his May sermon James Harvey of the UFC hailed the strike's defeat a 'victory for God' while John White of the Kirk took a more conciliatory line, referring to the 'great work' which remained to be done 'for the cause of labour'. When the Mining Association and Minister of Labour Sir Arthur Steel-Maitland (a Kirk elder) lobbied against the National Union of Scottish Mine Workers' being received by both Churches, John White protested to Baptist Sir Adam Nimmo that surely there was:

> some way of placing the industry on a basis that would pay a living wage, and give a moderate return to capital. Are we after all only a nation of amateurs? To say that there is no way out is a confession of economic failure, or worse still it is to say that Britain's day as an industrial force is at an end.[101]

On 7 June, meanwhile, Stanley Baldwin paid an unprecedented visit to both General Assemblies and received a hero's welcome as an 'apostle of peace'.[102] The Church of Scotland and United Free Church finally reunified in 1929.

What of the individuals prominent in the final days of the general strike? Mr Justice Astbury always claimed within earshot of Sir Henry

Slesser that 'he it was who had saved the nation'.[103] Havelock Wilson, the trade unionist who prompted Astbury's *obiter dicta*, won favour among shipowners but pariah status within the Labour movement and died in 1929.[104]

Sir Henry – who lived to see Margaret Thatcher assume office in 1979 – rightly dismissed the 'legend' that Sir John Simon's speeches had ended the general strike.[105] Having failed to become Liberal leader following Asquith's resignation, Simon's political career languished until the national and coalition governments of 1931–45 gave him a remarkable second wind as, successively, Foreign Secretary, Home Secretary, Chancellor and finally Lord Chancellor. This was all the more remarkable given his unpopularity. 'I am always trying to like him,' remarked Neville Chamberlain in 1928, 'and believing I shall succeed when something crops up to put me off.'[106]

The National Government formed in 1931 also saw Sir Herbert Samuel return to frontline politics as Home Secretary. He became *de facto* leader of the pro-government Liberals until they quit the government in 1933.[107] The philosophical treatise interrupted by the general strike was finally published in 1937 as *Belief and Action: An Everyday Philosophy*. It became the most popular of Samuel's many books, eventually selling nearly a hundred thousand copies. He joined the House of Lords as Viscount Samuel the same year and died in 1963.[108] Samuel's finest and most sympathetic biographer judged that during the general strike, as in Palestine, his 'Olympian above the fray' posture had relied too much on traditional Liberal devices – constitutions, frameworks, formulas – papering over conflicts without resolving them.[109]

At the 1945 general election Winston Churchill enjoyed a nation's gratitude but not its electoral confidence, and a majority Labour government full of strike veterans assumed office: Clement Attlee, whose political career almost foundered on his actions during the nine days; Ellen Wilkinson (who became Minister of Education) and Aneurin Bevan (Minister of Health). In a curious role reversal, Labour had by then assumed the position of patriotic defenders of the British constitution and Churchill that of an Edwardian throwback who warned that a socialist government would give rise to 'some sort of gestapo'.

Towering over most of the Cabinet physically as well as politically was Ernest Bevin as Foreign Secretary. In February 1946 he went straight from the first meeting of the United Nations' General Assembly at Westminster's Methodist Central Hall to a Commons debate on the repeal of the *Trade Disputes and Trade Unions Act 1927*. 'They cast the trade unions for the role of enemies of the State,' he told MPs. 'I am fighting to remove the stigma which the Tory Party in 1927 put upon me, as the leader of a trade union.'[110] In 1947 Britain's coal industry was finally nationalized. The Miners' Federation of Great Britain became the National Union of Mineworkers while the Mining Association, rendered largely irrelevant by state control, was dissolved in 1954.

The general strike now entered its commemorative phase amid relatively harmonious relations between trade unions and both main political parties. In April 1966 – four decades on – Lord Snowdon photographed the seventy-eight-year-old Lord Citrine and seventy-seven-year-old Lord (J. C. C.) Davidson for the *Sunday Times Magazine*. 'The strike that was,' read the cover caption, 'the revolution that wasn't.'[111] Six years later, A. J. P. Taylor described the 1972 miners' strike and pay settlement as having 'avenged the defeats of 1921 and 1926'.[112]

There was greater coverage for the strike's fiftieth anniversary, not only a plethora of historical studies but a major gathering in Margate at which the veteran Communist Robin Page Arnot criticized the TUC's weakness and Charles Clarke, President of the National Union of Students and a future Cabinet minister, apologized for his members having been 'first among the blacklegs' in May 1926.[113] When Greater London Council voted to contribute £10,000 towards a commemorative exhibition at Covent Garden, a Conservative alderman called it a 'stirring up of trouble on a political basis'.[114]

The industrial and political battles of the 1920s continued to resonate in a decade still marred by strikes and economic instability. Britain's final state of emergency was proclaimed on 13 November 1973 following disputes involving miners and electricity power workers.[115] In 1975, Patrick Renshaw pointed to a recent general strike in Northern Ireland which brought down the short-lived Northern Ireland Executive,[116] and indeed there was a certain irony in such a crisis finally reaching – and succeeding in – a part of the United Kingdom left relatively untouched in 1926. On 19 May 1974 the Secretary of State for Northern Ireland authorized another emergency proclamation,[117] the last in any part of the UK.

By the miners' strike of 1984–5, the events of nearly sixty years before were fading from the public consciousness. Like her predecessor Edward Heath, Margaret Thatcher channelled Stanley Baldwin by framing it as a battle between a democratically elected government and what she called 'the enemy within'. And, like Baldwin, it worked. The then Labour leader Neil Kinnock also evoked Ramsay MacDonald in steering a careful course between moderation and support for the miners. Again, this proved modestly successful. His party gained twenty seats at the 1987 election and took office with a landslide a decade later.

Now, a century on, only ghosts of that past epoch remain. The *Civil Contingencies Act 2004* removed the sovereign from any involvement in emergencies but, curiously, gathered dust during the Covid-19 pandemic of 2020–23, an experience which brought its own regulations, rumours and restrictions on 'normal' life. In September 2015 the Conservative MP Robert Jenrick felt able to brag about his great-grandfather (James Barrett) having led the general strike in Manchester,[118] and when Labour took office after the 2024 general election, Chancellor Rachel Reeves chose a portrait of 'Red' Ellen Wilkinson to adorn Number 11 Downing Street.[119] The UK's last coal power station at Ratcliffe-on-Soar ceased operations a few months later.[120] On a visit to Port Talbot in June 2025, the Reform leader Nigel Farage spoke of his ambition to 'reindustrialize' Wales including, so far as possible, by mining what he called 'our own coal'.[121]

17

THE GENERAL STRIKE RECONSIDERED

In the immediate wake of the general strike it was the habit of some to congratulate themselves on how the United Kingdom *as a nation* had dealt with the crisis. Everyone had been so well behaved; not a single shot had been fired; and so on. This was permeated with a strong sense of British exceptionalism. Imagine a general strike in Italy, it was suggested, or, worse, in France. May 1926 had not turned into Russia's February 1917 because of innate *English* 'common sense'. For the Solicitor General Sir Thomas Inskip, it had been 'worthwhile having a General Strike to really appreciate what the British nation is'.[1]

Yet it was one thing to applaud the handling of and response to a crisis not of one's own making, quite another to revel in that following a failure of governance and of public policy. That failure was not limited to one party: the government had intervened both too little and too late, the trade unions lacked a clear goal, while the miners believed that compromise could be avoided indefinitely. The strike, meanwhile, dramatically revealed the existence of what Disraeli called 'two nations', rich and poor, industrial and leisured.

Was this failure avoidable? Only to a degree. For many, some sort of confrontation had appeared inevitable since the 1910s. The First World War then acted as a catalyst for a series of economic, political and social events much as the Great Financial Crash would almost a century later. The Great War did not create new problems but sharpened old ones, and these played out during much of the 1920s: political realignment, economic turbulence, industrial and class tension.

Indeed, structural changes in both government and trade unions positively exacerbated this industrial fatalism. Liberal, Conservative and even Labour governments prepared and sustained emergency machinery from 1919, while the Trades Union Congress streamlined its organization and concentrated ultimate power in the hands of its General Council. Form ultimately followed function. As Keith Laybourn concluded in his study of the general strike, the TUC and the government ended up on 'a collision course, despite their hopes for industrial peace, and ... the coal dispute provided the flash-point for conflict'.[2]

In his memoirs, Harold Macmillan was clear the conflict was one into which 'both sides had drifted helplessly to disaster' through the intransigence of their respective and so-called 'allies'. Even a Conservative government despaired of (but felt allied to) the Mining Association of Great Britain while the TUC was exasperated by (but felt solidarity with) the Miners' Federation. As Macmillan observed:

> If the owners had unequivocally accepted and if the Government had undertaken to give immediate effect to the recommendations of the Samuel Commission as to the reorganisation of the industry – still better, had they gone even further than the actual Report along the lines of compulsory unification [of royalties] – the moral position of the Miners' Federation would have been much weakened, and the hands of the T.U.C. leaders strengthened.

Crucially, however, Conservative opinion was 'not yet prepared for so drastic an interference of the State with industry'.[3] Still governed by old economic and political orthodoxies, the strike occurred too soon for the UK's natural party of government to approach it with the imagination and pragmatism the situation demanded.

Tom Jones, the Deputy Cabinet Secretary, believed that, had the memorandum produced by Sir Herbert Samuel towards the end of the strike formed part of his Commission report published before it, then the government's 'troubles would have been fewer, and perhaps the General Strike itself would have been avoided'. But that is to inhabit the world of 'what if'.[4] The central problem was the mutual intransigence of miners and mine owners. Even had the miners accepted Samuel's initial recommendations, the coal owners would have rejected them – and vice versa. There was never an easy solution hiding in plain sight.

Macmillan's point about the unintentional 'drift' towards a breakdown is supported by the events of 1–2 May 1926. Although both the government and TUC worked genuinely hard to reach an accommodation, misconceptions arising from tangled discussions between exhausted and anxious men made this impossible. Given the scattered nature of its organization, the General Council felt it necessary to despatch telegrams on the Saturday evening to ensure strike action, if necessary, by the evening of Monday 3 May. The government was similarly motivated in its proclamation of a state of emergency and mobilization of its Civil Commissioners on 30 April. Both moves were essentially precautionary and provisional, yet when the TUC learned of the proclamation and the Cabinet was alerted to the strike telegrams, the resulting suspicion had a predictable outcome.

It is impossible a century later, meanwhile, not to admire the risks taken by rank-and-file trade unionists in response to the TUC's call. As Alan Bullock observed in his biography of Ernest Bevin, many risked secure jobs and pensions:

> They did so with their eyes open, knowing that if the strike failed, they would have great difficulty in getting their jobs back; might see themselves replaced by younger men; might be ... reduced to the ranks of the unemployed. Working men do not go on strike lightly, least of all when unemployment is high, trade slack and there is no dispute in their own industry. Too much was at stake for them and the families dependent on them to indulge in gestures.

The response was therefore a 'remarkable demonstration of working-class unity and of unselfish support for the miners'.[5] The 'Big Three' – Ernest Bevin, Jimmy Thomas and Arthur Cook – also remain a remarkable generation who had overcome more obstacles by the age of ten than others did in an entire lifetime, and certainly more than those sitting round the Cabinet table who judged them to be wild, irresponsible figures. And while sympathy for the working conditions endured by miners – who constituted around a tenth of the adult working male population – extended to the King and his Prime Minister, this was essentially hollow in the absence of any tangible improvements to their terms and conditions.

As Tom Jones observed in an aide-memoire composed after the strike, the 'battle' then proceeded on two fronts:

> the material front, by the provision of essential services by the Government's control, and local, official and voluntary organisations, and, secondly, the moral front, by speeches and messages and pledges, by means of the official newspaper [the *British Gazette*] and by broadcasting.[6]

In modern parlance, these were the Ground War and the Air War. The government's preparations for the former remain impressive. The enormous range and magnitude of the emergency machinery was a tribute to the agency of the interwar British state, not to mention the ingenuity of Whitehall and the still fledgling Cabinet Secretariat. Although its 'voluntary' wing, the Organisation for the Maintenance of Supplies, quickly proved inadequate, the Home Office responded nimbly by mobilizing thousands of special constables and other volunteers across Great Britain. That not everybody who signed up had something to do does not neutralize that point, even if the notion – posited at the time – of near 'normal' railway and bus services lacked credibility.

From the other side, the strike was more effective than is often supposed, even if communications between the TUC and local strike committees – often called 'Councils of Action' – did not always function adequately.[7] Ernest Bevin, the General Council's most disciplined and dynamic figure, moved quickly to rectify an initially chaotic atmosphere at Eccleston Square by concentrating decision-making in fewer hands. This decisiveness, however, masked the central problem: that the TUC's precise goal and the terms by which its success might be assessed were never clear. Realizing this, Bevin et al. began searching for an off ramp before the general strike was even a few days old.

Much was made, at the time and in its wake, of the strike's relatively orderly and even-tempered nature, but as Charles Ferrall and Dougal McNeill have observed, this should not be allowed to obscure the violence that took place during the nine days. Thousands were arrested for breaches, often tenuous, of Emergency Regulations or the ordinary criminal law; dissenting leaflets and publications were confiscated; while riots in normally peaceful cities like Edinburgh were put down by mounted police and baton charges.[8] Several people also lost their lives due to volunteer railwaymen whose enthusiasm proved no substitute for decades of technical skill.

Would the outcome have differed had the strike lasted another week? Perhaps, but as Leo Amery memorably observed, even then it would have remained 'technically out of date':

> Thirty years earlier the cessation of public transport services and means of disseminating information would have been far more effective. The small private car and the wireless had tilted the scale in favour of the middle class and of the Government.[9]

The American academic Wilfrid Harris Crook concurred as to the importance of modernity:

> Oil-burning ships, no longer dependent upon the frequent replenishment of their coal-bunkers; canned food supplies that did not require refrigeration for their preservation; aeroplanes for the swift movement of governmental executives, medical supplies and important mail; radio to the homes of most citizens ... but above all the automobile itself, in all its forms from private car to freight truck or army tank.[10]

Had the TUC foreseen this governmental advantage, then a much more effective and less self-defeating tactic might have been to confine strike action to the handling and transport of coal. That was, after all, what the dispute was all about.[11]

Tom Jones also noted the 'immense value' of the wireless to the government,[12] indeed it proved decisive in the Air War. Here Stanley Baldwin's more impressive qualities become clear. His move to 'frame' the strike as a constitutional rather than industrial battle from the moment negotiations broke down was a stroke of genius. As soon as this was done, noted Alan Mason, the TUC were cornered:

> They could either retreat and be humiliated or stand and fight for which they were totally unprepared. A short general strike, called off as soon as it could decently be done, was a kind of ironic compromise.[13]

Using his communication skills to great effect in a radio broadcast midway through the strike, Baldwin sought to rally those on the side of 'constitutional' government and maintain their morale.

The technique is more familiar today than it was in 1926: the importance of narrative, of telling and sustaining a political story simple enough to be understood by voters who did not, after all, pay close attention to miners' pay scales, trade union rules or indeed government policy.

In this respect the Prime Minister and the nascent British Broadcasting Company proved a perfect match. Baldwin was the first commanding figure of the political-media age, a surrogate 'father of the nation' who rose to the occasion, even if there is evidence that it brought him under huge psychological pressure. For it was a colossal gamble. As one biographer noted, 'safety first' was the least appropriate slogan for a career which encompassed so many throws of the political dice: ending the Conservative–Liberal coalition in 1922, tariffs in 1923, the political levy and coal subsidy in 1925, and above all the general strike in 1926.[14]

He did not get everything right. Baldwin's role in suppressing the Archbishop of Canterbury's appeal unwittingly elevated an intervention which might otherwise have proved a damp squib, while his contemplation of incendiary anti-union legislation at the height of the strike could have destroyed his government's authority with potentially destructive consequences. In the event, Baldwin's moderate instincts saw it delayed (if not shelved), but it was a close-run thing. As the historian Charles Loch Mowat has observed, it was ironic that the premier's 'greatest failure in leadership – the coming of the general strike – was transformed, by the constitutional issue, into one of his greatest successes'.[15]

This acknowledged that the Prime Minister's skill in telling a political story did not necessarily make it true. The TUC was neither assaulting the 'community' nor the British constitution – it was the coal owners they were attempting to coerce. Yet it was clear from the first pre-strike exchanges in Parliament that the Labour movement was alive to the difficulties of the dispute being framed in such a way. Government rhetoric cleverly exploited uneasiness about radical industrial action and its impact on the forward march of Labour in electoral terms. Spirited rebuttals followed, but they had little effect.

How was the British constitution perceived in 1926? It rested upon A. V. Dicey's twin concepts of parliamentary sovereignty and the rule of law. Whatever was enacted by the Crown-in-Parliament was the constitution, and that was largely decided by whichever party 'commanded' the confidence of the elected House of Commons. Since the election of October 1924 that was indisputably the Conservative Party. Yet the constitutional status quo included the trade unions, something facilitated as much by the Conservatives (in the late nineteenth century) as Labour. And while Tory diehards complained about Liberal governments having placed organized labour 'above' the law, it was an inconvenient truth that the *Trade Disputes Act 1906* had been passed by a sizeable parliamentary majority.

Nor was the British constitution somehow beyond challenge. As a postal worker put it during the strike itself:

> What was this constitution which should not be challenged? Freedom meant the right to disagree with a thing, not always to agree. Did Cromwell challenge the Constitution? Did Lord Birkenhead and Carson challenge the constitution?[16]

The last reference was well aimed. Little more than a decade before the general strike's supposed assault on the constitution, Birkenhead, the Marquess of Londonderry and even the then Unionist leader Andrew Bonar Law had supported Sir Edward Carson's and Ulster's right to resist Home Rule for Ireland, if necessary by extra-parliamentary – even paramilitary – means. Their hypocrisy was often highlighted during the nine days, and they had no ready response. In 1914 there had been 'things stronger than parliamentary majorities' but not, it seemed, in 1926.

If anything, it was the Conservative government rather than the TUC which came close to behaving 'unconstitutionally' during the general strike: Emergency Regulations granted Ministers of the Crown and the police sweeping and often arbitrarily exercised powers; junior ministers styled 'Civil Commissioners' ran the UK's nations and regions as they saw fit; soldiers and gunboats were distributed around the country in a show of force; special constables were handed responsibility for law and order; while a government newspaper produced by His Majesty's Stationery Office was little more than propaganda. The Archbishop of Canterbury and Leader of the Opposition – both central components of the constitution – were gratuitously excluded from the fledgling British Broadcasting Company, which had pretensions to speak impartially on behalf of the nation.

Even the King does not emerge unblemished from a crisis he felt more deeply than most. Despite efforts by his official biographer to depict George V as consistently tempering the reckless policy of his ministers, the Royal Archives tell a different story of a monarch torn between sympathy for the underdog but also appalled by disorder, 'constantly on the alert to prevent the government, through timidity or slackness, from failing in its duty to suppress what the king saw as genuinely revolutionary elements'.[17] Thus George was not the first sovereign, as some have argued, to have fully accepted the principle of constitutional monarchy – limited and apolitical – in the modern sense of the term. Indeed, the idea of urging the Home Secretary to arrest certain individuals or demanding emergency legislation would have been anathema to Queen Elizabeth II, who was born shortly before the strike began.

Also objectionable was the government's cynical exploitation of Sir John Simon's declaration that a general strike was illegal and those taking part liable to damages of their 'uttermost farthing'. Not only had prejudice and political ambition evidently interfered with the former Attorney General's legal judgement, but a government with its share of eminent barristers knew it not to be true: why else did it toy with legislation providing for the very thing it was suggested already existed? Even more revealingly, at no point were the Law Officers of the Crown asked to provide a formal opinion.

That towards the end of the strike such claims were blessed by the judiciary hardly improved matters. Mr Justice Astbury arguably weaponized *obiter dicta* to political ends and within months of the strike's conclusion the weight of academic and legal opinion had weighed in against both him and Simon. Their interventions were undoubtedly effective volleys in the Air War but not good law. Even an internal Ministry of Labour post-mortem concluded there was 'little in the contention that the General Strike was unconstitutional'. Striking, it added correctly, was 'a well-recognised means' *within* the British constitution for improving working conditions.[18]

To have been on the receiving end of the full force of the state during that period must have done incalculable damage to any concept of an enlightened and 'perfect' constitution. This is not to excuse the acts of some of those involved in the strike; those who smashed up – and even set alight – 'blackleg' omnibuses in central London or attempted to derail volunteer-controlled trains caused damage both criminal and physical. Yet for many more, it must have appeared that almost every organ of local and central administration, the police and Army, radio and newspapers, was 'united as one instrument against the Labour movement'.[19]

But it remains the case that the government insisted upon unconditional surrender and got exactly that. The Trades Union Congress, so decisive and united at the beginning of the general strike, emerged with little credit from its undeniably messy denouement. There is therefore much in Fenner Brockway's pithy observation that the explanation for the end of the general strike was that it 'was led by people who did not believe in it'.[20] And having accepted early on that an exit strategy was necessary, Ernest Bevin, Jimmy Thomas and even the usually methodical Walter Citrine applied astonishingly little rigour once they had settled upon Sir Herbert Samuel as the person who might lead them out of the quagmire.

It was most likely wishful thinking combined with Thomas's ability to persuade his colleagues that His Majesty's former High Commissioner in Palestine had sufficient authority to compel His Majesty's government to act upon his proposals. No matter how many times Samuel reiterated his lack of standing, the TUC's General Council fixated on process at the expense of substance, even disdaining Herbert Smith and Arthur Cook of the Miners' Federation when they correctly identified the central weakness of the whole exercise. Sir Herbert, too, was naïve, placing his faith in the 'ultimate reasonableness of men' while taking insufficient account of the 'collective hatreds' which had emerged from interwar politics.[21] Albeit unwittingly, Samuel allowed himself to be 'used' by a government whose hands remained unbound by conditions or pledges.

More broadly, the TUC called off the strike because it saw no prospect of success.[22] The Ministry of Labour was again on the money when it asked (in an internal memo) why had there been:

> no definite statement as to the length to which the strike would be pushed or of the precise terms upon which it would be called off? ... why did the [General] Council, before they called the strike off, not make more certain that the Samuel terms would be agreed to by the Government? And why when they met the Prime Minister was their attempt to impose any conditions at all with regard to [the] return to work so very half-hearted?[23]

The General Council only felt able to articulate another justification for its actions eight months later: the miners' refusal even to consider the question of wages. The responsibility of carrying on the strike, concluded the TUC leadership, required greater justification than a 'mere slogan' – 'not a penny off the pay, not a minute on the day':

> The Council were satisfied that, however long they continued the strike, they would still be in the same position so far as the attitude of the miners' executive was concerned, and consequently the Council were not justified in permitting the unions to continue the sacrifice for another day.[24]

Paradoxically, although the General Council had embarked upon the strike with 'utmost reluctance' and exited it with equal quantities of trepidation, after the event it remained sure the whole enterprise had nevertheless been 'morally justified'.[25] Solidarity was not an unworthy quality, especially considering what was at stake.

The general strike's many afterlives also highlighted contradictions on the 'winning' side. While Stanley Baldwin basked fleetingly in 'man of the hour' plaudits, rather than spend his considerable political capital on the sort of decisive intervention the moment so obviously required, he legislated sporadically, grew increasingly exasperated at the coal owners and, most seriously, lost control of a Conservative Party he ought to have dominated. The Prime Minister had little choice but to introduce punitive legislation in the spring of 1927 which, among other things, finally exposed the hollowness of his own government's cry of 'illegality' a year earlier.

As the Liberal statesman Philip Kerr put it in his post-strike analysis, the government had two options for uniting the 'two nations' in the wake of the nine days: 'either prove to the Labour world that their diagnosis is wrong or set to work to alter an economic and social system which can produce such unjust and preposterous effects'.[26] Baldwin, or perhaps more fairly his party, chose unwisely. And as one of his biographers concluded, the Conservative leader went on 'talking of peace' while his methods became increasingly 'alienated from his actions'.[27]

Not for the first time, the Labour leader Ramsay MacDonald made the correct strategic call, even if this infuriated some colleagues. Appalled by the general strike not only as a doomed political weapon but as a potential challenge to his positioning of Labour as a moderate, constitutional party of progressive change, he worked hard during the strike and after to keep his party united while drawing a distinction between an impressive display of solidarity and the strike's ultimate lack of utility. In this delicate task he was undoubtedly successful. The Conservatives' trade union reforms damaged Baldwin's authority and established a clear electoral dividing line which favoured the opposition, as did continuing Liberal infighting exacerbated by the general strike. In that context, Labour's victory at the 1929 general election resembles Clement Attlee's in 1945. In both cases the electorate was sophisticated, perfectly able to separate respect for a Prime Minister's rhetoric and leadership in a crisis from their ability to deliver a broader programme of reform.

Nor, surprisingly, did the general strike discernibly weaken trade unionism. As several scholars have concluded, it marked not a turning point in British industrial relations but, rather, consolidated an existing trend towards a more constructive form of collective bargaining later symbolized by beer and sandwiches at Number 10 Downing Street. If the strike had served a purpose, it was in demonstrating that the practical reality of such action was considerably more challenging than the theory. In Earl Winterton's vivid conclusion, with the end of the strike 'an abscess burst, which in time healed, and organised Labour has been healthier ever since'.[28]

A. J. P. Taylor only exaggerated slightly when he observed that the general strike seemed to have produced 'a lessening of class antagonism':

> The middle-class blacklegs, performing manual labour for the first and only time in their lives, learnt to respect those who did it always; the workers recognized that the leisured classes, too, were human beings. Hence the paradoxical outcome. The general strike, apparently the clearest display of the class war in British history, marked the moment when class war ceased to shape the pattern of British industrial relations.[29]

Thus the strike's chief effect, to quote Gordon Phillips, was to alter the 'rhetorical style' of trade unionism as well as the broader tone of its public discourse.[30] Its leadership became more realistic and more technocratic, and within a few years there was little space for the likes of Arthur Cook or Herbert Smith, the two individuals who had dominated the Miners' Federation of Great Britain. Subsequent events also created the space for more pragmatic understanding between Number 10 Downing Street and the Labour movement, beginning with the 'national' governments of the 1930s and followed by the exceptional demands of wartime. By the time a majority Labour government came to repeal the *Trade Disputes and Trade Unions Act 1927* and nationalize the coal industry, there was remarkably little controversy. That new orthodoxy endured until another coal dispute incurred a Conservative government's wrath nearly half a century after the first.

Today, even the industrial battles of the 1970s look like an alien world let alone those of a hundred years ago. Perhaps inevitably, the general strike – if it is thought about at all – long ago became a national myth. Only certain images, incidents and ideologies persist: photographs of office workers crammed into cars; food convoys hurtling through central London; and premonitions, however specious, of imminent revolution, all signifiers, as one study put it, 'of a particular comforting narrative of Englishness and English history'.[31] It has, in short, been treated like a football match with the implicit assumption that one must pick a side.

Yet if this centenary study has a purpose, it is to illustrate that the general strike remains relevant, and not just historically. Its politics is still recognizable, its economic challenges familiar, and the often-quixotic demands made by electors of those who govern in certain respects unchanged. The dramatic events of those nine days in May arguably represented a constitutional moment in the life of the United Kingdom. For those who cared to look beyond the noise and the fury, it revealed a great deal about the country, its leaders – both political and industrial – and perhaps most of all its people.

APPENDIX

The text of Ramsay MacDonald's proposed BBC 'talk'. This was sent to John Reith on 10 May 1926 but never broadcast:

> So much has been said of a hostile character to Labour in recent days that it has been felt that the fairminded and reasonable public ought to hear a different note struck and my colleagues who have laboured with me for peace and a humane settlement and are still doing so, have asked me to do it.
>
> The country is passing through a fiery trial which the Labour movement both industrial and political has striven with might and main, night and day, to avert.
>
> The miners' standard of life, already deplorably low, has been attacked by proposals that calm-minded and impartial men have called disgraceful. We believe that negotiations could have settled the difficulty, but time was wasted and opportunities lost for which we were not responsible. Lock-out notices became effective even before any reasonable offer was made to us, at 1.25 on Friday a week ago. Against our pleadings negotiations were ended, and the coal industry was paralysed.
>
> The whole Trade Union movement has been deeply moved by all this and was determined to give the miners every possible support. Rightly or wrongly they decided that the best way to do this was to strike in sympathy. I am in a position to give the public a most categoric assurance that it never entered into the mind of the Trades Union Council to challenge the Government or the constitution. It is not a political strike nor has it in any sense a revolutionary significance. It can and will be terminated the instant the Trade Unions have some certainty that by a reorganisation of the mining industry protection will be guaranteed against a further lowering of the

standards of the lives of the miner, his wife, and his children. To do that and to do that alone is its intention.

The weekend has shown a temper in general of which our nation and our people may well be proud. Why? Because, I make bold to say, it is a strike of goodwill conducted by men and women of goodwill. I appeal to the whole nation to see to it that the folly and criminality of ill will is kept far from us and that the hands and the work of the peacemaker are generously maintained.[1]

ENDNOTES

1. 'The Great Trek'

1. *The British Worker*, 6 May 1926.
2. Robert Rhodes James (1969), *Memoirs of a Conservative: J. C. C. Davidson's Memoirs and Papers, 1910-37*, London: Weidenfeld & Nicolson, p. 250.
3. R. J. Cootes (1966), *The General Strike (1926)*, London: Longmans, p. 28.
4. PP MS 14/001/044, Papers of Sir Charles Stewart Addis, London: SOAS Archives & Special Collections.
5. Julian Symons (1957), *The General Strike*, London: Cresset Press, p. 57.
6. D4016/6, Miscellaneous papers, Gloucester: Gloucestershire Archives.
7. Hamilton Fyfe (1926), *Behind the Scenes of the Great Strike*, London: Labour Publishing Company, pp. 9–10.
8. *Daily Mail*, 5 May 1926.
9. R. H. Haigh, Dave Morris and Anthony Peters (eds) (1988), *The Guardian Book of the General Strike*, London: Avebury, p. 146.
10. AMT/K/1/17, The Papers of Alan Mathison Turing, Cambridge: King's College Archive Centre.
11. Keith Laybourn (1996), *The General Strike: Day by Day*, Stroud: Sutton Publishing, p. 59.
12. *Socialist Review*, June 1926.
13. *Scotsman*, 5 May 1926.
14. A. J. Cook (1927), *The Nine Days*, London: Co-operative Printing, p. 16.
15. DD2560/1/7, William Thomas Pickbourne papers, Nottingham: Nottinghamshire Archives.
16. *The Times*, 4 May 1926.
17. 10 a.m. BBC news broadcast, 4 May 1926.
18. Julian Symons, *The General Strike*, pp. 58–9.
19. Charles Loch Mowat (1964), *Britain Between the Wars 1918–1940*, London: Methuen, p. 311.
20. Simon Heffer (ed.) (2021), *Henry 'Chips' Channon – The Diaries: 1918–38*, London: Hutchinson, p. 213.

21 Norman and Jeanne MacKenzie (eds) (1984), *The Diary of Beatrice Webb*, Volume Four, *1924-1943 'The Wheel of Life'*, London: Virago, p. 77.
22 *Daily Mail*, 5 May 1926.
23 Hamilton Fyfe, *Behind the Scenes*, p. 7.
24 *Socialist Review*, June 1926, and Fenner Brockway (1942), *Inside the Left: Thirty Years of Platform, Press, Prison and Parliament*, London: George Allen & Unwin, p. 189.
25 Keith Middlemas (ed.) (1969), *Thomas Jones: Whitehall Diary*, Volume II, *1926-1930*, London: Oxford University Press, p. 36.
26 RA QM/PRIV/QMD/1926, Queen Mary papers, Windsor: Royal Archives (RA).
27 HC Deb 3 May 1926 Vol 195 c72 [Prime Minister's Statement].
28 H. H. Asquith (1928), *Memories and Reflections 1852-1927*, Volume 2, London: Cassell, p. 234.
29 *Daily Herald*, 4 May 1926.
30 Bernard Wasserstein (1992), *Herbert Samuel: A Political Life*, Oxford: Clarendon Press, p. 283.
31 Henry Pelling (1987), *A History of British Trade Unionism* (4th edition), London: Palgrave Macmillan, p. 175.
32 C. L. Mowat, *Britain Between the Wars*, pp. 311-12.
33 MSS.292/252.62/20/5, Trades Union Congress Papers, Warwick: Modern Records Centre.
34 Walter Citrine (1964), *Men and Work: The Autobiography of Lord Citrine*, London: Hutchinson, p. 129.
35 J. H. Thomas to E. C. Sewell, D4016/6.
36 Simon Heffer, *Channon Diaries*, p. 213.
37 John Barnes and David Nicholson (eds) (1980), *The Leo Amery Diaries*, Volume I, *1896-1929*, London: Hutchinson, p. 452.
38 John Julius Norwich (ed.), *The Duff Cooper Diaries 1915-1951*, London: Weidenfeld & Nicolson, p. 213.
39 *Daily Mail*, 5 May 1926.
40 R. J. Cootes, *The General Strike*, p. 30.
41 MSS.292/252.62/13/25, TUC Papers, Warwick: Modern Records Centre.

2 The Origins of the General Strike

1 Board of Trade (1940), *Statistical Abstract for the United Kingdom for each of the fifteen years 1924 to 1938*, London: HMSO.
2 TUC/GS/03/002, TUC Papers, London: London Metropolitan University Archives.

3   Northern Ireland had just two coalfields, Ballycastle and Coalisland.
4   R. J. Cootes (1966), *The General Strike (1926)*, London: Longmans, pp. 14–16.
5   Henry Pelling (1987), *A History of British Trade Unionism* (4th edition), London: Palgrave Macmillan, pp. 180–82.
6   W. H. Marwick (1967), *A Short History of Labour in Scotland*, Edinburgh: Chambers, p. 70.
7   *Taff Vale Railway Co v Amalgamated Society of Railway Servants* [1901] UKHL 1.
8   *Amalgamated Society of Railway Servants v Osborne* [1910] AC 87.
9   Lord Birkenhead (1930), *Last Essays by the Earl of Birkenhead*, London: Cassell, p. 167.
10 J. D. B. Mitchell (1964), *Constitutional Law*, Edinburgh: W. Green, p. 290.
11 *The Times*, 3 August 1916.
12 See David Torrance (2024), *The Wild Men: The Remarkable Story of Britain's First Labour Government*, London: Bloomsbury Continuum, pp. 173–9.
13 John Maynard Keynes (1925), *The Economic Consequences of Mr Churchill*, London: Hogarth Press.
14 HC Deb 6 March 1925 Vol 181 cc833-41 [Prime Minister's Speech].
15 Acc 9851/1/1/7, Archive of the Joynson-Hicks family, Viscounts Brentford (Jix Archive), Brighton: The Keep.
16 G. M. Young (1952), *Stanley Baldwin*, London: Rupert Hart-Davis, p. 99.
17 *Daily Herald*, 31 July 1925.
18 A. Mason (1969), 'The Government and the General Strike, 1926', *International Review of Social History* 14:1, p. 7.
19 In 2008 Lord Selsdon admitted that Sir William was 'one of the reasons' he was in the House of Lords, as his grandfather had, during the general strike, forced 'people to go back to work' (HL Deb 24 April 2008 Vol 700 c1675).
20 Keith Jeffery and Peter Hennessy (1983), *States of Emergency: British Governments and Strikebreaking Since 1919*, London: Routledge & Kegan Paul, pp. 88–98.
21 Ian MacDougall (ed.) (1979), *Essays in Scottish Labour History: A Tribute to W. H. Marwick*, Edinburgh: John Donald, pp. 172–3.
22 COM/13/4/43a, Government of Northern Ireland records, Belfast: Public Record Office of Northern Ireland.
23 *The Times*, 28 April 1926.
24 Jeffery and Hennessy, *States of Emergency*, p. 101.

25 Alan Bullock (1960), *The Life and Times of Ernest Bevin*, Volume One, Trade Union Leader 1881–1940, London: Heinemann, p. 292.
26 Walter Citrine (1964), *Men and Work: The Autobiography of Lord Citrine*, London: Hutchinson, pp. 149–50.
27 It was the best-selling publication of its sort until the Beveridge Report in 1943.
28 Royal Commission on the Coal Industry (1926), Volume 1, *Report*, Cmnd 260, London: HMSO, p. 230.
29 Keith Laybourn (1993), *The General Strike of 1926*, Manchester: Manchester University Press, p. 37.
30 John Murray (1951), *The General Strike of 1926: A History*, London: Lawrence and Wishart, p. 70.
31 Keith Laybourn, *The General Strike of 1926*, p. 37.
32 Stuart Ball (ed.) (1992), *Parliament and Politics in the Age of Baldwin and MacDonald: The Headlam Diaries 1923–1935*, London: The Historians' Press, pp. 82–3.
33 John Ramsden (ed.) (1984), *Real Old Tory Politics: The Political Diaries of Sir Robert Sanders, Lord Bayford, 1910–35*, London: The History Press, p. 226.
34 *Observer*, 2 May 1926.
35 Bernard Wasserstein (1992), *Herbert Samuel: A Political Life*, Oxford: Clarendon Press, pp. 282–3.
36 *Answers*, January 1927.
37 Alan Bullock, *Life and Times of Ernest Bevin*, p. 298.
38 The Labour Representation Committee (later the Labour Party) had been founded at a meeting there on 27 February 1900. The hall was demolished in 1968.
39 Alan Bullock, *Life and Times of Ernest Bevin*, p. 302.
40 Ian MacDougall, *Essays in Scottish Labour History*, pp. 170–71.
41 Philip Williamson (ed.) (1987), *The Modernisation of Conservative Politics: The Diaries and Letters of William Bridgeman 1904–1935*, London: The History Press, p. 227.
42 MS.292/252.61/29/9, TUC Papers, Warwick: Modern Record Centre (MRC).
43 Ibid.
44 Walter Citrine, *Men and Work*, pp. 159–60.
45 Robert Taylor (2005), 'Citrine's Unexpurgated Diaries, 1925–26: "The Mining Crisis and the National Strike"', *Historical Studies in Industrial Relations* 20, p. 82.
46 Stuart Ball, *Parliament and Politics in the Age of Baldwin and MacDonald*, p. 84.

47 Robert Taylor, 'Citrine's Unexpurgated Diaries', p. 86.
48 Stuart Ball, *Parliament and Politics in the Age of Baldwin and MacDonald*, p. 85.
49 Philip Williamson, *The Modernisation of Conservative Politics*, pp. 194–5.
50 Alan Bullock, *Life and Times of Ernest Bevin*, pp. 307–8.
51 Acc 9851/1/1/7, Jix Archive, Brighton: The Keep.
52 Robert Taylor, 'Citrine's Unexpurgated Diaries', p. 85.
53 Alan Bullock, *Life and Times of Ernest Bevin*, pp. 309–10.
54 Walter Citrine, *Men and Work*, p. 165.
55 Alan Bullock, *Life and Times of Ernest Bevin*, p. 311.
56 John Barnes and David Nicholson (eds) (1980), *The Leo Amery Diaries*, Volume I, *1896–1929*, London: Hutchinson, p. 451.
57 Leo Amery (1953), *My Political Life*, Volume II, *War and Peace 1914–1929*, London: Hutchinson, pp. 483–4.
58 RMD/1/4/37, James Ramsay MacDonald Papers, Manchester: John Rylands Research Institute and Library. Isaacs later served as a minister in the governments of Clement Attlee. NATSOPA stood for 'National Society of Operative Printers and Assistants'.
59 Templewood/V/File 6, Templewood Papers, Cambridge: Cambridge University Library.
60 *New Statesman*, 22 May 1926. Churchill considered taking legal action but was advised turning it into a 'cause célèbre' by the Attorney General (Martin Gilbert, ed., 1979, *Winston S. Churchill*, Volume V, *Companion Part 1 – The Exchequer Years 1922–1929*, London: Heinemann, pp. 726–7).
61 Charles Loch Mowat (1955), *Britain Between the Wars 1918–1940*, London: Methuen, p. 309.
62 *Answers*, January 1927.
63 Walter Citrine, *Men and Work*, p. 171.
64 MS.292/252.62/13/17, TUC Papers, Warwick: MRC.
65 G. M. Young, *Stanley Baldwin*, p. 116.
66 Keith Middlemas (ed.) (1969), *Thomas Jones Whitehall Diary*, Volume II, *1926/1930*, Oxford: Oxford University Press, p. 33.
67 *Scottish Worker*, 13 May 1926.
68 A. J. Cook (1927), *The Nine Days*, Co-operative Printing, p. 13.
69 PRO 30/69/1753, James Ramsay MacDonald Papers (JRMP), Kew: The National Archives (TNA).
70 *The Times*, 4 May 1926.
71 Simon Heffer (ed.) (2021), *Henry 'Chips' Channon – The Diaries: 1918–38*, London: Hutchinson, pp. 212–13.

72 Paul Davies (1987), *A. J. Cook*, Manchester: Manchester University Press, p. 98.
73 David Marquand (1977), *Ramsay MacDonald*, London: Jonathan Cape, p. 436.
74 Walter Citrine, *Men and Work*, pp. 173–4.
75 Stuart Ball, *Parliament and Politics in the Age of Baldwin and MacDonald*, p. 87.
76 HC Deb 3 May 1926 Vol 195 cc71-72 [Prime Minister's Statement].
77 Barnes and Nicholson, *The Leo Amery Diaries*, Volume I, p. 452.
78 HC Deb 3 May 1926 Vol 195 cc81-82.
79 HC Deb 3 May 1926 Vol 195 c115.
80 A. J. Cook, *The Nine Days*, pp. 14–15.
81 Barnes and Nicholson, *The Leo Amery Diaries*, Volume I, p. 452.
82 Walter Citrine, *Men and Work*, pp. 175–6. The 1911 siege of Sidney Street was an east London gunfight between a combined police and army force and two Latvian revolutionaries. Churchill had been Liberal Home Secretary at the time.
83 Harold Nicolson (1952), *King George the Fifth: His Life and Reign*, London: Constable, p. 417.
84 PRO 30/69/1753, JRMP, Kew: TNA.
85 Gregory Blaxland (1964), *J. H. Thomas: A Life for Unity*, London: Frederick Muller, p. 195.
86 *Socialist Review*, June 1926.
87 Julian Symons (1957), *The General Strike: A Historical Portrait*, London: Cresset Press, p. 53.

3 'THE ROAD TO ANARCHY AND RUIN'

1 Lord Vansittart (1958), *The Mist Procession: The Autobiography of Lord Vansittart*, p. 355.
2 Ibid., p. 355.
3 *Sunday Times Magazine*, 10 April 1966.
4 Philip Williamson (2007), *Stanley Baldwin: Conservative Leadership and National Values*, Cambridge: Cambridge University Press, p. 189.
5 Stuart Ball, 'Baldwin, Stanley, first Earl Baldwin of Bewdley (1867–1947)', ODNB.
6 T 172/1558, Treasury records, Kew: The National Archives.
7 Walter Citrine (1964), *Men and Work: The Autobiography of Lord Citrine*, London: Hutchinson, p. 184.
8 PP MS 14/008/01/186, Papers of Sir Charles Stewart Addis, London: SOAS Archives & Special Collections.

ENDNOTES

9 Philip Williamson (ed.) (1987), *The Modernisation of Conservative Politics: The Diaries and Letters of William Bridgeman 1904–1935*, London: The History Press, p. 196. 'Cant' means hypocritical or sanctimonious talk.
10 STAT 14/1496, Records of the Stationary Office, Kew: TNA.
11 5th BBC news bulletin, 8 May 1926.
12 G. D. H. Cole (1937), *A Short History of the British Working Class Movement 1789–1937*, Volume III, *1900–1937*, London: George Allen & Unwin, p. 208.
13 *British Gazette*, 6 May 1926.
14 Robert Rhodes James (1969), *Memoirs of a Conservative: J. C. C. Davidson's Memoirs and Papers, 1910-37*, London: Weidenfeld & Nicolson, p. 253.
15 Horne, reported the British Embassy in Paris, had said 'something to the effect that the Prime Minister was threatened by a break-down and that the Premiership might have to be put into commission' (DAV/173, Papers of John Campbell Davidson, London: Parliamentary Archives).
16 PRO 30/69/1753, JRM Papers, Kew: TNA.
17 DAV/173, Papers of John Campbell Davidson (PJCP), London: PA.
18 Reuters, 11 May 1926.
19 4629/1/1926/37, Records of the Bridgeman Family, Shrewsbury: Shropshire Archives.
20 Keith Middlemas (ed.) (1969), *Thomas Jones Whitehall Diary*, Volume II, *1926/1930*, Oxford: Oxford University Press, p. 44.
21 Philip Ziegler (1990), *King Edward VIII: The Official Biography*, London: Collins, pp. 184–5.
22 Keith Middlemas, *Thomas Jones*, p. 43.
23 Christopher Farman (1972), *The General Strike May 1926*, London: Rupert Hart-Davis, p. 114.
24 Julian Symons (1957), *The General Strike: A Historical Portrait*, London: Cresset Press, p. 25.
25 John Wheeler-Bennett (1962), *John Anderson: Viscount Waverley*, London: Macmillan, p. 106.
26 Templewood/V/File 6, Templewood Papers, Cambridge: Cambridge University Library.
27 Rodney Lowe, 'Wilson, Sir Horace John [civil servant] (1882–1972)', ODNB.
28 T 172/1558, Treasury records, Kew: TNA.
29 AIR 2/8507, Air Ministry records, Kew: TNA.
30 J 86/37, Records of the Supreme Court of Judicature, Kew: TNA.

31 Leonard D. White (1933), *Whitley Councils in the British Civil Service: A Study in Conciliation and Arbitration*, Chicago: University of Chicago Press, pp. 283–4.
32 *British Gazette*, 12 May 1926.
33 Richard Temple, 'Brown, William John (1894–1960)'.
34 FO 366/838, Foreign Office records, Kew: TNA.
35 *British Gazette*, 8 and 11 May 1926.
36 John Campbell (1985), *F. E. Smith, First Earl of Birkenhead*, London: Jonathan Cape, p. 769.
37 Philip Williamson, *The Modernisation of Conservative Politics*, p. 232.
38 John Campbell, 'Smith, Frederick Edwin, first earl of Birkenhead (1872–1930)', ODNB.
39 F. E. Smith (1913), *Unionist policy and other essays*, London: Williams & Norgate, pp. 1–20.
40 John Campbell, 'Smith, Frederick Edwin, first earl of Birkenhead (1872–1930)', ODNB.
41 COOKE/22, Arthur Ebenezer Cooke Papers, London: London School of Economics.
42 John Campbell, 'Smith, Frederick Edwin, first earl of Birkenhead (1872–1930)', ODNB.
43 HL Deb 5 May 1926 Vol 64 c60 [Emergency Regulations].
44 Philip Williamson, *The Modernisation of Conservative Politics*, p. 233.
45 Viscount Templewood (1954), *Nine Troubled Years*, London: Collins, p. 31.
46 Stuart Ball (2013), *Portrait of a Party: The Conservative Party in Britain 1918–1945*, Oxford: Oxford University Press, p. 422.
47 *The Times*, 3 August 1925.
48 Monty Johnstone, 'Campbell, John Ross (1894–1969)', ODNB.
49 Antony Howe, 'Arnot, Robert Page [Robin] (1890–1986)', *ODNB*.
50 Acc 9851/1/1/7, Jix Archive, Brighton: The Keep.
51 Keith Laybourn (1993), *The General Strike of 1926*, Manchester: Manchester University Press, pp. 70–72.
52 John Murray (1951), *The General Strike of 1926: A History*, London: Lawrence and Wishart, p. 125.
53 1946/4/2F/2/16, Pleydell-Bouverie family papers, Chippenham: Wiltshire and Swindon History Centre.
54 *British Gazette*, 10 May 1926.
55 X274/2/Brown, I, Bill Moore collection, Sheffield: Sheffield City Archives.
56 Keith Laybourn, *The General Strike of 1926*, p. 71.

ENDNOTES

57 D/D Con 291/7, Glamorgan Constabulary papers, Cardiff: Glamorgan Archives.
58 Acc 9851/1/1/7, Jix Archive, Brighton: The Keep.
59 DAV/173, PJCP, London: PA.
60 H. A. Taylor (1933), *Jix, Viscount Brentford*, London: Stanley Paul, p. 197.
61 Walter Citrine, *Men and Work*, p. 183.
62 5th BBC news broadcast, 5 May 1926.
63 G. A. Phillips (1976), *The General Strike: The Politics of Industrial Conflict*, London: Weidenfeld & Nicolson, p. 160.
64 D/D Con 291/7, Glamorgan Constabulary papers.
65 Martin Gilbert (1976), *Winston S. Churchill*, Volume V, *1922–1939*, London: Heinemann, p. 164.
66 *Daily Mail*, 11 May 1926.
67 Templewood/V/File 6, Templewood Papers, Cambridge: Cambridge University Library.
68 Keith Jeffery and Peter Hennessy (1983), *States of Emergency: British Governments and Strikebreaking Since 1919*, London: Routledge & Kegan Paul, p. 121.
69 Ralph Miliband (1973), *Parliamentary Socialism: A Study in the Politics of Labour* (2nd edition), London: Merlin Press, p. 136.
70 KV 4/246, Records of the Security Service, Kew: TNA.
71 SD 1821/AWC-438-1, Revealing Voices Project, Stoke: Stoke-on-Trent City Archives.
72 5th BBC news broadcast, 7 May 1926.
73 WO 32/3455, War Office records, Kew: TNA.
74 Acc 9851/1/1/7, Jix Archive, Brighton: The Keep.
75 D2455/F7/2/1/16, Records of the Hicks Beach family, Gloucester: Gloucestershire Archives.
76 Ralph Miliband, *Parliamentary Socialism*, p. 136.
77 Robert Rhodes James, *Memoirs of a Conservative*, p. 253.
78 Acc 9851/1/1/7, Jix Archive, Brighton: The Keep.
79 G. A. Phillips, *The General Strike*, p. 162.
80 John Barnes and David Nicholson (eds) (1980), *The Leo Amery Diaries*, Volume I, *1896–1929*, London: Hutchinson, p. 453.
81 Jeffery and Hennessy, *States of Emergency*, p. 120.
82 G. A. Phillips, *The General Strike*, p. 164.
83 Stuart Ball, *Parliament and Politics in the Age of Baldwin and MacDonald*, p. 82.
84 HO144/7985, Home Office records, Kew: TNA.
85 MSS.292/252.62/32, TUC Papers, Warwick: Modern Records Centre.

86 G. A. Phillips, *The General Strike*, p. 165.
87 Keith Middlemas, *Thomas Jones*, pp. 45–7.
88 Stephen Roskill (1972), *Hankey: Man of Secrets*, Volume II, *1919–1931*, London: Collins, p. 425.
89 Barnes and Nicholson, *The Leo Amery Diaries*, pp. 453–4.
90 Keith Middlemas, *Thomas Jones*, p. 47.
91 John Barnes and David Nicholson (eds) (1980), *The Leo Amery Diaries*, Volume I, *1896–1929*, London: Hutchinson, p. 454.
92 Robert Rhodes James, *Memoirs of a Conservative*, p. 232.

4 'Anxious times'

1 R. H. Haigh, Dave Morris and Anthony Peters (eds) (1988), *The Guardian Book of the General Strike*, London: Avebury, p. 77.
2 Although this conference failed, the *Parliament Act 1911* constrained the veto powers of the Upper House.
3 STR/13/15/45, Papers of John St Loe Strachey, London: Parliamentary Archives (PA).
4 RA PS/PSO/GV/C/B/2052/13, KGV papers, Windsor: RA.
5 RA PS/PSO/GV/C/B/2052/14, KGV papers, Windsor: RA.
6 STR/13/15/45, Strachey Papers. Part of Stamfordham's reply paraphrased Lord Birkenhead's account of the negotiations (CAB24/179, Cabinet Conclusions, Kew: The National Archives).
7 *Manchester Guardian*, 10 May 1926.
8 RA PS/PSO/GV/C/B/2052/27, KGV papers, Windsor: RA.
9 *The Tatler (Emergency Number)*, 12–19 May 1926.
10 R. J. Cootes (1968), *The General Strike (1926)*, London: Longmans, p. 42.
11 *Socialist Review*, June 1926.
12 Jane Ridley (2021), *George V: Never a Dull Moment*, London: Chatto & Windus, p. 343.
13 H. C. G. Matthew, 'George V (1865–1936)', ODNB.
14 Duke of Windsor (1951), *A King's Story: The Memoirs of H.R.H. The Duke of Windsor*, London: Cassell, p. 217.
15 Kenneth Rose, *King George V*, London: Papermac, 1984, p. 342.
16 RA PS/PSO/GV/PS/MAIN/43053/11, King George V (KGV) papers, Windsor: RA.
17 RA PS/PSO/GV/C/B/2052/3, KGV papers, Windsor: RA.
18 RA GV/PRIV/GVD/1926, KGV papers, Windsor: RA. The King erroneously believed he had 'passed the [Defence of the Realm] act by order in Council'.

19 RA PS/PSO/GV/PS/MAIN/43053/1, KGV papers, Windsor: RA.
20 RA PS/PSO/GV/PS/MAIN/43053/3, KGV papers, Windsor: RA.
21 RA PS/PSO/GV/PS/MAIN/43053/2, KGV papers, Windsor: RA.
22 RA GV/PRIV/GVD/1926, KGV papers, Windsor: RA.
23 *Daily Chronicle*, 13 May 1926.
24 Duke of Windsor, *A King's Story*, pp. 217–18.
25 *Daily Mail*, 11 May 1926.
26 Acc 9851/2/2/11, Jix Archive, Brighton: The Keep.
27 *Evening News*, 11 May 1926.
28 RA PS/PSO/GV/PS/MAIN/43053/7, KGV papers, Windsor: RA.
29 RA PPTO/PP/WC/MAIN/NS/419, KGV papers, Windsor: RA.
30 RA GV/PRIV/GVD/1926, KGV papers, Windsor: RA.
31 RA GV/PRIV/GVD/1926, KGV papers, Windsor: RA.
32 *Sunday Times*, 9 May 1926.
33 Hamilton Fyfe (1926), *Behind the Scenes of the Great Strike*, Labour Publishing Company, p. 40.
34 KV 4/246, Records of the Security Service, Kew: The National Archives.
35 *British Gazette*, 8 May 1926. 'Most of his listeners smiled tolerably', noted the *Gazette*, 'and took no more notice of the foolishness.' As Royal Dukes, both the King's sons were members of the House of Lords.
36 J. R. Clynes (1937), *Memoirs 1924–1937*, London: Hutchinson, pp. 81–2.
37 *British Gazette*, 8 May 1926.
38 RA PS/PSO/GV/C/B/2052/23, KGV papers, Windsor: RA.
39 RA PS/PSO/GV/C/B/2052/25, KGV papers, Windsor: RA.
40 John Murray (1951), *The General Strike of 1926: A History*, London: Lawrence and Wishart, p. 137.
41 RA PS/PSO/GV/C/B/2052/9, KGV papers, Windsor: RA.
42 RA PS/PSO/GV/C/B/2052/12, KGV papers, Windsor: RA.
43 RA PS/PSO/GV/C/B/2052/11, KGV papers, Windsor: RA.
44 See Chapter 5.
45 RA PS/PSO/GV/C/B/2052/22, KGV papers, Windsor: RA.
46 RA PS/PSO/GV/C/B/2052/24, KGV papers, Windsor: RA.
47 RA PS/PSO/GV/C/B/2052/24, KGV papers, Windsor: RA.
48 4629/1/1926/36, Records of the Bridgeman Family, Shrewsbury: Shropshire Archives.
49 RA PS/PSO/GV/C/B/2052/29, KGV papers, Windsor: RA. The King had underlined 'second line of defence to-night'.
50 RA PS/PSO/GV/C/B/2052/34, KGV papers, Windsor: RA.

5 'Blacklegs'

1. Harold Macmillan (1966), *Winds of Change 1914–1939*, London: Macmillan, p. 217. A BBC bulletin on 8 May also alluded to a 'holiday spirit'.
2. Box No: P328, Private Papers of Commander J Murray RN, London: Imperial War Museum (IWM).
3. D.3.4, Baldwin Papers, Cambridge: Cambridge University Library (CUL).
4. Acc. 13934/7, William Burton Stewart papers, Edinburgh: National Library of Scotland.
5. EO/GEN/1/65, London County Council records, London: London Archives.
6. *Daily Telegraph*, 7 May 1926.
7. *Daily Mail*, 6 May 1926.
8. SD 1821/AWC-461-1, Revealing Voices Project, Stoke: Stoke-on-Trent City Archives.
9. GBR/0014/LASL II/1/6A, The Papers of Sir Alan Lascelles, Cambridge: Churchill College Archives (CCA).
10. Martin Pugh, 'Bentley Boys (act. 1919–1931)', ODNB.
11. D/EX239/1/7, Letters relating to the General Strike, Reading: Royal Berkshire Archives.
12. *British Gazette*, 8 May 1926.
13. *Aberdeen Press and Journal*, 5 May 1926.
14. MS 335 A2045/6/15, Correspondence of Henrietta Joseph, Southampton: University of Southampton Special Collections.
15. Rachelle Saltzman (2012), *A Lark for the Sake of Their Country: The 1926 General Strike Volunteers in Folklore and Memory*, Manchester: Manchester University Press, p. 6.
16. Jennie Lee (1963), *This Great Journey: A Volume of Autobiography 1904–45*, London: MacGibbon & Kee, p. 70.
17. Philip M. Williams (1979), *Hugh Gaitskell: A Political Biography*, London: Jonathan Cape, pp. 17–19.
18. A. J. P. Taylor (1983), *A Personal History*, London: Hamish Hamilton, p. 79.
19. MS.21/3285/1, TUC Papers, Warwick: Modern Records Centre (MRC).
20. Richard Hyman (1966), *Oxford Workers in the Great Strike*, Oxford: Centre for Socialist Education, p. 3.
21. *Daily Chronicle*, 12 May 1926.
22. JL/112/1926/6, East Yorkshire Regiment papers, Beverley: East Riding Archives.

23 Peter Stansky (2003), *Sassoon: The Worlds of Philip and Sybil*, New Haven: Yale University Press, p. 121.
24 COLL MISC 0760, Dover Dockers, London: London School of Economics Library Archives and Special Collections.
25 DAV/173, Papers of John Campbell Davidson MP, London: Parliamentary Archives.
26 Lord Hailsham (1990), *A Sparrow's Flight: The Memoirs of Lord Hailsham of St Marylebone*, London: Collins, pp. 47–8.
27 *Daily Graphic*, 11 May 1926.
28 Julian Symons (1957), *The General Strike*, London: Cresset Press, p. 96.
29 Philip S. Bagwell (1963), *The Railwaymen: The History of the National Union of Railwaymen*, London: George Allen & Unwin, p. 480.
30 Ian MacDougall (ed.) (1978), *Essays in Scottish Labour History: A Tribute to W. H. Marwick*, Edinburgh: John Donald, p. 182.
31 BR/LNE/8/263, Records of British Railways Board, Edinburgh: National Records of Scotland. At a later inquiry the breakdown squad claimed they *had* assisted.
32 1784/3, Personal Records of RJ Cogswell, Chippenham: Wiltshire & Swindon History Centre.
33 GBR/0014/ELMT 10/7, The Papers of Thomas Elmhirst, Cambridge: CCA.
34 09/74/1, Private Papers of Major D. Allhusen, London: IWM.
35 *Daily Mail*, 11 May 1926.
36 Philip Bagwell, *The Railwaymen*, p. 477.
37 MS.292/252.62/16/9, TUC Papers, Warwick: MRC.
38 Frank McLynn (2012), *The Road Not Taken: How Britain Narrowly Missed a Revolution*, London: The Bodley Head, p. 448.
39 Simon Heffer (ed.) (2021), *Henry 'Chips' Channon – The Diaries: 1918–38*, London: Hutchinson, p. 214.
40 MEPO 2/7296, Metropolitan Police records, Kew: The National Archives.
41 Simon Heffer, *Chips Channon*, pp. 214–15.
42 Ibid., p. 215.
43 Rachelle Saltzman, *A Lark for the Sake of Their Country*, p. 95.
44 Lord Macmillan (1952), *A Man of Law's Tale*, London: Macmillan, p. 190.
45 *British Gazette*, 11 May 1926.
46 Ibid.
47 788/150, Liberty & Co. Ltd papers, London: Westminster City Archives.
48 David Howell (2002), *MacDonald's Party: Labour Identities and Crisis, 1922–1931*, Oxford: Oxford University Press, p. 325.

49 DDQ/9/63/13, Garnett of Quernmore papers, Preston: Lancashire Archives.
50 *Daily Graphic*, 11 May 1926.
51 Charles Ferrall and Dougal McNeill (2015), *Writing the 1926 General Strike: Literature, Culture, Politics*, Cambridge: Cambridge University Press, p. 36.
52 Evelyn Waugh (1962), *Brideshead Revisited*, London: Penguin Books, pp. 194–5.
53 https://libcom.org/article/diary-virginia-woolf-during-1926-general-strike.
54 Peter Stansky, *Sassoon*, p. 121.
55 Lord Vansittart (1958), *The Mist Procession: The Autobiography of Lord Vansittart*, London: Hutchinson, p. 345.
56 *British Gazette*, 8 May 1926.
57 GWY 8/3/1, Gwynne family of Folkington papers, Brighton: The Keep.
58 MS Add. 9454/36, Siegfried Sassoon: Letters to Glen Byam Shaw, Cambridge: CUL.
59 These were finally published in *New Statesman* on 30 April 1976.
60 Ferrall and McNeill, *Writing the 1926 General Strike*, pp. 1, 9.
61 Julian Symons, *The General Strike*, p. 66.
62 Ibid., p. 151.
63 *British Gazette*, 11 May 1926.
64 Ferrall and McNeill, *Writing the 1926 General Strike*, p. 10.
65 Duke of Windsor (1951), *A King's Story: The Memoirs of H.R.H. the Duke of Windsor*, London: Cassell, p. 217.
66 *The Tatler (Emergency Number)*, 12–19 May 1926.
67 HALIFAX/A2/280/2, Halifax Family and Estate Archive, York: Borthwick Institute for Archives.
68 MS Add.9790/1/6, Ruth Darwin: correspondence and papers, Cambridge: CUL.
69 PP MS 14/186, Papers of Sir Charles Stewart Addis, London: SOAS Library and Special Collections.
70 Robert Skidelsky, *John Maynard Keynes*, Volume Two, *The Economist as Saviour 1920–1937*, London: Macmillan, pp. 250–51.
71 TUC/GS/03/002, TUC Papers, London: London Metropolitan University Archives.
72 Keith Laybourn (1993), *The General Strike of 1926*, Manchester: Manchester University Press, p. 56.
73 Torquil Cowan (2011), *Labour of Love: The Story of Robert Smillie*, Glasgow: Neil Wilson, p. 372.
74 Frank McLynn, *The Road Not Taken*, p. 453.

75 David Kirkwood (1935), *My Life of Revolt*, London: George G. Harrap & Co., p. 232.
76 Harold Macmillan, *Winds of Change*, p. 217.

6 'Napoleon-Churchill'

1   CHAR 12/6/40-49, The Churchill Papers, Cambridge: Churchill College Archives.
2   *The Nation*, 7 July 1926.
3   Lord Moran (1966), *Winston Churchill: The Struggle for Survival, 1940-1965*, London: Constable, p. 247.
4   Paul Addison, 'Churchill, Sir Winston Leonard Spencer (1874–1965)', ODNB.
5   Philip Williamson (ed.) (1987), *The Modernisation of Conservative Politics: The Diaries and Letters of William Bridgeman 1904-1935*, London: The History Press, p. 233.
6   Stuart Ball, *Parliament and Politics in the Age of Baldwin and MacDonald*, p. 87.
7   G. M. Young (1952), *Stanley Baldwin*, London: Rupert Hart-Davis, p. 116.
8   Robert Rhodes James (1969), *Memoirs of a Conservative: J. C. C. Davidson's Memoirs and Papers, 1910-37*, London: Weidenfeld & Nicolson, p. 238.
9   TUC/GS/13, TUC Papers, London: London Metropolitan University Archives (LMUA).
10 Walter Citrine (1964), *Men and Work: The Autobiography of Lord Citrine*, London: Hutchinson, p. 177.
11 *The Labour Magazine*, June 1926.
12 Scott Nearing (1926), *The British General Strike: An Economic Interpretation of its Background and its Significance*, New York: Vanguard Press, p. xiv.
13 *British Gazette*, 12 May 1926.
14 STAT 14/1498, Records of the Stationary Office, Kew: The National Archives (TNA).
15 Christopher Farman (1972), *The General Strike May 1926*, London: Rupert Hart-Davis, p. 124.
16 Templewood/V/File 6, Templewood Papers, Cambridge: Cambridge University Library (CUL).
17 Martin Gilbert (1979), *Winston S. Churchill*, Volume V, *Companion Part I: The Exchequer Years 1922-1929*, London: Heinemann, p. 695.

18 Despite 1,182 of its 1,379 employees going on strike, the *London Gazette* continued to appear (STAT 14/1497, Kew: TNA), but for the first time in its history the *Edinburgh Gazette* was typed and duplicated, though when the father of the local chapel drowned himself on 7 May the men returned to work (STAT/17/16, Records of the Stationary Office, Kew: TNA; *Scotsman*, 8 May 1926).
19 Templewood/V/File 6, Templewood Papers, Cambridge: CUL.
20 Robert Rhodes James, *Memoirs of a Conservative*, p. 237. The Duke of Northumberland, a prominent coal owner in that part of England, had acquired an interest in the *Morning Post* in 1924.
21 Martin Gilbert (1976), *Winston S. Churchill*, Volume V, *1922–1939*, London: Heinemann, p. 157.
22 Robert Rhodes James, *Memoirs of a Conservative*, p. 238. Captain Douglas Hacking, the Civil Commissioner for the North Eastern Division, refused to distribute the *Gazette* in preference to the *Yorkshire Post*, which had remained in operation (N. J. Crowson, 'Hacking, Douglas Hewitt, first Baron Hacking (1884–1950)', ODNB).
23 Martin Gilbert (1976), *Winston S. Churchill*, p. 158.
24 Robert Rhodes James, *Memoirs of a Conservative*, p. 238.
25 DAV/173/U12, John Campbell Davidson Papers, London: Parliamentary Archives.
26 Hamilton Fyfe (1926), *Behind the Scenes of the Great Strike*, London: Labour Publishing Company, p. 25.
27 Robert Rhodes James, *Memoirs of a Conservative*, p. 242. Davidson kept all the 'blue-pencilled' drafts. Unhappily, these were destroyed during the war. He recalled that they included 'about ten or twelve galley proofs of leading articles written by Winston, which I would not allow to be published'.
28 HC Deb 7 May 1926 Vol 195 c654 [Industrial Crisis].
29 Robert Rhodes James, *Memoirs of a Conservative*, p. 243.
30 *Daily Mail*, 28 June 1926.
31 Keith Middlemas (ed.) (1969), *Thomas Jones Whitehall Diary*, Volume II, *1926/1930*, Oxford: Oxford University Press, p. 44.
32 Robert Rhodes James, *Memoirs of a Conservative*, p. 240.
33 WHS N/boy 145, W. H. Smith Business Archive, Reading: University of Reading Special Collections (URSC).
34 D.3.4, Baldwin Papers, Cambridge: CUL. Other, more welcome, visitors included Samuel Hoare, Sir William Mitchell-Thomson and the Prime Minister, who visited 'the heads of the various sections and commended their work and that of their volunteer staffs' (WHS N/ket 113, W. H. Smith Business Archive).

ENDNOTES

35 Keith Middlemas, *Thomas Jones*, p. 44.
36 Ibid.
37 John Julius Norwich (ed.) (2007), *The Duff Cooper Diaries 1915-1951*, London: Weidenfeld & Nicolson, p. 214.
38 Robert Taylor (2005), 'Citrine's Unexpurgated Diaries, 1925-26: "The Mining Crisis and the National Strike"', *Historical Studies in Industrial Relations* 20, p. 90.
39 STAT 14/1498, Records of the Stationary Office, Kew: TNA.
40 WHS N/ket 113, W. H. Smith Business Archive, Reading: URSC.
41 WHS 154/3, W. H. Smith Business Archive, Reading: URSC.
42 Templewood/V/File 6, Templewood Papers, Cambridge: CUL.
43 AIR 8/84, Air Ministry records, Kew: TNA.
44 Walter Citrine, *Men and Work*, pp. 181-2.
45 Hamilton Fyfe, *Behind the Scenes*, p. 35.
46 Walter Citrine, *Men and Work*, pp. 181-2.
47 Keith Middlemas, *Thomas Jones*, p. 38.
48 G. A. Phillips (1976), *The General Strike: The Politics of Industrial Conflict*, London: Weidenfeld & Nicolson, p. 171.
49 H. B. Grimsditch, revised by A. J. A. Morris, 'Fyfe, (Henry) Hamilton (1869-1951)', ODNB.
50 Hamilton Fyfe, *Behind the Scenes*, p. 33.
51 Ibid., p. 54.
52 *The Labour Magazine*, June 1926.
53 Ibid.
54 *British Worker*, 7 May 1926.
55 TUC/GS/07/007, TUC Papers, London: LMUA.
56 See Chapter 13. STAT 14/1498, Kew: TNA.
57 Ian MacDougall (ed.) (1978), *Essays in Scottish Labour History: A Tribute to W. H. Marwick*, Edinburgh: John Donald, p. 189.
58 Fenner Brockway, *Inside the Left*, p. 188.
59 Alun Burge (1992), 'The 1926 General Strike in Cardiff', *Llafur* 6:1.
60 Anonymous (1967), *The Glorious Privilege: The History of "The Scotsman"*, Edinburgh: Nelson, pp. 95-8.
61 *Glasgow Herald*, 1 May 1976.
62 Hywel Francis (1976), 'South Wales' in M. Morris, *The General Strike*, London: Penguin Books, p. 421.
63 ZBEN/14/12/4, The Bolton Evening News Archive, Bolton: Bolton History Centre.
64 L.1.1, Baldwin papers, Cambridge: CUL.
65 MSS.292/252.62/106, TUC Papers, Warwick: Modern Records Centre.
66 AIR 8/84, Air Ministry records, Kew: TNA.

67 GBR/0014/BULL 5/16, The Papers of William Bull, Cambridge: Churchill College Archives.
68 *Daily Mail*, 11 May 1926.
69 D/EX239/1/1, Letters relating to the General Strike, Reading: Royal Berkshire Archives.
70 Christopher Farman, *The General Strike May 1926*, p. 140.
71 Julian Symons (1957), *The General Strike: A Historical Portrait*, London: Cresset Press, p. 164.
72 Harold Macmillan (1966), *Winds of Change 1914–1939*, London: Macmillan, p. 219.
73 Anonymous (1926), *Strike Nights in Printing House Square: An Episode in the History of The Times*, London: The Times.
74 Martin Gilbert (1979), *Winston S. Churchill*, Volume V, *Companion*, p. 714.
75 STAT 14/1498, Records of the Stationary Office, Kew: TNA.
76 Patrick Renshaw (1975), *The General Strike*, London: Eyre Methuen, p. 197.
77 Martin Gilbert (1979), *Winston S. Churchill*, Volume V, *Companion*, p. 720.
78 Stuart Ball, *Parliament and Politics in the Age of Baldwin and MacDonald*, p. 87.
79 John Barnes and David Nicholson (eds) (1980), *The Leo Amery Diaries*, Volume I, *1896–1929*, London: Hutchinson, p. 454. 'To bell the cat' means to attempt, or agree to perform, an impossibly difficult task.
80 Robert Rhodes James, *Memoirs of a Conservative*, p. 245.
81 Hamilton Fyfe, *Behind the Scenes*, p. 87.

7 'Raised passions and frayed tempers'

1 *Guardian*, 3 May 1926.
2 *The Times*, 3 May 1926.
3 HC Deb 3 May 1926 Vol 195 c69 [Prime Minister's Statement]. Baldwin ignored him.
4 Marc Wadsworth (2020), *Comrade Sak: A Political Biography*, Leeds: Peepal Tree Press, p. 54.
5 Sehri Saklatvala (1991), *The Fifth Commandment: A Biography of Shapurji Saklatvala*, Salford: Miranda Press, pp. 307–8.
6 Rodney Mace (1976), 'The Strike in the Regions … Battersea' in M. Morris (ed.), *The General Strike*, London: Penguin Books, p. 381.
7 Keith Laybourn (1996), *The General Strike: Day by Day*, Stroud: Sutton Publishing, pp. 60–61.

8 Sehri Saklatvala, *The Fifth Commandment*, p. 308.
9 Marc Wadsworth, *Comrade Sak*, p. 55.
10 Sehri Saklatvala, *The Fifth Commandment*, p. 309.
11 Ibid., pp. 310–11.
12 Marc Wadsworth, *Comrade Sak*, p. 56.
13 HC Deb 7 May 1926 Vol 195 cc601-03 [Imprisonment Of Member].
14 Leonard D. White (1933), *Whitley Councils in the British Civil Service: A Study in Conciliation and Arbitration*, Chicago: University of Chicago Press, pp. 3–4.
15 H. J. Wilson, revised by Mark Pottle, 'Whitley, John Henry (1866–1935)', ODNB.
16 HC Dec 19 June 1928 Vol 218 c1597 [Mr Speaker's Retirement].
17 Asa Briggs (1961), *The History of Broadcasting in the United Kingdom*, Volume 1, *The Birth of Broadcasting*, London: Oxford University Press, p. 374.
18 Robert Taylor (2005), 'Citrine's Unexpurgated Diaries, 1925–26: "The Mining Crisis and the National Strike"', *Historical Studies in Industrial Relations* 20, p. 88.
19 HC Deb 7 May 1926 Vol 195 c642 [Industrial Crisis].
20 BBC news broadcast, 4 May 1926.
21 John Murray (1951), *The General Strike of 1926: A History*, London: Lawrence and Wishart, p. 130.
22 MS 1066 1/706, Papers of Waldorf Astor, 2nd Viscount Astor, Reading: University of Reading Special Collections.
23 See Chapter 13.
24 HC Deb 7 May 1926 Vol 195 cc642-43 [Industrial Crisis].
25 HC Deb 6 May 1926 Vol 195 cc439-40 [Parliamentary Papers (Distribution)].
26 MSS.292/252.62/114, TUC Papers, Warwick: Modern Records Centre.
27 Notices of Motions 1071, London: House of Commons Library.
28 STAT 14/1497, Records of the Stationary Office, Kew: The National Archives (TNA).
29 Sehri Saklatvala, *The Fifth Commandment*, p. 311.
30 HC Deb 3 May 1926 Vol 195 cc34-35 [Members of Parliament (Travelling Facilities)].
31 CHAR2_147_89, The Churchill Papers, Cambridge: Churchill Archives Centre.
32 HC Deb 3 May 1926 Vol 195 cc35-9 [Emergency Powers Act (Royal Proclamations)].
33 HO 144/6116, Home Office papers, Kew: TNA.
34 *The Journalist*, July 1926.

35 PRG/13/2, House of Commons Parliamentary Press Gallery Papers, London: Parliamentary Archives.
36 *Carlisle Journal*, 11 May 1926.
37 Andrew Sparrow (2003), *Obscure Scribblers: A History of Parliamentary Journalism*, London: Politico's, p. 73.
38 Asa Briggs, *History of Broadcasting*, p. 270.
39 Harold Macmillan (1966), *Winds of Change 1914–1939*, London: Macmillan, p. 216.
40 John Murray, *The General Strike of 1926*, p. 130.
41 *British Gazette*, 8 May 1926.
42 Julian Symons (1957), *The General Strike: A Historical Portrait*, London: Cresset Press, p. 121.
43 JHW/4/1/68, John Henry Whitley Archives, Huddersfield: Heritage Quay. Elizabeth had married the Romanian diplomat Prince Antoine Bibesco in 1919.
44 *Daily Mail*, 5 May 1926.
45 *British Gazette*, 8 May 1926.
46 PRO 30/69/1171, James Ramsay MacDonald Papers (JRMP), Kew: TNA.
47 Harold Macmillan (1966), *Winds of Change 1914–1939*, London: Macmillan, pp. 217–19.
48 See David Torrance (2011), *Noel Skelton and the Property-Owning Democracy*, London: Biteback.
49 *The Times*, 11 May 1926.
50 *British Gazette*, 10 May 1926.
51 Keith Middlemas (ed.) (1969), *Thomas Jones Whitehall Diary*, Volume II, *1926/1930*, Oxford: Oxford University Press, p. 39.
52 Ibid., p. 409.
53 John Julius Norwich (ed.) (2005), *The Duff Cooper Diaries 1915–1951*, London: Weidenfeld & Nicolson, p. 215.
54 Anthony Eden (1962), *The Eden Memoirs: Facing the Dictators*, London: Cassell, p. 6.
55 *Daily Telegraph*, 7 May 1926.
56 HC Deb 5 May 1926 Vol 195 cc421-22 [Strike Negotiations].
57 Margaret Bondfield (1948), *A Life's Work*, London: Hutchinson, p. 269.
58 Norman and Jeanne MacKenzie (eds) (1985), *The Diary of Beatrice Webb*, Volume Four, *1924–1943 'The Wheel of Life'*, London: Virago, p. 78.
59 Roy Jenkins (1998), *The Chancellors*, London: Macmillan, p. 186.
60 MS.292/252.62/20/8, TUC Papers, Warwick: Modern Record Centre.

61 David Marquand (1977), *Ramsay MacDonald*, London: Jonathan Cape, pp. 434–5.
62 David Howell (2002), *MacDonald's Party: Labour Identities and Crisis, 1922-1931*, Oxford: Oxford University Press, p. 100.
63 David Marquand, 'MacDonald, (James) Ramsay (1866–1937)', ODNB.
64 J. Ramsay MacDonald (1912), *Syndicalism: A Critical Examination*, Chicago: Open House, p. 62.
65 PRO 30/69/1436, JRMP, Kew: TNA.
66 *Socialist Review*, June 1926.
67 PRO 30/69/1436, JRMP, Kew: TNA.
68 PRO 30/69/1171, JRMP, Kew: TNA.
69 *Evening News*, 7 May 1926.
70 RMD/1/4/16, JRM Papers, Manchester: JRRIL.
71 PRO 30/69/1753, JRMP, Kew: TNA.
72 Norman and Jeanne MacKenzie, *Diary of Beatrice Webb*, Volume Four, p. 78.
73 John Paton (1936), *Left Turn! The Autobiography of John Paton*, London: Martin Secker & Warburg, pp. 246–7.
74 David Kirkwood (1935), *My Life of Revolt*, London: George G. Harrap & Co., pp. 231–2.
75 G. A. Phillips (1976), *The General Strike: The Politics of Industrial Conflict*, London: Weidenfeld & Nicolson, p. 221.
76 *British Gazette*, 8 May 1926.
77 Hamilton Fyfe (1926), *Behind the Scenes of the Great Strike*, Labour Publishing Company, p. 58.
78 *British Gazette*, 11 May 1926.
79 John Campbell (1977), *Lloyd George: The Goat in the Wilderness 1922–1931*, London: Jonathan Cape, p. 136.
80 Hamilton Fyfe, *Behind the Scenes*, p. 74.
81 Harold Macmillan, *Winds of Change*, p. 215.
82 Harold Nicolson (1952), *George V: His Life and Reign*, London: Constable, p. 418.
83 Robert Rhodes James (1969), *Memoirs of a Conservative: J. C. C. Davidson's Memoirs and Papers, 1910-37*, London: Weidenfeld & Nicolson, pp. 260–61.
84 John Campbell, *Lloyd George*, pp. 136–8.
85 LG/G/5/1/9, The Lloyd George Papers, London: Parliamentary Archives.
86 John Campbell, *Lloyd George*, pp. 139–40.
87 *Daily Chronicle*, 12 May 1926.

8 'The Big Three'

1. *Socialist Review*, June 1926.
2. Alan Bullock (1960), *The Life and Times of Ernest Bevin*, Volume One, *Trade Union Leader 1881–1940*, London: Heinemann, p. 318.
3. MSS.292/252.62/100, TUC Papers, Warwick: Modern Records Centre.
4. Christopher Loughlin (2018), *Labour and the Politics of Disloyalty in Belfast, 1921–39: The Moral Economy of Loyalty*, London: Palgrave Macmillan, p. 109.
5. Walter Citrine (1964), *Men and Work: The Autobiography of Lord Citrine*, London: Hutchinson, pp. 178–9.
6. Keith Middlemas (ed.) (1969), *Thomas Jones: Whitehall Diary*, Volume II, *1926–1930*, London: Oxford University Press, p. 38.
7. Hugh Armstrong Clegg (1985), *A History of British Trade Unions Since 1889*, Volume II, *1911–1933*, Oxford: Clarendon Press, p. 404.
8. John McLean (1976), *The 1926 General Strike in Lanarkshire*, History Group of the Communist Party, p. 8.
9. Walter Citrine, *Men and Work*, pp. 177–8.
10. HO144/10670, Home Office records, Kew: The National Archives (TNA).
11. TO134, Treasury records, Kew: TNA.
12. David Howell (2002), *MacDonald's Party: Labour Identities and Crisis, 1922–1931*, Oxford: Oxford University Press, p. 100.
13. Frank McLynn (2012), *The Road Not Taken: How Britain Narrowly Missed a Revolution*, London: The Bodley Head, p. 395.
14. Robert Taylor (2005), 'Citrine's Unexpurgated Diaries, 1925–26: "The Mining Crisis and the National Strike"', *Historical Studies in Industrial Relations* 20, p. 76.
15. RMD/1/4/57, JRM Papers, Manchester: JRRIL.
16. Robert Taylor, 'Citrine's Unexpurgated Diaries', p. 79.
17. David Kirkwood (1935), *My Life of Revolt*, London: George G. Harrap & Co., p. 231.
18. Arthur Horner (1960), *Incorrigible Rebel*, London: MacGibbon & Kee, p. 72.
19. Fenner Brockway, *Inside the Left*, p. 193.
20. David Howell (2002), *MacDonald's Party: Labour Identities and Crisis, 1922–1931*, Oxford: Oxford University Press, p. 120.
21. Hywel Francis, 'Cook, Arthur James (1883–1931)', ODNB.
22. *Daily Herald*, 27 April 1926.
23. Paul Davies (1987), *A. J. Cook*, Manchester: Manchester University Press, p. 102.

24 *British Worker*, 10 May 1926.
25 Robert Taylor, 'Citrine's Unexpurgated Diaries', p. 74.
26 Stuart Ball, *Parliament and Politics in the Age of Baldwin and MacDonald*, p. 84.
27 Frank McLynn, *The Road Not Taken*, pp. 392 and 409.
28 KV 4/246, Records of the Security Service, Kew: TNA.
29 Frank McLynn, *The Road Not Taken*, p. 395.
30 Philip Williamson, 'Thomas, James Henry [Jim, Jimmy] (1874–1949)', ODNB.
31 Julian Symons (1957), *The General Strike: A Historical Portrait*, London: Cresset Press, p. 6.
32 Egon Wertheimer (1929), *Portrait of the Labour Party*, London: G. P. Putnam's Sons, p. 178.
33 *Answers*, January 1927.
34 Lord Birkenhead (1924), *Contemporary Personalities*, London: Cassell, p. 185.
35 *Answers*, January 1927.
36 Walter Citrine, *Men and Work*, pp. 178 and 235.
37 Hamilton Fyfe (1926), *Behind the Scenes of the Great Strike*, Labour Publishing Company, p. 15.
38 Gregory Blaxland (1964), *J. H. Thomas: A Life for Unity*, London: Frederick Muller, p. 188.
39 *Answers*, January 1927.
40 Walter Citrine, *Men and Work*, pp. 179–80.
41 *British Worker*, 10 May 1926.
42 Alan Bullock, *Life and Times of Ernest Bevin*, pp. 365–6.
43 Ibid., p. 319.
44 Chris Wrigley, 'Bevin, Ernest (1881–1951)', ODNB.
45 John Paton (1936), *Left Turn! The Autobiography of John Paton*, London: Martin Secker & Warburg, pp. 257–8.
46 Alan Bullock, *Life and Times of Ernest Bevin*, p. 320.
47 Ibid., pp. 323–4.
48 Norman and Jeanne MacKenzie (eds) (1984), *The Diary of Beatrice Webb*, Volume Four, *1924-1943 'The Wheel of Life'*, London: Virago, pp. 126–7.
49 Tom Buchanan, 'Citrine, Walter McLennan, first Baron Citrine (1887–1983)', ODNB.
50 Walter Citrine, *Men and Work*, pp. 182–4, 196.
51 G. A. Phillips, 'Pugh, Sir Arthur (1870–1955)', ODNB.
52 *Answers*, January 1927.
53 John Hodge (1931), *Workman's Cottage to Windsor Castle*, London: Sampson Low, Marston & Co., p. 363.

54 R. W. Postgate, Ellen Wilkinson and J. F. Horrabin (1927), *A Workers' History of the Great Strike*, London: The Plebs League, p. 27.
55 Michael Foot (1997), *Aneurin Bevan 1897–1960*, London: Victor Gollancz, p. 45.
56 G. A. Phillips (1977), 'The Labour Party and the General Strike', *Llafur* 2:2.
57 John Bew (2016), *Citizen Clem: A Biography of Attlee*, London: Riverrun, p. 138. Attlee won on appeal two years later.
58 Patricia Ryan (1976), 'The Poor Law in 1926' in M. Morris, *The General Strike*, London: Penguin Books, pp. 361-66.
59 Bernard Donoughue and G. W. Jones (2001), *Herbert Morrison: Portrait of a Politician*, London: Phoenix Press, p. 80.
60 Scott Nearing (1926), *The British General Strike: An Economic Interpretation of its Background and its Significance*, New York: Vanguard Press, pp. xii–xvii.
61 Margaret Bondfield (1948), *A Life's Work*, London: Hutchinson, pp. 266-9.
62 R. W. Postgate et al., *A Workers' History of the Great Strike*, p. 46.
63 Robert Rhodes James (1969), *Memoirs of a Conservative: J. C. C. Davidson's Memoirs and Papers 1910-37*, London: Weidenfeld & Nicolson, p. 243.
64 Keith Middlemas and John Barnes (1969), *Baldwin: A Biography*, London: Weidenfeld & Nicolson, p. 411.
65 Julian Symons (1957), *The General Strike: A Historical Portrait*, London: Cresset Press, p. 142.
66 DCON/291/7, Glamorgan Constabulary Records, Cardiff: Glamorgan Archives.
67 Julian Symons, *The General Strike*, p. 198.
68 HO144/6898, Home Office records, Kew: TNA.
69 *Evening News*, 11 May 1926.
70 Hugh Armstrong Clegg, *A History of British Trade Unions*, p. 404.
71 G. A. Phillips (1976), *The General Strike: The Politics of Industrial Conflict*, London: Weidenfeld & Nicolson, p. 143.
72 Christopher Loughlin, *Labour and the Politics of Disloyalty in Belfast*, p. 109.
73 *British Gazette*, 11 May 1926.
74 MS.292/252.62/20/15, TUC Papers, Warwick: Modern Records Centre.
75 *Scottish Worker*, 11 May 1926.
76 John Paton (1936), *Left Turn! The Autobiography of John Paton*, London: Martin Secker & Warburg, p. 264.

9 'The stupidest men in England'

1. John Campbell (1985), *F. E. Smith: First Earl of Birkenhead*, London: Jonathan Cape, p. 777.
2. Norman and Jeanne MacKenzie (eds) (1984), *The Diary of Beatrice Webb*, Volume Four, *1924-1943 'The Wheel of Life'*, p. 75.
3. G. D. H. Cole (1937), *A Short History of the British Working Class Movement 1789-1937*, Volume III, *1900-1937*, London: George Allen & Unwin, p. 203.
4. Keith Middlemas (ed.) (1969), *Thomas Jones: Whitehall Diary*, Volume II, *1926-1930*, London: Oxford University Press, p. 12.
5. Ibid., p. 19.
6. Keith Robbins, 'Lister, Philip Cunliffe, first earl of Swinton (1884-1972)', ODNB.
7. John Murray (1951), *The General Strike of 1926: A History*, London: Lawrence and Wishart, p. 68.
8. TUC/GS/03/002, TUC Papers, London: London Metropolitan University Archives.
9. Quoted in William Wallace (1926), *The Great Strike: Its Causes and Consequences*, New York: American Management Association, p. 4.
10. Keith Middlemas, *Thomas Jones*, p. 18.
11. G. A. Phillips (1976), *The General Strike: The Politics of Industrial Conflict*, London: Weidenfeld & Nicolson, p. 34.
12. CAB 27/317, Cabinet Conclusions, Kew: The National Archives.
13. G. W. McDonald (1976), 'The Role of British Industry in 1926' in M. Morris, *The General Strike*, London: Penguin Books, pp. 294-5.
14. Royal Commission on the Coal Industry (1926), Volume 1, *Report*, Cmnd 260, London: HMSO, p. 111.
15. Keith Middlemas, *Thomas Jones*, p. 12.
16. William Alexander Lee (1954), *Thirty Years in Coal*, London: Mining Association of Great Britain, pp. 208-9.
17. Sir Evan Williams, Dictionary of Welsh Biography.
18. Sankey Commission (1919), *Interim Report of*, Cmnd 84, p. IX.
19. Barry Supple (1984), '"No bloody revolutions but for obstinate reactions"? British coalowners in their context, 1919-20' in D. C. Coleman and Peter Mathias (eds), *Enterprise and History: Essays in Honour of Charles Wilson*, Cambridge: Cambridge University Press, p. 214.
20. John Williams, 'Williams, Sir Evan, baronet (1871-1959)', ODNB.
21. Robert Taylor (2005), 'Citrine's Unexpurgated Diaries, 1925-26: "The Mining Crisis and the National Strike"', *Historical Studies in Industrial Relations* 20, p. 97.

22 G. W. McDonald, 'The Role of British Industry in 1926', p. 295.
23 Robin Page Arnot (1926), *The General Strike, May 1926: Its Origin and History*, London: Labour Research Department, p. 46.
24 Keith Middlemas, *Thomas Jones*, p. 12.
25 Quentin Outram, 'Sir Adam Nimmo'.
26 William Alexander Lee, *Thirty Years in Coal*, p. 209.
27 Quentin Outram, 'Sir Adam Nimmo'.
28 *The Times*, 20 March 1924.
29 *The Times*, 22 January 1925.
30 *The Times*, 26 January 1925.
31 Keith Middlemas, *Thomas Jones*, p. 19.
32 Cameron Hazlehurst, 'Pease, Joseph Albert [Jack], first Baron Gainford (1860–1943)', ODNB.
33 G. A. Phillips, *The General Strike*, p. 34.
34 94/161, Lord Gainford (LG) papers, Oxford: Nuffield College Library (NCL).
35 94/163, LG papers, Oxford: NCL.
36 *Daily Mail*, 5 May 1926.
37 Osbert Sitwell (1949), *Laughter in the Next Room*, London: Macmillan, pp. 223–4.
38 Christopher Farman (1972), *The General Strike May 1926*, London: Rupert Hart-Davis, p. 114.
39 Keith Middlemas, *Thomas Jones*, p. 10.
40 Alvin Jackson, 'Stewart, Charles Stewart Henry Vane-Tempest-, seventh marquess of Londonderry', ODNB.
41 *The Times*, 14 August 1925.
42 *The Times*, 17 August 1925.
43 Neil Fleming (2023), 'Paternalism, Conflict and Decline: The seventh Marquess of Londonderry and the Coal Industry, 1906–1947', *Journal of the Durham County Local History Society* 88.
44 *Daily Mail*, 11 May 1926.
45 Stewart Mews (1976), 'The Churches' in M. Morris, *The General Strike*, p. 326.
46 Neil Fleming, 'Paternalism, Conflict and Decline'.

10 The Archbishop, the Cardinal and the Moderator

1 Stuart Mews (1976), 'The Churches' in M. Morris (ed), *The General Strike*, London: Penguin Books, p. 320.
2 G. K. A. Bell (1935), *Randall Davidson: Archbishop of Canterbury*, Volume II, London: Oxford University Press, p. 1305.

ENDNOTES

3 HL Deb 5 May 1926 Vol 64 cc48-51 [Emergency Regulations].
4 Vol 273, Randall Thomas Davidson (RTD) papers, London: Lambeth Palace Library (LPL). In 1947 the Ecclesiastical Commissioners became the Church Commissioners.
5 *Daily Telegraph*, 7 May 1926.
6 Vol 273, RTD papers, London: LPL.
7 *The Labour Magazine*, June 1926.
8 Stuart Mews, 'The Churches', pp. 323–5.
9 G. K. A. Bell, *Randall Davidson*, pp. 1306–7.
10 Vol 164 f191, George Bell papers, London: LPL.
11 *Daily Chronicle*, 12 May 1926.
12 Matthew Grimley, 'Henson, Herbert Hensley [Bishop of Durham] (1863–1947)', ODNB.
13 Vol 273, RTD papers, London: LPL.
14 Philip Williamson (ed.) (1988), *The Modernisation of Conservative Politics: The Diaries and Letters of William Bridgeman 1904–1935*, The History Press, p. 197.
15 Charles Stuart (ed.) (1975), *The Reith Diaries*, London: Collins, p. 94.
16 Vol 273, RTD papers, London: LPL.
17 Charles Stuart, *The Reith Diaries*, p. 94.
18 CO 26, British Broadcasting Company papers, Caversham: BBC Written Archive Centre.
19 Vol 273, RTD papers, London: LPL.
20 J. C. W. Reith (1949), *Into the Wind*, London: Hodder & Stoughton, p. 109.
21 Asa Briggs (1961), *The History of Broadcasting in the United Kingdom*, Volume 1, *The Birth of Broadcasting*, London: Oxford University Press, p. 379
22 The headline in the *British Worker* was 'PEACE CALL SILENCED Plan of Churches Not Broadcast IS IT FAIR?'
23 G. K. A. Bell, *Randall Davidson*, p. 1311.
24 https://libcom.org/article/diary-virginia-woolf-during-1926-general-strike.
25 Vol 273, RTD papers, London: LPL.
26 Henry Slesser (1941), *Judgment Reserved*, London: Hutchinson, pp. 160–61.
27 Vol 273, RTD papers, London: LPL.
28 Martin Gilbert (1979), *Winston S. Churchill*, Volume V, *Companion Part 1: The Exchequer Years 1922–1929*, pp. 717–18. Both were finally printed in the *Gazette* on 12 May, the last day of the strike.

29 Robert Rhodes James (1969), *Memoirs of a Conservative: J. C. C. Davidson's Memoirs and Papers, 1910–37*, London: Weidenfeld & Nicolson, p. 249.
30 Frank McLynn (2012), *The Road Not Taken: How Britain Narrowly Missed a Revolution*, London: The Bodley Head, p. 445.
31 G. K. A. Bell, *Randall Davidson*, p. 1312. The Church Assembly was later renamed the General Synod.
32 Hamilton Fyfe (1926), *Behind the Scenes of the Great Strike*, Labour Publishing Company, pp. 59–74.
33 3rd BBC bulletin, 8 May 1926.
34 *New Republic*, 7 July 1926.
35 Private Papers XV, RTD papers, London: LPL.
36 Vol 213 f276, RTD papers, London: LPL.
37 Stuart Mews, 'Davidson, Randall Thomas, Baron Davidson of Lambeth (1848–1930)', ODNB.
38 Rene Kollar, 'Bourne, Francis Alphonsus (1861–1935)', ODNB.
39 Michael Walsh (2008), *The Westminster Cardinals: The Past and the Future*, London: Burns & Oates, pp. 98–100.
40 Bo. 5/77 – STRIKE, Cardinal Bourne (CB) papers, London: Westminster Diocesan Archives (WDA).
41 Bo. 5/77, CB papers, London: WDA.
42 Vol 273, RTD papers, London: LPL.
43 Stuart Mews, 'The Churches', p. 330.
44 Bo. 5/77, CB papers, London: WDA.
45 *Daily News*, 12 May 1926.
46 *Yorkshire Post*, 1 June 1926.
47 Bo. 5/77, CB papers, London: WDA. Gordon added that her stepfather had told her judges at Lincoln's Inn 'were all going to become RC's in consequence!!!'
48 Bo. 5/77, CB papers, London: WDA.
49 Ibid.
50 Ibid.
51 *The Christian Democrat*, July 1926.
52 Bo. 5/77, CB papers, London: WDA.
53 *British Worker*, 12 May 1926. The Labour MPs were John Scurr, Hugh Murnin, Joe Tinker, Martin Connolly and Joseph Sullivan.
54 Neil Riddell (1997), 'The Catholic Church and the Labour Party, 1918–1931', *Twentieth Century British History* 8:2, pp. 165–93.
55 Stuart Mews, 'The Churches', pp. 332–3.
56 The honourable exceptions are Stewart J. Brown and Ian MacDougall.

57 MS WHI Box 10/2, John White Papers, Edinburgh: New College Archives & Library.
58 Stewart J. Brown (1991), '"A Victory for God": The Scottish Presbyterian Churches and the General Strike of 1926', *Journal of Ecclesiastical History* 42:4, pp. 603-4.
59 https://www.scribd.com/doc/152217519/Menace-of-the-Irish-Race-to-our-Scottish-Nationality
60 Stewart J. Brown, 'A Victory for God', p. 601.
61 *Scotsman*, 10 May 1926.
62 Acc.5695/2, J. P. M. Millar papers, Edinburgh: National Library of Scotland.
63 *Scotsman*, 10 May 1926.
64 G. K. A. Bell, *Randall Davidson*, p. 1315.
65 Stewart J. Brown, 'A Victory for God', pp. 605-6.
66 Ibid., pp. 616-17.

11 'That Wuthering Height'

1 *The Times*, 18 January 1926. Knox later imagined a successful general strike. This included a Compulsory Employment Act and 'distressed' mine owners (Ronald Knox, 1932, 'If the General Strike had Succeeded', in J. C. Squire, ed., *If It Had Happened Otherwise: Lapses Into Imaginary History*, London: Longmans, pp. 277-89).
2 http://news.bbc.co.uk/newswatch/ukfs/hi/newsid_4080000/newsid_4081000/4081060.stm
3 Asa Briggs (1985), *The BBC: The First Fifty Years*, Oxford: Oxford University Press, p. 97.
4 TUC/GS/13, TUC Papers, London: London Metropolitan University Archives.
5 Asa Briggs (1961), *The History of Broadcasting in the United Kingdom*, Volume 1, *The Birth of Broadcasting*, London: Oxford University Press, p. 17.
6 Ian McIntyre, 'Reith, John Charles Walsham, first Baron Reith (1889–1971)', ODNB.
7 Patrick Renshaw (1975), *The General Strike*, London: Eyre Methuen, p. 199.
8 Ian McIntyre (1993), *The Expense of Glory: A Life of John Reith*, London: HarperCollins, pp. 140-41.
9 Charles Stuart (ed.) (1975), *The Reith Diaries*, London: Collins, pp. 92-93. Reith's account is confused as the first edition of the *British Gazette* did not appear until 5 May.

10 *St Martin's Review*, June 1926.
11 Asa Briggs, *History of Broadcasting*, p. 361.
12 Charles Stuart, *The Reith Diaries*, pp. 93–4.
13 Ian McIntyre, *The Expense of Glory*, pp. 142–3.
14 CO 30, British Broadcasting Company (BBC) papers, Caversham: BBC Written Archives Centre (BWAC).
15 Robert Rhodes James (1969), *Memoirs of a Conservative: J. C. C. Davidson's Memoirs and Papers, 1910–37*, London: Weidenfeld & Nicolson, p. 247.
16 Robert Rhodes James, *Memoirs of a Conservative*, p. 246.
17 Asa Briggs, *History of Broadcasting*, p. 367.
18 J. C. W. Reith (1949), *Into the Wind*, London: Hodder & Stoughton, pp. 107–8.
19 Charles Stuart, *The Reith Diaries*, p. 96.
20 Asa Briggs, *History of Broadcasting*, pp. 368–9.
21 See David Torrance (2024), *The Wild Men: The Remarkable Story of Britain's First Labour Government*, London: Bloomsbury Continuum, p. 216.
22 Keith Middlemas (ed.) (1969), *Thomas Jones: Whitehall Diary*, Volume II, *1926–1930*, London: Oxford University Press, p. 38.
23 J. C. W. Reith, *Into the Wind*, p. 110.
24 Keith Middlemas, *Thomas Jones*, p. 41. Kerr succeeded as the 11th Marquess of Lothian in 1930 and in 1939 he became the UK's ambassador to the United States.
25 Robert Rhodes James, *Memoirs of a Conservative*, p. 254.
26 Charles Stuart, *The Reith Diaries*, p. 95.
27 Keith Middlemass, *Thomas Jones*, p. 43.
28 https://libcom.org/article/diary-virginia-woolf-during-1926-general-strike.
29 Ian McIntyre, *The Expense of Glory*, p. 144.
30 Charles Stuart, *The Reith Diaries*, p. 95.
31 J. C. W. Reith, *Into the Wind*, p. 111. Reith refused.
32 Charles Stuart, *The Reith Diaries*, pp. 95–6.
33 GBR/0014/MCHL 5/1/66, The Papers of Lady Soames, Cambridge: Churchill College Archives.
34 SD 1821/AWC-437-2, Revealing Voices project, Stoke: Stoke-on-Trent City Archives.
35 Asa Briggs, *History of Broadcasting*, p. 374.
36 Stephen Usherwood, 'The B.B.C. and the General Strike', *History Today*, December 1972.

37 Andrew Boyle (1972), *Only the Wind Will Listen: Reith of the BBC*, London: Hutchinson, p. 198.
38 Philip S. Bagwell (1963), *The Railwaymen: The History of the National Union of Railwaymen*, London: George Allen & Unwin, p. 475.
39 Asa Briggs, *History of Broadcasting*, p. 371.
40 BDX 79/10/26/4, Senogles Papers, Barrow: Barrow Archive Centre.
41 See Chapter 12.
42 CO 27, BBC papers, Caversham: BWAC.
43 Charles Stuart, *The Reith Diaries*, p. 96.
44 PRO 30/69/1753, James Ramsay MacDonald Papers, Kew: The National Archives.
45 John Barnes and David Nicholson (eds) (1980), *The Leo Amery Diaries*, Volume I, *1896–1929*, London: Hutchinson, p. 454.
46 Charles Stuart, *The Reith Diaries*, p. 96.
47 See Chapter 13.
48 Asa Briggs, *History of Broadcasting*, p. 366.
49 J. C. W. Reith, *Into the Wind*, p. 109.
50 CO 28, BBC papers, Caversham: BWAC.
51 J. C. W. Reith, *Into the Wind*, p. 109.

12 The Civil Commissioners

1 MS. 9663/59, Archive of Edward Turnour, 6th Earl Winterton, Oxford: Bodleian Archives & Manuscripts.
2 Not examined individually in this chapter are Oliver Stanley (Midland Division), Douglas Hacking (North Eastern) and Douglas King (North Midland).
3 *Guardian*, 3 May 1926.
4 Earl Winterton (1953), *Orders of the Day*, London: Cassell, p. 136.
5 Kenneth Rose, revised, 'Turnour, Edward, sixth Earl Winterton (1883–1962)', ODNB.
6 MS. 9663/59, Archive of Edward Turnour, 6th Earl Winterton.
7 As this was an Irish peerage Winterton was not obliged to relinquish his Commons seat.
8 Kenneth Rose, 'Turnour, Edward, sixth Earl Winterton', ODNB.
9 MS. 9663/33, Archive of Edward Turnour, 6th Earl Winterton.
10 Earl Winteron, *Orders of the Day*, pp. 139–40. The 'showdown' was the armed protection of food convoys from London's docks.
11 MS. 9663/59, Archive of Edward Turnour, 6th Earl Winterton.
12 Earl Winteron, *Orders of the Day*, p. 138.
13 MS. 9663/59, Archive of Edward Turnour, 6th Earl Winterton.

14 Earl Winteron, *Orders of the Day*, p. 138.
15 Julian Symons (1957), *The General Strike: A Historical Portrait*, London: Cresset Press, p. 26.
16 RA PS/PSO/GV/C/B/2052/1, King George V papers, Windsor: Royal Archives.
17 HO 317/73, Home Office records, Kew: The National Archives.
18 MS.172/GS/4, TUC Papers, Warwick: Modern Records Centre (MRC).
19 *Daily Telegraph*, 7 May 1926.
20 Ernie Trory (1975), *Brighton and the General Strike*, Brighton: Crabtree Press, pp. 14–15.
21 Andy Durr (1976), *Who Were the Guilty? General Strike Brighton May 1926*, Brighton: Brighton Labour History Press, pp. 24–5.
22 Ernie Trory, *Brighton and the General Strike*, pp. 15–16.
23 *Guardian*, 31 December 2016.
24 Ellen Wilkinson, *Peeps at Politicians*, pp. 75–6.
25 Templewood/V/File 6, Templewood Papers, Cambridge: Cambridge University Library (CUL).
26 G. C. Peden, 'Wood, Sir (Howard) Kingsley (1881–1943)', ODNB.
27 Hugh Gault (2017), *Kingsley Wood: Scenes from a Political Life 1925–1943*, Cambridge: Gretton Books, p. 26.
28 George Short (1970), 'The General Strike and Class Struggles in the North-East. 1925–28', *Marxism Today*, October 1970.
29 HC Deb 6 May 1926 Vol 195 cc486-87 [Emergency Powers].
30 HC Deb 10 May 1926 Vol 195 c687 [Essential Services (Newcastle)].
31 Julian Symons, *The General Strike*, pp. 125–9.
32 Editors (1977), '1926 Remembered and Revealed', *Llafur* 2:2, 1 April 1977.
33 Hugh Gault, *Kingsley Wood*, p. 207.
34 Tony Mason (1970), *General Strike in the North East*, Hull: University of Hull Publications, p. 64.
35 Editors (1977), '1926 Remembered and Revealed', *Llafur* 2:2, 1 April 1977.
36 HO144/6894, Home Office records, Kew: TNA.
37 R. H. Haigh, Dave Morris and Anthony Peters (eds) (1988), *The Guardian Book of the General Strike*, London: Avebury, p. 24.
38 Haigh et al., *Guardian Book*, pp. 42–3.
39 D. E. Baines and R. Beani (1969), 'The General Strike on Merseyside, 1926' in J. R. Harris (ed.), *Liverpool and Merseyside: Essays in the Economic and Social History of the Port and Its Hinterland*, London: Frank Cass & Co., pp. 251–9.

40 Hywel Francis (1976), 'South Wales' in J. Skelley (ed.), *The General Strike 1926*, London: Lawrence and Wishart.
41 Alun Burge (1992), 'The 1926 General Strike in Cardiff', *Llafur* 6:1.
42 Ibid.
43 Tony Peters, 'The Volunteer's Story', Glamorgan Archives website.
44 LG/G/17/7/1, The Lloyd George Papers, London: Parliamentary Archives.
45 Alun Burge, 'The 1926 General Strike in Cardiff'.
46 The Parliament of Northern Ireland was then temporarily housed at the Union Theological College in Belfast. What became known as 'Stormont' was under construction on the outskirts of the city.
47 HC Deb (NI) 5 May 1926 Vol 7 cc977-81 [Emergency Powers Bill].
48 HC Deb (NI) 11 May 1926 Vol 7 c1081.
49 COM/13/4/43a, Government of Northern Ireland (GNI) records, Belfast: Public Record Office of Northern Ireland (PRONI).
50 HA/32/1/501, GNI records, Belfast: PRONI.
51 COM/13/2/47, GNI records, Belfast: PRONI.
52 Richard Hawkins, 'Barbour, Sir John Milne', Dictionary of Irish Biography website.
53 HA/32/1/498, GNI records, Belfast: PRONI. On 18 May the Attorney General, 'having considered all the circumstances', directed that no prosecution be instituted against Midgley.
54 CAB/9/R/39/1, GNI records, Belfast: PRONI.
55 Eugene Kiernan (1986), 'Drogheda and the British General Strike, 1926', *Saothar* 11, pp. 19–26.
56 MSS.292/252.62/124, TUC Papers, Warwick: MRC.
57 Eugene Kiernan, 'Drogheda and the British General Strike, 1926'.
58 BBC bulletin, 11 May 1926.
59 W. V. Ball, 'Watson, William, Baron Thankerton (1873–1948)', ODNB.
60 The other district commissioners were C. H. Marshall (Dundee), G. Bennett Mitchell (Aberdeen) and J. L. Robertson (Inverness).
61 *De facto* Deputy Prime Minister to Margaret Thatcher between 1979 and 1988.
62 HH56/38, Scottish Office records, Edinburgh: National Records of Scotland.
63 *Scotsman*, 10 May 1926.
64 *Daily Telegraph*, 7 May 1926.
65 *Scotsman/Emergency Press*, 7 May 1926.
66 *British Worker*, 7 May 1926.
67 1st BBC news broadcast, 8 May 1926.

68 Ian MacDougall (ed.) (1979), *Essays in Scottish Labour History: A Tribute to W. H. Marwick*, Edinburgh: John Donald, p. 178.
69 *Socialist Review*, June 1926.

13 'An utterly illegal proceeding'

1 John Julius Norwich (ed.) (2007), *The Duff Cooper Diaries 1915–1951*, London: Weidenfeld & Nicolson, p. 215.
2 HC Deb 6 May 1926 Vol 195 cc581-85 [Emergency Powers].
3 John Julius Norwich, *Duff Cooper Diaries*, p. 215.
4 Harold Macmillan (1966), *Winds of Change 1914–1939*, London: Macmillan, p. 215.
5 Roy Jenkins (1998), *The Chancellors*, London: Macmillan, p. 379.
6 Ellen Wilkinson (1930), *Peeps at Politicians*, London: Philip Allan, p. 44.
7 D. J. Dutton, 'Simon, John Allsebrook, first Viscount Simon (1873–1954)', ODNB.
8 Christopher Farman (1972), *The General Strike May 1926*, London: Rupert Hart-Davis, p. 203.
9 Frank McLynn (2012), *The Road Not Taken: How Britain Narrowly Missed a Revolution*, London: The Bodley Head, p. 437.
10 *British Gazette*, 10 May 1926.
11 Christopher Farman, *The General Strike*, p. 211.
12 Templewood/V/File 6, Templewood Papers, Cambridge: Cambridge University Library (CUL).
13 Henry Slesser (1941), *Judgment Reserved*, London: Hutchinson, p. 156.
14 Ibid., p. 157. This was published by the *British Gazette* on 11 May: 'There has recently arisen for consideration the question how far a strike called for political objects ... can be said to be a strike in contemplation or furtherance of a trade dispute ... I have very little doubt that such a strike would not be covered by the words in the definition of the Trade Disputes Act.'
15 RMD/1/4/7, JRM Papers, Manchester: JRRIL.
16 Henry Slesser, *Judgment Reserved*, pp. 157–8. The Conservative MP Cuthbert Headlam recalled Slesser 'button-holing everyone' in the Commons on 5 May 'to see whether no way of a decent climb down for his leaders could be effected' (Stuart Ball, *Parliament and Politics in the Age of Baldwin and MacDonald*, p. 87).
17 HC Deb 10 May 1926 Vol 195 cc787-93 [Industrial Crisis].
18 Henry Slesser, *Judgment Reserved*, pp. 158–60.

19 HC Deb 10 May 1926 Vol 195 cc793-97 [Industrial Crisis]. There is no trace among the Law Officers' records at The National Archives of an opinion as to the legality of the general strike.
20 *Scottish Worker*, 10 May 1926.
21 Add. 8990/468, Sir Owen Seaman: Letters to him, Cambridge: CUL.
22 G. A. Phillips, 'Wilson, Joseph Havelock (1858–1929)', ODNB.
23 G. D. H. Cole (1937), *A Short History of the British Working Class Movement 1789-1937*, Volume III, *1900-1937*, London: George Allen & Unwin, p. 214.
24 *National Sailors and Firemen's Union of Great Britain and Ireland v G. Reed and others* [1926] HCJ (CD).
25 R. W. Postgate, Ellen Wilkinson and J. F. Horrabin (1927), *A Workers' History of the Great Strike*, London: The Plebs League, p. 106.
26 HC Deb 11 May 1926 Vol 195 cc860-72 [Illegality of Proceedings].
27 A. L. Goodhart (1927), 'The Legality of the General Strike in England', *Yale Law Journal* 36:4, pp. 464–85.
28 Henry Slesser, *Judgment Reserved*, pp. 155–9.
29 He was, to be fair, supported by the eminent English jurist Sir Frederick Pollock in his *Law Quarterly Review*.
30 Harold J. Laski, 'The General Strike and the Constitution', *The Labour Magazine*, June 1926.
31 *The Economist*, 22 and 29 May 1926.
32 A. L. Goodhart, 'The Legality of the General Strike in England'.
33 *Socialist Review*, July 1926.
34 R. W. Postgate et al., *Workers' History of the Great Strike*, p. 107.
35 CO 34, British Broadcasting Company papers, Caversham: BBC Written Archive Centre. As Ramsay MacDonald later pointed out to Reith, Astbury had not given a judgment on the general strike but had merely 'referred to it … in a most improper way' (CO 27).
36 *Daily Mail*, 11 May 1926.
37 John Paton (1936), *Left Turn! The Autobiography of John Paton*, London: Martin Secker & Warburg, p. 259.
38 MSS.292/252.62/27, TUC Papers, Warwick: Modern Records Centre. Knight
39 MSS.127/NU/1/4/13B, National Union of Railwaymen papers, Warwick: Modern Records Centre.
40 CAB 23/52/28, Cabinet Conclusions, Kew: The National Archives (TNA).
41 CAB 23/52/29, Cabinet Conclusions, Kew: TNA.

14 The Judgement of Samuel

1. WALLAS 1/69, Graham Wallas papers, London: London School of Economics Archives and Special Collections.
2. Viscount Samuel (1945), *Memoirs*, London: Cresset Press, p. 187. Segrave had recently set his first land speed record of 152.33 miles per hour.
3. Bernard Wasserstein, 'Samuel, Herbert Louis, first Viscount Samuel (1870–1963)', ODNB.
4. Viscount Samuel, *Memoirs*, p. 187.
5. Keith Middlemas (ed.) (1969), *Thomas Jones Whitehall Diary*, Volume Two, *1926/1930*, Oxford: Oxford University Press, p. 42.
6. Keith Middlemas, *Thomas Jones*, p. 44.
7. *Daily News and Star*, 14 May 1926.
8. R. W. Postgate, Ellen Wilkinson and J. F. Horrabin (1927), *A Workers' History of the Great Strike*, London: The Plebs League, p. 80.
9. Walter Citrine (1964), *Men and Work: The Autobiography of Lord Citrine*, London: Hutchinson, pp. 185-86.
10. Ibid., p. 186.
11. PRO 30/69/1753, James Ramsay MacDonald (JRM) Papers, Kew: The National Archives (TNA).
12. Walter Citrine, *Men and Work*, pp. 186-7.
13. PRO 30/69/1753, JRM Papers, Kew: TNA.
14. RMD/1/4/62, JRM Papers, Manchester: JRRIL.
15. Walter Citrine, *Men and Work*, p. 188-93. Princess Mary was the twenty-nine-year-old Princess Royal, the only daughter of King George V and Queen Mary. She had two infant sons.
16. Keith Middlemas, *Thomas Jones*, p. 45.
17. Gregory Blaxland (1964), *J. H. Thomas: A Life for Unity*, London: Frederick Muller, pp. 199–200.
18. Patrick Renshaw (1975), *The General Strike*, London: Eyre Methuen, p. 220.
19. Osbert Sitwell (1949), *Laughter in the Next Room*, London: Macmillan, pp. 236-8.
20. Simon Heffer (ed.) (2021), *Henry 'Chips' Channon – The Diaries: 1918-38*, London: Hutchinson, p. 215.
21. Robert Taylor (2005), 'Citrine's Unexpurgated Diaries, 1925–26: "The Mining Crisis and the National Strike"', *Historical Studies in Industrial Relations* 20, p. 96.
22. Bernard Wasserstein (1992), *Herbert Samuel: A Political Life*, Oxford: Clarendon Press, p. 285.

23 Alan Bullock (1960), *The Life and Times of Ernest Bevin*, Volume One, *Trade Union Leader 1881–1940*, London: Heinemann, p. 326.
24 Walter Citrine, *Men and Work*, p. 194.
25 Viscount Samuel, *Memoirs*, p. 190.
26 A. J. Cook (1927), *The Nine Days*, London: Co-operative Printing, p. 18.
27 Walter Citrine, *Men and Work*, pp. 195–6.
28 PRO 30/69/1753, JRM Papers, Kew: TNA.
29 Walter Citrine, *Men and Work*, p. 196.
30 PRO 30/69/1753, JRM Papers, Kew: TNA.
31 Walter Citrine, *Men and Work*, p. 204.
32 PRO 30/69/1753, JRM Papers, Kew: TNA.
33 Walter Citrine, *Men and Work*, pp. 196–7.
34 The full letter is reproduced in Julian Symons (1957), *The General Strike: A Historical Portrait*, London: Cresset Press, pp. 240–47.
35 MSS.126/TG/11/1/24, Transport and General Workers' Union papers, Warwick: Modern Records Centre (MRC).
36 Alan Bullock, *Life and Times of Ernest Bevin*, p. 331.
37 Bernard Wasserstein, *Herbert Samuel*, p. 287.
38 Walter Citrine, *Men and Work*, p. 197.
39 Philip S. Bagwell (1963), *The Railwaymen: The History of the National Union of Railwaymen*, London: George Allen & Unwin, p. 483.
40 G. A. Phillips (1976), *The General Strike: The Politics of Industrial Conflict*, London: Weidenfeld & Nicolson, p. 240.
41 Robert Taylor, 'Citrine's Unexpurgated Diaries', p. 96
42 Bernard Wasserstein, *Herbert Samuel*, p. 287.
43 Alan Bullock, *Life and Times of Ernest Bevin*, pp. 327–32.
44 5th BBC bulletin, 11 May 1926.
45 MSS.292/252.62/130, TUC Papers, Warwick: MRC.
46 Bernard Wasserstein, *Herbert Samuel*, p. 288.
47 PRO 30/69/1753, JRM Papers, Kew: TNA.
48 1st BBC news broadcast, 12 May 1926.
49 PRO 30/69/1753, JRM Papers, Kew: TNA.
50 Philip S. Bagwell, *The Railwaymen*, p. 483.
51 Bernard Wasserstein, *Herbert Samuel*, p. 287.
52 Walter Citrine, *Men and Work*, pp. 198–201.
53 PRO 30/69/1753, JRM Papers, Kew: TNA.

15 'A GROTESQUE TRAGEDY'

1. 3rd BBC Bulletin, 11 May 1926.
2. Hugh Armstrong Clegg (1985), *A History of British Trade Unions Since 1889*, Volume II, *1911-1933*, Oxford: Clarendon Press, p. 408.
3. CSAC 80.4.81/A.25 f6, Lord Cherwell Papers, Oxford: Nuffield College Library.
4. *Financial News*, 12 May 1926.
5. Walter Citrine (1964), *Men and Work: The Autobiography of Lord Citrine*, London: Hutchinson, p. 201.
6. *Financial News*, 12 May 1926.
7. A. J. Cook (1927), *The Nine Days*, Co-operative Printing, p. 22.
8. J2/A-10, Jix Archives, Brighton: The Keep.
9. Walter Citrine, *Men and Work*, p. 201.
10. Alan Bullock (1960), *The Life and Times of Ernest Bevin*, Volume One, *Trade Union Leader 1881-1940*, London: Heinemann, p. 334.
11. Walter Citrine, *Men and Work*, pp. 201-2.
12. Philip Williamson (ed.) (1988), *The Modernisation of Conservative Politics: The Diaries and Letters of William Bridgeman 1904-1935*, The History Press, pp. 197-98.
13. John Campbell (1985), *F. E. Smith, First Earl of Birkenhead*, London: Jonathan Cape, p. 775. Birkenhead's remark was not meant snobbishly.
14. MS.292/252.61/29/15, TUC Papers, Warwick: Modern Records Centre; Walter Citrine, *Men and Work*, p. 203. The full shorthand notes of this meeting were released to the press.
15. Walter Citrine, *Men and Work*, p. 203.
16. Ibid.
17. Bernard Wasserstein (1992), *Herbert Samuel: A Political Life*, Oxford: Clarendon Press, p. 288.
18. R.H. Haigh, Dave Morris and Anthony Peters (eds) (1988), *The Guardian Book of the General Strike*, London: Avebury, pp. 127-8.
19. Asa Briggs (1961), *The History of Broadcasting in the United Kingdom*, Volume 1, *The Birth of Broadcasting*, London: Oxford University Press, p. 375. In his diary, Reith erroneously remembered leaving the live microphone to take a call from Downing Street.
20. Charles Stuart (ed.) (1975), *The Reith Diaries*, London: Collins, p. 97.
21. *British Gazette*, 12 May 1926.
22. RA PS/PSO/GV/C/B/2052/33, King George V (KGV) papers, Windsor: Royal Archives (RA).

ENDNOTES

23 RA GV/PRIV/GVD/1926, KGV papers, Windsor: RA. 'Showery day', noted Queen Mary in her diary. 'Walked with G. at 1.30. G. informed me the strike was off' (RA QM/PRIV/QMD/1926).
24 Templewood/V/File 6, Templewood Papers, Cambridge: Cambridge University Library.
25 RA PS/PSO/GV/C/B/2052/35, KGV papers, Windsor: RA.
26 RA PS/PSO/GV/C/B/2052/37, KGV papers, Windsor: RA.
27 RA PS/PSO/GV/C/B/2052/36, KGV papers, Windsor: RA. Earl Winterton thought this 'rather banal' as well as 'premature' (MS. 9663/33, Archive of Edward Turnour, 6th Earl Winterton, Oxford: Bodleian Archives & Manuscripts).
28 Haigh et al., *Guardian Book of the General Strike*, p. 128.
29 HC Deb 12 May 1926 Vol 195 cc877-79 [Appeal To Nation].
30 PRO 30/69/1753, James Ramsay MacDonald (JRM) Papers, Kew: The National Archives (TNA).
31 Alan Bullock, *Life and Times of Ernest Bevin*, p. 337.
32 Walter Citrine, *Men and Work*, p. 203.
33 MSS.292/252.62/3, TUC Papers, Warwick: Modern Records Centre
34 Robert Taylor (2005), 'Citrine's Unexpurgated Diaries, 1925-26: "The Mining Crisis and the National Strike"', *Historical Studies in Industrial Relations* 20, p. 94.
35 Jennie Lee (1963), *This Great Journey: A Volume of Autobiography 1904-45*, London: MacGibbon & Kee, p. 83.
36 COLL MISC 0760, Dover Dockers, London: LSE Library Archives and Special Collections.
37 Viscount Samuel (1945), *Memoirs*, London: Cresset Press, p. 192.
38 Ian McIntyre (1993), *The Expense of Glory: A Life of John Reith*, London: HarperCollins, pp. 145-6. Baldwin's message had concluded: 'Our business is not to triumph over those who have failed in a mistaken attempt but it is rather to rally them together with the population as a whole in an attempt to restore the well being of the nation' (RMD/1/4/36, JRM Papers, Manchester: JRRIL).
39 David Marquand (1977), *Ramsay MacDonald*, London: Jonathan Cape, p. 339.
40 Charles Loch Mowat (1964), *Britain Between the Wars 1918-1940*, London: Methuen, p. 327.
41 D5922 2/25, Martyns archive, Gloucester: Gloucestershire Archives.
42 M.D.31., TUC Papers, London: London Metropolitan University Archives.
43 Walter Citrine, *Men and Work*, p. 206.

44 RA GV/PRIV/GVD/1926, KGV papers, Windsor: RA.
45 D/EX239/1/11, Letters relating to the General Strike, Reading: Royal Berkshire Archives.
46 PRO 30/69/1753, JRM Papers, Kew: TNA.
47 *Daily Mail*, 14 May 1926.
48 WORK 21/247, Works departments records, Kew: TNA.
49 PRO 30/69/1753, JRM Papers, Kew: TNA.
50 HC Deb 13 May 1926 Vol 195 cc1043-50 [Prime Minister On Dangers Of Present Situation].
51 Bernard Wasserstein, *Herbert Samuel*, p. 289.
52 MS.292/252.62/20/18, TUC Papers, Warwick: Modern Records Centre.
53 Viscount Samuel, *Memoirs*, p. 193. Sir Stuart Samuel was just short of his seventieth birthday.
54 PRO 30/69/1753, JRM Papers, Kew: TNA.
55 John Julius Norwich (ed.) (2005), *The Duff Cooper Diaries 1915-1951*, London: Weidenfeld & Nicolson, p. 219.
56 Fenner Brockway, *Inside the Left*, p. 192.
57 Julian Symons (1957), *The General Strike: A Historical Portrait*, London: Cresset Press, p. 222.
58 RA GV/PRIV/GVD/1926, KGV papers, Windsor: RA.
59 Norman and Jeanne MacKenzie (eds) (1984), *The Diary of Beatrice Webb*, Volume Four, *1924-1943 'The Wheel of Life'*, London: Virago, p. 82.

16 Afterlives

1 Norman and Jeanne MacKenzie (eds) (1984), *The Diary of Beatrice Webb*, Volume Four, *1924-1943 'The Wheel of Life'*, London: Virago, p. 84.
2 RMD/1/4/72, JRM Papers, Manchester: JRRIL.
3 RMD/1/4/101, JRM Papers, Manchester: JRRIL.
4 Keith Laybourn (1993), *The General Strike of 1926*, Manchester: Manchester University Press, p. 101.
5 LAB2 12/3/8, Ministry of Labour records, Kew: The National Archives.
6 G. M. Young (1952), *Stanley Baldwin*, London: Rupert Hart-Davis, p. 121.
7 Walter Citrine (1964), *Men and Work: The Autobiography of Lord Citrine*, London: Hutchinson, p. 205.
8 G. A. Phillips, 'Pugh, Sir Arthur (1870-1955)', ODNB.
9 Paul Davies (1987), *A. J. Cook*, Manchester: Manchester University Press, p. 190.

10 Hywel Francis, 'Cook, Arthur James (1883–1931)', ODNB.
11 *The Times*, 19 July 1926.
12 Martin Gilbert (ed.) (1979), *Winston S. Churchill*, Volume V, *Companion Part I: The Exchequer Years 1922–1929*, London: Heinemann, pp. 865–6.
13 Roy Jenkins (2001), *Churchill*, London: Macmillan, p. 410.
14 Philip Williamson and Edward Baldwin (eds) (2004), *Baldwin Papers: A Conservative Statesman 1908–1947*, Cambridge: Cambridge University Press, pp. 184–8.
15 Spencer later established the breakaway Nottinghamshire and District Miners' Industrial Union.
16 Frank McLynn (2012), *The Road Not Taken: How Britain Narrowly Missed a Revolution*, London: The Bodley Head, pp. 467–8.
17 Robert Rhodes James (1977), *The British Revolution*, Volume Two, *From Asquith to Chamberlain 1914–1939*, London: Hamish Hamilton, p. 208.
18 Williamson and Baldwin, *Baldwin Papers*, pp. 181–2.
19 Stanley Baldwin (1928), *Our Inheritance: Speeches and Addresses by the Right Honourable Stanley Baldwin, M.P.*, London: Hodder & Stoughton, p. 223.
20 L.1.1, Baldwin Papers, Cambridge: CUL.
21 Harold Macmillan (1966), *Winds of Change 1914–1939*, London: Macmillan, p. 221.
22 D.3.1, Baldwin Papers, Cambridge: CUL.
23 Harold Nicolson (1952), *King George the Fifth: His Life and Reign*, London: Constable, p. 421.
24 R. H. Haigh, Dave Morris and Anthony Peters (eds), *The Guardian Book of the General Strike*, London: Avebury, pp. 173–4.
25 HO 144/12050, Home Office papers, Kew: TNA.
26 Home Office (1928), *Criminal Statistics: Statistics relating to Criminal Proceedings, Police, Coroners, Prisons, and Criminal*, Cmnd 3055, London: HMSO, p. 5.
27 LCO 2/918, Records of the Lord Chancellor's Office, Kew: TNA.
28 Their powers and responsibilities passed to local and national government bodies under the *Local Government Act 1929*.
29 Sir William Joynson-Hicks (1926), *Communist Plotting: Lessons from the General Strike*, London: NUCUA, p. 11.
30 Edward Hallett Carr and R. W. Davies (1976), *A History of Soviet Russia: Foundations of a Planned Economy 1926–1929*, Volume Three – II, London: Macmillan, pp. 319–40.

31 Earl Winterton (1953), *Orders of the Day*, London: Cassell, pp. 140–41.
32 MS. 9663/59, Archive of Edward Turnour, 6th Earl Winterton, Oxford: Bodleian Archives & Manuscripts.
33 HO 144/6116, Home Office records, Kew: TNA.
34 HH56/37, Scottish Office records, Edinburgh: National Records of Scotland.
35 Paul Stocker (2016), 'Importing fascism: reappraising the British fascisti, 1923–1926', *Contemporary British History* 30:3, pp. 331–2.
36 HALIFAX/A4/410/14/2, Halifax Family and Estate Archive, York: Borthwick Institute for Archives.
37 PWO/20/14, Parliamentary Works Office papers, London: Parliamentary Archives.
38 H. J. Wilson, revised by Mark Pottle, 'Whitley, John Henry (1866–1935)', ODNB.
39 HC Deb 25 June 1926 Vol 197 c733 [Communist Propaganda And Trade Agreement].
40 Sehri Saklatvala (1991), *The Fifth Commandment: A Biography of Shapurji Saklatvala*, Salford: Miranda Press, p. 327.
41 Norman and Jeanne MacKenzie, *Diary of Beatrice Webb*, p. 86.
42 David Marquand (1977), *Ramsay MacDonald*, London: Jonathan Cape, pp. 441–2.
43 RMD/1/4/71, JRM Papers, Manchester: JRRIL.
44 *Forward*, 22 May 1926.
45 *Socialist Review*, June 1926.
46 MSS.126/EB/GS/7/26, Ernest Bevin Papers, Warwick: Modern Records Centre (MRC).
47 Alan Bullock (1960), *The Life and Times of Ernest Bevin Volume One: Trade Union Leader 1881–1940*, London: Heinemann, p. 350.
48 David Marquand, 'MacDonald, (James) Ramsay (1866–1937)', ODNB.
49 LP/JSM/STR/123i-ii, J. S. Middleton Papers, Manchester: Labour History Archive & Study Centre.
50 *Daily Herald*, 19 May 1926
51 G. A. Phillips (1977), 'The Labour Party and the General Strike', *Llafur* 2:2.
52 PRO 30/69/1171, James Ramsay MacDonald (JRM) Papers, Kew: TNA.
53 G. A. Phillips (1977), 'The Labour Party and the General Strike'.
54 PRO 30/69/1753, JRM Papers, Kew: TNA.
55 John Simon (1926), *Three Speeches on the General Strike*, London: Macmillan, p. 44.

56 Lord Birkenhead (1930), *Last Essays by the Earl of Birkenhead*, London: Cassell, p. 187.
57 John Campbell (1977), *Lloyd George: The Goat in the Wilderness 1922–1931*, London: Jonathan Cape, pp. 140–46
58 Viscount Simon (1952), *Retrospect: The Memoirs of The Rt. Hon. Viscount Simon*, London: Hutchinson, p. 140.
59 Lord Oxford and Asquith (1928), *Memories and Reflections 1852–1927*, Volume 2, London: Cassell, p. 247.
60 Robert Boothby et al. (1927), *Industry and the State: A Conservative View*, London: Macmillan.
61 John Ramsden (1978), *The Age of Balfour and Baldwin 1902–1940*, London: Longman, p. 282.
62 Melvin C. Shefftz (1967), 'The Trade Disputes and Trade Unions Act of 1927: The Aftermath of the General Strike', *The Review of Politics* 29:3, pp. 387–406.
63 Stuart Ball, 'Baldwin, Stanley, first Earl Baldwin of Bewdley (1867–1947)', ODNB.
64 Christopher J. V. Loughlin (2018), *Labour and the Politics of Disloyalty in Belfast, 1921–39: The Moral Economy of Loyalty*, London: Palgrave Macmillan, p. 110.
65 Z/3798/10/3/4, Furness Collection, Barrow: Barrow Archive Centre.
66 Stuart Ball, *Parliament and Politics in the Age of Baldwin and MacDonald*, p. 89.
67 Viscount Simon, *Retrospect*, p. 164.
68 Simon Heffer (ed.) (2021), *Henry 'Chips' Channon – The Diaries: 1918–38*, London: Hutchinson, p. 216.
69 *Evening Standard*, 18 May 1926.
70 RA PS/PSO/GV/C/N/2556/44, King George V papers, Windsor: Royal Archives.
71 https://glamarchives.wordpress.com/2016/05/20/the-volunteers-story/.
72 Lord Macmillan (1952), *A Man of Law's Tale*, London: Macmillan, p. 190.
73 HO144/10671, Home Office records, Kew: TNA.
74 A/TOY/21, Toynbee Hall archive, London: London Archives.
75 DDQ/9/63/14, Garnett of Quernmore papers, Preston: Lancashire Archives.
76 Templewood/V/File 6, Templewood Papers, Cambridge: CUL.
77 *British Gazette*, 13 May 1926.
78 Martin Gilbert (1979), *Winston S. Churchill*, p. 174.
79 WHS 154/3, W. H. Smith Business Archive, University of Reading Special Collections.

80 HC Deb 7 July 1926 Vol 197 cc2216-18 [Emergency Services].
81 David Kirkwood (1935), *My Life of Revolt*, London: George G. Harrap & Co., p. 235.
82 Hamilton Fyfe (1949), *Sixty Years of Fleet Street*, London: W. H. Allen, p. 199.
83 R. W. Postgate, Ellen Wilkinson and J. F. Horrabin (1927), *A Workers' History of the Great Strike*, London: The Plebs League, p. 92.
84 MSS.292/252.62/44, TUC Papers, Warwick: MRC.
85 Thanks to my colleague Corie Chambers for tracking this down. The Newspaper Society complained to the Librarian of the House of Commons that the *Scotsman*'s claim could not 'be accepted as correct' as several other newspapers had been published as normal.
86 Anonymous (1967), *The Glorious Privilege: The History of "The Scotsman"*, Edinburgh: Nelson, pp. 99–100.
87 D.3.4, Baldwin Papers, Cambridge: CUL.
88 DAV/173/U22, John Campbell Davidson Papers, London: Parliamentary Archives. 'I will be responsible henceforward for … our friend Reith,' added Mitchell-Thomson, 'so we will revert to the old role & keep him out of politics altogether.'
89 D.3.4, Baldwin Papers, Cambridge: CUL.
90 J. C. W. Reith (1949), *Into the Wind*, London: Hodder & Stoughton, p. 113.
91 Charles Stuart (ed.) (1975), *The Reith Diaries*, London: Collins, p. 97.
92 CO 36, British Broadcasting Company (BBC) papers, Caversham: BBC Written Archives Centre (BWAC).
93 CO 27, BBC papers, Caversham: BWAC.
94 Asa Briggs (1961), *The History of Broadcasting In The United Kingdom*, Volume 1, *The Birth of Broadcasting*, London: Oxford University Press, p. 378.
95 *Radio Times*, 28 May 1926.
96 CO 37, BBC papers, Caversham: BWAC.
97 CO 34, BBC papers, Caversham: BWAC.
98 G. K. A. Bell (1935), *Randall Davidson: Archbishop of Canterbury*, Volume II, London: Oxford University Press, p. 1316.
99 Stuart Mews, 'Davidson, Randall Thomas, Baron Davidson of Lambeth (1848–1930)', ODNB.
100 Stuart Mews (1976), 'The Churches' in M. Morris, *The General Strike*, London: Penguin Books, p. 335.
101 MS Gen 523_49, John White Papers, Edinburgh: New College Archives & Library.

102 Stewart J. Brown (1991), '"A Victory for God": The Scottish Presbyterian Churches and the General Strike of 1926', *Journal of Ecclesiastical History* 42:4, pp. 606–10.
103 Henry Slesser (1941), *Judgment Reserved*, London: Hutchinson, p. 155.
104 G. A. Phillips, 'Wilson, Joseph Havelock [trade unionist and politician] (1858–1929)', ODNB.
105 Henry Slesser, *Judgment Reserved*, pp. 154–5. 'I have spoken to most of the leading characters in the affair', added Slesser, 'and never found one who admitted it.'
106 Roy Jenkins (1998), *The Chancellors*, London: Macmillan, pp. 366–7.
107 Sir John Simon led the breakaway Liberal National Party and Lloyd George a small group of Independent Liberals.
108 Twenty years after the strike, the Viscounts Samuel and Simon relitigated its legality during a Lords debate on the Attlee government's trade union legislation (HL Deb 30 April 1946 Vol 140 cc945-50 [Trade Disputes and Trade Unions Bill]).
109 Bernard Wasserstein (1992), *Herbert Samuel: A Political Life*, Oxford: Clarendon Press, p. 291.
110 HC Deb 13 February 1946 Vol 419 c399 [Trade Disputes and Trade Unions Bill]. The equivalent legislation in Northern Ireland was only amended in 1958.
111 *Sunday Times Magazine*, 10 April 1966. Citrine lived until 1983; Davidson until 1970.
112 *The Times*, 22 February 1972
113 *The Times*, 1 March 1976.
114 *The Times*, 31 March 1976.
115 There was a total of six under the *Emergency Powers Act 1964* and the same number under its 1920 predecessor (HC Deb 19 November 1984 Vol 68 c58W [Emergency Powers]).
116 Patrick Renshaw (1975), *The General Strike*, London: Eyre Methuen, p. 194.
117 Under the *Emergency Powers Act (Northern Ireland) 1926*, as amended by Stormont in 1964.
118 HC Deb 14 September 2015 Vol 599 c789 [Trade Union Bill].
119 https://www.ncl.ac.uk/press/articles/archive/2024/11/conversationredellen/.
120 'UK's last coal-fired power station set to close', BBC News online, 27 September 2024.

121 'Restart coal mining and bring back traditional steelmaking to Wales, says Nigel Farage', ITV Wales website, 9 June 2025.

17 The General Strike Reconsidered

1. C152/17/1/28, Halifax Family and Estate Archive, York: Borthwick Institute for Archives.
2. Keith Laybourn (1993), *The General Strike of 1926*, Manchester: Manchester University Press, p. 6.
3. Harold Macmillan (1966), *Winds of Change 1914–1939*, London: Macmillan, pp. 216–17.
4. Keith Middlemas (ed.) (1969), *Thomas Jones Whitehall Diary*, Volume Two, *1926/1930*, London: Oxford University Press, p. 49.
5. Alan Bullock (1960), *The Life and Times of Ernest Bevin*, Volume One, *Trade Union Leader 1881–1940*, London: Heinemann, p. 316.
6. Keith Middlemas, *Thomas Jones*, p. 51.
7. Keith Laybourn, *The General Strike of 1926*, p. 6.
8. Charles Ferrall and Dougal McNeill (2015), *Writing the 1926 General Strike: Literature, Culture, Politics*, Cambridge: Cambridge University Press, p. 4.
9. Leo Amery (1953), *My Political Life*, Volume Two, *War and Peace 1914–1929*, London: Hutchinson, p. 485.
10. Wilfrid Harris Crook (1934), 'Social Security and the General Strike', *Political Science Quarterly* 49:3, p. 413.
11. Isador Lubin and Helen Everett (1927), *The British Coal Dilemma*, London: Macmillan, p. 102.
12. Keith Middlemas, *Thomas Jones*, p. 53.
13. A. Mason (1969), 'The Government and the General Strike, 1926', *International Review of Social History* 14:1, p. 14.
14. Stuart Ball, 'Baldwin, Stanley, first Earl Baldwin of Bewdley (1867–1947)', ODNB.
15. Charles Loch Mowat (1964), *Britain Between the Wars 1918-1940*, London: Methuen, p. 310.
16. MSS.148/UCW/2/13/7, Union of Communication Workers records, Warwick: Modern Records Centre.
17. Harry Hearder (1974), 'King George V, the General Strike, and the 1931 Crisis' in H. Hearder and H. R. Loyn (eds), *British Government and Administration: Studies Presented to S. B. Chrimes*, Cardiff: University of Wales Press, p. 241.

18 LAB 2/1207/IR745/1926, Ministry of Labour records, Kew: The National Archives (TNA).
19 John Foster (1976), 'British Imperialism and the Labour Aristocracy' in J. Skelley (ed.), *The General Strike 1926*, London: Lawrence and Wishart, p. 3.
20 Fenner Brockway, *Inside the Left*, p. 193.
21 Bernard Wasserstein (1992), *Herbert Samuel: A Political Life*, Oxford: Clarendon Press, p. 373.
22 Keith Laybourn, *The General Strike of 1926*, p. 6.
23 LAB 2/1207/IR745/1926, Ministry of Labour records, Kew: TNA.
24 *The Times*, 21 January 1927.
25 G. A. Phillips (1976), *The General Strike: The Politics of Industrial Conflict*, London: Weidenfeld & Nicolson, p. 274.
26 GD40/17/413, Private and political Papers of Philip Kerr, 11th Marquess of Lothian, Edinburgh: National Records of Scotland.
27 Roy Jenkins (1995), *Baldwin*, London: Papermac, p. 108.
28 Earl Winterton (1953), *Orders of the Day*, London: Cassell, p. 142.
29 A. J. P. Taylor (1978), *English History 1914–1945*, Oxford: Clarendon Press, p. 250.
30 G. A. Phillips, *The General Strike*, pp. 293–5.
31 Ferrall and McNeill, *Writing the 1926 General Strike*, p. 181.

Appendix

1 RMD/1/4/10, James Ramsay MacDonald Papers, Manchester: John Rylands Research Institute and Library.

BIBLIOGRAPHY

PRIMARY SOURCES

Papers of Sir Charles Stewart Addis, London: SOAS Special Collections
Air Ministry records, Kew: The National Archives
Private Papers of Major D. Allhusen, London: Imperial War Museum
Baldwin Papers, Cambridge: Cambridge University Library
Ernest Bevin Papers, Warwick: Modern Records Centre
The *Bolton Evening News* Archive, Bolton: Bolton History Centre
Cardinal Bourne Papers, London: Westminster Diocesan Archives
British Broadcasting Company Papers, Caversham: BBC Written Archives Centre
Records of British Railways Board, Edinburgh: National Records of Scotland
The Papers of William Bull, Cambridge: Churchill College Archives
Records of the Bridgeman Family, Shrewsbury: Shropshire Archives
Cabinet Conclusions, Kew: The National Archives
Lord Cherwell Papers, Oxford: Nuffield College Library
The Churchill Papers, Cambridge: Churchill College Archives
Personal Records of R. J. Cogswell, Chippenham: Wiltshire & Swindon History Centre
Arthur Ebenezer Cooke Papers, London: London School of Economics Library Archives and Special Collections
Ruth Darwin: Correspondence and Papers, Cambridge: Cambridge University Library
Papers of John Campbell Davidson, London: Parliamentary Archives
Randall Thomas Davidson Papers, London: Lambeth Palace Library
Dover Dockers, London: London School of Economics Archives and Special Collections
East Yorkshire Regiment Papers, Beverley: East Riding Archives
The Papers of Thomas Elmhirst, Cambridge: Churchill College Archives
Foreign Office records, Kew: The National Archives
Furness Collection, Barrow: Barrow Archive Centre
Lord Gainford Papers, Oxford: Nuffield College Library.
Garnett of Quernmore Papers, Preston: Lancashire Archives

King George V Papers, Windsor: Royal Archives
Glamorgan Constabulary Records, Cardiff: Glamorgan Archives
Government of Northern Ireland Records, Belfast: Public Record Office of Northern Ireland
Gwynne Family of Folkington Papers, Brighton: The Keep
Halifax Family and Estate Archive, York: Borthwick Institute for Archives
Records of the Hicks Beach Family, Gloucester: Gloucestershire Archives
Home Office Records, Kew: The National Archives
Correspondence of Henrietta Joseph, Southampton: University of Southampton Special Collections
Archive of the Joynson-Hicks Family, Viscounts Brentford (Jix Archive), Brighton: The Keep
The Papers of Sir Alan Lascelles, Cambridge: Churchill College Archives
Letters Relating to the General Strike, Reading: Royal Berkshire Archives
Liberty & Co. Ltd Papers, London: Westminster City Archives
The Lloyd George Papers, London: Parliamentary Archives
London County Council Records, London: London Archives
Records of the Lord Chancellor's Office, Kew: The National Archives
Private and Political Papers of Philip Kerr, 11th Marquess of Lothian, Edinburgh: National Records of Scotland
James Ramsay MacDonald Papers, Manchester: John Rylands Research Institute and Library
James Ramsay MacDonald Papers, Kew: The National Archives
Martyns Archive, Gloucester: Gloucestershire Archives
Queen Mary Papers, Windsor: Royal Archives
Metropolitan Police Records, Kew: The National Archives
J. S. Middleton Papers, Manchester: Labour History Archive & Study Centre
J. P. M. Millar Papers, Edinburgh: National Library of Scotland
Ministry of Labour Records, Kew: The National Archives
Miscellaneous Papers, Gloucester: Gloucestershire Archives
Bill Moore Collection, Sheffield: Sheffield City Archives
Private Papers of Commander J. Murray RN, London: Imperial War Museum
National Union of Railwaymen Papers, Warwick: Modern Records Centre
Parliamentary Works Office Papers, London: Parliamentary Archives
William Thomas Pickbourne Papers, Nottingham: Nottinghamshire Archives
Pleydell-Bouverie Family Papers, Chippenham: Wiltshire and Swindon History Centre

Revealing Voices Project, Stoke: Stoke-on-Trent City Archives
Siegfried Sassoon: Letters to Glen Byam Shaw, Cambridge: Cambridge University Library
Scottish Office Records, Edinburgh: National Records of Scotland
Sir Owen Seaman: Letters to him, Cambridge: Cambridge University Library
Records of the Security Service, Kew: The National Archives
Senogles Papers, Barrow: Barrow Archive Centre
W. H. Smith Business Archive, Reading: University of Reading Special Collections
The Papers of Lady Soames, Cambridge: Churchill College Archives
Records of the Stationary Office, Kew: The National Archives
William Burton Stewart Papers, Edinburgh: National Library of Scotland
Papers of John St Loe Strachey, London: Parliamentary Archives
Records of the Supreme Court of Judicature, Kew: The National Archives
Templewood Papers, Cambridge: Cambridge University Library
Toynbee Hall Archive, London: London Archives
Trades Union Congress Papers, London: London Metropolitan University Archives
Trades Union Congress Papers, Warwick: Modern Records Centre
Transport and General Workers' Union Papers, Warwick: Modern Records Centre
Treasury Records, Kew: The National Archives
The Papers of Alan Mathison Turing, Cambridge: King's College Archive Centre
Union of Communication Workers Records, Warwick: Modern Records Centre
Graham Wallas Papers, London: London School of Economics Archives and Special Collections
War Office Records, Kew: The National Archives
John White Papers, Edinburgh: New College Archives & Library
Archive of Edward Turnour, 6th Earl Winterton, Oxford: Bodleian Archives & Manuscripts
Works Departments Records, Kew: The National Archives

SECONDARY SOURCES

Leo Amery (1953), *My Political Life*, Volume II, *War and Peace 1914–1929*, London: Hutchinson
Anonymous (1926), *Strike Nights in Printing House Square: An Episode in the History of The Times*, London: The Times

BIBLIOGRAPHY

Anonymous (1967), *The Glorious Privilege: The History of 'The Scotsman'*, Edinburgh: Nelson

H. H. Asquith (1928), *Memories and Reflections 1852-1927*, Volume 2, London: Cassell

Philip S. Bagwell (1963), *The Railwaymen: The History of the National Union of Railwaymen*, London: George Allen & Unwin

Stanley Baldwin (1928), *Our Inheritance: Speeches and Addresses by the Right Honourable Stanley Baldwin, M.P.*, London: Hodder & Stoughton

Stuart Ball (ed.) (1992), *Parliament and Politics in the Age of Baldwin and MacDonald: The Headlam Diaries 1923-1935*, London: The Historians' Press

Stuart Ball (2013), *Portrait of a Party: The Conservative Party in Britain 1918-1945*, Oxford: Oxford University Press

John Barnes and David Nicholson (eds) (1980), *The Leo Amery Diaries*, Volume I: *1896-1929*, London: Hutchinson

G. K. A. Bell (1935), *Randall Davidson: Archbishop of Canterbury*, Volume II, London: Oxford University Press

John Bew (2016), *Citizen Clem: A Biography of Attlee*, London: Riverrun

Lord Birkenhead (1924), *Contemporary Personalities*, London: Cassell

Lord Birkenhead (1930), *Last Essays by the Earl of Birkenhead*, London: Cassell

Gregory Blaxland (1964), *J. H. Thomas: A Life for Unity*, London: Frederick Muller

Margaret Bondfield (1948), *A Life's Work*, London: Hutchinson

Robert Boothby et al. (1927), *Industry and the State: A Conservative View*, London: Macmillan

Andrew Boyle (1972), *Only the Wind Will Listen: Reith of the BBC*, London: Hutchinson

Asa Briggs (1961), *The History of Broadcasting in the United Kingdom*, Volume 1, *The Birth of Broadcasting*, London: Oxford University Press

Asa Briggs (1985), *The BBC: The First Fifty Years*, Oxford: Oxford University Press

Fenner Brockway (1942), *Inside the Left: Thirty Years of Platform, Press, Prison and Parliament*, London: George Allen & Unwin

Alan Bullock (1960), *The Life & Times of Ernest Bevin*, Volume One, *Trade Union Leader 1881-1940*, London: Heinemann

John Campbell (1977), *Lloyd George: The Goat in the Wilderness 1922-1931*, London: Jonathan Cape

John Campbell (1985), *F. E. Smith: First Earl of Birkenhead*, London: Jonathan Cape

Edward Hallett Carr and R. W. Davies (1976), *A History of Soviet Russia: Foundations of a Planned Economy 1926-1929*, Volume Three – II, London: Macmillan

Walter Citrine (1964), *Men and Work: The Autobiography of Lord Citrine*, London: Hutchinson

Hugh Armstrong Clegg (1985), *A History of British Trade Unions Since 1889*, Volume II, *1911-1933*, Oxford: Clarendon Press

J. R. Clynes (1937), *Memoirs 1924-1937*, London: Hutchinson

G. D. H. Cole (1937), *A Short History of the British Working Class Movement 1789-1937*, Volume III, *1900-1937*, London: George Allen & Unwin

D. C. Coleman and Peter Mathias (eds) (1984), *Enterprise and History: Essays in Honour of Charles Wilson*, Cambridge: Cambridge University Press

A. J. Cook (1927), *The Nine Days*, London: Co-operative Printing

R. J. Cootes (1966), *The General Strike (1926)*, London: Longmans

Torquil Cowan (2011), *Labour of Love: The Story of Robert Smillie*, Glasgow: Neil Wilson

Paul Davies (1987), *A. J. Cook*, Manchester: Manchester University Press

Bernard Donoughue and G. W. Jones (2001), *Herbert Morrison: Portrait of a Politician*, London: Phoenix Press

Andy Durr (1976), *Who Were the Guilty? General Strike Brighton May 1926*, Brighton: Brighton Labour History Press

Christopher Farman (1972), *The General Strike May 1926*, London: Rupert Hart-Davis

Charles Ferrall and Dougal McNeill (2015), *Writing the 1926 General Strike: Literature, Culture, Politics*, Cambridge: Cambridge University Press

Michael Foot (1997), *Aneurin Bevan 1897-1960*, London: Victor Gollancz

Hamilton Fyfe (1926), *Behind the Scenes of the Great Strike*, London: Labour Publishing Company

Hugh Gault (2017), *Kingsley Wood: Scenes from a Political Life 1925-1943*, Cambridge: Gretton Books

Martin Gilbert (1976), *Winston S. Churchill*, Volume V, *1922-1939*, London: Heinemann

Martin Gilbert (ed.) (1979), *Winston S. Churchill*, Volume V: *Companion Part 1 – The Exchequer Years 1922-1929*, London: Heinemann

R. H. Haigh, Dave Morris and Anthony Peters (eds) (1988), *The Guardian Book of the General Strike*, London: Avebury

Lord Hailsham (1990), *A Sparrow's Flight: The Memoirs of Lord Hailsham of St Marylebone*, London: Collins

J. R. Harris (ed.) (1969), *Liverpool and Merseyside: Essays in the Economic and Social History of the Port and Its Hinterland*, London: Frank Cass & Co.

Harry Hearder and H. R. Loyn (eds) (1974), *British Government and Administration: Studies Presented to S. B. Chrimes*, Cardiff: University of Wales Press

Simon Heffer (ed.) (2021), *Henry 'Chips' Channon – The Diaries: 1918-38*, London: Hutchinson

John Hodge (1931), *Workman's Cottage to Windsor Castle*, London: Sampson Low, Marston & Co.

Arthur Horner (1960), *Incorrigible Rebel*, London: MacGibbon & Kee

David Howell (2002), *MacDonald's Party: Labour Identities and Crisis, 1922-1931*, Oxford: Oxford University Press

Richard Hyman (1966), *Oxford Workers in the Great Strike*, Oxford: Centre for Socialist Education

Keith Jeffery and Peter Hennessy (1983), *States of Emergency: British Governments and Strikebreaking Since 1919*, London: Routledge & Kegan Paul

Roy Jenkins (1995), *Baldwin*, London: Papermac

Roy Jenkins (1998), *The Chancellors*, London: Macmillan

Sir William Joynson-Hicks (1926), *Communist Plotting: Lessons from the General Strike*, London: NUCUA

David Kirkwood (1935), *My Life of Revolt*, London: George G. Harrap

Keith Laybourn (1993), *The General Strike of 1926*, Manchester: Manchester University Press

Keith Laybourn (1996), *The General Strike: Day by Day*, Stroud: Sutton Publishing

Jennie Lee (1963), *This Great Journey: A Volume of Autobiography 1904-45*, London: MacGibbon & Kee

William Alexander Lee (1954), *Thirty Years in Coal*, London: Mining Association of Great Britain

Christopher Loughlin (2018), *Labour and the Politics of Disloyalty in Belfast, 1921-39: The Moral Economy of Loyalty*, London: Palgrave Macmillan

Isador Lubin and Helen Everett (1927), *The British Coal Dilemma*, London: Macmillan

Ian MacDougall (ed.) (1979), *Essays in Scottish Labour History: A Tribute to W. H. Marwick*, Edinburgh: John Donald

Ian McIntyre (1993), *The Expense of Glory: A Life of John Reith*, London: HarperCollins

Norman and Jeanne MacKenzie (eds) (1984), *The Diary of Beatrice Webb, Volume Four, 1924–1943 'The Wheel of Life'*, London: Virago

John McLean (1976), *The 1926 General Strike in Lanarkshire*, History Group of the Communist Party

Frank McLynn (2012), *The Road Not Taken: How Britain Narrowly Missed a Revolution*, London: The Bodley Head

Harold Macmillan (1966), *Winds of Change 1914–1939*, London: Macmillan

Lord Macmillan (1952), *A Man of Law's Tale*, London: Macmillan

David Marquand (1977), *Ramsay MacDonald*, London: Jonathan Cape

W. H. Marwick (1967), *A Short History of Labour in Scotland*, Edinburgh: Chambers

Tony Mason (1970), *General Strike in the North East*, Hull: University of Hull Publications

John Maynard Keynes (1925), *The Economic Consequences of Mr Churchill*, London: Hogarth Press

Keith Middlemas (ed.) (1969), *Thomas Jones: Whitehall Diary*, Volume II, 1926–1930, London: Oxford University Press

Keith Middlemas and John Barnes (1969), *Baldwin: A Biography*, London: Weidenfeld & Nicolson

Ralph Miliband (1973), *Parliamentary Socialism: A Study in the Politics of Labour* (2nd edition), London: Merlin Press

J. D. B. Mitchell (1964), *Constitutional Law*, Edinburgh: W. Green

Lord Moran (1966), *Winston Churchill: The Struggle for Survival, 1940–1965*, London: Constable

Margaret Morris (1976), *The General Strike*, London: Penguin Books

Charles Loch Mowat (1964), *Britain Between the Wars 1918–1940*, London: Methuen

John Murray (1951), *The General Strike of 1926: A History*, London: Lawrence and Wishart

Scott Nearing (1926), *The British General Strike: An Economic Interpretation of its Background and its Significance*, New York: Vanguard Press

Harold Nicolson (1952), *King George the Fifth: His Life and Reign*, London: Constable

John Julius Norwich (ed.) (2005), *The Duff Cooper Diaries 1915–1951*, London: Weidenfeld & Nicolson

Lord Oxford and Asquith (1928), *Memories and Reflections 1852–1927*, Volume 2, London: Cassell

Robin Page Arnot (1926), *The General Strike, May 1926: Its Origin and History*, London: Labour Research Department

John Paton (1936), *Left Turn! The Autobiography of John Paton*, London: Martin Secker & Warburg

Henry Pelling (1987), *A History of British Trade Unionism* (4th edition), London: Palgrave Macmillan

G. A. Phillips (1976), *The General Strike: The Politics of Industrial Conflict*, London: Weidenfeld & Nicolson

R. W. Postgate, Ellen Wilkinson and J. F. Horrabin (1927), *A Workers' History of the Great Strike*, London: The Plebs League

John Ramsden (1978), *The Age of Balfour and Baldwin 1902–1940*, London: Longman

John Ramsden (ed.) (1984), *Real Old Tory Politics: The Political Diaries of Sir Robert Sanders, Lord Bayford, 1910–35*, London: The History Press

J. C. W. Reith (1949), *Into the Wind*, London: Hodder & Stoughton

Patrick Renshaw (1975), *The General Strike*, London: Eyre Methuen

Robert Rhodes James (1969), *Memoirs of a Conservative: J. C. C. Davidson's Memoirs and Papers, 1910–37*, London: Weidenfeld & Nicolson

Jane Ridley (2021), *George V: Never a Dull Moment*, London: Chatto & Windus

Kenneth Rose (1984), *King George V*, London: Macmillan

Stephen Roskill (1972), *Hankey: Man of Secrets*, Volume II, *1919–1931*, London: Collins

Rachelle Saltzman (2012), *A Lark for the Sake of Their Country: The 1926 General Strike Volunteers in Folklore and Memory*, Manchester: Manchester University Press

Viscount Samuel (1945), *Memoirs*, London: Cresset Press

John Simon (1926), *Three Speeches on the General Strike*, London: Macmillan

Viscount Simon (1952), *Retrospect: The Memoirs of The Rt. Hon. Viscount Simon*, London: Hutchinson

Osbert Sitwell (1949), *Laughter in the Next Room*, London: Macmillan

Robert Skidelsky, *John Maynard Keynes*, Volume Two, *The Economist as Saviour 1920–1937*, London: Macmillan

Henry Slesser (1941), *Judgment Reserved*, London: Hutchinson

F. E. Smith (1913), *Unionist Policy and Other Essays*, London: Williams & Norgate

J. C. Squire (ed.) (1932), *If It Had Happened Otherwise: Lapses Into Imaginary History*, London: Longmans

Peter Stansky (2003), *Sassoon: The Worlds of Philip and Sybil*, New Haven: Yale University Press

Charles Stuart (ed.) (1975), *The Reith Diaries*, London: Collins
Julian Symons (1957), *The General Strike*, London: Cresset Press
A. J. P. Taylor (1978), *English History 1914–1945*, Oxford: Clarendon Press
A. J. P. Taylor (1983), *A Personal History*, London: Hamish Hamilton
H. A. Taylor (1933), *Jix, Viscount Brentford*, London: Stanley Paul
Viscount Templewood (1954), *Nine Troubled Years*, London: Collins
David Torrance (2024), *The Wild Men: The Remarkable Story of Britain's First Labour Government*, London: Bloomsbury Continuum
Ernie Trory (1975), *Brighton and the General Strike*, Brighton: Crabtree Press
Lord Vansittart (1958), *The Mist Procession: The Autobiography of Lord Vansittart*, London: Hutchinson
William Wallace (1926), *The Great Strike: Its Causes and Consequences*, New York: American Management Association
Michael Walsh (2008), *The Westminster Cardinals: The Past and the Future*, London: Burns & Oates
Bernard Wasserstein (1992), *Herbert Samuel: A Political Life*, Oxford: Clarendon Press
Evelyn Waugh (1962), *Brideshead Revisited*, London: Penguin Books
Egon Wertheimer (1929), *Portrait of the Labour Party*, London: G. P. Putnam's Sons
John Wheeler-Bennett (1962), *John Anderson: Viscount Waverley*, London: Macmillan
Leonard D. White (1933), *Whitley Councils in the British Civil Service: A Study in Conciliation and Arbitration*, Chicago: University of Chicago Press
Ellen Wilkinson (1930), *Peeps at Politicians*, London: Philip Allan
Duke of Windsor (1951), *A King's Story: The Memoirs of H. R. H. The Duke of Windsor*, London: Cassell
Philip M. Williams (1979), *Hugh Gaitskell: A Political Biography*, London: Jonathan Cape
Philip Williamson (ed.) (1987), *The Modernisation of Conservative Politics: The Diaries and Letters of William Bridgeman 1904–1935*, London: The History Press
Philip Williamson and Edward Baldwin (eds) (2004), *Baldwin Papers: A Conservative Statesman 1908–1947*, Cambridge: Cambridge University Press
Philip Williamson (2007), *Stanley Baldwin: Conservative Leadership and National Values*, Cambridge: Cambridge University Press

Earl Winterton (1953), *Orders of the Day*, London: Cassell
G. M. Young (1952), *Stanley Baldwin*, London: Rupert Hart-Davis
Philip Ziegler (1990), *King Edward VIII: The Official Biography*, London: Collins

GOVERNMENT PAPERS

Board of Trade (1940), *Statistical Abstract for the United Kingdom for each of the fifteen years 1924 to 1938*, London: HMSO
Home Office (1928), *Criminal Statistics: Statistics relating to Criminal Proceedings, Police, Coroners, Prisons, and Criminal*, Cmnd 3055, London: HMSO
Sankey Commission (1919), *Interim Report*, Cmnd 84, London: HMSO
Royal Commission on the Coal Industry (1926), *Volume 1: Report*, Cmnd 260, London: HMSO

JOURNAL ARTICLES

Stewart J. Brown (1991), '"A Victory for God": The Scottish Presbyterian Churches and the General Strike of 1926', *Journal of Ecclesiastical History* 42:4, pp. 596–617
Alun Burge (1992), 'The 1926 General Strike in Cardiff', *Llafur* 6:1, pp. 42–61
Wilfrid Harris Crook (1934), 'Social Security and the General Strike', *Political Science Quarterly* 49:3, pp. 411–20
Editors (1977), '1926 Remembered and Revealed', *Llafur* 2:2, 1 April 1977, pp. 9–30
Neil Fleming (2023), 'Paternalism, Conflict and Decline: The seventh Marquess of Londonderry and the Coal Industry, 1906–1947', *Journal of the Durham County Local History Society* 88, pp. 7–43
A. L. Goodhart (1927), 'The Legality of the General Strike in England', *Yale Law Journal* 36:4, pp. 464–85
Eugene Kiernan (1986), 'Drogheda and the British General Strike, 1926', *Saothar* 11, pp. 19–26
A. Mason (1969), 'The Government and the General Strike, 1926', *International Review of Social History* 14:1, pp. 1–21
G. A. Phillips (1977), 'The Labour Party and the General Strike', *Llafur* 2:2, pp. 44–58
Neil Riddell (1997), 'The Catholic Church and the Labour Party, 1918–1931', *Twentieth Century British History* 8:2, pp. 165–93

Melvin C. Shefftz (1967), 'The Trade Disputes and Trade Unions Act of 1927: The Aftermath of the General Strike', *The Review of Politics* 29:3, pp. 387–406

Paul Stocker (2016), 'Importing fascism: reappraising the British fascisti, 1923–1926', *Contemporary British History* 30:3, pp. 326–48

Robert Taylor (2005), 'Citrine's Unexpurgated Diaries, 1925–26: "The Mining Crisis and the National Strike"', *Historical Studies in Industrial Relations* 20, pp. 67–102

ACKNOWLEDGEMENTS

This book was completed not far from a part of London known as Elephant and Castle. A century ago this experienced some of the worst violence of the general strike; today, it is being transformed into a 'new town centre'. There are no longer any trams – several of which were obstructed in May 1926 – but commuter trains continue to pass through Elephant and Castle Station. I doubt, however, many in the area would notice if they woke up one morning to find no printed newspapers.

As ever, it has been fun to take a deep dive into an era, or more specifically a crisis, I hitherto knew little about. In doing so, I have incurred the usual debts. First of all, to my agent Matt Cole for nudging me into pitching a 'sequel' to *The Wild Men: The Remarkable Story of Britain's First Labour Government* while that book enjoyed gratifyingly good reviews; second to Tomasz Hoskins, Katherine Macpherson, Octavia Stocker and the fine team at Bloomsbury Continuum for embracing it so enthusiastically. It is a joy to work with a publisher which takes such good care of its authors as well as its products. Richard Collins also provided his usual eagle-eyed and sympathetic copy-editing.

One of the great thrills of researching a book like this is the primary research, which in this case took me to every part of the United Kingdom as well as towns and archives which were either unfamiliar or completely new. All were superb, and I must pay tribute to the dedication and care of hundreds of archivists and librarians who ensure historians have access to the raw material with which to carry out their tasks. I must also thank His Majesty King Charles III for kind permission to quote from material held in the Royal Archives at Windsor.

Current and former colleagues at the House of Commons Library also warrant a mention. Edward Hicks for identifying journal articles, Georgina Sturge for some invaluable number crunching on the proportion of miners in 1926, Greg Howard and Paul Little for tracking down books, pamphlets and other paraphernalia, and Penny McMahon for facilitating access to the Parliamentary Archives during a logistically challenging period which will see that invaluable collection relocate to the National Archives at Kew.

Much of this book was drafted at the home of another colleague, Hazel Armstrong, in Ecclefechan, which is not far from the birthplace of the now largely forgotten Victorian historian Thomas Carlyle. He postulated the 'Great Man' theory, an historical philosophy which contended that major events are shaped by exceptional individuals. The men – and they were largely men – in this book are generally flawed rather than great, but I hope I have done them justice.

Dr David Torrance
Peckham, London
6 October 2025

INDEX

A
Ablett, Noah 112
Acland, Sir William 76
Addis, Sir Charles Stewart 1, 27, 66–7
Addison, Paul 69
Admiralty, First Lord of the *see* Bridgeman, William
 the Admiralty 39, 53, 73, 143, 146, 166
Air Union 79
Aitchison KC, Craigie 173
Aliens Act 33
Alington, Dr 63
Allhusen, Major Des 60–1
Amalgamated Society of Railway Servants (ASRS) 104–5
Amery, Leo 5, 19, 22, 40, 41, 80–1, 150, 209, 227
Amies, E.L. 54
Anderson, Sir John 29, 166
Answers magazine 207
Argus Press 75–6
Armed Forces, British 3–4, 35, 37–8, 46, 48–9, 167, 205, 229
Army, British 35, 38, 163–4, 197
Arnot, Robin Page 33, 119, 159–60, 161, 221
arrests and imprisonments 37, 83–5, 157, 163, 168, 210, 212–13, 215, 216, 226
Asquith, Countess of Oxford 65
Asquith, Lord Oxford and 4, 44, 85, 96, 97, 121, 127, 214
Asquith, Princess of Bibesco, Elizabeth 65, 89
Astbury, Mr Justice John Meir 174–9, 219–20, 230
Astor, Lady 89
Astor, Viscount 75, 80
Attlee, Clement 110, 220
Auden, W.H. 65

B
Bagwell, Philip 60
Baldwin, Alfred 25
Baldwin, Betty and Diana 59, 79
Baldwin, Lucy 21–2, 28
Baldwin, Oliver 94
Baldwin, Stanley 4, 7, 11, 12, 16, 17–20, 21–2, 23, 25–9, 39, 40, 41, 45, 46, 50–1, 59, 70, 74, 81, 90, 91, 92, 96–7, 100, 103, 106, 108, 115–16, 117, 119, 121, 122–3, 124, 127, 128, 129–30, 132, 133, 135, 143–8, 150, 166, 179, 183, 186, 194, 196, 197–201, 203–5, 209–10, 212, 215, 219, 222, 227–8, 232–3

Balfour Declaration (1917) 183
Balfour, Earl of 40, 46, 91
Bank of England 11, 75
bank transfers, curtailing of 39
Barr, Rev. James 86
Barrow 37
'Battle of Lewes Road,' Brighton 157–8
BBC (British Broadcasting Company) 1, 3, 28, 38, 61, 86, 88, 121, 128, 129–31, 132, 141–51, 177, 199, 202, 212, 217–18, 228, 229
Beatty, Earl 38
Beaverbrook, Lord 80
Belfast 13, 37, 165–6
Belfast Telegraph 79, 135
Bennett, Arnold 65
Bentinck, Lady 66
'Bentley Boys' 55
Betjeman, John 57
Bevan, Aneurin 110, 220
Beveridge, Sir William 103
Bevin, Ernest 15, 16, 18, 20, 22, 23, 99–100, 105, 106–8, 109, 187, 191, 192, 197–8, 202–3, 207–8, 213, 221, 225, 231
bicycle sales 55
Birkenhead, Lord 18, 19, 30–2, 39, 105, 115, 146, 150, 154, 170, 183, 197, 200, 214, 229
Biron, Sir Chartres 84–5
'Black Friday' 9, 104, 118–19
'blackleg' volunteers *see* volunteer workers
Blackwall Tunnel, London 3
Blain, H.E. 214
Boards of Guardians 110, 211
Bolitho, William 6
Bonar Law, Andrew 11, 25, 31, 33, 229
Bondfield, Margaret 92, 111
Bourne, Cardinal 132, 133–8, 218–19
Bramley, Fred 109
brewing industry, Scotland's 168
Brideshead Revisited (E. Waugh) 63–4
Bridgeman, William 16, 17, 27, 28, 29, 31, 32, 41, 51, 69–70, 129
Briggs, Asa 131, 144, 148, 199
Brighton 157
British Fascists (BF) 13, 84, 212
British Gazette 5, 48–9, 61, 65, 70, 71–6, 80–1, 96, 113, 131–2, 143–4, 148, 149, 171, 199, 204, 216–17, 226, 229
British Worker 57, 60, 76–8, 81, 131, 203

297

Broadcasting the Barricades BBC wireless broadcast 141
Brockway, Fenner 4, 24, 78, 99, 102, 205, 231
Bromley, Jack 51, 94–5, 185
Brooklands Squad 55
Brown, Isabel 34
Brown, Stewart J. 140
Brown, William 30
Buchanan, George 48, 89
Buckingham Palace 16, 43, 45, 48, 102, 203
Bullock, Alan 225
bus and tram conductors, volunteer 53–4, 216
Bute, Marquess of 116
Butler, Lady Betty 66
Butt, Sir Alfred 65

C
Cabinet, the British 13, 17–21, 23, 29, 30–1, 33, 35, 39–41, 44, 49, 50, 74, 80–1, 93, 115, 116, 128, 131, 144–5, 146, 150–1, 179, 187, 195, 197–8, 204, 225
    see also Baldwin, Stanley; Bevin, Ernest; Birkenhead, Lord; Churchill, Winston; Cunliffe-Lister, Philip; Davidson, J.C.C.; Gilmour, Sir John; Hankey, Sir Maurice; Hoare, Samuel; Jones, Thomas 'Tom'; Joynson-Hicks, Sir William 'Jix'
Caird, Sir Andrew 71–2, 73
Caledon, Earl of 61
Caledonian Press 78
Cambridge University 58–9
Campbell, John Ross 33
Canterbury, Archbishop of 74, 97, 124–5, 127–33, 134–6, 138, 139, 149, 201, 218–19, 228, 229
Cardiff 78, 163–4
Carlton Club 64
Carnac, Rivett 187
Carson, Sir Edward 229
Casson, Sir Lewis 65
Catholic Church 133–8, 140, 218–19
Catholic Social Guild 137
Cave, Lord 39, 40, 46
Cecil, Hugh 91, 92, 127
Chamberlain, Neville 19–20, 40, 183, 220
Chambers, Kathleen 137
channel crossings 54–5
Channon, Henry 'Chips' 3, 5, 22, 62, 188, 215–16
Chartist movement 10
Chester races 47, 56
Church of England 116, 127–33, 135–6, 140, 218–19
Church of Scotland 138–40, 219
Churchill, Clementine 69, 200
Churchill, Winston 5, 7, 11, 19–20, 23, 26, 29, 32, 33, 35, 36, 37, 40, 56, 78, 84, 87, 123, 141, 144–6, 148, 158, 195, 198–9, 208, 220
    British Gazette 69–70, 71–6, 80–1, 132, 216–17

Citrine, Walter 5, 13–14, 16–17, 18, 20, 21, 22, 35–6, 70, 76–7, 100, 101, 106, 166, 178, 186–7, 188, 189, 190, 191, 192, 194, 195–9, 201, 208, 210, 221, 231
Civic Press 78
Civil Commissioners system 12–13, 153–4, 211–12, 229
    Eastern Division 158–9
    London and Home Counties Division 156–7
    North Western Division 162–3
    Northern Division 159–62
    Northern Ireland Division 164–6
    Scotland Division 167–8
    South Midland Division 154–5
    South Wales Division 163–4
Civil Constabulary Reserve (CCR) 37, 38
Civil Contingencies Act 2004 222
Civil Servants 29–30, 35, 40, 215
    see Hankey, Sir Maurice; Jones, Thomas 'Tom'
Civil Service Clerical Association 30
Clarendon, 6th Earl of 163–4, 211
Clarke, Charles 221
'Clubland,' London 64
Clynes, J.R. 48
Coal Industry Commission 9
Coal Mines Act 1926 208–9
coal mining industry 9, 11–12, 14–24, 214, 221, 222, 223–34
    government subsidies 12, 18–19, 97, 102, 116, 119, 128, 129, 193, 205
    mine owners 7, 9, 12, 14–15, 16, 115–25, 129, 205, 208–9
    the miners 2, 4, 9, 11, 12, 14–15, 17, 94–5, 205, 209, 219, 232
    see also Cook, Arthur James; Gainford, Lord; Londonderry, 7th Marquess of; Miners' Federation of Great Britain (MFGB); Nimmo, Sir Adam; Samuel Commission and Report; Samuel Memorandum; Samuel, Sir Herbert; Smith, Herbert; Trades Union Congress (TUC) and General Council; Williams, Evan
Codling, William 72, 78
Cogswell, R.J. 60
Coldstream Guards 38
Cole, G.D.H. 57, 115
Cole, Margaret 57
Collins, Sir Godfrey 97
Communist Bradford Strike Bulletin 34
Communist Party of Great Britain (CPGB) 33–4, 84, 100, 101, 211
communists/communism 33–5, 51–2, 83–5, 211, 221
Connaught and Strathearn, Duke of 58
Connolly, Martin 87, 160
Conservative-Liberal coalition government 11, 25

INDEX

Conservative Party and government 10–12, 13–24, 25–7, 40–1, 69, 72, 90–2, 121–2, 211, 213, 214–15, 221, 223–4, 229, 232, 233, 234
    see also Cabinet, the British; House of Commons; individual politicians by name
Constabulary (Ireland) Act 1922 165
Cook, Arthur James 2, 15, 21, 22, 23, 31–2, 92, 101–3, 116, 119, 124, 185–6, 188–90, 191, 193–4, 196, 208, 225, 231
Cooper, Duff 5, 91–2, 169, 170, 205
Cope, Major William 156
Councils of Action 100, 110, 201, 226
COVID-19 global pandemic 6, 222
Craig, Sir James 164, 166
Craik, Sir Henry 139
Cramlington Miners 216
Crawford, 27th Earl of 142–3
Crawford Commission and Report 142–3, 218
Crawford, Earl of 120
Crewe 111
cricket matches 55–6, 111–12
Cromer, Lord 40
Cunliffe-Lister, Philip 116, 196–7
Curran, Joseph B. 134
Cymric Federation Press 78

D

Daily Chronicle 97, 217
Daily Express 20, 66, 72, 80, 81
Daily Herald 4, 48, 70, 73, 76–8, 81, 105, 161, 217
Daily Mail 6, 19, 20, 37, 44, 55, 71–2, 79, 80, 83, 91, 177–8, 202
Daily News 135
Daily Record 79
Daily Telegraph 92
Davidson, J.C.C. 1, 28, 35, 38, 41, 59, 70, 71, 73–4, 81, 130, 132, 143–7, 149–51, 171, 221
Davidson, Randall *see* Canterbury, Archbishop of
Davies, Selwyn 188
Dawson, Geoffrey 80
Day-Lewis, Cecil 65
de la Warr, Lady 111
Defence of the Realm Act 1914 101
Denning, Lord 63
Derby, Lord 45
Dillon, Malcolm 122
dock workers 38–9, 160–1, 217
dock workers, volunteer 58–9, 202, 216
Dollan, Patrick 2, 168, 214
Dover Dockers 58–9, 202
Downing Street 2, 4, 17–19, 20, 44, 49, 130, 135, 147, 166, 195, 198–9, 217, 233, 234
    see also Cabinet, the British; individual politicians by name
drivers, volunteer 55, 57, 87, 216
Durham 116

Durham, Bishop of 129, 219
Durham, Lord 45
Durham miners' strike (1893) 128

E

East India Dock Road, London 3
Ecclesiastical Commissioners 128
Eckersley, Peter 141–2
Eden, Anthony 91–2
Edinburgh 2, 167–8, 201–2, 226
Edinburgh Evening Dispatch 79, 217
Edinburgh University 56–7
Education Act (Northern Ireland) 1923 123–4
Edward VII, King 43, 47
Edwards, James 164
Electrical Power Engineers' Association 5
electricity supplies 39, 90
Elizabeth II, Queen 4, 203, 215
Elliot, Walter 40–1
Elmhirst, Sir Thomas 60
Emergency Powers Act 1920 11, 16, 35, 37, 39, 45, 107, 153
Emergency Powers Act (Northern Ireland) 1926 165
Emergency Regulations 35, 37, 39, 76, 83–4, 87–8, 91, 100, 112, 127, 157–8, 163, 164–5, 210, 212, 226, 229
Evening News 94
Evening Standard 75
Ewer, W.N. 161
Eyres-Monsell, Bolton 40, 198

F

Farage, Nigel 222
Ferrall, Charles 65
First World War 11, 32, 154, 158, 174, 223
Flying Scotsman service 60, 62, 216
food supplies 38–9, 111, 112, 155, 159–61, 163, 164–5, 205
Foreign Cattle Market, Deptford 34–5
Foreign Office 30
France 11
Francis, Hywel 102, 163
Fraser, Sir John Foster 66
Fraser, Sir Malcolm 72, 74
Furness Strike Bulletin 149
Fyfe, Hamilton 2, 4, 48, 73, 77–8, 81, 96, 105–6, 132, 217

G

Gainford, Lord 118, 121–2, 130, 142, 145–6, 187–8, 218
Gaitskell, Hugh 57
Galsworthy, Sir John 65
Game, Kingsley 55, 203
Garnett, William 63
Garvin, J.L. 65
general strike, UK (1842), 'first' 10

299

George, David Lloyd 9, 11, 12, 74, 89, 96, 121, 158, 170, 214
George V, King 4, 7, 16, 20, 23, 32, 40, 41, 43–52, 87, 91, 96–7, 102, 127, 132, 156, 199–200, 203, 205, 210, 229–30
George VI, King 215
Gilmour, Sir John 196–7
Glamorganshire 112
Glasgow 2, 37, 99, 167, 168
Glasgow Herald 79
Gordon, Dorothy F. 136
Gorell, Lord 63
government, British
  the general strike reconsidered 223–34
  origins of the general strike 9–24
  see also Baldwin, Stanley; BBC (British Broadcasting Company); *British Gazette*; Cabinet, the British; Canterbury, Archbishop of; Civil Commissioners system; Downing Street; George V, King; House of Commons; House of Lords; Parliament; individual politicians by name)
Gower, Patrick 194
Graham, William 149, 218
Gray, Countess 66
'The Great Trek' 1–2
Greene, Graham 79–80
Greenwood, Arthur 161
Grey of Fallodon, Viscount 96, 148, 149, 150
Griffin, Chief Constable Charles 157
Grigg, P.J. 72
Guardian 2, 43, 83, 162
Guest, Freddie 26
Gwynne, Howell 73, 216

H
Halifax, Lady 66
Hall, Radclyffe 65–6
Hamilton, Duke of 116
Hankey, Sir Maurice 29, 40, 50
Hardinge, Lord 13
Harvey, Dr James 139, 219
Headlam, Cuthbert 14, 16, 17, 22, 39, 70, 80, 103, 215
Henderson, Arthur 23, 77, 89, 107, 172, 185, 186, 192, 203, 213, 214
Hennessy, Major George 162–3
Herbert, Captain 28
Herbert, Sidney 92, 186
Herschell, Lord 61
Hibberd, Stuart 199
HMSO (His Majesty's Stationery Office) 72, 73, 74, 78, 229
Hoare, Samuel 29, 33, 37, 72, 76, 144, 158–9, 171, 196–7, 199–200
Hodge, John 110
Hodges, Frank 113
Hogg, Quintin 59

Hogg, Sir Douglas 39, 50, 160, 173
Home Office 29, 35, 36, 100, 155, 161–2, 166, 226
Home Rule 31–2, 123, 229
Horne, Sir Robert 28
Horner, Arthur 102
horse racing 47, 56
House of Commons, Northern Ireland 164
House of Commons 16, 22–4, 26, 27, 31, 47, 50, 70, 72, 73–4, 83, 85–90, 91–2, 95–7, 128, 132, 160, 169–79, 182, 198, 200–1, 203–5, 212, 218, 221, 229
  peers' gallery 48, 65, 88–9, 201
  see also individual politicians by name
House of Lords 10, 32, 43, 87–8, 96, 122, 123, 127, 131, 133, 208, 220
Howell, David 100, 102
Hudson, Air Vice Marshal 76
Hull 37
Hyde Park, London 38

I
'Illegal Strikes Bill' proposed 39–41, 50
Imperial Airways 79
Incitement to Mutiny Act 1797 33
Independent Labour Party (ILP) 84, 85, 95, 101, 214
Inge, Dean 135–6
Inskip, Sir Thomas 223
Institute of Journalists 71
International Working People's Association (IWPA) 10
Irish Convention 123
Irish Free State 26, 166
Irish Home Rule 26, 31–2
Irish Trades Union Congress 166
Iron and Steel Trades Confederation (ISTC) 110, 208
Isaac, George 19
Isherwood, Christopher 65
Iveagh, Lady 66

J
Jenrick, Robert 222
Jockey Club 47, 56
Jones, Flo 55
Jones, Thomas 'Tom' 28–9, 30–1, 40, 44, 74, 75, 116, 118, 119, 120, 147, 188, 198, 224, 226, 227
Joseph, Henrietta 56
Joynson-Hicks, Sir William 'Jix' 13, 20, 32–6, 38, 39, 51–2, 59, 85, 136, 145, 150, 196–7, 210–11

K
Kenworthy, Joseph 73–4
Keynes, John Maynard 12, 67, 116, 214
Kindersley, Major 132

INDEX

Kinnock, Neil 222
Kintore, Earl of 64
Kipling, Rudyard 65
Kirkwood, David 68, 95, 102, 217
Knight, Holford 178
Knox, Father Ronald 141
Kyle, Sam 215

L

Labour governments 11, 26, 33, 86, 89, 104, 107, 120, 211, 224, 229, 234
Labour movement 14, 92, 132, 174, 228, 234, 235
Labour Party 22, 23, 26, 48, 49, 68, 70, 76, 84, 88, 89, 93–5, 97, 100, 107, 134, 149–50, 168, 170, 171–3, 208, 212–14, 215, 218, 220, 222, 228, 233
    see also MacDonald, James Ramsay
Labour Party, Northern Ireland 164, 215
Lambeth Conference (1920) 128
Lanarkshire 116, 120
Lanarkshire Coal Masters' Association (LCMA) 120
Lane-Fox, Colonel 129, 197
Lansbury, George 89
Lansbury's Weekly 78
Larkin, James 166
Lascelles, Alan 55
Laski, Harold 192–3
Lawrence, Susan 89, 112
Lawther, Will 215
Laybourn, Keith 14, 34, 68, 207–8, 224
Laycock, Herbert 90
Lee, Jennie 57, 201–2
Lee, William 22, 118, 120
Leeds 111
legality of the general strike 39–41, 50, 169–70, 171–9, 183–4, 188, 215, 230
Leith, the general strike 2
Liberal governments 10, 170, 223–4, 229
Liberal Party 26, 31, 33, 85, 95–6, 96–7, 121, 170–1, 174, 182, 214, 215, 220
Liberty & Co. 63
Lidgett, Dr John 128
Lindsay, A.D. 138, 155
Liverpool 4, 37–8, 76, 136, 162–3, 174
Liverpool, Bishop of 128
London, Bishop of 128
London County Council 54, 66, 110, 128, 157, 182
London Docks 38–9, 205
London General Omnibus Company 46–7, 54
London Municipal Society 21–2
London, the general strike 1–6, 38–9, 156–7
Londonderry, 7th Marquess of 64, 80, 122–5, 128, 187–8, 209, 229
Londonderry, Lady 124
Long, Sydney 72

Low, David 31, 148
Lyon, Hugh 112

M

MacDonald, James Ramsay 4, 7, 11, 14, 16–17, 19, 21, 22, 23, 28, 43–4, 45, 86, 89–90, 91, 92–5, 97, 102, 107, 108, 120, 124, 128, 171, 173, 177, 185, 186, 190–1, 193, 201, 202, 203–4, 207, 213–14, 215, 218, 229, 232–3, 235–6
Machine Managers' Union 87
Macmillan, Harold 53, 68, 80, 88, 90–1, 96, 170, 210, 214, 224–5
Macmillan, Lord 63
Macready, General Sir Nevil 37
Main, Professor Archibald 138
Manchester 2, 79, 222
Manchester, Bishop of 219
Manchester Guardian 44, 70, 97, 217
Manners, Lady 66
Marlowe, Thomas 19, 177
Marquand, David 93
Martin, Principal Alexander 139
Marxist Plebs' League 110
Mary, Queen 4, 44–5, 47–8, 199
Marylebone Cricket Club 55–6
Matthew, H.C.G. 45
McLynn, Frank 68, 132
McNeill, Dougal 65
Meath, Earl of 63
Melba, Dame Nellie 65
Merthyr Tydfil 112
Metropolitan Police 34, 35, 49, 155
Mews, Stuart 138
MI5 34–5, 48, 103
Middleton, Lady Sybil 66
Midgley, Harry 165
Miliband, Ralph 37, 38
Milne-Bailey, Walter 70, 142
Milne Barbour, Sir John 13, 164–5, 211
Milne, General 49
Miners' Federation of Great Britain (MFGB) 9, 12, 15, 16, 17, 18, 21, 22, 92, 93, 94–5, 101–3, 113, 116, 117, 119, 176, 185, 186, 189–94, 196, 197, 204, 208–9, 221, 224, 231
    see also Cook, Arthur James; Smith, Herbert
Mining Association of Great Britain (MAGB) 21, 115, 117–19, 120, 121, 130, 176, 204, 208–9, 219, 221, 224
Mining Industry Act 1926 208–9
Ministry for Air 29, 30
Ministry of Health 110, 155–6
Ministry of Labour 17, 22, 30, 191, 231
Ministry of Transport 87, 155–6
Mitchell-Thomson, Sir William 13, 155, 166, 181, 211–12, 217
Mitford, Jessica 66
Mond, Sir Alfred 92, 121

301

Monkswell, Lord 61
Morning Post 5, 72
Morrison, Herbert 213–14
motorcycle sales 55
Mountbatten, Edwina 66
Mowat, Charles 19–20
Murray, John 49, 88
Murray, Lieutenant Commander 53–4
Mussolini, Benito 13

N
Nall, Sir Joseph 132
Narborough, Rev. F.D.V. 134
The Nation 67
National Hunt Committee 56
National Liberal Club 64, 120
National Minority Movement 101–2
National Sailors' and Firemen's Union (NSFU) 5, 174, 175
National Society of Operative Printers and Assistants (NATSOPA) 19
National Union of Journalists (NUJ) 5, 71, 88
National Union of Railwaymen (NUR) 51, 60, 94–5, 99, 101, 104, 105–6, 207
National Union of Scottish Mine Workers (NUSMW) 219
Navy, Royal 3–4, 35, 37–8, 160–1, 163
New Leader 78
New Scotland Yard 34
New Statesman 19, 65, 133
New York Herald Tribune 28
Newcastle 76, 160–2
Newport, South Wales 37, 163
newspaper bias 70–1, 73–4, 77
newspaper/press industry 70–1, 78–80, 168, 217
 see also British Gazette; British Worker; individual newspapers by name
Newspaper Proprietors' Association 71
Newspaper Society 79
Nichols & Son 87
Nicol, Rev. D. Bruce 139
Nicolson, Harold 25
Nimmo, Sir Adam 115, 118, 119–20, 209, 219
Norman, Montagu 75
Northern Ireland 13, 71, 79, 99, 113, 123–4, 155, 164–6, 215, 221–2
 devolved Parliament 13, 71, 123, 164–6, 215
Northfleet papermaking works 76
Northumberland 116

O
Observer 75
Official Report (Hansard) 86, 87
Order Papers (Votes and Proceedings) 86–7
Orders in Council, Privy Council 50–1
Organisation for the Maintenance of Supplies (OMS) 13, 156, 159–60, 226
Osborne judgment (1910) 10

Oxford and Asquith, Lord *see* Asquith, Lord Oxford and
Oxford Labour Council 58
Oxford Trade Council 58
Oxford University 56–8, 155

P
Palestine 182–3
Parliament 2, 11, 26–7, 28, 31, 73–4, 84, 85, 86–9, 95, 142, 177, 200, 212, 215, 228–9
 see also House of Commons; House of Lords; individual politicians by name
Parliamentary Labour Party (PLP) 89
Paton, John 95, 108, 113, 178
Pease, Jack *see* Gainford, Lord
Peck, James 167
Pelling, Henry 10
the People 78
Percy, Eustace 81, 88
Phillimore, Lord 131
Phillips, Gordon 39, 77, 112–13
Phoenix Wharf 76
Pickbourne, William 2
picketing/protests 38–9, 49–50, 156–7, 164, 168
police force, British 3, 11, 34, 35, 36–7, 49–50, 76–7, 89, 111–12, 155, 156–7, 168
 Special Constables 11, 27, 36, 47–8, 62–3, 112, 155, 159, 163, 205, 216, 226, 229
Poor Law relief 110, 211
Portarlington, Lord 61
Prince of Wales, Edward 5–6, 29, 45, 47, 48, 66, 76, 89, 201
print workers 70–1, 78–9, 86–7
Printing and Kindred Trades Federation 88
Printing House Square 80
Privy Council 45, 50–1, 105, 208
protests/violence 3–4, 156–8, 164, 168, 226–7, 230
Pugh, Arthur 18, 20, 22, 75, 92, 109–10, 185, 187, 190, 191–2, 196, 197–8, 208
Punch 56, 173, 216

R
Racing and Football Outlook 78
Radio Times 218
Raglan, Lord 61
railway industry 9, 167, 204–5
railway workers, volunteer 59–61, 216, 227
Reading, Lord 188
'Red Friday' 12, 102
Reeves, Rachel 222
Reform Club 64, 181
Reform Party 222
Reith, John 7, 128, 129–31, 142–51, 177, 199, 202, 217–18, 235
Renshaw, Patrick 221–2
Republic of Ireland 26

302

INDEX

Reuters 28, 146
Ripon, Bishop of 128
Rose, Sir Arthur 167, 212
Roundell, Christopher 46–7
Royal Air Force 35
Royal Commissions 4, 12, 117, 181, 183, 185
    see also Samuel Commission and Report;
        Samuel, Sir Herbert
Royal Ulster Constabulary (RUC) 165
Ruhr, French occupation of 11
Russia, Prince George of 63
Ruthven, Lord 38

S

St Andrews, Scotland 56
St Helier, Lady 66
Saklatvala, Shapurji 83–5, 212–13
Salisbury, Alice Marchioness of 66
Samuel Commission and Report 12, 14–15,
    17, 18–19, 103, 117, 125, 176, 181, 188,
    209, 224
Samuel Memorandum 188–94, 201, 204, 224
Samuel, Sir Herbert 4, 12, 15, 19, 56, 181–6,
    188–94, 198, 201, 204, 214, 220, 231
Sankey Commission 116, 118, 120, 121
Sankey, Lord 9
Sassoon, Siegfried 64–5
Sassoon, Sir Philip 58, 158, 211
Scotland 13, 33, 78, 116, 155, 167–8
Scotsman 2, 79, 139, 217
Scott, C.P. 171
Scottish Emergency Organisation (SEO) 167
Scottish Horse and Motormen's Association
    (SHMA) 112
Scottish Office 41, 212
Scottish Trades Union Congress (STUC) 78, 15,
    99, 100
Scottish Worker 78, 113, 173
Seaman, Sir Owen 173–4
'The Secret People' (G.K. Chesterton) 53
Sharp, Clifford 133
Shaw, Glen 64
Sheffield 2
Shop Stewards Movement 85
Simon, Sir John 169–78, 184, 214, 220, 230
Simpson, James Young 93
Sitwell, Osbert 122, 187–8
Skelton, Noel 90–1
Slesser, Sir Henry 131, 171–3, 175–7, 220
Smillie, Robert 68, 120
Smith, Frederick Edwin *see* Birkenhead, Lord
Smith, Herbert 18, 22, 89, 92, 103, 116, 185–6,
    188–90, 191–4, 204, 231
Smith, Sir Allan 186
Snowden, Ethel 92, 187–8
Snowden, Philip 27, 92, 187
Socialist Review 213
South Wales 2, 79, 116, 156, 163–4

South Wales Coal Owners' Association 118
South Wales Miners' Federation (SWMF) 78, 101,
    112, 201
Southampton 2
Soviet Union 39, 45, 50–1, 210, 211
Special Constables Act 1923 11, 36
Spencer, George 209
sports, spectator 47, 55–6, 111–12
Stair, Earl of 13
Stamfordham, Lord 40, 43–4, 45, 46, 49–50, 51,
    199, 200
Stanley, Lady Maureen 80
State Bank of the Soviet Union 39, 50–1, 210
Steel-Maitland, Sir Arthur 23, 183–4, 196, 197,
    208, 219
Stewart-Liberty, Captain 63
Stewart, William Burton 54
Strachey, John St Loe 43–4, 186
Strickland, Sir Gerald 86
strike committees 34, 57, 100, 111, 112, 160–1,
    201–2
student volunteers 56–9, 155, 158–9, 163,
    202, 216
Suffragette movement 33
Sunday Times 48
    Magazine 221
Sunningend Aircraft Works 202–3
Supply and Transport Committee (STC) 12–13,
    35, 37, 144–5, 205
Sutherland, Duchess of 80
Symons, Julian 24, 59, 160–1

T

Taff Vale judgement 10
Tatler 45, 66
Tawney, R.H. 103
Taylor, A.J.P. 57, 221, 233
teachers, East End 54
Territorial Army (TA) 37
Thatcher, Margaret 222
The Times 2, 11, 70, 75, 79–80, 81, 91, 131, 135,
    174, 199
theatre and opera performances 65
Thomas, Jimmy 2, 5, 7, 14, 16, 18, 20, 21,
    23, 24, 35–6, 39, 48, 75, 91, 92, 100,
    104–6, 110, 128, 178, 181–2, 184–5,
    187–8, 189, 191, 194, 197–8, 204–5, 207,
    218, 225, 231
Thompson, Luke 128
Thorndike, Dame Sybil 65
Thring, Sir Arthur 87–8
Tillett, Ben 75, 210
Tonypandy riots (1910—1911) 101
Trade Disputes Act 1906 10, 36, 39, 49, 170,
    172–3, 175, 177, 229
Trade Disputes and Trade Unions Act 1927 215,
    221, 234
Trade Disputes and Trade Unions Bill 31, 215

Trade Union Act 1913 10
Trade Union Levy Bill (1925), proposed 12
trade unions 12, 15, 16–17, 19, 31, 39–40, 49–50, 75, 78, 99, 100, 102, 108, 110, 112, 149, 160–1, 166, 168, 169–79, 187, 190, 194, 204, 210, 219, 220, 221, 223, 225, 229, 233–4
   see also Miners' Federation of Great Britain (MFGB); National Union of Railwaymen (NUR) Trades Union Congress (TUC) and General Council; Transport and General Workers' Union (TGWU)
Trade Union Congress (TUC) and General Council 2, 4–5, 13–21, 22, 24, 26, 27–8, 30, 31–2, 34, 39, 41, 44, 50–1, 57, 61, 65, 70, 75, 76–8, 79, 86, 87, 91, 95, 99–101, 105–6, 108, 109, 110–13, 129, 149, 169–70, 175, 177–8, 181–2, 183–95, 207–8, 211, 215, 221, 224, 225, 228
   calling off the general strike 197–9, 201–5, 231–2
   talks with Sir Herbert Samuel and the Samuel Memorandum 181–2, 183–94, 196–7, 201–3, 224, 231
   see also Bevin, Ernest; Citrine, Walter; Pugh, Arthur
Trades Councils 100, 105, 160
train accidents 60, 62, 216, 226–7
Transport and General Workers' Union (TGWU) 15, 101, 106–7, 156, 160, 166, 202, 208
Treacy, Herbert 70–1
'Triple Industrial Alliance' 9, 15, 17, 102
Trory, Ernie 157
Troubridge, Una 66
Turing, Alan 2

U
Ulster crisis (1912—1914) 31
Ulster Unionists 31, 123, 165
Ulster Volunteer Force 31
United Free Church (UFC) 139–40, 219

V
Vansittart, Lord 25
Victoria House Printing Company 76–7
volunteer workers 53–64, 68, 87, 155, 157, 158–9, 163–4, 166, 167–8, 202, 205, 215–16, 221, 226, 230, 233

W
War Office 37, 38, 46, 49, 51
Waterhouse, Sir Ronald 49
Watson KC, William 167–8, 211
Waugh, Evelyn 63–4
Webb, Beatrice 3, 92, 95, 101, 109, 112, 115, 149, 182, 205, 207, 212–13
Webster, Sir Lonsdale 88
Wertheimer, Egon 104
Westcott, Bishop 128
Western Mail 79
Westminster, Duchess of 80
Weymouth, Lord 61
W.H. Smith 76
White, John 138–9, 219
Whitelaw, William 167
Whitley, John Henry 85–7, 89, 212
Wigan Coal and Iron Company 120
Wilkinson, Ellen 71, 110–11, 158, 170, 175, 177, 184, 218, 220, 222
William, E.T. 39
Williams, Evan 115, 118–19, 204, 209
Williams, Robert 76
Wilson, Joseph Havelock 5, 174–5, 220
Wilson, Sir Horace 17, 18, 19, 30, 147, 183, 197
Wimborne, Lord 187–8
Winterton, Edward Turnor, 6th Earl 153–4, 211
wireless broadcasts 2–3, 27–8, 36, 121, 141–51, 227–8
Wood, Edward 153, 154, 211
Wood, Sir Kingsley 90, 159–62, 211
Woolf, Leonard 65, 67, 131
Woolf, Virginia 64, 131, 147
Workers Chronicle 162
Workers Defence Corps 51
Workers' Union of Ireland 166
Worthington-Evans, Sir Laming 46, 198
writers and artists on the strike 63–6

Y
Yeovil 111
York, Archbishop of 128, 129, 136
York, Duke and Duchess of 4, 47, 48, 89, 201, 203
Younger of Leckie, Viscount 64

Z
Zinoviev Letter 19, 70, 107, 177
Zionist Movement 182–3